Control Balance

CRIME & SOCIETY
Series Editor
John Hagan, University of Toronto

Control Balance

Toward a General Theory of Deviance

Charles R. Tittle

WestviewPress

A Division of HarperCollins*Publishers*

Crime & Society

Copyright © 1995 by Westview Press, Inc., A Division of HarperCollins Publishers, Inc.

Published in 1995 in the United States of America by Westview Press, Inc., 5500 Central Avenue, Boulder, Colorado 80301-2877, and in the United Kingdom by Westview Press, 12 Hid's Copse Road, Cumnor Hill, Oxford OX2 9JJ

Library of Congress Cataloging-in-Publication Data
Tittle, Charles R.
  Control balance : toward a general theory of deviance / Charles R. Tittle.
    p.   cm. — (Crime & society)
  Includes bibliographical references and index.
  ISBN 0-8133-2631-1. — ISBN 0-8133-2632-X (pbk.)
  1. Deviant behavior.   2. Social control.   I. Title.   II. Series:
Crime & society (Boulder, Colo.)
HM 291.T565   1995
302.5'42—dc20   95-18229
                                                                        CIP

Printed and bound in the United States of America

The paper used in this publication meets the requirements of the American National Standard for Permanence of Paper for printed Library Materials Z39.48-1984.

10   9   8   7   6   5   4   3   2   1

Contents

Figures

Acknowledgments

For help on this book I owe the most to Debra Curran, who not only supported and encouraged me when I wanted to quit but who also served as a sharp critic, sounding board, proofreader, and general adviser. Raymond Paternoster, Harold Grasmick, David Ward, and Austin Turk read early versions of various sections of the manuscript and offered much constructive criticism. Critiques of the entire manuscript by Valerie Jenness and Jim (James F., Jr.) Short were very helpful and greatly appreciated. Jennifer Longmire is to be commended for her fine work in preparing the diagrams. Thanks are also owed to the staff of Westview Press, particularly Jill Rothenberg and Jennifer Blandford, and to Michele Wynn, the copy editor. None of these people, however, contributed to the book's shortcomings.

Charles R. Tittle

1

The Problem with Simple Theories

Most theories of deviant and criminal behavior are straightforward and uncomplicated, usually setting forth one or two explanatory principles involving only a few variables that are assumed to apply to all instances of the particular form of deviance being explained. These can be called simple theories. Conventionally, simple theories are classified into six or seven major categories, with sublistings of variations on themes. The most popular categorical schemes identify strain, learning, labeling, control, opportunity, psychodynamic, and biological categories as the major divisions, but according to Pearson and Weiner (1985), the most important specific simple theories are differential association (Sutherland and Cressey 1978), anomie (Merton 1957a), Marxian conflict (Bonger 1916; Quinney 1970), social control (Hirschi 1969), labeling (Becker 1963; Gove 1975, 1980; Schur 1971), utilitarian/deterrence (Andenaes 1974; Becker 1968; Cornish and Clarke 1986; Gibbs 1975; Tunnell 1992; Zimring and Hawkins 1973), and routine activities (Cohen and Felson 1979). Each of these leading theories has followers, enjoys some empirical support, and seems sensible, at least in prescribed usage and in application to particular kinds of deviance or crime. No simple theory in the crime/deviance area, however, has proven to be more than minimally satisfactory in overall explanatory ability, in applicability to a wide range of types of deviance, or in empirical support for its tenets. All are plausible, yet they fail as general theories. This is easily illustrated.

Simple General Theories

Differential Association

Consider first simple cultural learning theories, the prime example of which is Edwin Sutherland's differential association theory (Sutherland and Cressey 1978, chapter 4; see also Tittle et al. 1986; Jackson et al. 1986). These theories explain deviance as a product of the individual's having learned devio-genic (deviance-causing) attitudes and behaviors through extensive exposure to specific kinds of social messages or as a result of the individual's efforts to fulfill normative expectations in a devio-genic subculture (Miller 1958; Wolfgang and Ferricuti 1967). Sutherland's theory specifically postulates that the likelihood of criminal behavior (or by extension, deviance) varies with the individual's criminal attitudes, values, motivations, and skills, learned from "excess" exposure to crime-favorable messages or "definitions." Cultural messages can be supportive, neutral, or contradictory to crime, and they will have various degrees of influence depending upon their source, priority, intensity, and frequency. Thus, the ratio of "weighted" crime-relevant definitions can vary widely from person to person. Some will have ratios less than 1, others will have ratios above 1, and still others will have ratios that are far greater than 1. Presumably, the more the ratio of weighted crime-favorable messages to weighted noncrime messages exceeds unity, the greater are an individual's chances of learning criminal orientations and of committing crime.

Cultural learning theories have a commonsense, experiential character, especially when applied to things like gang fighting, drug abuse, or corporate price-fixing. Successful practice of these forms of deviance requires some learning of norms, techniques, and attitudes. In addition, they are activities requiring the cooperation of other people, and they are usually undertaken in company. Hence, it is reasonable to imagine that individuals do these things because they have been in situations where these, or similar, activities have been socially defined as appropriate and have been practiced by people who were known to, and perhaps admired by, the individual. Further, since they are group activities, it is logical to think that individual practitioners feel some pressure to meet group (normative) expectations and that if they do participate in deviant activities condoned by the group or culture they will be recognized, supported, accepted, and perhaps honored by those with whom they are associated.

A cultural learning theory, however, can hardly be used to explain criminal or deviant acts that are individualized in character. If there are no social contexts in which a given behavior is normative and if there are few social definitions of the behavior as acceptable, or fun, or indicative of some desired trait or status, then cultural learning can scarcely play an important part in its production. Extremely unconventional, bizarre behaviors, usually thought to be evidence of mental illness, for instance, do not seem to be products of cultural learning. Consider the eating of feces, an activity sometimes practiced by psychotic people. In the United States, and probably in all other places in the contemporary world, this is highly unacceptable. However, to explain it by Sutherland's differential association theory we would have to assume that the feces eater had been exposed to more social definitions favorable to feces eating than to messages unfavorable to the act. In any case, where would an individual encounter *any* social messages favorable to feces eating, much less an excess of such definitions? Similarly, in the United States, suicide, except for the altruistic type, is not normatively acceptable, and there are few social definitions of nonaltruistic suicide as appropriate behavior in any circumstances (however, it may be becoming acceptable to end one's life if one is suffering from an incurable, expensive-to-treat disease). It is difficult, therefore, to maintain that U.S. citizens who commit suicide have been exposed to an excess of suicide-favorable messages. In short, feces eating and suicide, and other individualized forms of deviance or crime, simply do not lend themselves to a cultural learning explanation.

Furthermore, differential association theory is not fully adequate to explain even those social acts to which it seemingly applies most directly. For one thing, it takes no account of opportunity for deviance. Even if individuals are confronted with "excess" social messages that produce devio-genic attitudes, skills, and desires propelling them toward deviant behavior, they cannot actually commit acts of crime or deviance without the opportunity to do so. Even if earlier interaction with a particular group has generated a strong desire to steal cars, and the individual has become extremely skilled at it, if there are no cars in or near the particular locale where that person ends up residing, then there is little likelihood that individual will commit auto theft. Similarly, some deviantly inclined individuals will, nevertheless, refrain from actual misbehavior when the chances of getting caught and punished are high. However, differential association theory takes little account of ongoing constraints on individual behavior that exist in the behavioral environment, recognizing only their influence as messages unfavorable to deviance that affect the presence or strength, or both, of internal motivations. Consequently, the theory's explanations must necessarily be incomplete.

In a similar way, Sutherland's formulation overlooks variations in learning ability among individuals, as well as differences in the degree of exposure to deviance-favorable messages required to produce various kinds of criminal or deviant behavior. Because some learn better and more quickly than others (Eysenck and Gudjonsson 1989; Wilson and Herrnstein 1985), individuals will differ in their deviant behavior, even with similar degrees of excess exposure to crime/deviance-favorable messages. In addition, it might take much greater exposure to homicide-favorable messages to produce murderous behavior than it takes of excessive definitions favorable to marijuana use to persuade individuals to smoke it. Finally, despite passing reference to differential social organization, Sutherland's theory does not explain why individuals have the associations they have or why the ratio of messages favorable to crime/deviance varies from one social context to another.

This brief overview shows that differential association, and other cultural learning theories, probably identify an important cause of crime, but it also shows that the theory is limited and incomplete.

Anomie

Robert Merton's (1957a) anomie theory of deviance is somewhat ambiguous because its author shifted explanations from one statement of the theory to another (see Chapter 3) and because it mixes macroexplanatory (structural conditions bearing on rates of crime/deviance) with microexplanatory (situational variables bearing on behavior of individuals) elements without fully explicating how the variables mesh. However, the theory is usually interpreted to explain individual criminal/deviant behavior as an adaptive response to the strain of incongruence between a person's internalization of culturally defined success goals and his or her possession of culturally approved means for achieving those goals. For example, U.S. society is said to prescribe financial success as the primary goal for all to achieve. However, not everybody has the means to achieve financial success. Those who embrace the goal of financial success and have access to the means to achieve that goal can be said to exhibit goals-means congruence, which leads to conformity. Others lacking such congruence, because they do not embrace the culturally prescribed goal of financial success or do not possess the appropriate means for achievement, are likely to engage in various kinds of deviance as adaptive responses.

One form of deviance—"innovation" (finding a new way to get to the goal, such as theft)—typically is manifested by those who internalize the success goals but lack either the means to achieve them or the moral inhibitions, or both, that might prevent them from innovating. "Ritualism" (going through the motions of conformity but lacking the emotional commitment—such as slavish or compulsive obedience to minute conduct standards) characterizes those who have internalized the goals but lack the means of achievement and are constrained from innovation by their moral inhibitions. Those who originally internalize the goals but repeatedly fail to achieve them "retreat" (withdraw from participation in the larger cultural system, for example, by becoming alcoholics or skid-row bums) by psychologically rejecting the goals and the means. Finally, some either fail to internalize the culturally dominant goals altogether, or later reject them because of the lack of means to achieve them, in favor of other goals and other means. This adaptation is called "rebellion" and is typical of revolutionaries.

Since everyone has been frustrated at one time or another by being required to do something they were not prepared to do, it is not hard to relate to the situations that Merton describes. It is easy to imagine conformity as being simple for those who inherit large financial resources and who have high intelligence, effective interpersonal skills, lucrative occupational or professional training, and good looks. In addition, the thought of cutting corners (innovation) will probably occur to most people when they feel an urgent need for money they cannot get or when they contemplate providing better for their families, selling more of a product, or rising to the top of their occupations but realize they probably can never achieve these things because of circumstances over which they have little control. Most people have personally observed individuals who upheld the virtues of work, saving, and self-discipline but who seemed indifferent to the goals for which the rest of us strive (ritualism). It is not rare to encounter people who seem so disoriented, perhaps by the recognition that things are hopeless, that they become inattentive to the goals and the culturally approved means (retreatism). In fact, much everyday conversation involves marveling at instances that come to light of people who adapt in these various ways.

Yet, even laypeople see the fallacy of the theoretical argument because most of the people they know conform despite their lacking the means necessary for financial success, and as often as not, those who "innovate" are high-status people who ostensibly have the means. So it is clear that the relationship between culturally defined goals and approved means is not all that is going on, and in fact, may not even be among the most important factors in explaining deviant behavior. On the one hand, many who, according to the theory, are prone to innovate actually refrain because of fear of legal punishment or reluctance to risk shaming their families, or because they have more important competing goals. On the other hand, some conform because they get few opportunities to innovate or because they lack the skills or intelligence to do so in effective ways. Finally, human behavior seems to depend, at least to some extent, upon people's personalities, the things they have learned, the kinds of social groups with which they are affiliated, and unusual provoking or activating circumstances, regardless of objective goals and means. Whether people conform or not seems to depend, particularly, on the accuracy with which they perceive reality, since relative deprivation (of the means) seems to be as potent as objective deprivation. However, none of this is built into anomie theory, and as a result, the best that it can claim is that a goals-means strain is one thing that may, under some circumstances, lead to deviance. Yet even this proposition is weak because the theory does not indicate who will experience various configurations of goals and means, nor does it detail the immediate provocative conditions under which those with various goals-means relationships are most likely to manifest their strain in actual deviance.

Nevertheless, since it can be construed to apply to almost any form of deviance, even that usually regarded as evidence of mental illness, anomie theory is more adequate as a general theory than differential association, at least in one sense. Yet it ultimately seems to do no more than identify one important factor possibly contributing to deviant behavior. Overall, it falls far short of being an adequate general theory because it leaves out too much and is too imprecise to specify which things it does include (see Agnew 1992).

Marxian Conflict

There are many versions of Marxian, or conflict, theory (Bohm 1982; Bonger 1916; Quinney 1970; Taylor et al. 1973) and most are designed to explain why crime rates vary among societies, not why individuals commit deviance. Nevertheless, a common theme—that exploitation (usually associated with a capitalist economic system) and its accompanying deprivation lead to inhumane relationships (deviance, crime) among societal members—can also be used to explain individual deviance. Wilhelm

Bonger (1916) probably articulates this theory best. According to his version, the profit motive that drives capitalism forces both capitalists and workers to become "de-moralized," that is, they lose moral feeling and sympathy for others.

Capitalist competition, according to Bonger, de-moralizes owners of the means of production toward each other because one owner's success may be bought at the expense of another owner's failure. In addition, to compete effectively, capitalists must pay workers the lowest wage possible. To get employees to accept such wages, they must create societal conditions of scarcity requiring workers to compete among themselves for survival. Doing this successfully depends on the capitalist's ability to squelch his or her own potential human sympathy for those being exploited. At the same time, workers become de-moralized toward capitalists, who they know are exploiting them, and since they are forced by competitive conditions to struggle among themselves for survival, they become "de-humanized" toward each other as well. The result is an entirely inhumane society, where owners of the means of production feel no moral obligation to their competitors or employees, and where workers forfeit human feelings toward their exploiters and fellow workers. Because all members of capitalist societies are motivated to use or defeat others and are freed from the constraining hold of sentiment, crime and deviance abound.

Following the logic of this argument, rates of crime and deviance should vary directly with the degree of capitalism characterizing societies, or more specifically, rates of crime should vary directly with overall deprivation and competition. By extending these arguments to the individual level, we would explain criminal/deviant behavior among those who do not own the means of production as a product of the degree of personal deprivation they experience: the greater the personal deprivation, the greater the probability of deviance. Among those who do own the means of production, crime stems from the strain of competition. Logically, those capitalists most committed to the ideal of success or those least successful in fulfilling it will feel the greatest strain and have the greatest probability of engaging in deviance.

This theory also has much to offer. It is easy to see that deprivation and struggle for survival or economic dominance can motivate much uncaring behavior, especially when people can compare themselves with others who may be faring better. Hence, the Marxian conflict formulation probably identifies an important component of crime causation, and it has the virtue of accounting for the degree of its prevalence from society to society. As a general theory of criminal behavior, however, the conflict argument is quite deficient. Like other theories being discussed here, it focuses almost totally on motivation for deviance while ignoring these other variables: variations in the constraining effects of potential sanctions; internalized moral commitments that some people, even in capitalist societies, have; influences of interpersonal social groups; and opportunities for crime/deviance. All of these may interact with deprivation or strain to affect the likelihood of crime/deviance. In addition, there is nothing in the theory that explains the conditions under which one type of crime/deviance is more likely to occur than another. Why, for instance, would one deprived worker or noncapitalist assault a comrade, whereas another would rob a bank? Why would one failing capitalist commit suicide, whereas another would murder a competitor? Moreover, the theory does not explain how individuals come to have various relationships to the means of production or why the degree of deprivation or strain varies from individual to individual within either the capitalist or the noncapitalist group. Finally, the theory does not recognize that strain stemming from competition or deprivation may result from things other than the conditions of capitalism, particularly if varied perceptions of reality are taken into account.

The Marxian conflict theory, then, probably has much validity, and it provides considerable insight about the potential consequences of unrestrained capitalism. It is not, however, a satisfactory general theory of deviance.

Social Control

All control theories play on the theme that deviance is mainly a function of the kinds of constraints to which people are exposed (Durkheim [1897] 1951; Hirschi 1969; Reckless 1967; Reiss 1951). The most well-known specific theory of this genre is Travis Hirschi's theory of social control (1969). It contends that everybody is motivated toward deviance, but only those who are relatively free of the bonds of commitment to, and belief in, the conventional order, attachment to others, and involvement with conventional institutions of society actually manifest their deviant motivation in unacceptable behavior.

It is certainly plausible and consistent with common sense to assert, as this theory does, that people are more likely to violate conventional social rules when they are free of constraining social bonds. Most of us realize that our beliefs, commitments, attachments, and involvements have great influence on our behavior. In fact as one of my colleagues phrased it, a lot of us learned in Sunday school or from our parents that we would go wrong if we did not believe in God; develop strong moral principles; attach ourselves to conventional social groups like the family, church, and school; and involve ourselves in wholesome activities and useful work. We can recall examples of those who did go wrong, apparently because they did not follow these dictates. In addition, most of us have probably been separated at one time or another from families, friends, and neighbors for varied lengths of time and have experienced the initial exhilaration and sense of freedom to do things we usually would not do. Moreover, everybody is familiar with individuals lacking familial, interpersonal, or professional reputations who, as a result, seem to care little about the consequences of their behavior.

It is clear, however, that the desire to offend is, for some individuals, so strong that social controls pale; some deviance is committed because the groups to which offenders are bonded actually exercise social control to encourage deviance; and some unbonded individuals nevertheless conform, perhaps out of habit, lack of alternatives, or internalized moral commitments. Most people agree that deviance is to some extent dependent upon opportunities and skills, as well as other factors. For instance, individual variation in accuracy of perceptions about how particular behaviors would be viewed by conventional others, or about the deviant orientations of groups to which one might be bonded, could affect delinquency. Moreover, although this theory implies equal ability to explain all forms of crime/deviance (though it specifically addresses only "delinquency"), it is quite likely that the constraints of social bonds are differentially effective for various kinds of crime/deviance and are probably more effective at preventing acts strongly disapproved by general opinion than acts that are only slightly disapproved. However, none of these components are encompassed within social control theory, and it neglects to account for variations in social bonds themselves.

Therefore, as sensible as the main proposition appears, social control theory fulfills few of the criteria for adequacy as a general theory. Like the others, it is more incomplete than incorrect, excluding more than it includes, and only imprecisely accommodating the interactions of its main variables with other conditions.

Labeling

Scholars differ in their interpretations of the labeling argument (see Gove 1980). Although some see it proposing an interrelated set of causal effects, others contend it is nothing more than a collection of "sensitizing" observations. I treat it as a general theory, in part because the majority of deviance scholars regard it as such, but also because it can be construed to explain at least some degree of repetitious deviance, regardless of disclaimers by those who claim it is only a sensitizer. As a theory, the formulation has two components, one concerning the application of labels, and the other about effect of labels on subsequent behavior. Supposedly, labels are created by public declarations, like those enunciated in arrest or judicial processing. Official actions stating that a person has committed deviance sometimes result in stigma (the label sticks). The theory states that whether public declarations are made, and whether such announcements succeed in creating stigma, depends upon the ability for resistance by those who are the objects of labeling attempts. Those with little power and few economic, personal, or interpersonal resources are least able to resist and are therefore more likely to be labeled. Being labeled, in turn, presumably undermines the victim's opportunities for conforming behavior and encourages that person to associate with those similarly labeled. In addition, stigma presumably causes a crisis of self leading to a deviant identity. Blocked opportunities and deviant identity then combine to produce recidivism ("secondary deviance"—that which is a product of the way in which primary deviance was dealt with).

Like the others, this theory has a lot of surface validity. Obviously public declaration of misbehavior may cause self-threatening embarrassment, humiliation, and stigma, and one may react by turning toward bitterness and determination rather than remorse. Everyday observation confirms that public identification as a deviant can close off opportunities for conventional activities and associations and that social involvements with others in similar circumstances can lead to new ways of thinking about oneself, which ultimately may produce recidivism. In addition, it is clear that the chances of public stigma with the consequences described above are not equal for all individuals or categories of persons, even when they commit similar acts. In view of stereotyping tendencies, it would be surprising if minorities, the poor, and those lacking conventional certification as responsible people were not especially vulnerable to stigma as criminals or deviants and if stigma for males and females did not vary with the type of alleged offense.

It is no wonder that labeling theory is intriguing, even captivating to some. It seems so reasonable and at the same time it contradicts academically unpopular ideas about deterrence (Tittle 1975a). However, as a general theory it is much too imprecise and weak. First, and foremost, it does not account for initial acts of deviance; it begins with the discovery (or at least the perceived discovery) and potential reaction to a deviant act.

Second, it does not recognize that labeling can sometimes deter, and it only obliquely (by using indeterminate language such as "may," or "can" rather than "will" or "with X probability under Z conditions") accommodates situations where labeling has no effect at all. Further, it does not address the possibility that, even among those affected in the specified way, the intensity of the effect may vary with personality, internalized moral commitments, and involvement with various kinds of social groups.

Third, it takes no account of the way in which the labeling process might vary from offense to offense. As far as the theory is concerned, the sequence of effects from labeling to transformation of self and ultimate secondary deviation is universal to all forms of deviance and of equal intensity. Nevertheless, being labeled as a murderer surely has quite different effects than being labeled as a marijuana user; certainly stigmatization as a white-collar criminal is different from stigmatization as an illegal-drug dealer.

Fourth, labeling theory recognizes none of the other reasons for or ways in which one might become a recidivist or adopt a deviant self-image. It is simply not reasonable, for example, to believe that the absence of labeling will lead to conformity. Is it sensible to imagine that theft of large sums of money without apprehension, labeling, or stigma is typically a singular event with little possibility of repetition? Moreover, there is much reason to imagine, and much evidence to indicate, that some people deliberately seek to establish deviant reputations and embrace deviant identities (see Katz 1988) because they serve as tools of defense or domination.

Fifth, the theory specifies none of the immediate conditions that bring forth deviance among those labeled, for, as even proponents concede, deviance is neither continuous nor does it necessarily follow from labeling or a deviant self-concept. Thus, even if the labeling process constitutes one avenue through which career deviance is stimulated and sustained, the labeling formulation is far too skimpy to serve as an adequate general theory.

Utilitarian/Deterrence

This theory is sometimes referred to as rational choice (Cornish and Clarke 1986) or "economic" theory (Yunker 1977), and often when the focus is exclusively on the effect of sanctions, it is called deterrence theory or doctrine (Gibbs 1975). The basic idea is that all human acts are decisional and that any behavior can be understood in terms of relative costs and benefits. When the cost of a given behavior exceeds the benefit (utility) for a particular individual, he or she decides to forgo it. When the benefits exceed the cost, the behavior follows. Therefore, if we can learn the costs and benefits of different courses of action, we presumably can explain and predict what will happen. There are two ways to use this basic cost-benefit formula. One is much like a closed system of religious philosophy, and the other is theoretical. I am concerned only with the theoretical aspects of rational choice theory, but because many scholars confuse a closed philosophical system with the theory, I want to make that distinction clear before I try to show the plausibility and value—and inadequacy—of this formulation.

A cost-benefit formula is like a closed philosophical system when every possible variable in human behavior is translated into the terminology of the formula as a cost or a benefit and when this translation is justified in tautological terms (compare Etzioni 1983). For example, a man goes berserk and shoots a number of people in a public place. He is caught, found to be psychotic, and incarcerated for life in an institution for the criminally insane. According to the closed philosophical system version of rational choice theory, this man has calculated the potential benefits of shooting those people, weighed them against the potential cost of being caught and incarcerated, and found the benefits of the killing to exceed the cost of lifelong incarceration. However, we might protest, what possible benefit could these shootings have for someone? One of several answers is given: (1) In the twisted mind of this psychotic, killing is extremely pleasurable, even to the extent of outweighing the incarceration, so he killed because the benefit outweighed the cost; (2) the killings were somewhat pleasurable, but the killer thought he would escape without paying any cost, therefore he did the killing because the perceived benefit still outweighed the potential cost; or (3) the killings were not pleasurable at all, but were actually a little bit costly because of the price of the rifle and bullets and the loss of social reputation, but the killer anticipated he would get free room and board in a hospital for the rest of his life, which was worth more to him than the cost of equipment and the loss of social reputation, and so forth. If you accept one or another of these rationales and ask how the theorist knows that the explanation offered is correct, the answer is tautological—the man did the killing, therefore it must have been more rewarding than costly.

With this gimmick, the job of the researcher becomes that of finding and construing evidence to fit the conclusion. The cost-benefit formula, in instances like this, is like a key that permits translation of mysteriously coded secrets into a coherent format. Being able to incorporate material into an understood language, however, does not explain how the material came into existence, what the ideas expressed in the translated material mean in an intellectual sense, or even that the key reveals the actual code used by the writer of the material—and to think it does is self-delusion of the highest sort.

Gimmicks like this are not helpful to science, which is why we distinguish theory from philosophy and evidence from faith. Most religions operate in the same mode as much economic theory. To the religious person, every event in life is seen as an act of God intervening in one's personal life, either to help the believer or to test the believer's faith. When good things happen to religious fanatics, they interpret them as rewards from God for their good works or favored status. When bad things happen, God is said to be testing faith. Believers claim that these divine interventions are empirical proof of God's existence and the truth of their philosophy, but a nonbeliever can quickly see that *every* event will fit into the interpretive scheme to confirm it. In short, given the prior faith and the interpretive device of translating all evidence into rewards or tests of faith, there is no possible way that negative evidence can intrude into the circular system of religious reasoning (see, for example, Lofland 1967). So it is with some versions of rational choice or economic theory—they are not theories at all. This can be seen from the above example of the psychotic killer. Within the parameters of true-believing economic theorists, there is no possible way that negative evidence can contradict rational choice interpretation. If one suggests that free room and board is hardly beneficial at the price of freedom, the response is likely to be that in the mind of a psychotic it is. If the killer fears incarceration and claims that he got no pleasure from the killing and knew that he would be caught, the response is that at the time of the killing he must have perceived that he would get great pleasure from it (otherwise he would not have done it), and so on.

Although utilitarian/deterrence thinking is often of the gimmicky variety, it not inherently so; there is a genuine theoretical component that conceives of most, if not all, human action as decision-making behavior in which cost-benefit calculations play an important part. This theoretical component is consistent with common sense. Everybody knows that most of the time cheating on one's federal income tax, defrauding a client in a confidence game, running an illegal gambling operation, and engaging in professional burglary all involve cost-benefit calculations in which an offender concludes that probable gains outweigh the potential costs. All the same, it strains imagination to think that this is always the case. For instance, some tax cheating is accidental, some cheaters do it out of conviction that the tax is used for immoral purposes, and some do it to spite the government or to prove bravery to others. Many people gamble illegally because it is a habit, or because it is fun, or because they are with others who are doing it, not because they rationally calculate that it is economically beneficial. It certainly stretches credibility to contend that impulsive or emotion-driven behaviors like most homicide, suicide, mutilation, or compulsive gambling can be explained as rational choices, unless one contends that the momentary pleasure or dynamic of the situation is so powerful that its benefits outweigh any possible costs. Falling back on this catch–22 invites tautology and demonstrates the failure of rational choice theory.

Moreover, as powerful as the idea of cost-benefit calculations is, only a very naive person would imagine that all, or even most, individuals perceive objective costs and benefits accurately enough to permit explanation in those terms. However, to substitute perceived for objective costs and benefits in rational choice theory requires a whole line of theorizing about how and why people perceive things the way they do. The conspicuous absence of this additional contingent of theory about perception is one of the key reasons that the utilitarian/deterrence model is inadequate as a general theory. In addition, rational choice theory takes the social structure, which creates and distributes costs and benefits, for granted, making it impossible to incorporate into the scheme deviant opportunities that are likely to be crucial in accounting for cases in which personal proclivities render deviance more beneficial than costly but in which individuals nevertheless conform.

Finally, the rational choice calculus resembles a mechanical gearbox that transforms inputs into particular kinds of outputs (compare Liska 1969). Without knowing how and why the inputs take on particular values, understanding the gearbox is of limited use in explaining and predicting behavior. For example, if one is trying to understand why and how automobiles move, it may be essential to gain a knowledge of how transmissions work, for surely the automobile cannot move unless the power generated by the engine is transformed into an appropriate mode for turning the wheels. Nonetheless, it would be silly to concentrate on the transmission and the intricacies of its operation. After all, without fuel, a mechanical device to transform the fuel into physical movement, and a drive shaft, a transmission would be useless. In what sense then would understanding the internal structure of a transmission explain the movement of the car? By analogy, even if economic theory were completely valid, it would be extremely limited as a general theory because it does little more than show how some inputs are translated into particular outputs.

Routine Activities

The latest contender among simple theories calls attention to a crucial, but usually neglected, variable—opportunity (Cohen and Felson 1979). Although routine activities theory primarily addresses variations in rates of predatory crime across ecological contexts or through time, it highlights aspects of the behavioral field that are implicated in individual explanations of crime and deviance. According to the theory, the way in which three variables converge in time and space determines the rate of predatory crime. These three variables are the presence of people motivated to offend, targets for predation, and absence of guardianship. In some social environments, such as the modern suburb, the routine activities of people (such as employment of all adults outside the home) interact with availability of suitable targets of predation (such as a large number of portable but quite valuable commodities) to create opportunities for those in the urban environment who are motivated to steal. The result is a high rate of burglary. From this, one can predict that rates of burglary will vary with suburbanization and labor-force participation of women and that they will also vary with other changes in the conditions of life that impinge on the three variables central to the theory.

Like all the theories being discussed here, this one has much inherent appeal, and its basic premises can be extended to many microlevel situations. For instance, few would deny that the chances of any given person's stealing money are greater when the loot is in paper form, already bagged, and lying in an easily accessible place, with nobody around, than if it is in metal form, in a locked box, and guarded by someone. Also, of course, if we already know that the individual in question has a strong desire for additional money and is willing to break the law, the prediction is even more likely to be correct. Similarly, prudent parents know that the chances of their teenage daughters' becoming sexually active vary somewhat with opportunities to be alone with slightly older males that they find attractive. In this situation we see a person highly motivated to break the rules that prohibit premarital sex (youthful sex drives are powerful), there is a suitable target (a desirable member of the opposite sex), and an absence of guardianship (no parents or adults around to find out or intervene). Thus, even though Lawrence Cohen and Marcus Felson have not claimed that their theory explains individual crime or deviance, or that it is a general theory, we can evaluate its potential in those terms, and if we do so, we will be impressed with its plausibility.

Nevertheless, despite the credibility and importance of the routine activities argument, it is inadequate as a theory capable of explaining variation in crime rates and as a potential base for a general theory of individual criminal or deviant behavior. Consider problems with the theory as a general scheme for explaining crime rate variations, for which it was intended. First, the key concept—routine activities—is ambiguous and unexplained. Humans perform many activities routinely; they go to work, wear clothes, brush their teeth, and so on. On the surface the theory seems to imply that any "routine activity" affects the crime rate. Yet it is hard to see how the general practice of toothbrushing can affect the crime rate. Actually, in examples given by the inventors of the theory, and in most tests of it, only particular kinds of routine activities are featured—those associated with, and reflecting, behaviors of people with particular demographic characteristics, which are basically activities stemming from the composition, distribution, and movement of populations, and from levels of technological functioning (like the separation of work from place of residence). In reality, then, proponents of the theory seem to imply that the routine activities that matter are those that, in fact, empirically affect one or another of the central variables. One would presumably rule out toothbrushing because it has not been shown empirically to affect the availability of motivated offenders, suitable targets, or guardianship, nor does it seem to have the logical likelihood of doing so.

The *theory* contains nothing that specifies which routine activities, or even which type of such activities, will affect crime rates and which will not. Evidently, one must leave theory and take up research to identify the routine activities that actually affect the crucial variables. Since there are literally thousands of possibilities to be examined, it is clear the theory does not do what theories should. The theory of routine activities seemingly does no more than simply postulate an additive effect of three central variables; it does not specify the causes of those three variables. Apparently, whenever the causes of the central variables are established empirically, those causal variables, whatever they might turn out to be, will then be classified as routine activities, whereas regular patterns of behavior that do not empirically affect the number of motivated offenders, availability of suitable targets, or the degree of guardianship will be called something else. Thus, rather than explaining crime rates, the theory merely identifies proximate variables and sets in motion a trial-and-error, empirical search for routine activities that affect the proximate variables.

Further, although the theory seems to explain two of its key variables—guardianship and availability of suitable targets—as products of routine activities, it leaves the third unexplained (see Felson 1986 for an effort to rectify that). It is hard to conceive how variations in the number of people motivated to offend can be a product of routine activities unless the term encompasses aggregated living, or urbanization. Even then, a lot would need to be filled in to explain why cities or certain areas of cities attract or generate motivated offenders, and such explanations would have to contend with the controversy about whether cities actually contain more potential offenders (see Archer and Gartner 1984; Fischer 1984; Tittle 1989a and 1989c).

Moreover, the routine activities formulation does not spell out the various ways in which its central variables might intersect to affect crime rates. Although additivity is plausible, it is nevertheless conceivable that one or another of the central variables is so important that it sets the parameters within which the other two can operate. Weak guardianship in combination with low target availability and few motivated offenders might produce as much crime as strong guardianship with high target availability and many motivated offenders, if there is anything to the deterrence argument. It is also possible that the conditional effects might be curvilinear. One could imagine that beyond a certain point the number of motivated offenders has a diminishing effect on the property crime rate as competition among potential offenders undermines the value of booty and leads to lethal conflict.

Finally, the theory is limited because, as currently formulated, it applies only to "ordinary" predatory crime. We need general ecological theories that allow explanation of rates of white-collar (such as contract fraud) and moralistic crimes (such as drug usage, driving while intoxicated, and prostitution) as well as other forms of deviance (like homosexual behavior or devil worship). Consequently, although the routine activity theory of crime-rate variations is fascinating and provocative, it falls short of what we need.

In the same way, an analogical theory of individual predatory behavior based on the principles of the routine activity formulation provides a lot of insight but still leaves much to be desired. Such a theory might contend that the probability of an individual's committing predatory criminal behavior varies directly with the combined magnitude of motivation, opportunity, and low risk. Drawing on the macrolevel theory, it would posit that the opportunities for and the low risk associated with predatory crime depend upon demographic and technological factors (routine activities) characterizing the population in the person's social and geographic domain.

However, such a theory would hardly be sufficient, for it would suffer from the same imprecision as the macrolevel version. It would not tell us which routine activities, in what amounts, would produce various levels of motivation or risk, or how they would do so. It would provide no explanation at all for motivation, and it would not move beyond the simple additive assumption about how the three variables might combine to affect the individual's responses. Moreover, this analogical theory would be limited to predatory crime, and it would not address how psychological variables, like aggression, intelligence, or perceptual ability, or other variables, such as moral commitment or group affiliations, might interact with the three central variables in affecting individual behavior.

Summary on Simple General Theories

All of the simple theories of crime/deviance are defensible in their own terms, but all are also incomplete. They are limited in applicability, and even in instances where a given theory logically applies to a particular criminal or deviant behavior, the explanatory power of the theory is typically not very great. These theories leave too many questions unattended, and they neglect to connect the variables they deal with fully and logically. As a result, each of the simple theories leaves us intellectually unsatisfied and incapable of adequately explaining or predicting criminal/deviant behavior. This is reflected in research showing that empirical predictions drawn from them prove correct only a little more often than chance—most cases do not fit the pattern predicted by the theory. Indeed, it is rare for any of the deviance theories to generate hypotheses that achieve even 30 percent accuracy in any test. Although some of this inaccuracy may be due to technical deficiencies of measurement, most is not. The deficiency is mainly theoretical.

Plan of the Book

In the remainder of this book, I try to overcome some of these theoretical deficiencies. In Chapter 2, I delineate four features that must be incorporated in successful general theories, and I highlight those features by reassessing the simple theories described in this chapter in terms of them. Chapter 3 discusses two popular methods—invention and elaboration—for building better theory; Chapter 4 evaluates the less popular technique of theoretical integration. In both chapters the practice and promise of each of the respective methods of theory building are evaluated against the backdrop of the four elements for successful theory laid out in Chapter 2. That assessment leads me to advocate theoretical integration as an approach for building general theory. However, since theoretical integration has not yet fulfilled its promise, I set forth a framework for integrating theories. After that I report my own attempt to specify a central causal process called "control balance," around which the paradigm for integrating theory can be focused. Chapter 5 defines the dependent variable in the theory, and Chapter 6 is devoted to clarifying the concepts with which the control balance theory deals. Chapter 7 describes the central causal process of the proposed integrated theory, and Chapter 8 identifies the contingencies under which the control balance process is likely to operate with greater or lesser force. Chapter 9 evaluates the extent to which the control balance process is consistent with the current evidence about deviant behavior and outlines the kind of research that must be undertaken to evaluate the theory effectively. Finally, Chapter 10 shows how the paradigm for theoretical integration introduced in Chapter 4 has been implemented and assesses control balance theory in terms of the criteria of adequate theory set forth in Chapter 2.

2

Features of Adequate Theory

The central ideas of the most popular simple theories of deviance identify variables or processes that are probably important in the production of deviant behavior. Yet each of the theories is incomplete, and so far they have not been combined into a more general formulation to compensate for that deficiency. Moreover, the simple theories individually and collectively exhibit other deficiencies that highlight the need for better theory. Theories of deviance should provide satisfactory explanations for all forms of the phenomena within the various domains addressed by the field, which is to say that theories should answer the questions why and how—adequately and with breadth. I will show that the simple theories reviewed previously do not do this, and by such application, I hope to illuminate the features that we should use to guide efforts to build general theory.

The most important task for theory is to generate explanations of the phenomena to which it is addressed. A theory of deviant behavior must help satisfy intellectual curiosity about the origins and forms of the conduct under consideration—ideally it completely quenches the thirst for understanding, that is, it provides answers to the questions why and how that are pleasing to an audience trained in skepticism and commissioned to seek solutions to intellectual puzzles. In short, theories must specify the causes of things within their domains, and so they must be differentiated from (1) perspectives, which represent broad orientations or approaches to a subject matter; (2) philosophies, which encompass moral positions about what ought to be, and theologies that assume a single, divine cause of all things; (3) taxonomies, which systematically classify phenomena into categories; (4) descriptions, which portray the static features of existing objects, thoughts, or arrangements; and (5) definitions, which represent declarations of the meanings of things or assertions about the nature of things.

"Breadth" refers to the capacity of a theory to explain a variety of specific instances within a given domain of phenomena. Ideal theories of individual deviance will encompass all forms of deviant behavior. But since theory building is always in process rather than complete, no theory is ideal. Instead, breadth, and the other features of good theory to be discussed, represent continua. A theory should be evaluated by the extent to which it possesses each of the characteristics being described here.

In addition to breadth, a unitary feature, deviance theories should explain their subject matter adequately. Adequacy involves three distinct components: comprehensiveness, precision, and depth. Comprehensiveness refers to the number and inclusivity of causal elements that might be operating. The more comprehensive a theory, the more complete the explanations it can generate because more of the various causal forces that can come into play are accommodated within its framework. Thus, if strain sometimes affects deviance, a comprehensive theory should recognize this and spell out how and when strain has that effect. If the learning of patterns of deviant behavior through differential association sometimes affects deviance, a comprehensive theory will also incorporate that element, along with strain, and show how and when it comes into play, and so on, for other causal elements that might operate. The ultimate outcome is a completely comprehensive theory that incorporates all causal elements necessary to achieve full explanation.

Second, adequate theories should identify the conditions that influence exactly when and to what degree the causal processes will unfold, the nature of the causal effects, and the time interval between the proposed causes and the expected effects. This feature I call "precision." Rarely does an independent variable always affect a dependent variable to the same degree, even when they are causally linked. The extent to which some variable, or some interaction among causal variables, affects some dependent variable will depend on the time lag, the degree of exposure, and the presence of conditional, or contingent, elements that vary from unit to unit and from situation to situation (Birbeck and LaFree 1993). Moreover, not all causal effects are monotonic, or linear in their influence; many take other forms. A precise theory stipulates the magnitude of the causal intervals and spells out how much exposure, under what conditions, produces various degrees of the dependent variable, and with what form. In addition, a precise theory identifies other variables that impinge on the causal process, specifying how they influence or set the parameters within which the causal variables of the theory operate.

Adequate theories must also answer the question *why* systematically and exhaustively so that outcomes can be understood as products of dynamic sequences of events, or interactions of variables. It is necessary to specify that A has a causal effect on B, but it is better to go on to show why and how A has the value and valence it does in given instances and how or why A affects B. It is still more useful to show how A and X jointly affect B, or how A and B might be reciprocally influencing each other. In other words, a good theory specifies the full causal process and provides logical rationales for the connections among the parts—a feature I refer to as *depth*.

Comprehensiveness, then, refers to the inclusion of all possible causal variables; precision concerns how well a theory specifies the conditions for the operation of the causal effects as well as the nature and form of the causal relationships; and depth indicates how well the causal variables are logically interlinked to form a meaningful and systematic whole.

We must design theories general enough to explain all forms of deviance in a way that is simultaneously comprehensive, precise, and deep. It is hardly debatable that simple theories fail by those standards. However, the extent to which they fall short, and the pejorative consequences of those deficiencies, are not often recognized. This is shown by the popular argument that theories should be evaluated only on their own terms. Following that line of reasoning, a consumer of theory should ask first what the theorist "intended" to do and then judge whether the product lives up to that standard. Hence, if the labeling theorists "intended" only to sensitize the discipline to some things that might be operative, it is presumably unfair to judge labeling theory by other criteria.

That approach places priority on evaluation of the theorist (being fair, granting recognition, praising a good effort) rather than on the merit of the theory. The goal for a community of scholars must be to explain and understand the phenomena within its domain. Since theory is the primary means to that end, a given formulation should be evaluated by how well it advances the collective agenda, regardless of the limited intent of the theorists.

Consider an example. Suppose a community is situated on the edge of a river. To progress economically and socially it needs a bridge across the river, although some residents may deny the need, claiming that the community has survived up to that point without it. To inspire citizens to undertake the task, the community authorizes a governing body to request blueprints for a bridge, with rewards to be given for effective plans. In response, a particular architect submits a plan to build a toolshed. The evaluation committee examines the plan and collectively concludes that it is a very good blueprint; consequently, most members of the committee argue that a reward should be given to the architect. Other members of the committee, however, dissent, pointing out that the plan will never produce a bridge, and despite the excellent way in which the architect accomplished what he or she set out to do, the plan is not adequate to the goals to which the community is committed.

I endorse the board's minority opinion. The objective of the contest, specified as vital to the future of the community, was not even addressed, much less accomplished by the toolshed architect. Certainly the committee might want to congratulate the architect for developing a good blueprint for a structure that would ultimately come in handy during actual construction of the bridge, once it got a workable plan for it; after all, any large building project needs a place to store tools. But the committee would deceive itself, the community, and the architect if it promoted the idea that a blueprint for a toolshed is an adequate response to the need for a bridge. By its actions, the committee would encourage other architects to aim low, and it is a good bet that after rewarding the toolshed architect, the committee would be inundated with limited, off-target, inadequate plans, each justified on such grounds as "All I intended to do was draw a plan for a road to the bridge" ("a house for the foreman," "an on-ramp for the bridge," "a boat for helping build supports," and so forth). As a result the bridge would probably never be built, or if it were, the final product would take an inordinately long time.

Conversely, if the committee took the board's minority point of view to its extreme, rejecting any submission that was not a full-blown blueprint for the most elegant bridge imaginable, it would stifle the bridge project. An extremely strict standard would discourage architectural efforts, and it might cause the committee to dismiss something useful. To succeed, the bridge committee must keep the final goal clearly in mind in evaluating submissions. It must not allow individual architects to set the standards in terms of their own idiosyncratic intents, yet it cannot afford to impose unrealistic, self-defeating standards.

The study of crime/deviance is analogous. As a community of scholars we desperately need an adequate general theory, although like a few citizens of the community on the river, some will deny the need. I believe we must encourage the general theoretical endeavor, and we must keep our eyes focused on the objective. In the process, we ought to recognize and encourage any achievements that move us closer to the goal, but at the same time, we must not be afraid to criticize products that fall short. Only by setting forth the criteria for a good theory and judging contenders by those standards can we generate the awareness to improve. Yet, recognizing the overall deficiencies of theoretical entities does not mean that they contain nothing of value. Indeed, I believe that our objective cannot be achieved without joining the disparate, separately incomplete, explanatory strands contained in the various explanations and formulations making up our theoretical arsenal.

Let us, therefore, consider the criteria of good theory in more detail. Although the main criterion is, of course, actual explanation, the following discussion will not focus on explanation per se. Rather, it will highlight features of theory that bear on the quality of explanations generated by theories. The simple formulations reviewed in Chapter 1, as well as other formulations to be discussed in subsequent chapters, unquestionably offer answers to the questions of *why* and *how*, though the answers may not be totally adequate.

Breadth

The theoretical weakness easiest to appreciate is lack of breadth; simple theories cannot account for the full range of phenomena that interest students of crime/deviance. Each simple theory applies to some forms of deviance but not to others, and often the range of kinds of deviance covered is quite narrow. This constitutes a major deficiency of theories of deviance for three specific reasons. First, permitting theories to be narrowly focused violates a major assumption of scientific work—that the field to be studied is composed of systematically and coherently interlinked entities—and in my opinion deviance can and should be studied scientifically. If deviance scholars do not assume an orderly structure to the phenomena they study, they run the risk that their work will be ephemeral and particularistic, much like description of transitory events, with no long-range import or continuity. In addition, if the scientific assumption that the social world is tied together in a meaningful and coherent way is true, then explanations of behavior, whether they be of deviance or of conformity, must accommodate that order. To do that, theories must make it possible to understand and predict all forms of behavior within a common framework. Differentiating deviant behavior from conforming behavior is counterproductive, and further dividing deviant behaviors into subtypes to be accounted for with distinct and separate theories is a serious mistake.

The danger is not in the failure to embrace scientific assumptions per se; rather, it is in the strategy of work that follows from it. Unless there is an initial commitment to the scientific mode, we cannot make informed decisions about whether the main operating assumption of science is correct for the crime/deviance domain. To discover whether science is appropriate, we must act as if its central assumption is valid. We may ultimately find that a scientific approach does not work, and if so, downshifting to a more limited, particularistic mode can be accomplished easily. However, developing multiple theories, each of which is limited to some particular number of deviant behaviors, without first stretching to reach the general formulation, precludes ever learning whether the scientific assumption is correct. Thus, by exclusive attention to the limited case, we run the risk of being extremely wrong. More important, we will not know we are wrong.

Consider the opposite scenario. Suppose the assumption that deviant behavior is of one cloth, explicable with a systematic, coherent general theory, does turn out to be correct. There will be a tremendous payoff in the power of general theories built on that assumption. In short, embracing scientific procedures and attempting to build general theories accordingly will enable us to find out if the scientific assumption applies, and if it does, there will be much benefit from having built general theories. If we start by rejecting science and building particularistic theories, we will be stuck with them without even knowing that they are ill informed. Therefore, at this point, good theories of deviance should have wide breadth.

Second, it is already clear that the many theories in existence do not cover unique phenomena and that the explanatory principles of various theories overlap (Akers 1985, 1990; Pearson and Weiner 1985; Wilson and Herrnstein 1985). Students of deviance make a major error in assuming that general theories can only apply to behaviors that are manifestly similar. Theories are built around abstractions, which permits them to transcend the confines of raw empirical reality. Things that seem dissimilar when viewed through the lenses of everyday conceptualization and discourse may be basically alike on a more abstract level. One example is rape. Before feminist writers began to raise the awareness of scholars, rape was treated theoretically as it appeared empirically—as an act of passion, the object of which is for a male to penetrate a female to achieve orgasm for his own sexual pleasure—and particularistic theories were developed to explain it. Feminist thought, however, forced scholars to redefine this act as a vehicle of violence used by one person to exert dominance over another person (usually, but not always in the form of a male dominating a female). With reconceptualization, rape began to appear like many other forms of violence, and the possibility of explaining it with the same kind of theory one would use to explain assault, gang violence, extortion, and contests of moral dominance became apparent.

Subsequent discussion of existing theories will show that particularistic applications are artificial. In fact, I contend that restricted theories are not necessary even when deviant acts are conceived in their most obvious empirical form. Limited breadth, therefore, is a primitive fetish, constituting an impediment to effective theory.

Third, adequate theories must have wide breadth because that is more parsimonious. Any fair survey of the theoretical literature will reveal much redundancy. Theories supposedly limited to different forms of deviance turn out looking a lot alike, even though they purportedly explain quite different things (see Tittle 1972 concerning the similarity of two theories). Many theories of "delinquency" could just as easily be regarded as theories of crime (Agnew's general strain theory was initially thought to apply only to delinquency), just as so-called theories of crime could just as well be regarded as theories of deviance (see Tittle and Ward 1993). In the same way, theories of drug usage may easily be applied to theft, and theories supposedly designed to explain theft apply to drug usage (Akers 1985, 1990; Gottfredson and Hirschi 1990; Katz 1988). If we build general theories that have appropriate breadth, we can eliminate much of this excess baggage.

Breadth is important, then, because it resonates with the basic strength of the scientific approach, it exposes latent traits of existing theories, and it leads to parsimonious general theories. These advantages can be illustrated by considering the breadth present in the most popular simple theories.

Illustrations

As noted previously, differential association appears limited to deviance involving group contexts of learning and action, and it cannot account for individualized acts totally lacking normative acceptability. These exclusions encompass acts often attributed to mental illness (partly because they do not appear to be socially normal); suicide, in societies where taking one's own life is not culturally prescribed; uncouth behaviors like public nose picking; and forms of self-imposed social isolation (such as living as a hermit). Narrowly considered, the theory is even more particularistic than that because Sutherland explicitly described it as a theory of "criminal behavior."

Actually, with broader vision, the learning principles on which differential association theory is based probably can be extended to any form of behavior. After all, humans must learn an enormous number of things just to function in the culture where they are born, and learning conceivably involves no more than exposure to excess definitions favorable to those behavioral patterns (although contemporary psychological research contradicts this). For instance, a simple thing like eating with a fork, neither a deviant nor a criminal act in most Western societies, requires learning that is probably based on exposure to more messages endorsing fork usage than messages supporting other ways of eating. In a similar way, the individualistic behaviors that seem to be excluded from Sutherland's formulation could have been incorporated within the premises of differential association had its author recognized the need for breadth and had he been more attuned to comprehensiveness and precision. This is clear from modern learning theories that have been used to restate and improve his basic argument (Akers 1985; Wilson and Herrnstein 1985). In fact, modern learning theories purport to explain all behavior, conforming and deviant as well as normal and "abnormal." Although, as will be seen later, such theories may promise more than they deliver in actually providing a satisfactory explanation of all forms of behavior, they at least have wide breadth.

Hirschi's theory of social control is deliberately narrow, applying as it does only to "delinquency," although there is no necessity to limit its principles to the misbehavior of youth (a fact now recognized by Hirschi [1992]). Still, it is hard to know what adult deviances it should explain, and even though delinquency sometimes encompasses a broad range of different kinds of behavior—including crime, social and moral delicts, and a number of individualistic acts that adults think may damage a youth's health, mental condition, or future preparation for adult responsibility—the breadth of the theory is not clear. In addition, ostensibly it does not seem to apply to behaviors of the mentally ill, to white-collar or professional types of deviance, or to instances of overconformity as deviance.

This is unfortunate. Social control theory postulates that involvement in, acceptance by, and dependence on a given group renders a person susceptible to control by that group. Such notions have been used to explain many kinds of behavior (Cullen 1984:137–42), heroic as well as criminal (Durkheim [1897] 1951). If integration with a conventional social group helps prevent suicide (Durkheim [1897] 1951) and "delinquency" (Hirschi 1969) and motivates people to fight (Stouffer et al. 1949), make sacrifices for a community (Kephardt and Zellner 1994), or commit deviant acts on behalf of a subcultural group (Lofland 1967), it should affect almost all forms of deviance. The absence of social integration with conventional groups should be influential in psychotic behavior (unless that specific behavior is organically determined and totally uncontrollable); without integration into nonbusiness groups, entrepreneurs, who are highly motivated to turn a profit, should be free to engage in price fixing; and strong social integration with any group should inspire some to excess zeal in fulfilling what they perceive as group expectations (overconformity), which may result in various forms of deviance. Since Hirschi's version, the best-known expression of the social control argument, does not convey this breadth, it must be regarded as shortsighted. Even the proliferation of separate theories of social integration for various deviant and conforming acts (Reckless 1967; Tittle and Welch 1983; Stets 1991) illustrates the inefficiency of theory building in the social sciences and dramatically underscores the importance of constructing theories with breadth.

Because of imprecision and shallowness, it is difficult to say exactly what kinds of deviance labeling theory presumably explains, particularly since it only attempts to account for those forms of deviance that are "secondary" in nature. It might apply to any form of deviance that can be publicly recognized through the imposition of a label by duly authorized officials. This would include any behavior officially prohibited in the criminal law of a given society (labeled by criminal justice agents), any "abnormal" behavior regarded as evidence of mental illness (labeled by medical personnel), and any form of institutional misbehavior (labeled by school officials, church authorities, and so on). It may also apply to any form of social misbehavior that can be magnified in a public "event" or "episode" to which a social audience can respond by collectively stigmatizing an individual.

Presumably, it cannot explain private or secret acts undetected by authorities or unknown to the public, such as disloyalty to a friend or lack of sensitivity to a spouse or child, nor can it explain the many forms of primary deviance that escape stigma or even repetitive deviance that continues without the individual having been labeled deviant by a hostile audience (like habitual shoplifting). As it bears on secondary deviance, the labeling theory seems to have fairly broad coverage, but because it is extremely narrow otherwise, even if it were completely accurate in its account of secondary deviance, it would be inadequate as a general theory.

This may not be inherent, however. If the principles of labeling are conceived more generally, perhaps as reflected by theories of self-formation in the symbolic interaction tradition (Heimer and Matsueda 1994; Matsueda 1992), which is often hinted at, but not yet fully accomplished, the theory could explain all forms of behavior. Rather than thinking of "labeling" as something that officials or entire social "audiences" deliberately do, one could think of all social reactions to behavior as confirming, challenging, or being neutral to the self-implications of behavior emitted by a given individual. From the premise that everybody constantly checks their self-concepts against reactions of others to arrive at and sustain meaningful and workable self-images, one could account for any pattern of behavior.

Initially, to arrive at a tentative definition of self, infants and youths could be seen as emitting all kinds of behaviors to test the reactions of those nearby. Once a "self" began to crystallize, it would motivate behavior designed for confirmation. Since some initial "trial-and-error" acts would be deviant, social reaction could lead to a tentative "deviant" self-image. A deviant self-image would then inspire more deviant behavior as individuals struggled to confirm that they were the kind of people they were beginning to think they were. Labeling/self theory, so conceived, would explain primary and secondary deviance, and it would account for any form of deviance that might be within the cultural imagery of a given social context. Labeling theory would be much better if it had this kind of breadth.

If one interprets Marxian conflict theory in terms of the deprivation and exploitation presumably inherent in capitalism (but also possible in a wide variety of social contexts and economic systems), rather than in terms of capitalism per se, it explains all forms of exploitation and insensitive or de-moralized acts by one person against another—what Michael Gottfredson and Travis Hirschi (1990) refer to as acts of force or fraud pursued for self-interest—acts of protest or retaliation by workers against exploiters or symbols of oppression, as well as acts reflecting adaptive techniques for economic survival (such as prostitution). Even with a direct focus on exploitation/deprivation rather than capitalism, the theory still does not explain individualized acts of deviance that victimize only the perpetrator, "social deviance" like failure to observe religious rituals, or those forms of deviance like drug abuse that are sometimes called "moralistic offenses." Hence it has a broader focus than labeling but is narrower than differential association.

Like labeling theory, however, this one does not need to be so limited. If deprivation or being a victim of exploitation can free individuals to take advantage of others, it can also affect their psychological well-being. Constant distrust, fear, and insecurity can have devastating consequences for an individual's psychic health; indeed, when those attitudes dominate, paranoia is often diagnosed. Therefore, it is not much of a stretch to imagine that these same forces can alienate people to the point where they want to escape by suicide, drug abuse, or catatonia. Alienation can also lead to "irrational" acts of property destruction, symbolic acts of defiance like flag burning, and refusal to participate in conventional patterns of behavior as expressed in unusual modes of dress, "hippieism," and "swinging."

My point is that the same arguments that Marxian conflict theories use to explain inhumane acts in the struggle for survival can be extended to incorporate almost any form of deviance one can imagine. The failure of the Marxian theorists to make such extensions stems partly from their political agenda, which is to attack capitalism, not to understand deviance, whereas the failure of other theorists to expand the potential of conflict theory reflects a disciplinary flaw. The fact that there are distinct theories of psychological functioning to account for some deviant acts, other theories specifying the effect of competition on acts of predation, and still others to explain alienated behavior, when all could be accommodated within Marxian conflict theory, shows the weakness of our collective commitment to breadth.

The main strength of utilitarian/deterrence, or rational choice, theory is its purported breadth. Granting the premises of the theory, there is no deviance—indeed no behavior of any kind—that it cannot explain. Since every act can be conceived in terms of costs and benefits, the rational choice argument can be construed as an explanation of all deviance. However, as I explained earlier, many of these constructions are gimmicks. In reality, there appear to be many deviant acts that defy utilitarian/deterrence explanation. Some represent habitual patterns of conduct (such as failure to stop completely at traffic signs); others reflect illogical balances of cost and benefit (such as acts of rage that result in long-range costs so far outweighing the benefits in the immediate situation that it is questionable whether rational calculation was at work). In addition, some deviant behavior grows out of duty, performed at enormous personal cost without much benefit (such as euthanasia) (see Etzioni 1988), whereas other deviant activities seem to provide so many immediate benefits that perceptions of potential costs are blurred (like addictive drug use or risky sexual behavior). Finally, some deviant acts appear to represent outright miscalculation of costs and benefits (the prime example is compulsive gambling). Therefore, contrary to its claims, economic theory is quite narrow, being limited to those deviant acts usually subject to dispassionate calculation of instrumental gain relative to measurable cost—including much (but not all) property crime, many types of deception and lying, and a small percentage of first-degree homicides and assaults. Nevertheless, the prime virtue of the theory is its attempt at broad sweep, and one reason it has attracted a strong following in recent years is its promise of accounting for so many things within one explanatory scheme. Thus, even in failure, it asserts the importance of breadth.

Nevertheless, although the theory's attempt at breadth is virtuous, its weak execution is a vice. Utilitarian/deterrence theory is too simple to explain all forms of deviance, though it could account for a broad range of behaviors by treating the exceptions noted above as special instances to be brought into the explanatory scheme through additional theoretical principles that operate under specific intervening or conditional circumstances.

Since routine activities theory requires a suitable "target," it is almost inevitably limited to forms of deviance with a victim, or in a few cases a coconspirator such as a teenage sex partner. This excludes much deviance, but unnecessarily so. Why should routine activities bear only on predatory crime? With a little additional theoretical work, the formulation might come to grips with the question: What happens when there is a motivated (potential) offender but no suitable targets and lack of guardianship? One line of theoretical development in answer to that question might lead to explanations of symbolic, nonpredatory deviance, particularly if the theory maintains, as it seems to, that "offender motivation" is a constant, taken-for-granted condition that must somehow be expressed. Another line might lead to moralistic deviance, mental illness types of behavior, or social withdrawal, if the theory were to bring in conditional principles that show why some potential offenders attempt to suppress deviant motivations in the face of almost certain frustration of predatory efforts. This kind of expansion would make the theory far more useful, and certainly more complete; and it would contribute to efficiency in the overall theoretical enterprise.

Notwithstanding its flaws, Merton's anomie formulation is very broad and, possibly for that reason, has had more impact than any other simple theory. To the extent that it actually explains deviance, it appears to explain almost all kinds. The "innovation" adaptation seemingly includes all forms of theft, violence, and deception; "retreatism" covers suicide, social isolation, withdrawal, and acts regarded as evidence of mental illness. "Ritualism" and "rebellion" seem to pick up all of the residual forms of deviance not encompassed in the other two, cleverly including overconformity itself as deviance. Unfortunately, this breadth is bought at the price of precision and explanatory quality, a trade-off not to be encouraged.

Summary on Explanatory Breadth

In summary, then, adequate general theories of deviance should explain many different forms of deviance, ideally all possible forms, because this is consistent with scientific endeavors, it reflects the character of the collective body of theory already available, and it is parsimonious. However, all except one of the simple theories are quite restricted in what they can explain. Although anomie theory has the potential for the broad sweep needed, it acquires that breadth only by an imprecise explanatory scheme that fails to satisfy most criteria for adequate explanation. Most neglected by the simple theories are individualized forms of deviance, unusual acts often regarded as indicating mental illness, social deviances of alienation or protest, "moralistic" acts, and overconformity. Therefore, improving the breadth of deviance theories will require sensitivity to their explanation.

Comprehensiveness

The objective of a general theory is to account fully for the phenomena within its domain. "Accounting for" means to answer the questions *why* and *how*; it is not limited to "explaining variance" in a statistical sense. Indeed, explaining the variance probably has minimal relationship to explanation as conceived here. Even total statistical explanation of the variance may leave us intellectually unsatisfied about answers to how and why questions because statistical models do little more than confirm the importance of variables. Such models can show interconnections among variables only in a rudimentary way because they cannot tell us why the variables are so interconnected. Nevertheless, a good statistical model must incorporate all the important variables if it is to account for the variance in specific dependent variables, just as a theory, if it is to account fully for the phenomena within its domain, must incorporate all of the causal elements that might be operative. Beyond a point, additional causal elements may add only small increments to the overall explanatory power of a theory, but current formulations are far from diminishing returns. Moreover, causal elements are rarely additive in their effects. Instead, they are more likely to operate in interactive combinations, often with nonlinear manifestations. Therefore it is essential for theories to bring in a wide range of causal elements that potentially can be interlinked for depth.

Simple theories stress specific causal elements to the neglect of others. In reality, every deviant or criminal act probably involves some motivation as well as weak control, and every criminal or deviant act probably has some internal and some external elements. A full account of deviant behavior probably requires explanation using all these as well as other causal forces (Pearson and Weiner 1985), especially as they interlink. Indeed, there seem to be at least five things operative at the point of commission of any given act of deviance (Megargee and Hokanson 1970; Sheley 1983): motivation, opportunity, ability, constraint, and absence of alternative motivation.

There is no question but that simple theories picture the deviance-causing element too narrowly—both in the configuration of causal factors and the locale from which they emanate. Typically they portray the cause of deviance unitarily. Five of the seven most popular theories depict the cause of deviance as being mainly, if not exclusively, either unusual motivation toward deviance or unusual weakness of constraint. Differential association, anomie, labeling, and Marxian conflict emphasize motivation. Differential association sees the motivation in learned attitudes, values, and skills; anomie theory postulates that the motivating force is strain; labeling projects the motivators as stigma, blocked opportunities, and deviant self-identity; and Marxian conflict theories contend that the motivators for deviance are competition, deprivation, and struggle for survival. Social control exclusively stresses the absence of constraint and identifies the constraining social bonds that may be absent as belief, commitment, attachment, and involvement. Their absence is said to permit the deviant urges presumably present in everyone to be expressed in actual behavior.

The remaining simple theories bring in at least two causal factors, but both stop far short of the inclusivity necessary for full explanation. Moreover, even with more than one central variable, both of these "more complex" simple theories neglect one of the central factors featured in the other. Utilitarian/deterrence, or rational choice, theory encompasses both motivation and constraint because benefits (the motivators) are evaluated relative to costs (the constraints), but the theory neglects opportunity, which is pivotal for routine activity theory. Routine activity theory, in turn, incorporates constraint (absence of guardianship) along with opportunity (availability of suitable targets), but it takes motivation for granted.

At the point of behavior, simple theories also tend to emphasize causal elements located either in the person or in the social situation rather than in both places. Three of them (differential association, social control, labeling), though recognizing the influence of external, environmental influences in producing the internal variables, stress causal foci within or characteristic of the individual, paying minimal attention to how the effects of those individualistic elements on deviant behavior might be affected by the ongoing social situation. The other four (anomie, utilitarian/deterrence, Marxian conflict, and routine activities) treat variations in the social environment as paramount while largely ignoring individual variables.

Illustrations

Sutherland's differential association theory narrowly emphasizes "push" in leading to crime/deviance and locates the causal element almost exclusively inside the individual. The theory does acknowledge the importance of the social environment in presenting "definitions" to the individual that lead to attitudes, desires, values, and skills that ultimately cause deviant behavior. At the point of commission, however, the individual's internalized attitudes and desires propel that person toward crime or deviance. The theory, therefore, is incomplete because it does not take account of potential variations in opportunity, risk, or precipitating conditions that might evoke or stifle behavioral impulses reflecting the individual's own personal "definitions" about crime/deviance. As a result, it will frequently fail when criminally motivated people refrain from actual criminal behavior, perhaps because they are not in situations where acts can be committed, because the chances of getting caught and punished are too high, or because they have other, more important things to do when they encounter criminal opportunities. Further, it will also fail when those not particularly motivated toward crime/deviance nevertheless commit it, perhaps because the deviance promises unusually strong rewards or there is unusually strong provocation to act in anger or to compensate for humiliation (Katz 1988). Unfortunately, this would still be true even if "excess definitions favorable" to crime or deviance are interpreted in the most comprehensive way to accommodate situational variables, because the theory does not explicitly reveal how one is to know that "definitions" are favorable or unfavorable to crime or deviance.

Social control theory obviously lacks comprehensiveness. It does not depict how its main variables (elements of social bonds) are caused, instead taking them as givens. Like differential association, its point-of-behavior causal variables are all traits of individuals, either internalized factors like belief, commitment, and attachment, or static features of individuals' involvements with social entities. It too makes no attempt either to spell out situational conditions that might invoke delinquency among those not well bonded or to recognize that actual deviance, whether among socially bonded or unbonded individuals, to some extent reflects opportunities and risks in the immediate behavioral field. Thus, the focus is narrowly on constraint flowing from individual attributes.

Labeling theory, too, pulls one element out of a larger pool of potential causal elements, and at the point of behavior, it locates that causal factor inside the individual, with too little regard for external social circumstances. It does recognize the preliminary impact of social situations influencing whether one will be labeled, the effects of labeling on a stigmatized person's options, and social response molding deviant identities. However, labeling theory's answer to the question What causes deviant career behavior? is quite likely to be: "a deviant self-identity." Such an answer grants no recognition to social situations that might deny self-identified deviants opportunities for affirming their identities through deviance, nor does it show regard for the possible risks in various situations or for provocative circumstances that might make one acutely anxious to express behavior consistent with a deviant identity.

Merton's anomie theory limits itself to one central motivational variable located in the social environment—strain from inconsistency between culturally defined goals and available means. It largely ignores variable constraints and opportunities in immediate social contexts that might affect strain as well as inhibit or encourage various kinds of adaptation, focusing attention instead on more or less stable structural features of social contexts. As a result there is no place in the theory for point-of-commission features of the individual or the social situation. If individuals are strained by having been exposed to success goals over a long period of time without the acceptable means to achieve them, why don't they constantly commit acts of deviance? Shouldn't things going on in the immediate situation, such as perceived need to project a deviant self or to bear testimony to one's religious convictions, affect whether strain leads to deviance? Furthermore, there are probably many characteristics of individuals, in addition to strain, that would help explain deviant adaptation, although Merton only hints at internalized values as one possibility. Hence, even if strain is an important motivator, anomie theory is too narrow to provide much general understanding of its operation or of the way it is linked with deviant behavior. It ignores several critical variables in its emphasis on strain, and it locates its central causal process in the social structure while paying no attention to the individual or the immediate behavioral field.

Similarly, Marxian conflict theory locates the cause of individual deviance almost completely in the social structure external to the individual. Capitalist economic relationships presumably de-humanize and demoralize both workers and capitalists. The more intense the competition between one capitalist and another, and the more a worker must struggle against other workers for subsistence, the more likely each is to engage in various forms of exploitation and predation (Bonger 1916). However, the theory ignores other features of the larger social structure as well as the immediate social situation that must come into play, since even the most deprived people deviate only sporadically. Furthermore, in its overemphasis on the larger social structure, Marxian conflict theory overlooks individual variations in personality, perceptions of reality, and moral constraints against exploitation or predation, which probably bear on behavioral probabilities.

Although the two remaining simple theories are more complex, they are still limited in their configuration of causal processes and in their imbalanced emphasis. The utilitarian/deterrence, or rational choice, argument focuses on the simultaneous operation of motivation and constraint (although much research on the deterrence question assumes the relevance only of cost, or constraint) but neglects the distribution of opportunities for benefits to exceed costs; likewise, it ignores other variables, like the ability to carry out an act, that probably influence whether a favorable balance of rewards to costs actually results in specific forms of behavior. The theory merely asserts that the probability of deviance reflects the extent to which motivation (benefits) exceeds constraint (cost). Furthermore, although the mental process of calculating a cost-benefit ratio is no doubt affected by personality, ability to perceive reality, intelligence, and other things, the causal forces are portrayed as being outside the individual in the immediate social environment where dynamic circumstances reflecting potential benefits and costs are at work.

In like manner, an analogical extension of routine activities theory to individuals' behavior would stress the social situation almost exclusively. Motivation to offend is assumed; guardianship and availability of suitable targets are seen as variables in the environment that constitute constraint and opportunity, respectively. Nowhere in the theory is there a place for individual variables like moral commitments, personality, and strain that might affect whether guardianship is ignored or underestimated, nor is there a place for ability to perform various criminal acts that would affect whether targets are perceived as available or suitable. Moreover, it is clear that this theory excludes crucial variables in the situation, like peer expectations and behavior, that would affect whether a motivated potential offender acts, even when presented with suitable targets without guardians.

Implications

Clearly none of the simple theories include all of the five types of causal elements mentioned earlier, and certainly none of them show appreciation for the interdependency of causal forces. Motivation, opportunity, ability, alternative motivation, and constraint represent variables that operate with greater or lesser force in any immediate context in which deviant or criminal behavior could occur, and they interact or interlink in the production of crime/deviance. A theory or explanation that takes account of only one or two of these forces will inevitably fall short. For example, imagine an individual, Y, who is usually strongly motivated to commit a particular act. If we were trying to predict whether Y actually would commit this crime/deviance using a theory like differential association, anomie, or labeling that attributes the main cause of deviance to the strength of motivation, we would predict a high likelihood. However, imagine that Y constantly faced a high probability of being arrested or of experiencing informal rejection from peers for that act and that these were even more compelling in Y's mind than the motivation for this particular form of deviance. In this instance, if we were to observe data concerning Y's actual crime/deviance, we would probably find no evidence of the type in question despite Y's strong motivation. The empirical evidence in this case would *appear* to contradict the theory, but such negative evidence would not prove the theoretical principle per se to be wrong. Instead, empirical failure would reflect the incompleteness of the theory, which emphasized only one variable.

Simultaneous operation of the forces of motivation and constraint can be diagrammed by using the length of a forward arrow to represent the strength of Y's motivation to commit the particular act in question and using the length of a backward arrow to represent the strength of constraints in Y's life against the deviance. As diagram a shows, for Y the strength of constraint against a particular act exceeds the strength of motivation to do it. Hence Y would probably not commit the act in question.

Motive   Constraint

(a) Individual Y ——————→ ←——————————

Now consider a second example involving individual Z, whose motivation is slight, much less than it was for Y in the example above. Again, if we only take into account the strength of motivation, as some simple theories mandate, we would predict little likelihood of the crime/deviance. Next, imagine that for Z the constraint against this particular behavior is almost nonexistent. The actual probability of deviance would likely turn out to be quite high despite rather low absolute motivation. By taking into account only the motivational factors, we would again predict incorrectly, and that failure would challenge the validity of the theory from which the prediction was derived. Again, the poor prediction would not necessarily indicate that the theory is wrong, only that it leaves out something important. This second example is shown in diagram b:

Motive   Constraint

(b) Individual Z ——————→ ←——————

Comparing diagrams a and b reveals a further weakness of simple theories that give priority to motivational elements. If motivation is the main factor determining deviant behavior, Y should have a greater probability of deviating than Z, because Y has stronger absolute motivation. Yet, if we compare the lengths of the motivational arrows in diagrams a and b, relative to the respective constraint arrows, that suggests that the situation is actually reversed. Individual Z has stronger *relative* motivation than Y despite Z's weaker absolute motivation. Thus, though motivation is important, unitary theories that treat it in isolation from constraint will prove inadequate.

These same considerations also demonstrate the inadequacy of Hirschi's social control theory, which attempts to explain deviance by considering only variations in constraint. Imagine that individual Q is strongly bonded to conventional groups and society and that in Q's life pattern the chances of getting caught and punished by the law are high. Constraint theories would suggest little likelihood of Q committing the deviance in question. However, if Q also has an extremely strong desire to commit the act, a desire that exceeds the level of constraint, then Q likely will deviate. Yet, looking only at the extent of constraint would lead to a predictive error that would misleadingly contradict constraint theory. Instead, it would reflect the narrowness of the theory in not recognizing the simultaneous operation of motivation and constraint. This example appears in diagram c:

Motive   Constraint
(c) Individual Q

Contrast this with individual R, who faces few constraints. Constraint-based unitary theories would predict offending by R. However, if R has very little motivation toward this deviance, R probably would not commit it despite weak controls. This would be another instance in which the theory fails because it overlooks the interaction of important forces. This example is shown in diagram d:

Motive   Constraint
(d) Individual R ⟶ ←

Comparing diagrams c and d also reveals another potential misleading interpretation. If constraint is the main factor in deviance, individual R should have a greater chance of deviating than Q because controls on R are so much smaller in absolute terms than those on Q. Yet, the constraint on R, relative to motivation, is much greater than the relative constraint on Q. Accurate predictions and reasonable explanations in these cases depend on consideration of the joint strengths of motivation and constraint.

Similar misapplications occur when motivation- or constraint-focused theories fail to take account of other variables. Consider Q in diagram c, who is heavily constrained but whose motivation is even stronger. A simple theory stressing motivation would predict deviance by Q. However, if Q rarely has any opportunity to commit the kind of deviance at issue, Q is unlikely to deviate despite strong motivation, and predicting deviance solely from Q's level of motivation would prove empirically incorrect.

One reason simple theories have limited explanatory and predictive power, then, is their exclusion of many important variables. Even if Sutherland were totally correct about learning and criminal behavior, his theory could not predict well. Two individuals could be equally exposed to an excess of crime-favorable messages from which they learn criminogenic attitudes, but one of them may encounter numerous criminal opportunities, whereas the other rarely has such chances. As a result the two will differ dramatically in actual probability and frequency of criminal behavior despite possessing equal amounts of the supposed causal variable. Similarly, two individuals rationally calculating the chances of being caught and punished for misbehavior will not possess the same quality information; one may have accurate data the other lacks, or one may correctly perceive the chances of punishment and the other may misperceive them. Consequently, individual behavior is often at odds with predictions from economic theory.

At this point some readers may object that simple theories implicitly assume the operation of many other things, but because of their limited goals in showing the import of their primary variables or processes, they fail to make the other interactive or causal elements explicit; that is, simple theories operate with an implicit assumption that "all other things are equal." Accordingly, to give differential association its due, one should presumably measure all essential variables, including constraint and opportunity (ability, motivation, and alternative motivation are incorporated as things learned in differential association) and observe the effect of differential association and its intermediate products on deviance, holding constant, or removing the effects of, constraint and opportunity. Under these conditions, defenders might say, differential associations will co-vary with the likelihood of deviance or crime, as the explanation offered by the theory predicts. Similarly, it could be said that to assess Hirschi's theory of social bonds one should measure motivation, opportunity, alternative motivation, and ability in order to remove their effects while observing the capacity of social bonds to predict delinquency or other forms of deviance. Under such "controlled" conditions, empirical outcomes will presumably validate the explanation offered by the theory.

I agree that the appropriate test for a narrowly focused theory is one that removes, or holds constant, the effects of "all other variables." But finding support for a theory with this kind of test is not the same as certifying the *adequacy* of a theory for explaining crime or deviance. Clearly all other things are *not* equal, and it is only when we grasp the way in which theoretical variables or processes operate in conjunction with variations in "all other things" that we can account for crime and deviance. Moreover, without specific theoretical guidance, a researcher cannot identify "all other things" in order to measure and control them. Therefore, neglect of the simultaneous operation of a variety of forces is a theoretical failure.

Since there are a number of crucial point-of-commission forces that interact to influence the likelihood of crime/deviance, theory must be more inclusive than it usually is if the needed explanatory and predictive power is to be gained. Still, it is not enough to say simply that deviance is caused by a multitude of elements and to throw them together in a haphazard or undisciplined way. We must develop complex theories that specify the relative importance of these forces under various conditions and that articulate how they are interlinked to produce the effects to be explained or predicted.

Precision

This brings us to the third major feature of adequate theory, precision. To fully serve our purposes, a theory should identify the contingencies that influence the strength with which the causal processes operate, the form of the causal effect, and the time lag between the occurrence of the cause and the expected effect. A major reason for the inadequacy of simple theories of deviance is their postulation of processes that presumably produce effects in a monolithic, linear fashion and in the same way in all circumstances. One form this imprecision takes is a failure to incorporate statements specifying their scope, or the conditions for the full operation of the causal effects (Cullen 1984; Gibbs 1972b; Walker and Cohen 1985). Instead, simple theories set forth causal effects that are assumed to vary little from individual to individual, from social context to social context, or from situation to situation. Another expression of the imprecise character of simple theories is their neglect of the form of the supposed causal effect. The theories leave the impression that any increment in their proposed causal variable leads to an equal or proportional increment in the postulated effect. Further, simple theories do not specify the magnitude of the intervals between their postulated causal variables and their effects, leaving the consumer to guess whether particular variables will produce their effects immediately, within days, after months, or with the passage of years.

Illustrations

Sutherland's differential association theory ignores differences in the ability of individuals to learn, whether the subject might be mathematics, history, or definitions favorable to criminal or deviant behavior (see Eysenck and Gudjonsson 1989; also Wilson and Herrnstein 1985). Rather, the theory implicitly assumes that equal degrees (weighted by the modalities) of excessive exposure to crime-favorable definitions will produce the same amount of criminal behavior in all people. Similarly, differential association takes no account of the possibility that greater exposure to excessive definitions, for example, those favorable to homicide as opposed to marijuana use, might be necessary to induce individuals to adopt the particular behavior, or that differential association might simply be irrelevant for some criminal/deviant acts like necrophilia. Furthermore, Sutherland's theory does not explicitly recognize that the degree of learning of deviance-favorable definitions, as well as the degree to which things learned are expressed in deviance, might vary across societies, social groups, or demographic categories.

In addition, Sutherland's portrayal of the form of the relationship between differential association and deviant behavior is ambiguous. He usually spoke simply of "excess definitions," as if any ratio of crime favorable to anticrime messages exceeding unity would produce the same amount of criminal behavior. At times, however, he seemed to suggest that the term "excess" really implies a continuous variable with greater amounts of crime-favorable excess leading to greater probabilities of criminal behavior in a linear, even monotonic fashion (Tittle et al. 1986).

Finally, the theory largely ignores causal intervals, except for vague suggestions that priority and duration affect the weight of messages bearing on criminal behavior, leaving one to guess the extent to which differential association produces immediate or long-range effects.

In reality, however, even if differential association and the learning that results from it are key causes of crime/deviance, they are probably more or less effective for different individuals, for those of diverse social categories, and from society to society. After all, some people learn more easily than others and at different speeds (Eysenck and Gudjonsson 1989). Furthermore, given the influence of peer groups and other close associates, differential association probably produces short-range effects as often as long-range ones, despite Sutherland's contention that priority and duration are modalities for the effectiveness of social messages. Moreover, the effect of social messages may vary with frequency and duration in ways not anticipated by Sutherland. Messages too frequently conveyed can become boring and ineffective, sometimes even causing hostility and rejection. As a result, differential association and crime may be linearly related only up to a point, after which diminishing effects may appear, perhaps even reversing at the extreme.

As noted earlier, Merton's anomie theory does not show clearly why one form of deviant adaptation is chosen rather than another. Since the stipulated causal factors appear most straightforward for those embracing the goals but lacking the culturally approved means to achieve them, the theory probably should specify that the causal factors will work better for innovation than any of the other forms of deviance, though even such a contingency statement would not be enough. For one thing, since the causal variables can only work if people perceive the relationship between goals and means correctly, perceptual ability should probably be stated as a contingency. In addition, the theory's effects would seem to be contingent on the degree of homogeneity of culturally defined goals in various societies and to apply more to males than females. Finally, since the theory hinges on the extent to which dominant cultural themes are communicated to all, its effectiveness will probably vary with the sophistication of the system of mass communication in various societies. This theory is even less clear than differential association in indicating causal intervals. It offers no clues as to how long one has be exposed to inconsistent goals and means before the motivation to innovate is strong enough to produce deviance. Conceivably it could be a few minutes in contrived laboratory experiments or, in ordinary societal circumstances, years. Without theoretical guidelines, a researcher might assume causal intervals that are completely unrealistic and thereby produce misleading evidence.

Finally, since the theory says nothing about the form of the causal relationships it postulates, one is left to assume a simple linear effect. Is it realistic to think that a unit of goals-means discrepancy is the same when there is little overall discrepancy as when there is a great deal? Goals-means discrepancies may have larger and larger effects up to some point beyond which further increments make no difference, or perhaps extreme discrepancies produce hopelessness and inaction (retreatism?). However, Merton was interested in valences (directions), not degrees of commitment to goals and means, so the theory is doubly deficient. Since precision is necessary for effective explanation as well as for proper evaluation of a theory's main causal claims, is it any wonder that anomie enjoys scant empirical support?

Hirschi's theory of social control makes no attempt to spell out the circumstances within which social bonds will have more or less effect in restraining deviance. Individuals vary in how accurately they perceive the likely responses of others to particular behaviors, so strong social bonds may sometimes fail to restrain deviance. Moreover, the constraints of social bonds are probably more effective for some kinds of crime/deviance, perhaps more so for acts strongly disapproved by general opinion than acts that are only slightly disapproved. In addition, adults may be restrained more by social bonds than young people because maturation in modern societies requires a transition period of ambivalent status that makes affiliations with conventional groups become less important. No doubt other contingencies could be identified, but the theory itself makes no effort to do so. As a result, those who apply this theory must assume universality, which leads to disappointing results.

The theory is also imprecise in its failure to specify causal intervals. How long must a person be free of social bonds before delinquency is likely—days, weeks, months, or years? Perhaps bonds can be temporarily broken to permit almost instantaneous deviance (maybe that is what is involved in "neutralization" [Sykes and Matza 1957]). The causal interval may depend on the number and kind of opportunities for deviance presented by the youth's social environment, or perhaps, on the strength of the person's motivation toward a particular form of deviance. In any case the theory would be better if it specified the causal intervals and provided some theoretical linkages to account for the varied conditions under which the lag varied.

This theory also neglects the form of the supposed causal relationship, leaving one to assume a linear effect. Given the theory's assumption of invariant motivation toward deviance, postulation of linearity may be a logical assumption, but it would be better if that were explicit. Better yet, the theory could incorporate motivation as a variable and then detail the variety of forms the causal relationship might take. If theorists were to contemplate the nature of the causal relationship between social bonds and deviance, they might entertain the notion of a curvilinear effect. After all, high rates of violence among some tightly knit communities of primitives, as well as among dyads and families in contemporary societies, suggest that at some levels social bonding can create tension resulting in deviance.

Major criticisms of labeling theory have always included imprecision among its flaws (Gibbs 1966, 1972a; Tittle 1975b). Because the theorists seem to have used indeterminate language intentionally, consumers of labeling theory are provided with few guidelines about the conditions under which the causal processes are most likely to result in further deviance. It is said that labeling *may* lead to stigma, that stigma *can* inhibit opportunities, and that it *might* cause a transformation in self-identity. The theory does not say explicitly what circumstances must prevail for labeling to lead to stigma or for stigma to lead to self-transformations. Defenders claim that labeling theory has no obligation to specify these things because it was developed to "sensitize" the field to the possible unintended consequences of official processing of deviants. Yet the labeling argument has been used as if it were more. Unfortunately, however, it is inadequate, at least partly because the assumption of universality that must accompany a "non-conditionalized" theory has proved untenable.

If the labeling process (the sequence of effects from official labeling to secondary deviance) is valid, it is probably more likely to occur when the labeling is for some kinds of deviance rather than for others. Labeling a man for assaulting an adult no doubt has different effects than labeling him for assaulting a child. A criminal label for a male probably has far less effect than a criminal label for a female because such a label is more consistent with the masculine role. Also, being labeled deviant in small, homogeneous societies may have more consequences than labeling in large, heterogeneous ones because of greater opportunities to remain anonymous in the more-complex society, or because smaller communities are more likely to practice "shaming and reintegration" (see Braithwaite 1989). Furthermore, some individuals have exceptionally strong egos that lead them to resist accepting and acting on labels. Some who are officially labeled may escape tendencies toward secondary deviation because of their involvements with strong families, religious groups, or spouses. In fact, labeling can, under some circumstances, produce less rather than more deviance (Berk et al. 1992; Tittle 1975a).

Labeling theory could also benefit greatly by clarifying the causal intervals implied by its argument. Does it take a week, a month, a year, or several years for a label to lead to secondary deviation? And if that causal interval is determined by particular conditions, what are they?

Finally, labeling would be a much better theory if it recognized that the effects of audience labeling may be nonlinear. If labeling is a continuous rather than a discrete variable, at low levels it might inspire denials and efforts to prove the label wrong, but at higher levels it might produce transformations of self and association with other deviants. Thus, labeling might have opposite effects within different zones of a continuum, leading to secondary deviation only at high levels and beyond a threshold.

Marxian conflict theory paints with a broad stroke but neglects precision. Capitalism causes competition and material deprivation, which demoralize people, leading them to commit acts of deviance against others. The central causal variables of competition and deprivation apparently always cause deviance. However, it is more credible that they cause predatory deviance than what is sometimes called "moralistic deviance." The logical linkage between competition/deprivation and drug usage, for example, is tenuous. Although some defenders may claim that strain causes some to seek escape through drugs, the theory says nothing about the conditions under which competition/deprivation would cause an individual to prey on others rather than try to escape. Furthermore, if demoralization is the intervening variable, it is hard to sustain the idea that loss of feeling for fellow humans generates a desire for drug usage oriented to pleasure rather than escape. In addition, although material deprivation may logically lead to predatory acquisition of food, shelter, and other comforts of living, it is difficult to imagine it would lead to rape. Thus, the theory should contain contingency statements about the kinds of deviance to which it applies most effectively.

Another possible contingency for a causal linkage between deprivation and deviance involves a process urged by Marx on a grand scale, but which occurs naturally in some smaller locales—worker organization. Deprived people sometimes band together in informal self-help groups to share meager resources. Collective misery can cause collective solutions and in the process draw people together in tightly knit communities where predation becomes less likely. Relative isolation in a confined geographic area, coupled with universal deprivation, may be necessary for worker organization to bloom spontaneously, and it may be a condition specifying when the conflict process is less likely to unfold. Even without isolation and physical proximity, relative deprivation may be more potent than absolute deprivation.

The unmitigated effect of competition among capitalists depicted by conflict theory also appears too universalistic. Competition may have different effects for private-owner capitalists than for stock-owner capitalists, and its effects may vary with individual greediness. Surely some capitalists escape the compulsion to struggle for ever-greater wealth through cutthroat methods. Although it might be rare, there are probably some whose moral compunctions restrain total exploitation of their employees. Therefore, competition may not necessarily produce de-moralized individual behavior. Whether it does could depend on many things, including moral concerns and actual degrees of success. Profits may be large enough and so easy to achieve that deviance is simply not "needed" by capitalists, and individuals sometimes win without becoming exploitative or "de-moralized."

These contingencies, of course, are not exhaustive or even necessarily accurate. Much careful theorizing would be required to specify all of the conditions affecting the causal process portrayed by Marxian conflict theory and how they operate. I have simply illustrated some of the likely ones.

Second, the Marxian conflict theory does not state the causal intervals among the various effects that it hypothesizes. It is silent concerning how much competition must transpire before exploitation occurs, how long one can be exploited before deprivation is felt, the length of time a person has to be deprived before de-moralization sets in, and how long one must be de-moralized before criminal behavior results. Furthermore, though the theory seems to imply that the effects of its variables are all monotonic and linear, deprivation and crime might be causally linked in a curvilinear pattern. Deprivation may increase criminal behavior up to a point, beyond which it might immobilize people, thereby decreasing criminal behavior.

This theory is inadequate, then, partly because its imprecision precludes discovery of its true potential. A dearth of conditional statements, absence of attention to the form of causal relationships, and neglect of the time intervals linking the causal variables leave too much to the discretion of consumers and opens the door for misleading tests and interpretations that undercut the theory before it can be fully appreciated.

It is especially clear that the economic principles of utilitarian/deterrence theory could be transformed from a universalistic, imprecise theoretical argument to something better by supplying a set of meaningful contingency statements. For example, some misperceive reality and act in ways that seem most beneficial to them at the time, though such action might be regarded as irrational to observers. But rational choice theory, as it is usually conceived, can apply only where actors can and do perceive objective costs and benefits correctly. Furthermore the costs and benefits of different actions vary from individual to individual and from situation to situation. It is not enough just to measure them as they exist; a good theory should indicate when they will have particular value so that those conditions can be taken into account in larger explanation. Some individuals may typically think like classical economic automatons (probably economists or businessmen) by regularly assessing the tangible costs and benefits of all action, and the utilitarian/deterrence theory may apply quite well to them. Others, however, often act out of emotion or feeling; they do things because it feels like the right thing to do, because their emotions are not under good control, or because their sentiments and values compel them. Rational choice theory will not be effective in explaining or predicting deviance among such people.

Not only does rational choice theory seem to work better for some individuals, but it probably also explains "instrumental" deviance more effectively than "expressive" deviance (Chambliss 1967). Much theft is rational, but slugging a bank loan officer for refusing a loan is another thing. Similarly, contractually defrauding the government is sensible, given the instrumental character of contracts and the meager chances of actually being caught or having to endure a substantial penalty if caught, but using addictive drugs is hardly cost-effective. Indeed much deviance seems to have its own seductive appeal despite very costly consequences (Katz 1988).

Finally, this theory probably works better among those socialized to think of the "bottom line" than among those with a strong social consciousness or a sense of moral duty (Etzioni 1988). Most people cannot and will not commit some forms of deviance, no matter how favorable the cost-benefit equation might be. In modern advanced societies hardly anyone will eat human flesh. The few well-known cases of cannibalism pale in comparison with the number of instances in which groups of people have starved to death without eating each other. Indeed, in most Western societies people will not knowingly eat animals that have humanlike qualities, despite the potential economic benefit of using dogs, cats, or horses for food.

Utilitarian/deterrence theory, then, is deficient in part because it takes no account of contingencies affecting whether it works with greater or lesser force (see Tittle 1980a). Much empirical work has attempted to identify and elaborate such contingencies (for example, Bachman et al. 1992; Burkett and Ward 1993; Grasmick and Bursik 1990; Grasmick and Milligan 1976; Richards and Tittle 1981, 1982; Sherman et al. 1992), but the theory remains theoretically unconditionalized with no systematic rationale specifying when choices are likely to be rational.

The economic perspective also pays little attention to causal intervals, although an implication of instantaneous effects is clear. Humans presumably rapidly calculate the costs and benefits of their actions, so deviant behavior should follow quickly from realization of a favorable opportunity (see Gottfredson and Hirschi 1990; Wilson and Herrnstein 1985). Still, some decisions about deviance seem to entail long periods of thought. Hirschi and Gottfredson (1987) notwithstanding, many white-collar criminals plan long and hard before they commit fraudulent acts (Cressey 1953), so a favorable ratio of perceived benefit sometimes has a substantial causal lag, and if popular literature can be believed, adulterers often fantasize for years before acting on their perceptions that an affair would be more beneficial than costly. Therefore, rational choice theory needs more precision in specifying causal intervals than most of its proponents realize.

The same goes for the form of the causal relationship. The value of something depends on a number of factors, not the least of which are deprivation and saturation. Increasing benefit relative to cost, then, will not necessarily increase probabilities of deviance. There are a number of subtle cognitive and evaluative processes at work that have not yet been theoretically linked and have scarcely been recognized by economists or by criminologists. The "base-rate fallacy" literature on risk assessment (Nisbett and Ross 1980; Tversky and Kahneman 1974; Tyler 1980) suggests that many decisions are hardly rational at all, and at the very least the relationship between cost-benefit and behavior is anything but linear. When utilitarian/deterrence theory can accommodate and account for such anomalies, it will be much closer to the adequacy its proponents claim.

Routine activities theory needs to specify three kinds of contingencies. The first concerns which types of deviance are best explained. Even though a good theory should apply to all kinds of deviance, it will not work equally well for all of them. The convergence of motivation, suitable targets (opportunity), and weak constraint will probably produce predatory deviance by individuals more effectively than such convergence would for any other kind of misbehavior. For example, women who illegally abort themselves are motivated to do so; the fetus represents a suitable target, provided the means of abortion is at hand; and there must be a perception of possible escape from the watchful eyes of those who might prevent the abortion. Similarly, drug users are motivated toward pleasure or relief of withdrawal distress; their own bodies represent suitable targets of drug effects; and they are able to escape the controls that non–drug users face. However, such applications stretch the theoretical premises. One contingency that needs to be made explicit, then, is the greater applicability of an individual analogical extension of routine activity theory to predatory, as opposed to other, types of deviance.

Furthermore, as noted earlier, routine activity theory also needs to be "conditionalized" in terms of the circumstances in which motivation, target suitability, and weak guardianship are most and least likely to converge. So far, examples used by theorists and supportive researchers suggest that convergence is more likely among those who live in modern societies and in urban areas. In addition, there might be a greater chance of convergence for males, since they are typically under more pressure to succeed economically or to validate their masculine identities through physical violence, and they typically move about more freely than females. Convergence of the three conditions appears more likely among certain occupational categories and racial or ethnic groups, and among mobile individuals. Certainly the accuracy of the theory will be contingent on the awareness of individuals, as well as on their ability to perceive reality correctly.

Finally, this theory makes no statements about the length of time required for the convergence of the causal variables to produce any effects. Since the generic focus is aggregate populations, particularly those residing in cities, and the theory describes an ongoing process rather than particular events, one can understand the theorists' neglect of causal intervals. Nevertheless, convergence of the three factors is clearly postulated to be variable across population aggregates, so if the theory is to be applied effectively, there must be a way to predict how quickly the supposed effects will develop once convergence of the three key variables occurs, or begins to occur.

Precision in specifying the form of the causal relationship is also lacking in this theory since there is an implicit assumption of linearity. Yet, convergence of the motivation, opportunity, and weak guardianship may not have much effect until a threshold is reached. Furthermore, the meaning of "convergence" is not completely clear. Does it mean that all three variables have high values in the same population or geographic area, or by extension, in an individual event? If so, the problem is to decide what qualifies as "high." Does it mean that the three have similar values in a given situation, though all may be modest? Indeed, the magnitude and form of the causal effect might depend on which way, among a variety of ways, the three variables are configured. Does a very high score on opportunity (suitable targets) make up for a modest score on motivation and weak guardianship? Perhaps very strong motivation in combination with modest scores on the other two factors could produce deviance as readily as convergence of modest scores on all three.

Summary on Theoretical Precision

An adequate theory will reflect precision by containing statements about the contingencies under which it operates with greater or lesser force, revealing the time intervals between its causes and effects and spelling out the form of the causal relationships that it proposes. This means that it must accommodate a large number of variables to clearly specify exactly when and for whom the causal process will or will not result in various degrees of the predicted outcome. Precision, however, goes beyond mere postulation of causal effects under various conditions; it also tells the consumer how long it takes for the effects to occur under various conditions, and it reveals how much of the causal variable it takes to produce particular degrees of deviance.

Without these features, theories will always be incapable of generating good predictions, and they will not satisfy the need for effective explanation. Such is the plight of simple theories in crime and deviance. They all contain useful core ideas, but they lack the features of adequacy, including precision. Because of this their potential cannot be fully appreciated. This encourages the belief that general theory is not possible, and it discourages pursuit of scientific study of crime and deviance.

Depth

An explanation is an intellectual account of a specific phenomenon that satisfies the curiosities of those seeking it. Explanations vary in depth, sophistication, form, and adequacy, depending upon the characteristics of their consumers. When people explain to a child that the light comes on because a switch was flipped, they have provided a satisfactory explanation for that person at that time. Such an explanation will not do for most adults, however, and it certainly will not do for scientists. As they mature, children become more sophisticated intellectually; eventually most of them will want to know "why" the switch makes the light come on. At that point people might answer that the switch allows the flow of electricity to the light bulb. Again, this explanation might be adequate for that child, although it will still not be satisfying for older children, adults, and certainly not scientists. As people mature still further, particularly if they acquire a more "scientific" orientation, they will demand more sophisticated explanations of why the light burns, and they will be skeptical of many explanations offered. Eventually a well-educated person will reach the point where intellectual curiosity cannot be satisfied until the burning light is explained in terms of successive references to empirically validated explanatory principles governing all physical phenomena.

That is how it is with social science. An unsophisticated person may be satisfied when robbery is explained as a product of greed. Someone more sophisticated will wonder if this explanation is always true, and why some individuals are more greedy than others. If an explanation says that some are more greedy because they were deprived as children, a sophisticated thinker will further inquire as to why some are more deprived as children. This questioning and answering process goes on until the individual's intellectual curiosity is satisfied or until no further answer can be given to the question *why*. That limit reflects the knowledge and sophistication of the explanation seeker, not the phenomenon to be explained.

Scientific explanations differ from ordinary lay explanations in their effort to satisfy the intellectual curiosity of a community of informed, sophisticated thinkers who are trained to pose deeper and deeper "why" questions and who share a set of norms and values that makes inquiry and critical assessment of explanations offered by others a virtue. The scientific community is further distinguished by the shared belief that the portion of the world they choose to study is not fragmented and unrelated, but instead somehow fits together in a meaningful way. Hence, scientists usually believe that an adequate explanation ought to be part of a more general, abstract set of principles that permits understanding of a large number of different phenomena, of which the present instance is only one example.

The scientific process begins with observation of some regularity to be explained. An offered explanation is then tested, modified, and retested until the scientific community is confident of its accuracy. Eventually that explanation is joined with other explanations of other phenomena to produce a more general and comprehensive explanatory system—a theory. Theory synthesizes separate explanations and provides the basis for deriving additional explanations of still other phenomena. Explanations, in turn, can be deductively manipulated to yield hypotheses or empirical tests that will determine the adequacy of the explanations and the theory that gave rise to them. Data collected in the process of hypothesis testing can also be used to modify both explanations and the theory from which they were derived. This process of feedback, theoretical modification, hypothesis generation and testing, and further feedback goes on until an adequate and comprehensive, general and empirically established theory has been built (Braithwaite 1960; Freese 1972).

In the movement back and forth during the theory-building process, scientists are always trying to answer further "why" questions. The more scientists learn, the more demanding they are in their requirements for explanation, and the greater their intellectual curiosity to know more. Scientific theories, therefore, will be simplistic and narrowly focused at first, but later they will be incorporated into larger, more general theories. In other words, in the early stages of science, explanations are shallow and limited, but as a science matures, explanations acquire more depth, and through theory they become more comprehensive.

The difference between shallow and deep explanations can be grasped by contemplating causes of death. Imagine an intoxicated man driving late at night on an icy road. Mistakenly perceiving an object in the road, he brakes abruptly, causing the car to swerve, leave the road, and slam into a tree. His chest is crushed, but he continues to live. Eventually someone comes along and calls an ambulance, but because it is an especially busy night, the ambulance is slow to arrive. Moreover, the medics discover that someone forgot to replace an empty tank, so the injured man cannot be given oxygen. By the time the ambulance arrives at the emergency room, the man is dead.

What caused his death? Some would say it was caused by intoxication, which slowed his reactions, leading him to inappropriately apply the brakes. Others would say the poor design of the vehicle caused his death since it did not have air bags to prevent his body from being hurled onto the steering column. Still others would say that the negligence of the ambulance crew caused his death since he could have been saved with quicker action or with the aid of oxygen, and so on. Some would probably even contend that death was caused by the cessation of brain activity.

In some sense each of these explanations is correct. In this particular instance, and in general, intoxicated driving contributes to, or "causes" death. So does the absence of air bags, the negligence of ambulance crews, and ultimately the cessation of brain activity. None of these explanations in isolation is satisfying, for it is the process, or sequence of connected events, that provides intellectual satisfaction. Any explanations that cut into the sequence of causes without specifying the full chain are "shallow." Although cessation of brain activity may be the "necessary and sufficient condition" for death, such an explanation is not satisfying because it conceals a vast world of knowable causes that lead to brain failure. Likewise, even though intoxication is implicated in much death, focusing on it bypasses complex permutations of interactive conditions that must be operating for it to cause death. Similarly, medical scientists cannot be satisfied by the declaration that all death is caused by brain cessation, although for some technical purposes death might be defined as the cessation of brain activity.

No successful scientific discipline is content with shallow explanations. It is only the most primitive fields that tolerate explanations resting on obvious, surface-level accounts, or have a preponderance of theories that take for granted things that can be explained, or connect variables without providing a rationale that enables consumers of the theory to feel comfortable that they know *why* those variables intersect in the specified way.

Unfortunately the field of crime and deviance studies is primitive in exactly those ways. Most of our theories penetrate larger and more comprehensive, but unspecified, causal processes at some late-point, accepting the products of the unidentified processes at work up to that point as the taken-for-granted elements on which the specific theory being put forward rests. For example, only recently have scholars even begun to try to explain how early predispositions and training intersect with later events to account for life cycle patterns of crime and deviance (Laub and Sampson 1993; Sampson and Laub 1992, 1993). Indeed, the typical response to apparently conflicting evidence about whether crime/deviance follows a linear or curvilinear pattern throughout the life course has been to dispute the evidence rather than to look for theoretical linkages between the two phenomena (see the exchanges concerning this debate in the February 1988 issue of *Criminology*).

Not only do our simple theories fail to include all the necessary variables for reasonably deep explanation (they lack breadth), but they do not link their variables together in a coherent sequential fashion. The narrowness of simple theories in their exclusive focus on one or two point-of-commission variables, already shown, is accompanied by neglect of "second-tier" variables that set the parameters within which point-of-commission processes operate. Furthermore, simple theories are notorious for failing to fully spell out the logical connections among their variables, and they are shallow in that they almost always imply one-way causation (see Thornberry 1987). Although it is useful to imagine, for theoretical purposes, that some things affect other things in a straightforward, unidirectional manner, in reality such is rarely the case. Much contemporary research using advanced statistical methods for assessing causal interconnections among variables has demonstrated what many have long contended—that most of the more important causal processes involve reciprocality. A theory that correctly shows how X influences Y will nevertheless be inadequate if Y feeds back onto X, so that over a period of time one can say that Y also influences X, and the theory does not incorporate this into its explanatory structure.

Illustrations

Differential association theory cuts into the midpoint of a long, implicit causal chain, neglecting to elaborate that chain downward and upward. It does not explain why some individuals associate more extensively with crime-favorable messages than others; it simply takes that as given (al-

though there are passing references to "differential social organization").
Similarly, it does not attempt to explain why the proportion of social definitions that are "crime-favorable" varies from social group to social group
to constitute the "differential social organization" with which a collectivity of individuals can be differentially associated. Finally, it neglects to explain why social messages, both favorable and unfavorable, exist in the
first place, especially those that are embodied in norms. The theory begins with the existence and differential distribution of different kinds of
social messages, states its causal nexus at that point, and then stops, leaving much still to be explained after the elements of the theory have had
their effects.

Not every person exposed to an "excess" of crime- or deviance-favorable messages, weighted by the modalities that Sutherland stipulated, actually acquires attitudes, values, motivations, and skills linked with criminal or deviant behavior. It may depend partly on learning ability.
Further, not everybody with attributes favorable to crime/deviance actually commits crime or deviance. Whether or not they do depends somewhat on opportunity, constraints in the social environment, and their ability to perceive situations as crime salient. Hence, this theory is only a
fragment of what is needed to spell out the full chain of causes of crime
and deviance.

In addition, the supposed connections among the variables in differential association theory are not always obvious. Why and how, for example, does excess exposure to crime-favorable messages result in internal
criminal propensities? Sutherland merely states that this learning of criminal things takes place like any other kind of learning.

Finally, differential association, unlike its more sophisticated cousin,
social learning theory (Akers 1985), does not explicitly recognize the potential reciprocal linkages between social messages and deviance suggested by both empirical and theoretical considerations. Even when an
offender is caught and punished for a notorious crime in the United
States, that person is also likely to be rewarded with social recognition,
often gets to keep most of the financial fruits of the violation, and is sometimes accorded prestige and esteem. In addition, committing the crime
may have been thrilling or at least useful for overcoming "humiliation"
(Katz 1988). Thus, observing others profiting, being socially recognized,
or being thrilled may lead to actual offending by an individual so exposed, and the resulting criminal behavior may contribute to more excess
definitions favorable to further deviance by the individual. Although
Sutherland recognized that the rewards of crime enjoyed by one person
constitute part of the array of crime-favorable messages for others, the
theory did not foresee self-reinforcement and reciprocal relationships.

Anomie theory also provides only a few links in a lengthy causal
chain, since it makes no effort to explain why societies differ in their emphases on goals and means, how those goals and means get communicated to societal members, or how the goals and means are distributed

among individuals. After the components of the theory have done their work, much remains unexplained. Why, for instance, do some people with inconsistent goals and means nevertheless conform? Why do some with consistent and culturally congruent goals and means deviate? Why do those inclined by the goals-means schema to deviate do so under some conditions but not others? Moreover, Merton does not provide satisfactory accounts of the logical connections implied by his theory. Why or how, for example, does the strain of internalized goals and unavailable means produce motivations for "innovation"? Merton apparently thinks the answer is obvious. Still, it does not appear so to a lot of us, particularly since we know it often produces other kinds of motivations, such as the desire to get closer to God, to commit suicide, or to construct a social definition of the situation as one of virtuous, long-term suffering.

It is also obvious that the unidirectional causal scheme of the anomie argument is not the full story. If the strain of incongruence between internalized goals and the absence of objective means generates motivation toward innovative deviance, it is probably also true that innovative deviance creates more awareness in the individual of the gap between goals and means, thereby intensifying the motivation toward more deviance. In addition, it is possible that once this causal loop is fully operative, the causal effect from deviance back to the goals-means gap becomes predominant. For example, one consequence of "deviant" feminist activity may be to raise a woman's "consciousness," which, in turn, may make further deviance even more likely.

Hirschi's social control theory begins with the social bonds of individuals; it does not explain why some groups to which one can be bonded are conventional and some are not, and why some individuals are more bonded than others. Moreover, there is no recognition of other characteristics of individuals, provoking circumstances, perceptual variations in how circumstances are experienced by individuals, immediate opportunities or constraints in the behavior field, the valence of groups to which one might be bonded, or other variables that link together to give an in-depth account of delinquency or other forms of deviance.

Social control theory also neglects to satisfy our intellectual curiosity about how and why the variables are linked as they are said to be. Why, for instance, should attachment inhibit deviance? The connection between the two may be due to fear of disappointing those to whom one is attached or to a positive desire to please them, to fear of losing the economic or other advantages of those to whom one is attached, to a moral sense of obligation not to bring shame, and so forth. Obviously, there are a number of possibilities, but which one or which combination of possibilities is correct is not theoretically discernible.

Finally, social control theory is shallower than it could be because it does not recognize feedbacks. As Terence Thornberry (1987) has so brilliantly argued, every one of the social bond elements in Hirschi's theory logically bears a reciprocal relationship with each other and with delinquency.

Despite its flaws, labeling theory provides deeper explanation than any of the three theories just discussed, at least for repetitious deviance. Starting with a structural system organized to favor power that unfolds in differential response to individuals who either commit or are suspected of committing acts challenging the social order on which that structural system rests, it theorizes a sequence of consequences—blocked opportunity, likely association with others also labeled, crisis of self, transformation of self-identity, and finally additional deviance—all interacting in reciprocal networks. The theory, therefore, offers a reasonably deep explanation, at least in comparison with the other simple theories already discussed.

Nevertheless, it still falls short of ideal depth. It takes structural realities as given rather than explaining them, it ignores the causes of primary deviance, it fails to adjust for instances when conventional pathways are unblocked by labeling, when labeling does not lead to association with other deviants, when the crisis of self results in affirmation of a nondeviant identity, and when deviant self-identities lead to repentance. Moreover, there is no attention paid to circumstances likely to provoke deviance, opportunities in the behavioral field, internal and external constraints on deviance, and the import of perceptual variations. If we recall the intoxicated man who had an accident on an icy road discussed earlier, labeling theory could probably provide the equivalent of about three links in the chain—the accident, the crushed chest, and the delayed ambulance—but it would ignore the man's intoxication, his improper use of the brakes, the empty oxygen tank, the heavy caseload leading to the delayed ambulance, and the cessation of brain activity.

What part of the causal chain is missing in Marxian conflict theory? The theory begins with a structural condition of capitalism and portrays it leading to competition and exploitation, which in turn de-moralize participants, enabling them to commit acts of deviance in pursuit of greed or survival. However, the path to deviance through capitalism is only one of several such possibilities. Even the most egalitarian and socialistic societies have some competition, at least to see who can do the most for the group, and relative deprivation may be as potent as absolute deprivation in motivating deviance. Moreover, the theory makes no allowance for those who do not become de-moralized, those who become de-moralized but refrain from deviance, variations in opportunities for deviance, perceptual variations among individuals, and constraints in the behavioral environment, all of which can be regarded as linking parts in a network of causal connections, some of which may be reciprocal in nature.

Thus, competitive urges, as well as exploitative urges to some extent, may be influenced by particular kinds of child rearing, by preexisting biologically linked predispositions, or even by the cultural patterns to which children are exposed. Deprivation and criminal behavior could also be affected by such variables. Therefore, the causal links among the four major variables of the theory (competition, exploitation, deprivation, and crime) might be limited because much of the association among them is spurious. In a similar way, a number of intervening variables may influence the extent to which competition leads to exploitation and the subsequent extent to which deprivation leads to crime. They may include development of peer attachments that mute exploitative tendencies as well as the emergence of social networks that promote more equitable distribution of scarce resources to divert the criminal potential of deprivation.

Despite the often touted generality of rational choice theory, this utilitarian/deterrence approach provides a shallow explanation of deviance. In essence it identifies only one link, though perhaps a crucial one, in the chain of causes. Everything up to the situational costs and benefits, as well as everything thereafter, is left unattended. The theory simply says: Given that benefits, no matter what they are or how they came to be, exceed costs, no matter what they are or how they came to be, deviance will occur. This is equivalent to the explanation of the death of the intoxicated motorist as cessation of brain activity. It is hardly disputable, but it is also unenlightening and not very useful. To understand deviance, even if it can be described with a cost-benefit formula, one must know what goes into the calculation. Why do some fear punishment more than others; why do some regard particular things as costly that others regard as rewarding; why do actual punishment probabilities vary from situation to situation; and how do group sanctions interact with individual sanctions (see Heckathorn 1990)? Moreover, what are the circumstances that allow deviance to occur, given a favorable cost-benefit calculation, and how do we account for the distribution of costs and benefits in various societies and across social situations?

Rational choice theory also neglects antecedent and intervening variables that would help consumers identify exactly when effects will likely be forthcoming. For example, internalized moral commitments, possibly from early childhood religious training, may influence assessment of both benefits and costs, so that much of their observed association in a given instance may be spuriously attributable to this common factor.

Moreover, rational choice theories almost inevitably involve reciprocal relationships among variables that are not explicitly recognized. For instance, for many people, most forms of gratifying activity are pleasurable only up to a point. Beyond a certain satiation level, those gratifying activities become much less attractive, sometimes even repulsive, at least for a period of time. My children's annual Halloween chocolate-eating orgy usually resulted in several days of repulsion at the thought of chocolate. Had they been on an M & M behavioral modification conditioning program, its effects would have been quite different following Halloween than they were prior to Halloween. Still, it is sometimes true that "the more you get, the more you want," which is another way of saying that rewards and behavior may have a reciprocal relationship with each other.

Evidence of the transformation of costs into rewards or of the alteration of the cost-benefit meanings of things through availability is all around us. Prison officials, parents, and teachers all know the dangers of allowing privileges to become so plentiful that they become rights. At some point, a previous benefit becomes so routinized that failure to grant it is regarded as a punishment. Clearly, then, costs and benefits are not fixed quantities but are variable products of many other variables, even of their own past histories. Thus, versions of rational choice theory that accept costs and rewards as given are extremely shallow.

Routine activities theory goes a step beyond the economic argument by making some attempt to explain when there will be suitable targets and absence of guardianship. Yet this theory does not permit a rich account, even if we could be satisfied with the routine activities variable, because there is no effort to explain why particular activities become routine or to show why individuals are motivated to deviance. Furthermore, all of the personal and situational variables that affect whether the three causal factors—motivation, opportunity, and weak constraint—converge for individuals, as well as those variables that might affect whether deviance is expressed when that convergence occurs, are left unspecified. Further, the theory also neglects potential reciprocal effects since it does not explicitly recognize that transformation of individuals, objects, or dwellings into suitable targets may feed back to reduce guardianship or that the presence of motivated offenders can also influence the degree of guardianship as well as target suitability.

Summary on Theoretical Depth

All of the prominent simple theories of deviance put forth limited and incomplete explanations. In each case, the theories depict causal elements seemingly hanging in thin air, owing little or nothing to things above, below, or around, and with no reciprocal interconnections. Because of this attenuation, simple formulations appear shallow, naive, and inadequate to the job that theories should perform, and as a result many scholars reject them wholesale. Nevertheless, each embodies an important piece of the deviance-causing process, and within their own parameters, all individually appear quite powerful. Unfortunately, their "own parameters" preclude much depth.

General Conclusion

Adequate theory is essential for progress in understanding crime/deviance. To meet the need, theories must incorporate into coherent bodies of thought those broader explanatory processes that recognize a number of crucial variables. In addition, good theory must spell out the interconnections of its explanatory processes and crucial variables, while specifying the conditions under which the postulated causal processes are likely to apply with greater or lesser force. Furthermore, the kind of theories we need must indicate the causal intervals likely to be operative as well as the form of the relationships postulated. Finally, adequate theories must be general enough to at least encompass a range of different kinds of deviant behavior, if not also a range of nondeviant behaviors.

The basic theories within the field of crime/deviance, which I call simple theories, fail by these criteria of adequacy but illustrate why such features are important. Each theory identifies an important variable or process in the production of deviant behavior, but each also fails to capture the larger dynamics. This is like trying to explain the production of motion in an automobile. A theory claiming that burning fuel in the combustion chamber causes the motion would be right, in a sense, but it would also be inadequate. A theory portraying the cause as a transmission that allows the power of the crankshaft to be transmitted to the drive shaft would also be correct, but also insufficient. A theory suggesting the essentiality of wheels in allowing the movement of the vehicle would identify an important element, although one that alone would not provide understanding. There are many things necessary to make an automobile move, and those things interact rather than standing alone or simply forming an additive whole. They must be connected in a specified manner to produce the outcome, and they work better under some conditions than others. To account for this, a theory must have precision and depth. Furthermore, the things necessary to make automobiles move are not unique to automobiles, but instead are reflections of physical principles understandable within general theories of physics; in short, full understanding of the movement of automobiles involves a theory of physical phenomena with the breadth to include the dynamics operative in an automobile.

So it is with deviance. Simple theories do not provide the breadth permitting explanation of a full, or even reasonably wide, range of deviant behaviors. Moreover, such theories suffer from weak comprehensiveness since any one of them does not include enough explanatory elements to do the job. In addition, each and every one of the simple theories neglects to identify the contingencies under which its proposed causal processes are expected to hold with greater or lesser force or the extraneous or intervening factors that interact with the main causal forces. They also all fail to provide clear guidelines about the causal lags between their specified independent and dependent variables as well as the form of the postulated causal relationships; put another way, they lack precision. Finally, simple theories provide only partial explanations that encompass limited portions of larger but unspecified dynamic processes that often involve reciprocal relationships, and they usually fail even to make the connections among their variables clear; this means that they lack depth.

Some will view these criteria as excessively demanding and this assessment of basic theories as harsh and unfair because none of the theories under discussion was invented with the intent to accomplish all of those purposes. One of the oldest clichés in the social sciences is expressed in the admonition that "one should not criticize a theory or a piece of research for failing to do things it was not meant to do." However, adhering to that dictum dooms the enterprise because the sentiment expressed in it encourages small efforts with small objectives. As long as such premises are granted credence, theorists can always gain favor through limited formulations immunized from the corrective mechanism of criticism by claiming that whatever they did was all they intended to do, no matter how small or inadequate it might be. I believe we can, and should, strive to achieve more.

3

Conventional Methods
of Theory Building

Simple theories of deviance usually set forth good ideas, but they are limited or incomplete. They are not wrong; in fact, each one is, in its own way and as far as it applies, quite astute in pointing up one or more important factors probably implicated in the causation of deviant behavior. But this is not enough; progress requires more comprehensive theories with greater breadth, precision, and depth. Conventional methods of theory building, such as invention (Hirschi 1989) and elaboration (Thornberry 1989), however, probably cannot produce the needed theories. In this chapter the two approaches normally employed in building theory are described. For each one, I offer a few prominent examples of its use and assess its promise for improving the simple theories discussed in Chapter 1.

Invention

One method for improvement is to start from scratch, observe the phenomena of interest anew, and with the advantage of knowing the limitations of previous formulations, invent entirely unique theories. Advocates of this assume that clever thinkers can sweep aside old baggage and create fresh, different, and better theories (Glaser and Strauss 1967; Hirschi 1989; Polsky 1967). By examining the "results of research oriented more to the phenomenon and less to a priori theoretical explanations of it," it is said that theorists can fashion more adequate theories than we now possess (Hirschi 1989:48).

Although the idea of examining deviance with an open mind is appealing, and some work along that line has succeeded in generating provocative insights (see Katz 1988), it is unrealistic to depend on invention for building general theory. Invention requires rare abilities and, in practice, usually produces only bounded, deficient theories like the simple ones already in existence. Invention is impractical because its success does not rest on skills that can be taught to a substantial number of scholars; rather, the fate of the enterprise depends on the emergence of individuals with extraordinary creative talent who can conjure up unique ideas or offer genuinely novel interpretations. Using such a method, the community of crime/deviance scholars cannot *develop* better theory because training cannot play much of a role in theoretical improvement. Furthermore, even when visionaries arise, the likelihood that they can perceive unique relations in social phenomena, or invent truly new theory, is remote. This is because ideas cumulate. The longer the span of time over which scholarly work takes place, the larger the aggregate collection of ideas and the harder it is to formulate entirely neoteric theories. Even in earlier eras when the collective store of ideas was much smaller, almost every "new idea" eventually proved to have existed in one form or another. Indeed, experts in intellectual history (sometimes called "theorists") have often shown that contemporary ideas are really old ideas in camouflage (see Becker and Barnes 1961), and the similarity of ideas incorporated in various contemporary deviance theories is made clear in this book.

Skepticism about the prospects of unusual creativity, however, should not be taken as denial of the cleverness of some scholars or the outstanding contributions that inventive efforts have produced. In fact, the main advocate of theoretical invention, Travis Hirschi, is, in my opinion, a genius, as is Jack Katz, the premier practitioner of that art. The theory of self-control that Gottfredson and Hirschi (1990) have formulated is extraordinary and admirable. On close inspection, however, it turns out to be another instance of old wine in a new bottle, and it does not fully meet our theoretical needs. It illustrates what I believe to be an inherent, counterproductive tendency toward defensiveness by those who purport to invent theory. Katz's work also shows amazing insight and incredible depth, but in the end it constitutes a collection of inchoate interpretations that do not add up to a general theory.

Self-Control Theory

Gottfredson and Hirschi (1990) begin with a definition of crime that is independent of the law but which encompasses almost all things usually prohibited therein as well as those acts incorporated in most definitions of deviance. Their theory concerns acts of force or fraud undertaken in pursuit of self-interest (1990:15). They do not provide clear definitions of force and fraud, yet this conceptualization seems superior to many others as it brings great breadth to the theoretical enterprise. Although their definition does exclude some acts ordinarily prohibited in law but which are usually regarded as deviant (like those often referred to as "vice"), in application the theory is said to explain much criminal behavior as well as behaviors "analogous to crime," such as smoking, drug use, and promiscuous sex, which could all be regarded as instances of vice (Arneklev et al. 1993).

According to the theory, crime results when individuals with weak self-control encounter opportunities for self-gratifying force or fraud (see Grasmick et al. 1993). Opportunity refers to circumstances in which crime can easily produce quick gratification and there appears to be little short-range risk of detection or other cost. Thus, crime varies with two conditions, one a characteristic of the individual and the other a characteristic of social situations. Individuals with strong self-control are presumably unlikely to commit crime, whereas those with weak self-control may or may not commit crime, depending upon the kind of opportunities they encounter.

Since the key causal factor is the degree of self-control that individuals possess, Gottfredson and Hirschi attempt to explain why some people have more of it. They contend that self-control stems from child rearing, that it is set before adolescence, and that it remains stable throughout life. According to the theory, parents must do each of four things to produce strong self-control in their children: (1) care enough about the child to monitor its behavior, (2) actually monitor the child's behavior, (3) recognize misbehavior when it occurs, and (4) punish the child for wrongdoing. Failure or ineffectiveness in any of the four will presumably lead to weak self-control.

Strengths. The Gottfredson/Hirschi theory has broad application, aiming to account for self-gratifying force or fraud of all types; as a by-product, the theory also explains a wide range of crime-analogous deviant behaviors. It is more comprehensive than many others because it simultaneously takes into account more than one crucial variable or causal process, and it recognizes the simultaneous operation of internal as well as situational causal forces. The theory implies that every criminal act represents interaction between weak self-control and opportunities embedded in the situation or environment.

In addition, self-control theory is explicit about its main purported causal interval. It states that a person with low self-control is highly inclined toward immediate, impulsive resort to force or fraud when confronted with an opportunity where either of them can be used for quick gratification without much short-range chance of apprehension, punishment, or other cost. The causal interval is, therefore, quite short, if not instantaneous.

Finally, because the theory's account of "why" and "how" is generally persuasive and intellectually satisfying, it has more depth than many others. Accumulated evidence confirms the theory's contention that most "ordinary crime" is disorganized, impulsive, and of little long-range benefit to the offender. Most offenders do appear to conduct their lives in disorderly, uncontrolled, and self-gratifying ways. Moreover, this theory depicts a causal chain with at least three links: childhood experiences ⟶ self-control ⟶ criminal behavior. Further, it accounts for each step in the causal structure in terms of the previous steps, even adding an interactive element (opportunity) at the final stage. On balance, then, the self-control argument is a commendable advancement of the theoretical enterprise.

Weaknesses. Despite its virtues, however, this theory exhibits many of the deficiencies described earlier as characterizing simple theories, and in dramatic ways it illustrates the weaknesses of invention as an approach to theory improvement. First, despite the intended breadth of the theory, it actually falls short by "overexplaining" some instances of self-interested force and fraud that are *not* regarded as deviant or criminal by the U.S. population, and it miscarries in application to white-collar crime, organized crime, and the crimes of organizational entities.

How does it overexplain? Most advertising, ordinary salesmanship, political activity, and courtship involve fraud pursued for self-interest, and much force used by athletes in competitive games, by parents in coercing children to behave, and by businesses in collecting debts, foreclosing mortgages, and maintaining security on their property is in pursuit of self-interest. Yet it is a stretch to imagine that these acts of "crime" result from weak self-control. In fact, in most instances they seem to reflect the opposite. In addition, for conceptually similar, legally prohibited white-collar and organized crimes, which also ostensibly seem to involve strong self-control, Gottfredson and Hirschi try to prove that they are like other criminal behavior—impulsive, lacking long-range benefit, and "disorganized." Furthermore, these theorists contend that crime by organizational entities is really no more than crime by occupants of organizational positions, who, it seems, manifest the same behavioral traits as all ordinary criminals.

Despite adroit arguments, it is doubtful the criminological community will be swayed. If weak self-control explains all instances of force or fraud in pursuit of self-interest, then no "criminal" activity can be rationally organized and self-consciously planned and executed for instrumental purposes. This flies in the face of logic, evidence, and experience. Thus, much of the generality of the Gottfredson/Hirschi theory is bought at the expense of credibility, a trade-off especially likely when scholars invent self-reflective theories while remaining "at all times blind to the weaknesses of their own position and stubborn in its defense" (Hirschi 1989:45).

This defensive tendency by "inventors"—those who observe the facts and inductively derive explanations—to lose sight of the long-range goal of a scholarly/scientific community as they engage in the struggle to protect the ideas to which they have become committed is further illustrated by Hirschi and Gottfredson's perspective on age and crime (1983), which Hirschi uses to tout the advantages of inductive invention. It seems that he and Gottfredson examined all the data they could find, and from observing such facts decided that the form of the age-crime relationship is invariant (always an inverted J-curve) and inexplicable. After that, they unashamedly refused "to entertain with an open mind all of the many theories that might be advanced to explain the age-crime relation" (1989:46), a refusal they extended even to Hirschi's earlier-formulated theory of social bonds and now, it seems, to their own self-control theory (Gottfredson and Hirschi 1990:119, 168).

Observing "invariance" apparently made them decide that the age-crime relationship could not be explained but at the same time inspired them to invent an explanation of criminal behavior—the self-control theory under discussion here—that would accommodate both change over time (crime) and lifelong stability in criminal tendency (criminality). Strangely enough, however, the potential ability of self-control theory to account for the age-crime relationship—the inspiration for its invention— is evidently not recognized. Alternatively, perhaps Gottfredson and Hirschi do recognize the potential of self-control theory to explain the age-crime relationship, but in order to remain loyal to their earlier com- mitment to the idea of inexplicability, their recognition is deliberately shrouded in obfuscating language. In one place in their book, Gottfredson and Hirschi reaffirm statements made in 1983 about the inexplicability of the age-crime relation:

> An alternative interpretation of maturational reform or spontaneous desis- tance is that crime declines with age. This explanation suggests that matu- rational reform is just that, change in behavior that comes with maturation; it suggests that spontaneous desistance is just that, change in behavior that cannot be explained and change that occurs regardless of what else hap- pens. (1990:136)

Yet on the next page (Gottfredson and Hirschi 1990:137), the authors suggest that the reason "criminal events may vary over time and place without implying change in [individual's] self-control" is because self- control is only one element in the causal process, the other being a "pecu- liar set of necessary conditions (e.g., activity, opportunity, adversaries, victims, goods)." In other words, although these theorists never explicitly say so, the age-crime relationship may be a product of changing opportu- nities, or "peculiar conditions," for criminal behavior. Although one causal element, self-control, remains constant throughout a lifetime, the interactive element that permits weak self-control to express itself in ac- tual criminal behavior—the frequency of encountering situations where needs and desires can be gratified easily, quickly, and with minimum per- ceived short-range risk—may vary with age. Given the impressive lan- guage skills shown elsewhere by these authors, it is hard to escape the conclusion that their lack of clarity in applying the principles of self-con- trol theory in order to explain the age-crime relationship is due to their stubborn belief that all personally invented ideas (in this case, the idea that the inverted J-curve relationship between age and crime is inexplica- ble) must be maintained, no matter what.

   More evidence of the pejorative consequences of commitment to de- fend a particular formulation is the facility with which these authors en- dorse tautology to challenge evidence not fully supporting their theory (Hirschi and Gottfredson 1993). Despite their own criticism of biological positivism for reliance on tautology in equating aggression with criminal- ity (1990:66–68) and of the inability of psychologically oriented re- searchers to measure personality independently of the acts that it is meant to produce (1990:111), Gottfredson and Hirschi discount evidence contrary to their own scheme that is based on direct measures of self-control, contending that the only appropriate indicators are actual crime-like behaviors already exhibited by the individual. Were they not so intent on defense, such inconsistency would be unlikely.

The theory is more comprehensive than many, but it is still too simplistic. The argument simultaneously takes account of two of the central causal variables identified herein in Chapter 2—constraint (both internal and external) and opportunity—but it ignores others. There is no place for variation in the strength of motivation to commit crime, since the authors explicitly assume that people have a strong, ever-present desire to satisfy themselves with whatever gratifications potential force or fraud might produce. Still, we all know from experience that regardless of self-control, some people simply want or need some things more than other people do. Therefore, it is easy to imagine that the willingness of an individual to use force or fraud must depend to some extent on the magnitude of these desires or needs for gratifications of various kinds.

Similarly, self-control theory takes no account of potential alternative motivations that would divert people from the use of force or fraud, nor does it accommodate differences in people's abilities to use force or fraud for gratification. Presumably, when confronted with a chance to use force or fraud for easy gratification, anybody with weak self-control will coerce or deceive, despite any other possibilities for gratification available through alternative noncriminal behaviors. In addition, the theory seems to assume that all have equal skill and ability to use force or fraud. Both of these assumptions are unrealistic. Even those with poor self-control will find some things more gratifying than other things and will sometimes find noncriminal possibilities more compelling, even when the opportunity for force and fraud is there. Furthermore, a lot of people lack the skill, physical strength, or courage to perpetrate fraud or force, even when faced with opportunities where gratification appears easy and relatively risk free.

In addition, self-control theory falls short of fulfilling the criteria of general theory set forth earlier in two serious ways: It is not precise enough, and its depth, though great in comparison to many simple theories, is nevertheless deficient. Consider precision, which concerns how well a theory specifies the conditions under which its causal processes will operate with greater or lesser force, the size of the causal intervals, and the form of the relationship between the independent and dependent variables. Gottfredson and Hirschi do not state any contingencies under which the causal processes of their theory might be more or less likely to operate fully. In fact, they go to extraordinary lengths to argue that there are few conditions under which it might be modulated or enhanced. Readers are told that cultural variations, type of crime, age, gender, and race make no difference in the causal process; the only things that matter are the degree to which a person has weak self-control and the extent to which he or she confronts opportunities for criminal behavior. Apparently there are no individual, group, or organizational characteristics that might affect the extent to which a person's level of self-control interacts with criminal opportunities to produce actual criminal behavior. In short, the causal process in this theory is portrayed as being universal and invariant in strength. Given X amount of self-control and Y amount of opportunity, the result will almost always be Z amount of criminal behavior. The only variations that really matter are the magnitudes of X, because of individual family or cultural practices, and Y, because of social organization, culture, or luck.

To the extent that contingencies actually exist, then, the self-control theory is incomplete and perhaps misleading; certainly it will prove to be empirically weak, since researchers using traditional methods will not know what to hold constant or what comparisons to make to observe the theoretical process in its most favorable light. Clearly, numerous variables may enhance or detract from the interaction between self-control and opportunity, just as, according to Gottfredson and Hirschi's latest discussion of the age effect, "in some conditions, the effects of age may be muted. . . . we may find conditions in which age does not have as strong an effect as usual" (1990:128). For example, some poorly self-controlled individuals with good looks and charm probably forgo opportunities for fraud in seeking gratification of sexual needs simply because they can achieve such gratification without it, whereas some less attractive, weakly controlled individuals will nevertheless conform because they fail to recognize various opportunities for force or fraud that they encounter. Moreover, some people who are generally self-controlled sometimes encounter life circumstances where, for a time, they just stop caring (perhaps after a depressing divorce). In addition, one's companions or peers probably sometimes constrain impulsive tendencies (or perhaps encourage more impulsive behavior than would occur if the individual were alone).

By confusing generality with invariant universality, the authors have produced a less adequate theory than they might have. Had they been less determined to make it work the same way all the time, they could have allowed for contingencies. Then, statements like the following would have been possible: The interaction of self-control and criminal opportunity has a moderate positive effect on actual criminal behavior in the general case; an exceptionally strong positive effect under conditions X, Y, and Z; only a minimal positive effect under conditions Q, R, and T; no effect under conditions A, B, and C; and a negative effect under conditions D, E, and F.

The Gottfredson/Hirschi formulation exhibits further imprecision in not clearly portraying the form of the relationship between self-control and crime. On the one hand, the argument implies that any additional increment of self-control has a corresponding effect in reducing the probability of criminal behavior, no matter where on the continuum of self-control the additional increment occurs. On the other hand, the authors seem to de-emphasize the continuous qualities of a self-control trait, choosing instead to characterize it as a dichotomy. They typically refer to high or low self-control as if these were distinct categories, suggesting they may imagine a threshold above and below which increments of additional self-control make little difference, but such a threshold is not evident. Such lack of clarity precludes derivation of exact statements about the effects of self-control, with devastating consequences for strong tests because the implication of various kinds of evidence depends upon which form of the relationship the theory actually projects. Research using one measure of self-control may show less support than it would with another, and as a result, empirical feedback may be stifled, or the theory might be prematurely rejected (see Grasmick et al. 1993).

Finally, the theory is too shallow since it appears to omit or show ambivalence about a number of causal sequences that are essential for answering the questions *why* and *how*. Among other things, since it regards self-control as static after the childhood years, it makes no provision for the possible influence of later variables on the strength of self-control, and since it places all of its theoretical eggs in one basket, it cannot allow other variables to be implicated in the relationship between self-control and criminal behavior. Ironically, one of the variables excluded by that necessity is the extent or strength of adolescent or adult social bonds, whose causal role is relegated to early childhood (Hirschi 1992) or removed altogether as social bonds become passive products of self-control itself (Gottfredson and Hirschi 1990:119).

It seems likely, however, that other variables are operative and that self-control and crime may themselves reciprocally influence each other. Given the commitment of Gottfredson and Hirschi to rational choice assumptions, it seems strange that they overlook the possibility that sequences of negative consequences for various impulsive acts in the postchildhood years might strengthen self-control or that observing the rewards that others get from impulsive acts might cause those with high self-control to relent. In the same vein, life course events may well buffer or channel the effects of traits like self-control (Laub and Sampson 1993), and the connection between self-control, opportunity, and crime may also be interlinked with strain that the individual experiences (see Agnew 1992).

Summary on Self-Control Theory. Without question self-control theory, which is touted as inductive or "invented," enriches our theoretical repertoire, but it falls far short of what we need. Much of its generality is artificial or false; it ignores crucial variables, making its explanations less complete than they could be; it makes no provision for contingencies where the causal process applies with greater or lesser strength; and it is ambivalent about the form of the causal effect. Moreover, the theory adumbrates causal sequences and fails to recognize potential reciprocal effects between its prime independent variable and the dependent variable, crime.

Because of these deficiencies, self-control theory magnifies the problems with invention as a method for improving theory. Since originality presupposes proprietary ownership and commitment, Gottfredson and Hirschi are pledged to the theory's defense, resistant to contrary evidence, and reluctant to modify. Further, successful invention can only be accomplished by persons with extraordinary intellects. Although these authors certainly qualify on that count, it appears that the main ideas of self-control theory are not actually original.

Hirschi portrays the theory-building process as one "ultimately based on facts rather than data—that is, on the results of research oriented more to the phenomenon and less to a priori theoretical explanations of it" (1989:48). As I understand it, self-control theory involves three main ideas about criminal behavior: (1) Early child-rearing practices are crucial, (2) a personality characteristic produced by childhood experiences—self-control—is the prime determinant of criminal behavior, but (3) self-control must interact with several situational variables that together constitute opportunity for criminal behavior. As acknowledged by the authors, numerous scholars have emphasized the importance of the family and child rearing (Hagan et al. 1985; Kohlberg 1969; Nye 1958; Parsons 1955), not the least of whom are Sheldon and Eleanor Glueck (1950), Sampson and Laub (1993), and James Q. Wilson and Richard Herrnstein (1985), who are extensively cited by Gottfredson and Hirschi. Moreover, the main aspects of child rearing that Gottfredson and Hirschi emphasize—caring and supervision—are the ones also emphasized by many others (see Wells and Rankin 1988); in fact, the four-step process of successful socialization for self-control is the same as that set forth by Gerald Patterson and his colleagues on the basis of their research at the Oregon Learning Center (Patterson 1980). The idea of weak self-control as a factor in criminal behavior itself is heavily stressed by Wilson and Herrnstein (1985), who call it "impulsivity." Finally, as Gottfredson and Hirschi note, the idea of criminal opportunity as a characteristic of certain social environments is one of the key variables in the routine activities theory (Cohen and Felson 1979) that has become so prominent in recent years. Thus, it does not appear that the essentials of self-control theory grew out of observing the "facts"; rather it seems as though self-control theory is a creative combination of ideas borrowed from theoretical statements by others. Indeed, one might argue that the technique of theoretical "integration" was used to build self-control theory—the very approach that Hirschi (1979, 1989) adamantly opposes, or perhaps such a technique might be more accurately characterized as "cannibalizing" prior theories (Turk 1992:9). In any case, self-control theory fails as a persuasive illustration of the advantages of originating new ideas from inductive observation of the facts.

The Seductions of Crime: The Transcendence Theory

Perhaps the best usage of invention is by Jack Katz, who employs "the research tactic of defining the form of deviance to be explained from the inside and searching for explanations by examining how people construct the experience at issue and then, only as a secondary matter, turned to trace connections from the phenomenal foreground to the generational and social ecological background" (1988:317). Katz asks himself what domestic killers, shoplifters, those who posture as "badasses," fight in gangs, rob, pursue "sneaky thrills," and commit "cold-blooded" murder are trying to do. In answering these questions he attempts to view things through the deviant's eyes. Much of his work is about *how* the various forms of deviance are committed and what the existential requirements for accomplishing the tasks are, but he also formulates a series of specific explanations for the various kinds of crime/deviance he studies. In addition, these somewhat disparate, particularistic explanations are supplemented by an often obscure underlying theme that loosely applies to all the forms of deviance he examines—that deviants are trying to avoid or overcome limitations of one kind or another through the establishment or exercise of moral dominance.

From many kinds of information, but mostly from ethnographic and first-person material, Katz concludes that deviance is a functional device for those who perform it, and it often serves a symbolic purpose. Although he rejects the rational choice perspective that depicts criminal behavior in economic or materialistic terms, he emphatically views crime as purposeful, systematic, and meaningful despite its frequent appearance to nondeviants as impulsive and nonsensical. To Katz, all forms of criminal/deviant behavior at issue have their own seductive appeal as vehicles for achieving autonomy or exhibiting moral dominance. Yet, each type of deviance also has a unique purpose.

The typical homicide, involving spontaneous killing of friends, relatives, and acquaintances, is, according to Katz, provoked by some challenge to the person's status, rights, or dignity. Killing supposedly rectifies the affront, but it is enacted under the guise and with the belief that the killer is acting on behalf of the moral order that endows those statuses, rights, and dignities. Hence, "righteous slaughter" is motivated by the desire to escape humiliation but is infused with larger significance in the minds of killers who project themselves as guardians of abstract goodness. Vandalism, burglary, shoplifting, and joyriding, on the other hand, are all said to share a special fascination for young people as sneaky thrills. Katz describes each as involving a particular technique for defying convention and permitting youth to demonstrate competence and expand the boundaries of self. The youthful deviants accomplish this through hiding motives and thoughts from adults, practicing secret defilement, and transforming the prohibited acts into sexual metaphors. By committing deviance that permits use of these techniques, the young are able to transcend their vulnerability to total intrusion by external adult and conventional limitations. Therefore, sneaky thrills are liberating personal triumphs.

A syndrome of deviant behaviors characterized as "creating an awesomely deviant presence" through the role of the badass is interpreted as a mechanism by which males, particularly those who are black or of other minority status, escape the "rationality" and the "malleability" necessary for ordinary social relationships. The "badass" is unpredictable but fearsome in the potentiality of inflicting harm and creating social chaos, and because of this, people must take seriously those who otherwise would be held in low regard. Similarly those involved in gang activity "dramatize a superior moral ability to transcend local communal boundaries and move in a spirit of freedom and emphatic self-respect without accepting limitations" (Katz 1988:116). Thus, the violence, intergang warfare, and other criminal activities of "street elites" presumably represent assertions of sovereignty by those who are "humbled" by their inadequacy in dealing with modern, rationalized society.

Armed robbery, according to the Katz portrayal, is the ultimate test of being a "hardman," which is, in turn, the premier technique for achieving transcendence over the "chaos" of the criminal's social environment, an environment that normally reflects subordination to the larger society. Because stickups require much nerve and the ability to deal with uncertainty, they are performed mainly to establish the offender's reputation, from which the peculiar disorganized lifestyle of a hardman can emanate to declare independence from the constraints of ordinary living. Armed robbery, therefore, is not committed mainly to get money but rather to symbolically escape the boundaries that limit others.

Finally, "senseless, cold-blooded" murders are interpreted as a means by which the killers, through the medium of primordial religious ritual, are able to bring order out of their own chaotic subordination to circumstances. By engaging in unspeakable acts, and constructing a sense of purposiveness from them, such killers are supposedly able to demonstrate their "moral" transcendence through the negativity of an "awesome deviant presence."

Thus, Katz contends that criminal/deviant acts have purposive rationales that do not fit the usual assumptions of social scientists who impose their meanings on the criminal subjects. Moreover, those deviance-generating rationales are seen as relating in one way or another to individual efforts to be free of limitations on self, thought, and action. As such, they are usually undertaken by those whose status and life circumstance provide the greatest constraint on moral independence. Crime/deviance, then, is to be understood as a functional device for asserting autonomy.

Strengths. Unquestionably, Katz (1988) has succeeded in producing an original and important theoretical contribution. In ways not before imagined, he has illuminated the phenomenological world of the criminal/deviant to show a plausible version of how and why various forms of deviance are committed. Moreover, his underlying theme, despite being unsystematically pursued across offenses and often cloaked in obfuscative language, does appear to suggest a general "theory" representing an advance over some simple theories. Its superiority is evident in two specific ways: It has broader applicability than many, and it provides deeper explanation by incorporating a broad range of variables and showing how they interact to produce a sequence of events leading to deviant outcomes.

First, the general explanation of criminal/deviant behavior as purposeful action for overcoming limitations has potential applicability across many forms of deviance. If one counts all the deviant behaviors involved in pursuing sneaky thrills, establishing a badass reputation, attempting dominance through gang-inspired efforts, and sustaining a hardman image, as well as in the two kinds of homicide that Katz describes, it is clear that his theory of deviance as purposive transcendence is indeed far-reaching. However, this is not the end of it. Katz suggests that availability of appropriate information might show that white-collar crime has a similar transcendent rationale. Exactly how the transcendence argument might fit, or make sense of, white-collar crime is not clear, but the way in which a related idea encompasses and explains white-collar crime as well as other deviance will be appreciated later when I present my own "control balance theory," the main contribution of this book.

For now, the broad generality of the transcendent argument can be seen as it applies to disparate deviances like drug usage and child abuse, which Katz does not actually discuss. Both could possibly be interpreted as functional acts undertaken by their perpetrators to assert moral dominance and thereby transcend limitations of a constraining, humiliating situation. Such process appears evident in the talk, rationalizations, and other cultural accoutrements of drug users, who imagine themselves to be superior to those not "in the life." Addicts and other druggies often perceive that drugs liberate them from the aggravations and trivialities of ordinary existence that trap others (Finestone 1957; Tittle 1972), though outside observers, ironically, generally view drug addicts as having almost no autonomy. Similarly, child abusers may be engaging in self-defined uplifting behavior when they inflict severe punishments on their children in the guise of moral training, just as righteous slaughterers kill under the illusion that the act protects community standards or reaffirms sacred tenets.

Second, the seductions of crime argument implies deeper explanation than do some of the simple theories described in Chapter 1. It recognizes the importance of social background in generating a desire or need for transcendence, and it thrives on the theme that features of the immediate social situation (the foreground) activate various forms of deviance in addition to scripting the sequence of events that transpire in the deviant episode. At the same time, according to Katz's portrayal, the process of "transcending" is at least partially internal, involving mental constructions. Deviance, therefore, is depicted as arising from the interaction of a large number of variables, the alteration of any one of which could change the outcome. Furthermore, although the general argument is heavily bent toward deviant motivation (the person is impelled, or seduced, toward deviance by the appeal of the behavior as a means of overcoming or surpassing strains or limitations), it also emphasizes not only how controls (limitations) of one kind or another shape motivation but also how immediate situational controls can often intrude to prevent deviance. It certainly incorporates opportunity, ability, and alternative motivation, though in unsystematic ways.

Weaknesses. Katz's (1988) analyses prove that the method of invention can produce fascinating and useful theoretical products, but his work also demonstrates that his method probably cannot lead to an adequate general theory. Despite its provocativeness, breadth, and comprehensiveness, the argument fails as a general formulation. This is partly because its self-consciously intentional, unsystematic, and particularistic approach makes precipitating a general theory from his ad hoc "explanations," "interpretations," or "analyses" difficult. However, even when the veil is penetrated, the latent general theory turns out to be less comprehensive than needed, and it suffers dearly from imprecision and, to a lesser extent, from insufficient depth.

The most important shortfall is the unsystematic nature of the theory. Although with careful reading one can discern a general explanatory principle, Katz's interpretations seem quite particularistic in that he portrays each form of deviance as involving a more or less unique combination of situational, personal, and interpretive variables, often to achieve different kinds of transcendence. Indeed, Katz's portrayals of the variety of limitations that provoke deviance can easily mislead a reader to think there is no general theory at all. For example, he says on the one hand that those who commit righteous slaughter must experience humiliation to the point of rage, at which juncture they must somehow see themselves as acting to defend the larger moral order. Youths getting sneaky thrills, on the other hand, are presumably trying to "expand the boundaries of self," whereas the badass is trying to defy "rationality." Gangs presumably engage in their characteristic acts to establish sovereignty against a background of unpreparedness for a rationalized world, but hardmen and cold-blooded killers overcome chaos, the one by creating an image of awesome deviance, and the other through primordial religious rites. All of this might make some ask: Where is the similarity among humiliation, bounded selves, rationality, communal subordination, and chaos?

The essence of the theory, as distinct from the emergent particular interpretations, is the abstract proposition that by committing deviance all deviants are seeking to escape or overcome limitations of some kind. According to Katz, the details of how and when this occurs, of the limitations that might be relevant, or of the form particular transcendence might take, cannot be imagined or stated ahead of time; they can only be grasped from interpretive empirical analysis—in analyses that are extremely subjective both in what they observe and in what they conclude. In other words, the Katz "theory" does not actually explain crime/deviance; it only provides a vague guide as to where the explanation can be found if one undertakes the appropriate empirical analysis. Unfortunately, it appears that almost any set of circumstances and actions can be construed to force a given form of deviance into the general theoretical mold. In this sense, then, Katz's formulation has a gimmicky aspect, much like inappropriate versions of rational choice/economic theory. It is one thing to hypothesize that deviance is committed to enable one to transcend limitations; it is another to assert that a particular limitation, among the multitude of limitations that people experience, is the one that causes the individual to resort to deviance.

Even if one imposes a systematic, determinative structure on transcendence theory, the product turns out to be less comprehensive than it might be, and it appears exceptionally imprecise and shallower than general theory should be. Consider, for example, its incompleteness, or lack of comprehensiveness, as reflected in its exclusion of several specific but noteworthy causal processes. Katz's analysis of street elites shows how their defining behaviors are performed, and he almost convinces the reader that establishing local dominance helps these youths transcend the rationality of the modern world that they find daunting. Yet, it is also clear from Katz's descriptions that these patterns of behavior are familiar to all in the areas where they occur—to some extent they are emulations of already-existing cultural models. Katz, however, gives almost no credence to cultural transmission or learning; it is as if each individual, or cohort of individuals, learned anew how to transcend his circumstances. Even if deprived youths were attempting to achieve transcendence because they recognize its usefulness for avoiding a rationalized world, this would be only part of the motivation for street-elite behavior; they may also struggle to become street elites because they learn that this mode of behavior will bring status among peers and because they see others doing or attempting to do it.

A larger flaw in the transcendence argument is its imprecision. Remember that precision is the quality of specifying the conditions that influence exactly when and to what degree the theoretical causal processes will operate, the nature of the causal effect, and the magnitude of the time interval between the proposed cause and the expected outcome. Despite the power of crime seduction theory in reminding us of the allure of crime for enjoyment and problem solving, the formulation does not allow predictions about when limitations will produce crime, much less predictions about what kind of limitation will produce what kind of crime. Many people suffer humiliation but do not rage; most who rage do not kill. This is true of individuals similarly located in personal and structural networks. How does Katz's theory indicate who will or will not attempt to overcome humiliation through righteous slaughter? He suggests it may be those who suffer "hopeless" humiliation, but when humiliation will be perceived as hopeless is not clear. Similarly, almost all young people experience limited self boundaries imposed by the adult world but only some shoplift, joyride, burgle, or vandalize. A lot of people face personal chaos without resorting to primordial religious symbolism and senseless killing. Finally, the urge for autonomy is common but only rarely does it actually produce badasses or hardmen.

Imprecision is also evident in the failure of the theory to specify the form transcendence will take when it is provoked. Why would some youth, for instance, become badasses instead of seekers of sneaky thrills? Of those who are motivated to become badasses, why do some choose (or somehow end up) expressing "badass" in "conventional" ways such as professional fighting, nightclub bouncing, soldiering, or policing rather than in the unconventional ways Katz describes? Why would those suffering chaos or hopeless humiliation choose righteous slaughter rather than cold-blooded murder? For that matter, why wouldn't they choose suicide, since these actions are all infused with a sense of fatality anyway, or try to escape through drugs, satanic worship, or even conventional evangelical religion?

Even if Katz is generally correct, many contingencies probably affect the chances of, and form of, deviance that a person might commit to transcend situational constraints. The provoking elements that Katz identifies surely are not experienced or interpreted in the same way by all individuals. No doubt the same events or circumstances will be regarded by some as humiliating but by others as simply temporary unpleasantnesses, and the same social circumstances will generate a sense of chaos for some but not for others. How events and circumstances are interpreted will probably vary with individual personality, perceptual acuity, past experience, and so on. Hence, the likelihood that communal boundaries will lead to gang fighting and intra-area struggle for sovereignty probably depends greatly upon community organization within bounded areas (Cloward and Ohlin 1960; Bursik and Grasmick 1993).

Furthermore, even if deviance allows its practitioners to transcend various limitations, there is little in the Katz theory to help establish the form of the supposed causal effect or the causal interval. There does seem to be the assumption that various limitations like humiliation, bounded selves, or chaos bear a linear relationship with their characteristic crimes, but this is never explicit. Moreover, such an assumption may be wrong. I suspect that up to a certain point things that bind selves of adolescents and supposedly lead to sneaky thrills, external rationality that presumably provokes street-elite behavior, and chaos that is said to bring about cold-blooded murder motivate efforts to transcend, but that beyond that point, greater limitations inhibit transcendent efforts. Thus, adolescents with selves that are extremely bounded cannot even contemplate, much less undertake, sneaky thrills. Sneaky thrills are luxuries of the partially liberated self just as badass behavior and cold-blooded murder are possible only when rationality is incomplete, for complete rationality of the outside world would imply effective socialization and constraint for all.

The theory is also unclear about the implied causal interval between various limitations and the deviant outcomes they produce. How long does it take humiliation to produce righteous slaughter, or chaos to bring about cold-blooded murder, or humility concerning the rationalized world to produce street-elite behavior? Katz does not say; he merely identifies some markers, in some instances, that signify that it is about to happen.

Finally, though the theory is rich in its recognition of situational influences on behavior, especially in its accounts of *how*, it nevertheless has limited ability to answer the question of *why* systematically and exhaustively and in such a way that deviant outcomes can be understood as products of dynamic sequences of events or interactions of variables; that is, it is not as deep as a general theory needs to be. Like many simple theories, Katz's cuts into a longer causal chain at some midpoint; in his case that point is when the individual recognizes some limitation from his or her own situation. The theory makes little attempt to show how prior variables shape these situational limitations or the individuals' perceptions and interpretations of such limitations. In fact, Katz denigrates "sentimental materialism" as reflected in standard attempts to predict deviance from background factors (1988:313–317), yet it is clear that such background variables influence the foreground that Katz wants to emphasize.

Transcendence theory also fails to penetrate deeply enough into causal sequences because it seems to hinge on one-way causation. However, even Katz's own descriptions suggest that efforts to transcend often bring about, or at least intensify, the limitations that are supposedly at their root, suggesting reciprocal effects. For instance, sneaky thrills themselves sometimes provoke a sense of self-deprivation; and if they result in apprehension, they can lead to even more stringent boundaries on the development of adolescent autonomy. Similarly, righteous slaughter often backfires to produce even greater humiliation for the person, particularly if others reject the killer's claim to have acted out of indignation at the violation of community standards. In short, if the theory of transcendence is to serve as a general theory, it must recognize explicitly reciprocal causal effects, and it must specify the conditions under which one-way or reciprocal effects are most likely to result.

Summary on Transcendence Theory. Katz's analysis of the subjective elements of offender actions is exciting and informative, and it contains the germ of a general theory—that deviance is undertaken to transcend limitations. Moreover, his interpretation is general and somewhat deep. His use of invention, however, has not produced an adequate general theory. The Katz formulation is extremely unsystematic and imprecise, resting ultimately on subjective components to be discovered only by particularistic observation and interpretive understanding. It fails to incorporate situational, personal, and organizational variables that would permit prediction of deviance, and it neglects the forms of its central relationship as well as the magnitude of the causal interval. Finally, it adumbrates the causal sequences implied by analysis. In the end, transcendence theory is no more than a set of after-the-fact interpretations loosely tied together through a barely discernible underlying principle.

Katz's work, like that of Gottfredson and Hirschi, illustrates why invention is not the preferred method for remedying the defects of simple theories. Invention probably will do little to improve general theory because those qualified to practice it are scarce, it inherently encourages the production of self-absorbed but limited and incomplete schemes, and it can rarely lead to anything genuinely new. Katz's analyses should convince doubters that invention is the domain of creative geniuses, not the tool of ordinary scholars. Few could exercise the kind of insight he demonstrates, and his work, at least in its grasp of detail and application to a wide range of behaviors, appears to be original. Nevertheless, originality implies distinctiveness and separation, which produces limited and incomplete formulations. Those who traverse unexplored land cannot hope to benefit from equipment left by their predecessors, and to explore the wilds in a civilized world, one must exaggerate the uniqueness of the chosen path. So, although Katz is not so obviously defensive as Gottfredson and Hirschi, his elusive language distorts and mystifies a straightforward idea in ways that may be for self-aggrandizement, not general enlightenment. He seems to be saying to the community of scholars that mysterious limitations loom over the deviant to provoke his or her behavior, but they are so esoteric that only Katz can surmise what they are. Hence the seductions of crime theory illustrates again that invention encourages arrogance, leading away from adequate general theory, not toward it.

Finally, without slighting Katz's graphic interpretations, astute understandings, and unique handling of material, I must point out that his basic *theoretical* ideas are not totally new. The notion that deviant behavior is undertaken because it is useful, satisfying, or fun for the person is really quite mundane. Some formulations (Merton 1957a, 1957b) portray crime as a means of overcoming economic limitations (which Katz categorically rejects); others interpret crime/deviance as a way of countering failure, anticipated failure, or stresses (Agnew 1985; Cohen 1955). Still others present crime/deviance as expressions of anger and hostility toward more successful competitors or those who the perpetrators think are making life difficult for them (Agnew 1992; Yates 1962), as the means of escaping the drudgery or difficulties of everyday life (Finestone 1957; Miller 1958), as a way of defying authority (Brehm 1966), or to meet challenges in a tense situation (Luckenbill 1977, 1984; Short and Strodtbeck 1974). Much of Katz's work merely appears to be new because he labels in unusual ways the limitations giving rise to deviant solutions. Economic success and other socially prescribed goals are called rationality of the modern world; being controlled by circumstances and being outdone by rivals is referred to as humiliation, experiencing restrictions and control is portrayed as having a bounded self, and the general lack of meaning or direction in life is called chaos.

This illusion of originality is all the more important to note because, like all "inventors," Katz wishes to claim a larger domain of creativity than is warranted, and to defend it as his own. To do so he denies the value of what already exists by simplifying, degrading, and then rejecting all previous explanatory attempts, particularly "strain" theories. On close examination, however, his explanations look a lot like the very ones he savages. To claim originality, he must resort to semantic "sleight of tongue" to try to mislead those who are unwilling to struggle with his bewildering language.

This is not to deny some true inventiveness, only to demonstrate the general point that attempts at invention rarely produce really new theory. Katz's originality is in conceiving of all deviant solutions, and to some extent the limitations that provoke them, as subjective phenomena having meanings and values that are not obvious from the behavior. Hence, whereas thievery may have the outward, seemingly obvious value of providing money to the perpetrator, the more important, and perhaps the only real, function of theft may be to help thieves feel that they are not controlled by social circumstances; that they have risen above and triumphed over (transcended) economic limitations and their apparent superiors with greater resources.

Conclusions on Invention

Invention in its ideal form seems like a desirable method for producing better theory, and sometimes its practice results in stimulating and useful schemes or ideas, but it is impractical; it provokes an unfortunate tendency toward rigidity or idiosyncrasy, or both, that actually inhibits theoretical development; and its products are likely to be limited and incomplete. It is impractical because it cannot be taught, there are few who possess the necessary skills to do it, and the likelihood of truly new ideas is small. In addition, because "invented" theories are personal products to be distinguished by their originality, inventors become self-interested owners with commitments to differentiating, sanctifying, and defending them. The resulting schemes, therefore, are inherently limited and incomplete, often rigid and stultified. These weaknesses are clear in the best contemporary examples, the self-control theory of Gottfredson and Hirschi and the seductions of crime formulation by Katz.

Elaboration

A second way to build better theory is to modify and refine existing theories. This method assumes that empirical testing and logical criticism will reveal theoretical weaknesses that can be remedied by adding elements to existing theories to show how they apply in particular ways in some situations but in other ways in other situations or to more fully explicate their latent causal processes.

In its conceptually perfect form, the technique of theoretical elaboration is superior to invention, and in some respects it approaches the ideal implied by the scientific method. Theoretical elaboration has never been practiced in its conceptually perfect form, however, and even if it were employed in visionary style, it probably would still fail to produce the kind of general theory we need; certainly any progress it might bring would be slow and inefficiently achieved.

To some extent the success of elaboration has been stifled because of the way it has been practiced. Contrary to ideal mandates, the procedure has not been employed as a collective endeavor to modify central theories. Instead, individual scholars have elaborated parts of existing theories, usually for specific application to a localized issue or situation, with the objective of developing what they and others have come to regard as new and different theories. That is, the elaboration process has involved spin-off activity, which has produced a large number of smaller specific theories or critiques that have not been blended with the original statement to form an emergent, elaborated general product. Instead we now have a plethora of focused, partially redundant theory fragments. Moreover, at least partly because of spin-off activities, most deviance theories are specific rather than general and within each of a limited number of clusters, the specific theories are actually a lot alike (see, for example, Akers 1989, 1990).

But even without this misdirected practical application, elaboration suffers from a major defect. It inherently assumes that a given theory that is being modified and expanded will be dominant in any ultimately elaborated structure. Within the elaboration procedure, refinements are made to buttress, extend, or adorn the original theoretical scheme, not to change it. This precludes the possibility of subordinating a primary theoretical theme to a competitor, even if it has great potential for improving the overall emergent product. There is even little likelihood that secondary elements from theories that compete with the one being elaborated could be used in refinement, especially if the central arguments of competitive theories are potent. The practice of elaboration, therefore, blinds scholars to important possibilities, and it prevents them from arriving at the best general theory.

Not only is elaboration flawed by its basic commitment to primary theories (those that constitute the original focus on which elaboration builds), but it also suffers from intrinsic inefficiency. Even at its best, elaboration implies slow, isolated improvement. Detecting specific weaknesses, either through logical or empirical analysis, reformulating the weak part of the theory, then reanalyzing the logic and empirical standing of the newly elaborated structure in order to refine and modify the structure still more, without reference to, or absorption of, other theories or theory fragments, requires Jobian patience.

As practiced, elaboration involves much duplication of effort, which, along with the basic restraints of the method, makes for slow, and ultimately, incomplete theoretical development. At best, then, it is an inefficient method for improving theory. Even so, "best" is seldom employed, so theoretical elaboration usually results in the proliferation of limited theories and the preservation of a competitive atmosphere that probably cannot lead to the complex, contingent general theories that we need. This can be appreciated by examining the development of anomie theory.

The Elaboration of Anomie Theory

Strain theories, as exemplified by Merton's anomie formulation, contend that deviance results from, and often is performed, to solve problems that the individual experiences. Despite anomie theory's huge impact on the social science community at the time it was introduced (1938) and for the subsequent three decades (see Clinard 1964b), many of its defects were quickly recognized. As a result, various scholars urged elaboration or refinement of the original statement, either to correct its flaws or to apply its insights in a more complete and precise manner. None, however, actually attempted explicit elaboration, instead leaving that task for the original author, who, as early as 1949, began to make adjustments in his theory to deal with problems that came to light. Unfortunately, many of the changes he made were subtle, sometimes involving only a few words, and were not explicitly indicated in the various restatements and reprints of the original paper that appeared over the years (see Simon and Gagnon 1976). As a result, and partly because various interpreters have relied upon different versions of the theory, much confusion has prevailed about what the theory really says or means. There is no systematic, detailed account of how anomie theory has evolved, so I will try to track its elaboration, or more precisely, try to show how elaboration might have transpired had the scholarly community, and Merton, practiced it correctly.

Merton's Original Statement. In his first statement of the theory in 1938, Merton was concerned mainly with variations among groups or societies. He focused on the emphasis that different societies or groups place on culturally specified goals relative to social regulations concerning the achievement of those goals. His main point was that these two elements of social life can be mal-integrated with undue emphasis either on goals or on the norms regulating the achievement of those goals and that at least one form of such mal-integration would "exert pressure on certain persons in the society to engage in nonconformist behavior," resulting in higher *rates* of deviance than others. Although he stated that mal-integration can take the form of overemphasis on the cultural means to the neglect of goals, Merton was more interested in those groups that overemphasized goals. Even though he acknowledged that goals and means might take many forms in various "specific situations" (and he uses examples such as athletics and card playing), he focused on "economic activity in the broad sense," and on U.S. society as a whole, which he contended overemphasizes the goal of economic success. Thus Merton implied that in societies like that of the United States, which stresses goals relative to means, everybody has to seek some adaptation or accommodation to this general condition of mal-integration.

Individuals were said to have five options expressed in terms of simultaneous "acceptance" (sometimes he called it "assimilation") or "elimination" of the goals or the prescribed means. The most common adaptation was designated as conformity, but here as in subsequent modifications of the theory, Merton did not explain why someone would conform; he simply described this adaptation as acceptance of both the goals and means. However, in trying to account for the four deviant adaptations, Merton thought they all stemmed from the same conditions—"frustration . . . from the inaccessibility of effective institutional means for attaining economic or any other type of highly valued 'success.'" Hence by inference, since deviant adaptations grow out of inaccessible means, having access to effective means should lead individuals to conform.

Merton first planted seeds of confusion when he shifted from discussion of the conditions of societies or groups that produce differing rates of deviance to focus on the adaptations of individuals within mal-integrated societies or groups. The hiatus is this: His discussion of whole societies or groups suggests that all members of a mal-integrated society are liable to commit deviance because everybody must adapt to that mal-integration; yet, in discussing individual adaptations, Merton suggests that only some people in a mal-integrated society, those lacking access to effective means, will adapt deviantly. Thus Merton states that all of the four deviant adaptations are linked to individual inaccessibility to means, and by implication, conformity must ensue when an individual objectively has access to effective means to achieve goals. Moreover, this initial ambiguity is exacerbated by the use of "acceptance" and "elimination" to describe the adaptations, whereas terms like "inaccessible" and "internalized prohibitions" are used in trying to explain why individuals turn to specific adaptations. Since the terms describing the adaptations signify psychic or cognitive processes, and the terms used to explain adoption of one or another mode of adaptation seem to refer to objective conditions of deprivation or failure, consumers of anomie theory have never been able to use the theory without confusion.

Uncertainties surrounding the concept of conformity are probably not as important as other ambiguities, however, since Merton's primary focus is on deviant rather than conforming adaptations. At one point Merton says that *all* of the deviant adaptations, including ritualism, innovation, and rebellion, stem from the same conditions as retreatism (1938:678), an adaptation to which he paid special attention in the original statement. Retreatism presumably results when an individual initially strongly assimilates the goals and means but experiences repeated failure in achieving the goals. That is, the retreatist psychologically internalizes both the goals and the means but is objectively denied effective use of the means. Under such conditions a person with "internalized prohibitions" and "institutionalized compulsives," being psychically unable to resort to illegitimate means, would likely withdraw from active participation in the social system, psychologically rejecting the goals and the means.

Yet, despite having stated that all deviant adaptations stem from the same conditions—psychologically assimilating the goals and means but objectively experiencing the absence of effective means—and having suggested that whether one or another is chosen depends on "the particular personality, and thus, the particular cultural background involved"

(1938:678), Merton goes on to muddle the picture by discussing "innovation" as an adaptation in which an individual suffers from inadequate socialization that results in assimilating the goals but making no commitment to the means. This suggests that, unlike the retreatist, the innovator does not necessarily suffer from objective deprivation of effective means, but rather is psychologically deficient from the beginning in not having internalized the moral rules governing goal pursuit. Ritualism, also, is apparently not linked to objective deprivation of effective goals. Instead, according to Merton's discussion, the ritualist is one who suffers a different kind of inadequate socialization—one in which he or she overinternalizes the rules and regulations (the means) for achieving goals. Finally, because little is said about rebellion, one must infer from the logic of the other three deviant adaptations that it results from inadequate socialization wherein the individual has failed to internalize either the goals or the means but nevertheless fails in goal achievement.

Based on the original statement of anomie theory, then, one cannot ascertain whether deviance by an individual is theoretically caused by (1) the general conditions of living in an anomic society that overemphasizes goals relative to means, (2) the personal experience of not having access to effective means for goal achievement, (3) inadequate socialization that results in over- or underinternalization of goals or means, or (4) some combination of these with "personality." This causal elusiveness is particularly troublesome because almost all later interpretations of anomie theory (see Liska 1987) attribute the cause of individual deviance, particularly innovative forms of deviance, to inaccessibility of effective means for achieving culturally specified goals, and it is this causal hypothesis that represents the most enduring aspect—even the heart—of anomie theory. Yet, it appears from Merton's original statement that absence of access to effective means for goal achievement may be relevant only for two forms of deviance, retreatism and rebellion, whereas innovation (and ritualism) is the simple product of distorted socialization, albeit within a larger mal-integrated culture that overemphasizes goals. Moreover, it is not clear whether the concepts implicated in the supposed causes of deviance are of a cognitive-psychological or an objective nature.

To be sure, in this first statement, Merton introduced a number of provocative ideas around which a well-formulated theory could be developed, but his initial articulation of that potential theory was highly deficient. This statement, then, was a prime candidate for elaboration.

Merton's First Modifications. Eleven years after the appearance of anomie theory, its author must have realized some of its logical problems. Yet Merton's restatements of the theory, which appeared in two separate but almost identical sources published in 1949 (1949a and 1949b), though different from the original paper, did little to solve the most serious difficulties. The original paper contained two foci—cultural mal-integration, the more important issue, and investigation of how "some social struc-

tures *exert a definite pressure* upon certain [persons] in the society to engage in non-conformist" behavior. By 1949 (Merton 1949b), the main focus had shifted; now it was to locate groups, *within* social structures, that
were peculiarly subject to those social structural pressures that would
produce fairly high rates of deviant behavior. Showing "how deviations
had different shapes and patterns in different social structures" (Merton
1949b:125) became secondary. It was at this point that Merton began to
portray the groups especially subject to pressure toward deviance in social-class terms.

In addition, Merton began to formulate more explicitly how the family
serves as a transmission device connecting social status and the various
adaptations. In that endeavor, he changed the meaning of the minuses
used to signify the various adaptations from "elimination" to "rejection,"
and instead of goals and means, he wrote of "values." For example in
1949, ritualists were said to have internalized the institutional values and
learned the moral mandates of society, whereas before they had "assimilated the means to an extreme degree." Merton only minimally clarified
the theoretical causes of the various adaptations by introducing the "doctrine of luck," which he suggested was crucial in determining whether an
individual with inaccessible means rebelled or adapted in some other deviant way. The original statement had implied that rebels internalize neither the goals nor the means, so in the face of failure they try to alter the
social structure. In the 1949 statement, Merton suggested that rebels not
only fail to internalize the goals and means, but they also must attribute
actual failure to defects in the social structure. Others who fail attribute
their misfortune to fate and therefore seek accommodation in either innovation, ritualism, or retreatism, depending upon how strongly they have
internalized the goals and means.

Yet, Merton provided no theoretical guidelines as to the conditions that
would lead a person to attribute his or her predicament to the social
structure rather than fate. One is left to infer that absence of internalized
goals and means per se grants such insight. This, of course, implies that
internalizers of the goals or the means, or both, cannot perceive the social
structure as responsible for their condition and that noninternalizers will
inevitably make such attributions. Empirically, this inference is probably
wrong, and Merton would doubtlessly invoke a probabilistic rationale.
Nonetheless, he could have avoided the problem altogether by spelling
out additional theoretical bases for attribution of blame, thereby making
the theory more precise and deep.

Furthermore, the 1949 statement did not clarify whether the causal elements were cognitive or objective, nor did it spell out the import of inaccessible goals relative to socialization in leading to the various deviant
adaptations.

As messy as it was, however, other scholars began to criticize, borrow
from, remold, and extend the theory. Yet, much of the subsequent borrowing and expanding of Merton's scheme was less theoretical than expository and taxonomic, and most was aimed at developing more complete

and exhaustive classifications of types of anomie or adaptations to it. These efforts include those by Talcott Parsons (1951), Robert Dubin (1959), H. Taylor Buckner (1971), William Simon and John Gagnon (1976), and Merton himself (1964). I will not include these taxonomic expansions in tracing the elaborative history of anomie theory.

The Children's Bureau Conference. The first substantial effort by Merton to elaborate his theory appeared in 1956, in the form of proceedings of a conference sponsored by the U.S. Department of Health, Education, and Welfare. Partly in response to questions and criticisms from the participants, but also, no doubt, as a result of his own continuing efforts to justify the theory, Merton made two important modifications. First, without trying to rectify ambiguities in his earlier statement or to fill in the missing links about why various adaptations are embraced, he tried to make the theory deeper by calling attention to the possibility of reciprocal causation. He noted that "growth of patterns of 'illicit success' may progressively enlarge the degree of anomie in society so that others, who did not at first respond by personal deviant behavior to the initially low degree of anomie, may become liable to deviance as anomie is accentuated, this in turn creating an anomic situation for still others" (1956:38). Yet Merton did not say when this outcome was more or less likely to transpire or exactly how it was supposed to happen; it was simply portrayed as something that may sometimes happen. Moreover, this potential reciprocity was confined to the group level since no mention was made of the possibility that individual innovation might increase that same person's anomie, lack of access to means, or further rejection of the culturally prescribed means.

Second, Merton revealed awareness that his theory sorely neglected the process by which static conditions (like lack of access to means, or poor socialization) were translated into actual deviant adaptations of one kind or another. Although contending that anomie might play a part in the development of deviant subcultures, he fully granted (without direct reference to Sutherland's work on differential association) that delinquency could easily be explained, without direct recourse to anomie theory, as learned patterns of behavior, provided there was a preexisting subculture with deviant norms to which newcomers could be socialized. Apparently unaware of the work of Albert Cohen (1955), which was already in press, Merton called for a theory to explain how delinquent subcultures originate, crystalize, develop, and grow; presumably such a theory could be meshed with his own anomie formulation.

Cohen's Critique. Cohen, in *Delinquent Boys* (1955), and later in his explicit critique of anomie theory (1959), was the first to expose weaknesses in Merton's scheme in a cogent fashion while providing a basis for potential elaboration to correct them. Although Cohen did not offer his theory of subcultural formation and gang delinquency as a critique or application of anomie theory, it clearly serves that purpose, as recognized by many (see Clinard 1964b) and acknowledged by Merton. Thus:

Cohen does, in fact, examine the social and cultural sources of these pressures in much the same terms as those we have been considering. His thoroughly sociological analysis considerably advances our understanding of certain forms of deviant behavior commonly found in delinquency-groups and does so by extending the type of structural and functional theory now under review. (Merton 1957a:179)

Cohen's subcultural theory challenged the original anomie formulation by (1) arguing that the social process by which static structural conditions lead to deviant behavior must be spelled out in the theory, (2) showing that culturally prescribed success goals, even in the United States, must be interpreted according to varied contexts, and (3) demonstrating that individualized adaptations to strain, or to anomie, may be much less important than collective, organized adaptations by numerous persons in similar circumstances. In fact, one might say that Cohen identified a sixth adaptation, that of subcultural involvement, which combines some features of innovation, retreatism, and rebellion and which supersedes the five individualistic adaptations set forth by Merton (although Merton later describes subcultures as simple instances of rebellion, 1957b:191). Moreover, by actually specifying the conditions for, and the processes involved in, subcultural development, which would in turn permit individual involvement, Cohen offers a way to improve the original Mertonian argument. (Remember that Merton's statement provides no coherent theoretical basis for predicting when individuals will adopt one rather than another of the specified modes of adaptations.)

Cohen began by noting features of lower-class male delinquency that contradict predictions from various theories, including anomie. As Cohen interprets Merton, lower-class male delinquency should consist mostly of instrumental property crime, since those boys are deprived of financial success, presumably the overarching culturally prescribed goal to which they are taught to aspire. However, the evidence suggested to Cohen that most delinquent behavior by lower-class boys is noninstrumental property crime or physical aggression. He perceived that lower-class males are more interested in defying middle-class property values and in contradicting conventional rules against aggression than in achieving conventional success goals.

To make sense of this, Cohen theorized that lower-class boys lack the intellectual skills and preschool training necessary for effective competition in schools, which emphasize middle-class standards. As a result, deprived boys usually perform badly in the academic context and adjust poorly, both of which lead to loss of self-esteem. Since such boys normally reside in close proximity in urban neighborhoods, they can interact and share the common problem of school failure and poor self-esteem. Out of this "problem-sharing" interaction grows a subcultural solution, the delinquent gang, which allows the boys to reject and denigrate the middle-class standards by which they are unflatteringly judged and which replaces those standards with new goals and status criteria that are within their reach.

The logic of Cohen's theory suggests that the form and probability of delinquency will vary by gender, by social class, and by place of residence. It varies by gender because the success goals prescribed for males and females differ, with females being encouraged to attach themselves to successful males, ultimately for family building, whereas the males are expected to achieve high placement in the occupational-financial system. Differential difficulty in achieving these goals portends less delinquency among females overall, and when goal blockage does occur, it inspires gender-specific types of adaptations; males are provoked to find routes to financial success or to replace unachievable status criteria with achievable ones, whereas females are motivated to innovate new routes to attract and retain male attention.

Similarly, delinquency varies by social class, with the higher classes being less prone toward it, because family circumstances afford them greater skills for successful school performance, the main determinant of ultimate occupational placement. Further, goal blockage leads to individualized delinquency when experienced by the higher class but leads to gang delinquency when suffered by the lower class because of the opportunity for collective interaction around shared problems made possible by lower-class, proximate residential patterns, particularly in inner-city areas.

Finally, and following from the consequences of residential proximity, the form of delinquency varies by size of place, as larger, urban locales allow those with similar problems to seek mutual support in arriving at a collective, subcultural adaptation, yet residents of less dense, smaller settlements must endure their failures or resort to individualistic solutions.

Cohen's work suggested that anomie theory needed elaboration because a simple discrepancy between goals and means relevant to the larger culture will not necessarily lead to delinquency, even among those who presumably have not internalized rules prohibiting illegitimate means. There must also be contextual conditions that foster deviance, and the nature of those conditions will not only influence the likelihood of deviant adaptations but will affect their form as well. Moreover, the bridge between strain/anomie and deviance of particular types is not simply the presence of static conditions in the social environment but also involves social processes that unfold in a sequential pattern—processes ignored by Merton. Finally, Cohen's work shows that the theory should accommodate group or collective solutions, rather than focusing exclusively on individual adaptations, and he provides the subcultural theory that could be brought into an elaborated anomie formulation.

Merton's 1957 Response. By the late 1950s Merton had numerous guidelines for elaborating his anomie theory, and he had available to him at least two theory fragments—learning processes developed by Sutherland and processes of subcultural development and participation developed by Cohen—that could have been incorporated into the theory. However, he did very little to modify anomie theory along the indicated lines. In fact, he introduced further ambiguity by switching explanations for retreatism.

Recall that up to this point the conditions for retreatism are that both the goals and the means "have been thoroughly assimilated. . . . but accessible institutionalized avenues are not productive of success"; that is, the person has continuously failed to achieve the goal but cannot resort to illegitimate means because of internalized moral constraints (Merton 1957a:153). In addition, the conditions for ritualism are that a person who has assimilated the goals and the means be facing the prospect of failure. The retreatist apparently differs from the ritualist in that he or she has already failed, whereas the ritualist anticipates the possibility of failure. Due to moral training, neither can innovate.

In the 1957 revision, however, retreatism now is said to occur in response to an "abrupt break in the familiar and accepted normative framework and in established social relations," especially if perceived as likely to last a long time (Merton 1957a:188). Ritualism, on the other hand, now involves "the repeated frustration of strongly held goals or the continued experience of finding that reward is not proportioned to conformity" (1957a:185). Thus, what in earlier versions presumably explained retreatism (strongly internalized goals and means but actual repeated failure) now explains ritualism, and a new explanation (abrupt change in social arrangements) is offered for retreatism.

Merton did make a minor attempt to incorporate ideas about the process through which goals-means discrepancies are translated into deviant behavior. First, he explicitly noted the importance of social process since the "theoretical context requires us to see the emergence and growth of anomie as a resultant of ongoing social process and not simply as a condition that happens to obtain" (1957a:179). Second, he suggested that this process consists of deviance by some in response to a goals-means discrepancy; observation of this deviance by others causes them to more clearly perceive discrepancies between their own goals and means, which in turn creates more deviance in continuing reciprocation to the point of "cumulatively disruptive consequences" unless "counteracting mechanisms of control are called into play" (1957a:180). Third, he stated that there can be collective responses to anomie in the form of "subgroups, alienated from the rest of the community but unified within themselves," but he allowed that such "rebellion" tended to be unstable except when "the new groups and norms are sufficiently insulated from the rest of society which rejects them" (1957a:191). However, Merton did not say when any of these processes are more or less likely to transpire, nor did he show how they come about or how they might involve individuals. Hence, despite the presence of guidelines for correction, and with a new edition of his book in process, Merton failed to elaborate anomie theory in any meaningful way. In fact, he simply noted some ways that the theory needed alteration and modified some of the explanations by switching accounts of retreatism and ritualism and adding a new explanation for retreatism.

Cloward's Suggested Refinement. Two years later (1959) Richard Cloward provided still more material for elaborating anomie theory. He observed that the theory seemed to account for deviant behavior strictly in terms of motivation and constraint. Individuals who internalized success goals but who lacked access to means or who had failed to internalize moral prohibitions against deviance presumably innovated or retreated (note that Cloward here interprets the retreatist adaptation according to Merton's pre-1957 statements). However, accumulated research suggested to Cloward that individuals, at least those who develop recidivist patterns of criminal behavior, first have to learn criminal skills and then have to encounter opportunities for exercising those skills. Thus, even if anomie theory had been correct in its account of the motivation for criminal/deviant behavior, it was deficient, or at least incomplete, in not incorporating opportunity (or illegitimate means) into its theoretical structure. Of course, Cloward and Lloyd Ohlin later (1960) tried to specify how neighborhoods vary in providing illegitimate means for youth.

Like Cohen, Cloward identified a major deficiency in anomie theory that could have been corrected by elaboration. Clearly, Merton's formulation did not include enough causal elements. Learning to define crime as an appropriate response to strain, learning how to commit crime, and encountering situations where criminal skills could be brought into play all appear to be important interactants with goals-means discrepancies; at least they appear to constitute conditions under which anomie will have crime/deviance inducing effects. Without them, the theory is weak in its predictions, especially in predicting when goals-means discrepancies will result in specific forms of deviance.

Merton's 1964 Response. Despite the cogent criticisms noted above and the concrete developments of subtheoretical components by Cohen and Cloward and Ohlin, Merton continued to do little more than state that such elements were compatible with his theory and to state in broad terms that the processes identified by critics were relevant; he did not actually alter the theory or merge the insights or subtheories into the larger formulation. For instance, in supposedly demonstrating the incorrectness of Cohen's criticism of anomie theory as proposing static rather than interactive causes, Merton (1964:235) states:

> The men most vulnerable to the stresses resulting from contradictions between their socially induced aspirations and poor access to the opportunity structure are the first to become alienated. Some of them turn to established alternatives (Cloward's illegitimate opportunity-structure) that both violate the abandoned norms and prove effective in achieving their immediate objectives. A few others actually innovate for themselves to develop new alternatives. These successful rogues . . . become prototypes for others in their environment who, initially less vulnerable and less alienated, now no longer keep to the rules they once regarded as legitimate. This, in turn, creates a more acutely anomic context for still others in the local social system.

But in characteristic fashion, Merton still did not specify the conditions for occurrence of each of the three possibilities: turning to established alternatives, innovating for themselves, or conforming despite stresses stemming from discrepancies between aspirations and access. He apparently thought that identifying such possibilities was enough. Moreover, rather than theoretically developing the interlinkages between individual and social contextual conditions in their joint and interactive effects on deviant behavior, Merton ceded the problem to researchers. Indeed, using contingency tables and hypothetical figures, he simply identified a large number of possibilities (1964:229, 236, 237) that might be uncovered with empirical study. The prospect that such empirical regularities, once documented, would have to be explained did not seem to inspire him to enrich the theory.

Merton did use this occasion to elaborate his explanatory scheme in one respect. He noted that the anomic processes and their consequences, which supposedly lead to deviant behavior, are more likely in urban contexts, and to his credit, he provided a reasonable rationale for expecting this. Yet improving the theory's precision in this small way only accents the numerous ways in which the theory could be made more precise, comprehensive, and deep.

Post–1964 Developments. Although interest in anomie theory began to wane in the late 1960s and continued at a low ebb in the 1970s, several scholars subsequently pointed out additional ways strain theory could (or should) be elaborated (see Agnew 1985; Adler and Lauter 1994; Messner and Rosenfeld 1994; Stack 1984), and conditions under which anomie might have differing effects continue to be identified (Messner and Rosenfeld 1994; Stack 1984). These proposed elaborations mainly concerned the relativity of standards of comparison; some called attention to the possibility that goals to which individuals might be committed are not necessarily those that are generally prescribed in a culture, that commitments to culturally prescribed goals vary in strength from individual to individual, and that immediate goals may be more important than long-range ones. Even though several of these proposed revisions concerning goal orientation were made in the late 1960s, the 1968 edition of *Social Theory and Social Structure* contained no changes in anomie theory. Thus, despite many potential modifications and elaborations suggested by various scholars, anomie theory maintained its basic original form and content with only minor alterations. The potential elaborative elements remained scattered through the literature, often being referred to as if they were autonomous theories in their own right. It was not until the 1980s that a serious effort was begun to actually elaborate strain theory in a comprehensive way by systematically drawing together its component parts into one coherent statement (see Agnew 1985).

Agnew's Contribution. Robert Agnew's most complete effort to elaborate the strain argument is his "general strain theory" (1992). In essence, the theory states that negative relations with others, which involve their blocking one's goal achievement, their threatening the maintenance of valued stimuli, or their imposition of negative stimuli, as well as unpleasant stimuli from the physical environment or the body, provoke emotions, such as anger, that sometimes motivate individuals to use deviant behavior to deal with the negativity. Agnew assumes that strain is unpleasant and may upset an emotional equilibrium, so a strained individual will try to do something to alleviate the strain or correct the emotional disequilibrium that it creates.

Coping can take one of three broad forms: cognitive, behavioral, or emotional responses. In cognitive responses the person mentally reinterprets the situation; in behavioral responses the individual tries to do something to get rid of the source of the adversity or to accommodate to it; and in emotional coping the person employs various methods to relieve the internal discomfort. Each of these forms of coping can involve deviant or conventional modes. Most of the time, and for most people, strain produces conventional cognitive or nondeviant behavioral and emotional coping. However, sometimes, and under some conditions, strain leads to deviant behavior or unconventional, although not necessarily deviant, coping.

Agnew details aspects of strain that enhance the likelihood of its leading to deviant adaptations. He focuses particularly on cumulativity and the ratio of negative to positive factors, but he also notes the importance of the magnitude, recency, duration, and clustering of stress-inducing situations. He does not attempt to explain why one person experiences more stress than another. Rather, he takes strain as the starting point and proposes measuring its various characteristics, providing some guidelines as to those characteristics that enhance the chances of deviance. Agnew regards the main variables for explaining deviant behavior to be the conditions that make deviant rather than nondeviant coping more likely, and he catalogs conditions that *can* affect the type of coping likely to be employed. They include: personality and other characteristics of the individual; the kind of social support available to the person; the constraints on, or costs of, deviant coping; microlevel variables; the learning history of the person that may result in predispositions toward various kinds of coping; and peer influences. Thus, Agnew's theory consists mainly of a series of conditional statements, but there is an underlying assumption that whenever people can, they will cope cognitively with stress, so it is only when conditions preclude cognitive adaptations that strain causes deviant behavior.

In summary, Agnew describes the contribution of his general strain theory as (1) pointing to several sources of strain not encompassed within the Mertonian framework, (2) more precisely specifying the relationship between strain and delinquency, with particular focus on cumulative and threshold effects as well as on the relevant dimensions of strain that influence the likelihood that it will produce deviance, (3) providing more complete accounts of cognitive, behavioral, and emotional adaptations to strain, and (4) identifying the factors that affect the choice of delinquent rather than nondelinquent adaptations.

Yet, despite Agnew's compilation, expansion, and refinement of ideas about strain into a general statement, some may doubt whether his work actually represents an elaboration of anomie theory. For one thing, he does not build on previous leads in modifying and expanding Merton's ideas. The general strain theory accords only brief attention to social structural considerations (Agnew 1992:72), the main focus of Merton's original effort, and it even relegates immediate contextual factors to a relatively minor role in comparison to more psychological mechanisms. Indeed, Agnew's emphasis is mainly on the processes operating in the mind and personality of the individual, and as a result the lead provided by Cohen and acknowledged by Merton concerning collective solutions to individual problems is muted, as is the opportunity factor identified by Cloward. Nevertheless, Merton's main causal process—that strain provides a motive for deviance—is the basis of the general strain theory, and Agnew's scheme does encompass strain stemming from disjunctions between aspirations (or goals) and expectations or achievements (implying some connections with the effective means) that is at the heart of anomie theory. Moreover, Agnew identifies some cognitive or mental adaptations similar to the Mertonian types that may represent forms of deviance even when they involve no actual criminal or delinquent behavior. For instance, ritualism is regarded by Merton as a form of deviance in which the individual cognitively accepts the culturally mandated means and goes through the motions of conformity but psychologically rejects the goals of achievement. Agnew's formulation accommodates individuals who minimize strains by cognitively reducing the importance of the goals or values they cannot realize (1992:67), and his argument suggests that sometimes such individuals are in social contexts where the goals in question are normatively prescribed and where the very hint of weak commitment may be regarded as evidence of deviance (1992:72).

Even if Agnew's theory could be regarded as a revision of Merton's work that builds on and fully encompasses anomie theory's ideas and history, it is unlikely that the community of scholars will regard the general strain theory as a culmination of anomie thinking. In fact, if previous history is any indication, Merton's formulation will continue to be described as anomie theory, whereas Agnew's formulation will be regarded as a "new," separate theory.

Conclusions on Elaboration

Three weaknesses of elaboration as a method for improving theory are illustrated by the history of anomie theory. First, regardless of what elaboration could accomplish if employed in an ideal way, little is actually produced because the technique is almost never fully followed. Certainly it has not been well employed in the case of anomie, despite its almost perfect candidacy. Many scholars have highlighted the limitations of Merton's scheme, and several have offered additions that could have been incorporated into a growing but generic formulation. However, as is common with deviance theories, the original formulation has resisted transformation and revision, while our theoretical repertoire has become cluttered with anomie spin-offs that are regarded as separate, distinct theories. The closest thing to a coherent, elaborated anomie theory is Agnew's general strain argument, but it represents a departure from the main thrust of Merton's work, and in any case, like the other products of those who practice elaboration, it is coming to have an autonomous life of its own.

Second, the practical failure of elaboration probably reflects an inherent defect in its structure. Since elaborators begin committed to the worth or priority of a particular theory, idea, or causal argument, their efforts are limited to modification or extension; they cannot bring in additional elements that might compete with the original causal argument. Thus, this method of theory building prohibits its practitioners from substantially improving the basic theory beyond a certain point—the point at which alternative theoretical statements might undermine the priority of the central argument. In reality, effective elaboration quickly reaches the point where further progress requires elements from other theories. Either the elaborator stops the process in deference to the initial theory or moves into the realm of theoretical integration. If elaboration inevitably leads to theoretical integration, why not start by trying to integrate?

Agnew's general strain theory, whether or not it represents a culmination of anomie ideas, illustrates this point. He describes his work as an elaboration or refinement of strain theory, which he contends makes a contribution distinct from differential association (social learning) and social control (social bonds) theories. Yet, Agnew ultimately brings learning and bonding back in. He lists initial goals, values, and identities, individual coping resources, the larger social environment that influences the importance of and sensitivity to selected goals or values, and dispositions toward deviance as variables influencing whether the person uses conventional or deviant adaptations. All of these, however, are to some extent products of learning, so to fill out the explanatory terrain of Agnew's theory one would have to focus more fully on the learning process. Similarly, the general strain theory lists conventional social supports, social bonds themselves, characteristics of social environments that make unconventional coping likely, and association with delinquent peers as important variables channeling the direction that strain-induced coping can take. All of these directly or indirectly depend on linkage into various social networks, so full understanding, even of the effects of strain, requires incorporation of additional theory about social bonding. It appears, therefore, that Agnew's theory involves as much integration as elaboration, and certainly it seems that further development will require more merging of learning, bonding, and strain and perhaps other theoretical species as well.

Third, the elaboration process is inefficient. Conceding for the sake of argument that Agnew's scheme evolved through elaboration, and ignoring its reliance on learning and social bonds theory for much of its content, one would probably regard it as the best example of elaborated theory in the contemporary literature. As it has now been over fifty years since the original anomie formulation, the general strain theory should stand as an exemplar of what can be accomplished with this method of theory building.

Nevertheless, evaluating the theory in terms of the criteria set forth in Chapter 2 suggests that it does not constitute an adequate general theory, though it is a marked improvement over most theoretical efforts. It does have some breadth since it applies to a wide range of types of deviance, including much property crime, acts of violence or aggression, vandalism, drug use, various forms of contemptuous or defiant conduct, and bizarre behaviors normally associated with mental illness. Furthermore, it does not apply to most forms of white-collar, political, or business crime, to professional street crime, or to those aspects of organized vice practiced by providers (rather than consumers)—all forms of deviance that involve routinized, rationally chosen, culturally supported, learned methods of making a living—nor does it seem to apply well to collectively expressed deviance such as gang behavior, riots, or deviant religious practices. It is a broad theory, but it is not broad enough to encompass all that students of deviance wish to understand.

The general strain theory is also more comprehensive than anomie theory or any of the other simple theories, but it still far overemphasizes motivation to the neglect of other potential causal elements. Clearly, the main idea is that strain creates a motive, or impulse, toward action and that under some conditions that motive finds expression in deviant behavior. Agnew also brings in constraint to explain why the emotions generated by strain do not always result in deviance; he touches on alternative motivation that would relegate strain to an unimportant position; he calls attention to individual coping resources that influence one's ability to use conventional methods of dealing with strain; and he notes that some people lack the "illegitimate means" to employ unconventional coping methods.

Still, the general strain theory concerns itself with only one motive element, although others, like internalized deviant values, deviant self- identities, or the desire to meet normative expectations of a deviant group, probably operate directly rather than simply conditioning the direction that strain will take. In addition, constraints may directly influence not just the probability that strain, once experienced, will be expressed in deviant forms of coping, but also whether strain-inducing situations are even encountered. Similarly, alternative motivation may be linked to deviant behavior in a more straightforward way than simply determining the relative importance of strain in one's life; some personal goals help create strain. Further, opportunities are heavily underplayed in the general strain theory since their absence is regarded as a constraint on deviance, whereas their presence is not portrayed as a generator of strain, of other motives for deviance, or as having direct effects on deviance itself.

The general strain theory suffers most from lack of depth because its mode is static rather than dynamic. It posits one simple causal sequence:

strain ⟶ emotion ⟶ coping, and it identifies conditions that may or may not influence the form of coping. However, it does not fill out the causal chain by showing the how and why of strain—why one emotion rather than another emerges from strain, and how the various conditions might interact or interrelate in dynamic processes eventuating in deviance, including any possible direct effects of strain or other motivators on deviance or their indirect effects through other possible mediators. Moreover, no attention is paid to the possibility—even the likelihood—of reciprocal causation. After all, one of the prime creators of strain may be deviance itself that results from earlier strain-induced coping or from other causes. Nor is there much attention paid to how these processes might be influenced by life-course transitions.

Finally, Agnew's theory is imprecise. Although it identifies many conditions influencing the direction of possible coping, it does not spell out the contingencies under which the entire process underlying the theory operates with greater or lesser force. Furthermore, there is little theoretical guidance on the form of the postulated causal effects. Presumably all are linear and positive, and in some instances exponential or cumulative, but it is easy to imagine that the effects of strain on various emotions take other forms. Perhaps strain from the exposure to noxious stimuli at first evokes anger, which may dissipate, to be replaced with despair as exposure to the noxious stimuli continues. Perhaps emotions provoked by strain wax and wane in light of changes in the external context. Agnew notes possible interactive or additive, as well as threshold, effects, but he treats them as empirical rather than theoretical issues. Moreover, causal intervals are highly problematic since stress may have instantaneous or long-term effects.

General Conclusion

In concept, invention and elaboration seem promising as methods for building adequate general theory, but they fail in practice, and they contain inherent elements that impede their ultimate potential. Invention is impractical because it assumes rare and unteachable skills and because new ideas become less likely as knowledge accumulates. It is handicapped by the possessiveness and defensiveness of its practitioners, who almost inevitably isolate and protect their products, precluding cross-fertilization. Self-control and transcendence theories illustrate these points.

Despite the logical appeal of elaboration for theory building, and the obvious value of refining existing theories, this approach has not and probably cannot lead to the general theory we need. This is partly because the social organization of our work produces scholars more satisfied with elaborative spin-offs classified as new products than with modification of larger theoretical entities. Greater impediments, however, are the inefficiencies stemming from efforts to refine a number of theories simultaneously without threatening them with competition from more potent elements. Elaboration of any given theory ultimately reaches a point where additional refinement requires synthesis with other theories, and at that point no further progress can be made using the method of elaboration itself. Efforts to refine Merton's anomie theory show this.

If invention and elaboration are flawed procedures, and if both are stymied by an inability to borrow theoretical arguments, it follows that a method preserving their virtues but having the potential to overcome their weaknesses should be promoted. I believe theoretical integration, at least as I define it, is that method.

4

Theoretical Integration

A third way to build better theory is to combine, synthesize, or integrate one or more existing theories, or theory fragments, into more comprehensive or adequate formulations. Scholars disagree about how to accomplish this (Messner et al. 1989), but the basic idea is simple. In fact, theoretical integration is mandated by the logic of science. Observing regularities and seeking their explanation will eventually lead one to see that some explanations can be subsumed under more comprehensive general explanatory schemes, or theories. Theories represent integrations of a variety of explanations of one or more different phenomena. As the scientific process proceeds, it eventually becomes clear that some theories can be subsumed under more comprehensive general theories, just as several explanations can be subsumed under a single theory. Thus, integration is a sequential step in a process that begins with induction (invention), proceeds with elaboration, and finally moves to synthesis.

In addition, integration, though building on invention and elaboration, suffers fewer inherent procedural flaws. Unlike invention, an individualistic endeavor involving innate creativity to produce new ideas (that often turn out to be resistant to modification), integration (1) is a collective endeavor dependent on participation of many scholars, (2) uses trainable skills and aims for outcomes less dependent on idiosyncratic genius, (3) does not require completely new ideas, which are always in short supply, and (4) because the products of integration are not owned by individuals, they are flexible and capable of being modified in the interest of further improvement. Unlike elaboration, integration (1) leads to fewer but more comprehensive general theories that encompass many explanations of specific phenomena rather than leading to proliferation of many specifically focused spin-offs from the more general theories that were the object of the original attempts at elaboration and (2) discourages the redundancy of elaborating many separate theories by encouraging incorporation of competitive components into one scheme.

Whether such advantages accrue, however, depends on the meaning of integration, on the method used in trying to achieve it (Elliott 1985; Hirschi 1979; Messner et al. 1989), and on how closely the integrator attends to the defects of simple theories noted in the previous chapter.

Although there are now a number of so-called integrated theories, many of them scarcely improve the separate theories that preceded them, and even the best leave much to be desired because they perpetuate the weaknesses of simple theories. In addition, most contemporary "integrated" theories do not involve much integration. Instead of logical or abstract merging of elements from the component theories into organic entities, most so-called integrated theories simply string variables together in an ad hoc fashion to "explain more variance." Even the best still lack the comprehensiveness that general theories should have, mainly because they encompass only a few of the crucial variables implicated in causal processes, and most continue to explain only one or a few types of deviance. Furthermore, existing "integrated" theories fail to explicate full causal sequences, explain the how and why, or incorporate reciprocal effects. Finally, they provide few systematic specifications of contingencies under which the explanatory principles incorporated within them are likely to operate with greater or lesser intensity, they pay almost no attention to the form of the causal relationships, and they completely ignore the size of the causal intervals. Each of these weaknesses will be illustrated with actual or attempted integrations.

Modeling

Simple Multivariate Models

Some try to synthesize by specifying, and estimating the parameters of, statistical models showing the interconnections in a particular data set of variables suggested by different theories, lines of thought, or conventional practice. The simplest type of model brings together a number of predictors, and the researcher uses some form of regression, or higher-order correlation analysis, perhaps with a variety of arrangements of the data, to estimate the joint effects of the predictors, their relative strengths, interactions, and perhaps conditions under which they achieve or fail to achieve statistical significance. The results reveal how well various arrangements of the variables work, that is, which model is most adequate for the data at hand.

For example, Willie Edwards (1992) used variables suggested by anomie, social control, differential association, labeling, and self-esteem theories to predict the frequency and type of delinquency of a sample of institutionalized youth. Using correlations and logical reasoning, he specified a causal model in which anomie and social control were posited as occurring prior to differential association, which was prior to labeling, which in turn was portrayed as occurring prior to poor self-esteem, which finally was depicted as leading to delinquency. All of the variables were posited to affect all subsequent variables. Exactly why or how, or to what degree the different variables affect subsequent ones, was not spelled out, nor was the particular order of effects fully justified. The theory represented by the model, then, is only one plausible possibility among many that could be generated by arraying the variables in various orders.

Sophisticated Causal Models

Ad Hoc Models. More complex causal models specify the ways in which a series of variables in a specific set of data are interrelated in causal sequences, often drawing on the joint implications of various theories and on a series of trial-and-error arrangements of the variables. Then, using one of the statistical approaches for structural modeling developed in recent years (path analysis, two- or three-stage least squares, LISREL), the scholar estimates the strength and significance of the specified effects as well as the adequacy of the overall model. Since the variables used in empirically based modeling are usually to some extent relevant to more than one theory, the particular arrangements of variables and the interconnections among them that finally emerge from the modeling process are sometimes thought to constitute integrated theories.

An example is Richard Johnson's (1979) model of delinquent behavior, based partly on theories of delinquency but mainly on previous empirical findings. He postulates that social class affects parental concern for a child as well as the child's success in school. Parental concern, in turn, is posited to affect attachment of the child to the parent, the child's susceptibility to peer influence, and the child's school success. Success in school supposedly also affects the child's susceptibility to peer influence, attachment to school, and perceived strain. Following the presumed causal flow, Johnson specifies that perceived strain affects school attachment, whereas school attachment influences delinquent values, delinquent associates, and delinquent behavior. Furthermore, parental attachment is also said to affect attachment to school, delinquent associates, and delinquent behavior. Delinquent associates, in turn, affect anticipated peer approval for delinquency and perceived risk of apprehension for delinquency, both of which lead to delinquency, and anticipated peer approval affects delinquent values, which lead directly to delinquent behavior. Pictorially diagrammed (Johnson 1979:67), this model involves 12 separate variables interconnected through 22 causal links (with no reciprocal effects, however).

Models That Merge Competing Theoretical Claims. Structural modeling has not always been ad hoc, or based on a collection of variables that are seemingly obvious or at hand. Some scholars have employed the techniques to more directly spell out the empirical implications of variables from two or more particular theories. For example, David Ward and Charles Tittle (1993) specified a causal model merging the claims of parts of the economic theory with the claims of labeling theory, and for estimation purposes added other logical effects among six endogenous variables, to account for academic cheating among college students. The variables include primary deviance, informal sanctions, and labeling at time one; risk perception and deviant identity at time two; and subsequent deviance at time three. The resulting endogenous model incorporates 15 causal effects, one of which is reciprocal at time two. In addition, the estimated model encompasses 16 antecedent control/instrumental variables, including many that are often considered central to one or another theory (such as family closeness). Using two-stage least squares, they were able to estimate the strength of the causal effects suggested by the competing theories, concluding that the labeling effects were more viable than those suggested by the theory of specific deterrence in these particular data concerning this particular form of deviance.

Although Ward and Tittle did no more than consider simultaneously the implied causal effects suggested by labeling and deterrence theories in order to more adequately test the relative empirical strengths of the two, some contend that the products of efforts like theirs are "integrated theories." Indeed, some of the better-known "integrated theories" are little more than empirical models. Later in this chapter, I will describe some of those efforts as if they were genuine integrated theories, but they could easily be regarded as no more than sophisticated causal models.

Critique

Modeling is an important advancement of empirical work in the social sciences, enabling a clearer presentation and evaluation of the causal implications of sets of variables and theories. However, modeling is not theory building, nor can modeling substitute for theoretical integration. In modeling, (1) variables rather than concepts are the focus of attention, (2) at least some of the variables are joined by ad hoc reasoning or by the empirical necessities for estimation, and (3) the resulting models apply only to the particular situation or data set. In contrast, theory, and by extension integration, involves abstract concepts linked through a coherent set of general causal processes that provide an intellectual framework within which explanations of numerous specific, concrete phenomena can be incorporated. Therefore, no matter how sophisticated models may be, at best they express a set of potential effects implied by an underlying theory (or theories).

This contrast is vivid in comparisons of the criteria of successful modeling with those of successful theory building. Simple multivariate models aim to achieve as much "explained variance" as possible, whereas complex causal models aim to portray actual empirical relationships in a given set of data as accurately as possible, that is, their goal is efficient prediction. General theories, however, are expected to answer the questions *how* and *why* for a skeptical audience and to do this in an abstract manner so that the explanatory principles involved can be applied to a large number of phenomena. The ultimate goal is to produce intellectual accounts that satisfy scholars who are seeking to understand fully how effects within their domain of interest occur. Theories do not exist in the empirical world waiting to be discovered, as modeling assumes. Rather, theories are mental constructions that bring order to the empirical world.

Modeling can be useful for testing theories, but the procedures for successful model building can never produce adequate theories. One could conceivably build a good causal model using trial and error to isolate a large number of variables that would, in particular combinations and interlinkages, permit reasonably good prediction of some particular phenomenon, even though the modeler did not understand anything at all about how the variables produced the outcome or why the outcome follows. In contrast, a general theorist would be quite dissatisfied with mere prediction, regardless of its level of accuracy, and would insist on understanding the processes underlying those predictions (but see Elliott 1985 for a different perspective). In the case of crime, for instance, with careful modeling it is already possible to predict violation fairly well using demographic variables like age, gender, race, and place of residence in combination with the conditions of childhood training and various prior dispositions like intelligence, impulsivity, and aggressiveness, while including factors like prior offense, peer relationships, perceived chances of getting caught, and social bonds. Nevertheless, the whys and wherefores cry out to be explained.

To be sure, understanding the causal processes involved in a given phenomenon may lead to effective prediction, provided one can translate the concepts into measurable variables and can find the appropriate techniques for expressing the predictive expectation. Certainly, predictive ability is the acid test of whether a given theory is empirically accurate, but in theory building, prediction is a by-product of success; it is not success itself.

Integrating Theories

Narrowly Focused Integrations

Some syntheses of disparate, preexisting theories might be regarded as partial integrated theories (one is the opportunity theory of Cloward and Ohlin [1960] discussed in connection with elaboration of anomie theory), though many of them are not much different from empirical models, and most are narrow, with some focused specifically on "delinquency," or in some cases, on particular forms of delinquency. Two of the five "focused integrations" to be described are extremely constrained; one attempts to explain "repetitive, serious" delinquency (Colvin and Pauly 1983), and one aims to explain "differences" between males and females in nonserious, "common" delinquent behavior (Hagan 1989; Hagan et al. 1985). The other three collectively represent a trend of elaborative integration in which a beginning simple integration has been modified successively to move the entire structure toward greater adequacy. Nevertheless, the overall thrust of this "mainline delinquency integration" is still quite narrow since recent efforts were designed mainly to explain repetitive "sustained patterns of delinquent behavior" (Elliott et al. 1985) or "prolonged involvement in serious delinquency" (Thornberry 1987:867). As will be explained, these integrations are flawed in other ways as well.

The Mainline Delinquency Integration. Conger. Although his analysis
ended up testing competing claims of the two theories, Rand Conger's
(1976) discussion represents one of the earliest attempts to integrate
Hirschi's version (1969) of "social control" theory with "social learning"
theory as presented by Akers (1985) in 1973. Conger begins by noting the
inconsistency between social control theory, which predicts that attachment to peers will reduce delinquency, and research evidence suggesting
that such attachments, when the peers are themselves delinquent, actually increases the likelihood of delinquency. His examination of data from
Hirschi's study and from his own Seattle survey showed that the effect on
delinquency of peer attachment depends on delinquency of the peers and
the effect of attachment to parents depends on how rewarding interaction
with parents is for the child. Moreover, the influence of delinquent peers
was found to vary reciprocally with the parent-child relationship—as the
rewards of interaction with parents decrease, the influence of delinquent
peers increases. These results are interpreted as reflecting the strength of
reinforcement in the various conditions. Attachment to delinquent peers
apparently increases delinquency because peers reinforce delinquent conduct (reward it and punish resistance to doing it), but this happens
mainly when the rewards of parental interaction are few and the costs are
great, even with strong attachment to parents.

Conger concludes that "social learning provides information about the
'group processes' which Hirschi feels are needed but lacking in control
theory" (1976:35). He suggests that social learning principles extend or go
beyond the principles of social control, but he does not explicate a systematic theory integrating social control and social learning notions.
Furthermore, his discussion heavily favors social learning, almost hinting
that social control theory can be subsumed under it or absorbed by it.
Nevertheless, Conger's exposition suggests that concurrent consideration
of the two can produce superior explanation. Social learning theory does
not attempt to specify when individuals will be more or less positively or
negatively reinforced by factors in the social situation, nor does it identify
social contexts in which reinforcements will be most salient for deviant
behavior. It simply enunciates a behavioral principle that if an individual
is reinforced in one way or another, particular outcomes can be expected.
Therefore, incorporating the ideas of social control within a theory that
also includes social learning should improve social learning theory by
defining some of the conditions where differential reinforcements will
matter.

Similarly, a more general synthetic theory would be better than social
control alone because social learning spells out mechanisms for social
bonds to produce effects, and it helps elaborate variations in their effects.
Since social control theory assumes motivation, it predicts that strong
bonds will always reduce delinquency. Yet a consideration of social learning will lead to a variety of contingent predictions, as Conger shows.
Motivation toward delinquency may vary from individual to individual
depending on the inherent reinforcement value of the behavior as well as

on the differential likelihood of social rewards from peers. Therefore, the effect of social bonds should depend directly on the strength of motivation toward delinquency and indirectly on peer expectations. In addition, the ratio of rewards to costs of one set of social bonds may exceed that of another set, or such ratios may vary somewhat independently of social bonds. In the first instance we would expect different effects for some social bonds than others, especially when the behavioral expectations in different social relationships conflict, and in the second instance social bonds may be of secondary relevance.

Although this limited integration potentially improves theory, it clearly was not intended as a full integration and should not be evaluated as such. Rather, it has served as a platform on which others have tried to build.

Elliott et al. Using the logic of the separate theories, as well as cumulated empirical evidence concerning the components of various possible linkages among the variables implicated in them, Delbert Elliott and his associates (Elliott et al. 1979; Elliott et al. 1985; Elliott et al. 1989) have been working on "a conceptual framework in which traditional strain, social-learning, and social control perspectives are integrated into a single explanatory paradigm" (Elliott et al. 1979:4). To their credit, this synthetic model was not dogmatically enunciated and defended as initially stated, but rather has evolved, taking a somewhat different form in its more recent expressions than that with which it originally began.

In the initial statement, socialization was posited as the primary causal variable in a chain involving, successively, social bonds, variables that further strengthen or weaken the original level of bonds, and involvement with peer groups. Early socialization affects the strength of a child's external (integration) and internal (commitment) social bonds, but later experiences may strengthen or weaken initial bonds. Elliott identifies five variables that, depending on their valence, will modify social bonding in one direction or another: (1) the degree of success in conventional social contexts, (2) labeling experiences, (3) involvement in conventional activities and roles, (4) organization of the social contexts the person regularly confronts, particularly the neighborhood, and (5) changes in personal commitment.

The effect of social bonds, as modified by these variables, depends on whether the individual is exposed to, and becomes committed to, a peer group supporting sustained delinquent behavior. Those with strong bonds to the conventional world that are sustained by later experiences are unlikely to do delinquent things at all, whereas those with initially strong bonds that become weakened by one or more of the modifying variables are liable to engage in episodic "individual" delinquency but escape sustained delinquency unless they become involved with delinquent peers. Those individuals with initial weak social bonds who escape involvement with delinquent peers are said to be liable for "individual" delinquency as well, but those who become committed to delinquent peers are liable for sustained patterns of delinquency.

This "integrated" theory of delinquency is, thus, more comprehensive than many simple theories because it incorporates motivating and constraining elements. Yet it is not comprehensive enough because it barely accommodates ability and ignores opportunity altogether. Furthermore, it leaves out, or covers only in broad categories like "social disorganization," individual variables affecting how various situations might bear on social bonding, the susceptibility to delinquent peers, or even the potential rewards of delinquent conduct, as well as contextual variables like availability of drugs in the neighborhood or police surveillance that might affect the likelihood of delinquency, regardless of involvement with delinquent peers.

Elliott's scheme is also a bit more precise than most theories because it identifies contingencies that affect the operation of the main variables, and it recognizes the importance of the form of the causal effects, hinting that causal effects are interactive. Yet, this theory does not fully spell out when the various contingencies are likely to arise, only that if they arise, certain outcomes can be expected. Moreover, it describes its interactive causal processes in linear dichotomous form as if there were sharp differentiations between weak and strong social bonds, between conventional and delinquent peers groups, and between high and low probabilities of delinquent behavior patterns, and as if effects followed straightforward patterns. It also leaves the issue of causal intervals unattended.

Finally, although the Elliott model depicts a causal sequence with at least four steps and allows for varied directions of effects, it does not fully explain "how" and "why" at each step along the way (the authors acknowledge that it is not fully specified). Moreover, it attenuates the causal process by beginning with the nature of youths' social bonds as they emerge from childhood socialization. Even though the authors state that many of the effects may be reciprocal, they do not identify the ones that might be reciprocal or when they will feed back.

The imprecision and lack of depth of the theory, which preclude clear specification of its structure, were recognized implicitly by the authors (Elliott et al. 1985), who twice subsequently altered the sequence of variables and modified the structure of the causal model depicting the underlying theoretical argument (see Elliott et al. 1985:66, 146, and Elliott et al. 1989:138). The first modifications attempted to extend the depth of the theory by filling in some of the prior causes of social bonds, and the authors changed the location of strain and social disorganization in the causal chain. In the new model, strain and social disorganization were portrayed as occurring prior to weak conventional bonds and being of equal force with childhood socialization in producing social bonds, whereas before they were seen as coming into play later to alter initial levels of bonding. In addition, strain was now postulated as having a direct effect on delinquent bonding but not on delinquency. These adjustments, however, rendered the theory less precise because they eliminated any specific reciprocal effects.

Furthermore, from empirical results, Elliott and his associates further altered the theory, finally concluding that strain has only an indirect effect on delinquent behavior through its effect on weak conventional bonding, which in turn affects bonding to delinquent peers, which eventually leads to delinquent behavior. In addition, they specified that social disorganization indirectly affects delinquency through conventional bonding and bonding to delinquent peers. Finally, conceding the shallowness of the theory in its inability to explain its central causal variables, Elliott and his associates included a "catchall" variable—prior delinquency—in their model.

Still later, they (Elliott et al. 1989) altered the theory (or at least the structural model depicting its supposed effects) again. In this later modification, strain was portrayed as a consequence of socialization and social disorganization, whereas originally it had been conceived as an unaccounted-for modifier of the initial level of bonding, and in the 1985 modification, as an independent, unaccounted-for influence on social bonding.

This continuous jockeying of variables has done little to enhance the integrated *theory*, since the various revisions of the "model" have continued to exhibit the flaws of the 1979 effort and have added some new ones stemming from the elimination of reciprocal effects. In fact, the product of these efforts does not even meet the modelers' own criterion of "accounting for the variance." Thus, not only does the Elliott "integrated theory" turn out to be inadequate as a general theory and as an empirical model, but it dramatically illustrates the fallacy of equating modeling with theory building.

Synthesizing strain, control, and learning theories, certainly a worthy undertaking, must involve abstract articulation of the underlying ideas, not empirical puzzle solving with measured variables, as Elliott and his associates have been attempting. In building theory the interconnections of concepts are worked out in enough detail so that their implications are logically necessary; they cannot be "discovered" by examining empirical variables. Indeed, only when theoretical interlinkages are intellectually necessary can a meaningful empirical test even be performed, and only when several tests point in the same direction should a theory be modified to accommodate contrary results. Moreover, alterations in a theory, integrated or otherwise, must involve logical or theoretical changes in the underlying argument, not simple rearrangement of the variables. In contrast, modeling assumes that the interconnection of variables can be specified ad hoc, and that the causal implications of components of an underlying theory are directly reflected in the arrangement of empirical variables in a specific set of data.

Theories and models are different things; theories can lead to good models but models cannot produce good theories, particularly since any given empirical estimation may suffer considerable unreliability. Until Elliott and his associates recognize this, their "integrated models" are not likely to be satisfying or meet our needs for general theory, despite the diligence with which they are formulated and the brilliance of the reasoning behind them.

Thornberry. In an astute reworking of the basic Elliott et al. integration, Thornberry (1987) identified three weaknesses of extant integrations. First, the most important one concerns the absence of depth in the previous models that fail to fully appreciate or incorporate reciprocal causation. According to Thornberry, since all of the variables involved in delinquency are processual and interactive rather than static, an effective theory and the empirical models it prescribes must spell out reciprocal effects. Second, he argued that the processes involved in delinquency are somewhat different at different points in the adolescent's development, so an effective integrated theory must be precise enough to recognize that points in a developmental sequence represent contingencies for the operation of specified causal processes. Finally, Thornberry tried to extend the depth of the mainline delinquency integration by showing that the initial values of the variables in the theory are influenced, or systematically related to race, class, gender, and community of residence. However, since he did not show theoretically *how* the "start" values are determined, the demographic characteristics he mentioned are probably best regarded as conditional variables for the operation of the causal processes being theorized. Overall, then, Thornberry helped refine the basic mainline delinquency integration, but he also introduced further ambiguity because his arrangement of causal sequences departs somewhat from those specified in the previous Elliott models, particularly as they involve demographic and structural variables.

Summary on Mainline Delinquency Integration. The mainline delinquency integration that began with Conger, extended through the various works of Elliott and his associates, and culminated in Thornberry's statement represents a continuity in which theoretical integration is conceived in terms of, and is closely linked to, model building. Unfortunately, the result has not been satisfactory either as theory building or as modeling. This is indicated by disagreement among the various theorists or modelers about the arrangement of the common variables and their interconnections. The theory underlying the models is simply not well enough developed to provide compelling guidelines for the descriptive accounts that these authors seem to be seeking. Certainly this cumulative theory or model falls short of the general theory needed since it lacks breadth, and despite the use of variables from several theories, it still is not comprehensive enough to incorporate most of the causal elements potentially at work. Moreover, even within the domain it has claimed, the theory is not precise or deep.

Power/Control Integrations. Structural/Marxist Theory of Delinquency Production. Mark Colvin and John Pauly (1983) tried to merge the ideas of structural Marxist thinkers about social class in capitalist societies with Amitai Etzoni's organizational theory (1970), Hirschi's social control theory (1969), and Melvin Kohn's insights (1977) on parental values and child rearing to produce an "integrated structural-Marxist theory of delinquency production." This theory contends that "serious patterned delinquency" results from social-psychological consequences of occupying particular statuses in advanced capitalist systems.

Following the usual structural-Marxist orientation, Colvin and Pauly contend that modern capitalist societies rest on two modes of production, capitalist and petty commodity production. A capitalist class and a working class are the two major status divisions generated by the capitalist mode of production. Within each of these, there are minor subclass divisions. The capitalist class is composed of monopoly sector capitalists, competitive sector capitalists, and small employers, whereas the working class contains three "fractions," or components. One component (Fraction I) consists of workers with few skills who perform nonunion menial jobs in competitive industries (examples: southern (nonunion) textile workers, agricultural wage labor, service jobs) and those who are underemployed or not employed at all. A second working-class component (Fraction II) includes mainly unionized industrial workers, and the third part of the working class (Fraction III) is composed of technical staff employees, salaried professionals, state hires, and wage-earning skilled manual workers (such as building trade workers). Petty commodity production also encompasses two major parts—the petty bourgeoisie, such as small farmers who own their own means of production and sell on the open market, and their nonwage workers, such as family members.

According to Colvin and Pauly's theory, members of these various components of capitalist society experience different kinds of relationships within their work environments. Working-class people, in particular, are said to be controlled in qualitatively different ways on the job, depending upon which segment of the working class they occupy. Fraction I workers (low-skilled, nonunion, employed in competitive industries) face "simple control" or a coercive compliance structure that uses threat of dismissal from the job as the primary disciplinary tool. Fraction II workers (mainly unionized industrial workers), however, are controlled by a utilitarian structure that grants or withholds elements of material security (pay increments, steps up the seniority ladder) to get compliance. Fraction III workers (the more independent staff personnel, professionals, and skilled craftsmen) are exposed to a normative compliance structure, which secures conformity to the job requirements by allocating and manipulating rewards linked to concepts of moral obligation and commitment internalized by the worker.

These controls presumably create a social-psychological orientation to authority and a social bond reflecting the control structure to which one has been exposed—"an ideological orientation for the individual in relation to the agents and apparatuses of social control." Work-related coercive control, for instance, tends to create an alienated, or an intense negative, orientation toward work and work organizations. By contrast, the normative compliance schemes by which employees in Fraction III jobs are controlled foster positive bonds between the worker, the employer, and the organization. Utilitarian workplace controls (experienced by

Fraction II workers) tend to produce calculative orientations, but they are less intense than the other two and control is more tenuous because utilitarian systems depend "on continual remuneration and advancement up the pay ladder" (Colvin and Pauly 1983:513, 533).

Class position, orientation toward workplace "authority apparatuses," and serious delinquency are interlinked through the tendency of workers to re-create in the family the control structures of their work environment. Parents, consciously or unconsciously, teach their children that authorities are to be obeyed through either external compulsion (fear or utilitarian calculation) or internalized normative commitment. Parents in Fraction I of the workforce, who are controlled by the threat of dismissal, supposedly oscillate between physical harshness and laxity in disciplining their children. The utilitarian-controlled Fraction II parents employ disciplinary techniques encouraging calculation of material benefits and costs. Fraction III parents tend to appeal to conscience to control their children, just as they themselves are controlled in the workplace. Reflecting the same causal process that leads various workplace controls to be repeated in the family, various familial controls, in turn, produce different kinds of ideological bonds between parents and children. Coercively controlling parents produce intensely negative ("alienated") orientations in their children, utilitarian-controlling families are characterized by bonds of "intermediate intensity," whereas normatively controlling families have children with "positive bonds of high intensity" (Colvin and Pauly 1983:536).

The orientations of children are then translated into the school context, partly through performance on school system monitoring tests and behavioral cues that determine placement in various educational tracks, and partly through associative peer relations. Since school friendship networks reflect proximity, students from coercive environments who fail to impress school personnel and end up in the non–college preparatory tracks have associates who are similarly linked to school and family through negative bonds. These peer groups reinforce alienated orientations that, Colvin and Pauly contend, encourage serious, patterned delinquency. Students from families characterized by moderately intense, calculative bonds as well as those from normatively oriented families will likely be tracked less coercively, and as a result will form positively oriented friendship cliques that are far less likely to generate serious, repeated delinquency.

Colvin and Pauly, then, portray a causal chain operating in the context of a particular kind of economic system. Workplace control mechanisms influence parental methods of child rearing that, in turn, affect children's orientations and school experiences. These school and peer relationships ultimately reinforce orientations originating in the workplace that are then passed on to the child through family social control, leading to serious delinquency.

Although the Colvin and Pauly integration is an admirable merging of seemingly disparate theoretical strands, it is not an adequate theory. First, its numerous technical deficiencies (compare Paternoster and Tittle 1990),

especially conceptual imprecision, make discernment of the exact implication of the arguments almost impossible. For example, the authors
sometimes write as if the dependent variable were the frequency or probability of delinquency, but at other times they write as if the theory is to
explain the type of delinquency, and they make no distinctions that
would suggest how the concepts might be used to differentiate these two.
The main argument, specifying as it does a categorical effect of type of
workplace control on type of delinquency, implies two untenable assumptions: (1) the mode of child rearing is fixed by the type of social control imposed on workers in various Fractions and does not vary with
gender or age of the child, and (2) a delinquent's misbehavior is homogeneous with respect to type, that is, young people specialize in the type of
delinquency they commit. In addition, Colvin and Pauly fail to say
whether their argument concerns factors in the workplace that *actually*
control behavior, factors that are *intended* by employers to produce that effect, or whether it depends on employee *perceptions* of control in the
workplace. Consequently, the potential benefits of integration are muted
because this formulation is conceptually muddled and starts with assumptions already known to be false.

Even if these "technical" deficiencies were correctable, the Colvin and
Pauly formulation would still provide little advancement because it is so
narrowly focused on serious, patterned delinquency, which the authors
define as "repeated engagement of a juvenile in the FBI's Part One Index
crimes" (1983:513). Since this represents only a small proportion of all
delinquency (about 3 percent), and since delinquency represents only a
portion of all crime/deviance, their theory can apply to only a tiny part of
the crime/deviance domain. In addition, it explains this small portion of
crime only in capitalist societies and when manifested by children of the
working class. The scheme offers no explanation of, or even any reference
to, delinquency or other forms of deviance in noncapitalist societies, and
it has nothing to say about the children of capitalists or those in petty
commodity production. Indeed, it is so finely aimed that this integration
could probably best be regarded as an explanation of a specific phenomenon rather than as a theory. In this respect it represents no improvement
over the simple theories reviewed in Chapter 1.

It is possible, of course, to think of the formulation in more general
terms than the authors intend. The underlying general theme suggests
that the type and intensity of social control in any work environment will
shape the orientations of those exposed to them and that such orientations will carry over into other institutional domains. Thus, coercive controls produce alienated orientations that motivate people toward deviance, utilitarian controls lead to instrumental orientations that are
manifested in deviance whenever the person encounters the opportunity
to materially profit from the act and get away, and normative controls
lead to conformity through moral commitment. Following this argument,
one would expect some feedback to all institutional domains. Thus, alienated people are unlikely to be selected for responsible positions in the
community, to be put in leadership roles, to be able to borrow money, and

so on (just as the alienated youngster ends up in the noncollege track in the Colvin and Pauly scheme), but the morally committed are likely to perform all of those roles. Therefore, associative patterns in all institutional contexts reinforce basic orientations.

Hence, this theory need not be confined to workers in capitalist societies. Workers in socialist societies are subject to social control too, as are capitalists in capitalist societies. So the principles Colvin and Pauly enunciate ought to be generally operative. Furthermore, there seems to be no logical reason why the theory should apply only to serious patterned delinquency. If the authors are right about the effect of alienation on young people, it follows that alienated people generally ought to be more prone toward serious, patterned deviance of all types than are morally committed, positively bonded individuals. Moreover, the chances of instrumental deviance of all types should be greater for those with calculative orientations.

Unfortunately, even as more generally conceived, this theory does not go far. Granted, it provides deeper explanation than simple theories because it portrays deviance as the end product of a causal chain with the motivation for deviance starting in the work context of the individual or head of the family, proliferating through other institutional domains, and ending in the individual's psyche before finally being manifested. However, the theory does not incorporate other crucial variables. Constraint, for example, is conspicuously absent from the interior of the theory after having played such a large role in the beginning. Although it makes sense to argue that social controls experienced in the workplace produce basic orientations ultimately affecting the chances of deviance, an effective theory must explain why those orientations do not always produce the typical outcome. Some with alienated orientations nevertheless conform, perhaps because they fear the costs of nonconformity, lack opportunity, or have stronger alternative motivations. Likewise, positively bonded individuals sometimes deviate, perhaps because opportunity and absence of constraint are so compelling.

Similarly, even if workplace control is a crucial variable in producing basic orientations affecting the likelihood of deviance, other variables no doubt intrude. Personality, religious training, intelligence, the exact nature of work environments, social alliances among workers on the job, and numerous other things shape the effects that workplace control can have. For example, some jobs (perhaps assembling medical supplies for emergencies) are gratifying and useful, so even those controlled by the threat of dismissal may develop committed, positive orientations. Further, some workers are prideful, no matter how menial their jobs, because they believe work to be ennobling.

A second example illustrates how variations in perceptual acuity can foil the argument. Suppose a researcher, in trying to measure workplace control, looks at employer records to determine what typically happens when an employee of a particular type begins to do a poor job and finds that the worker is usually fired. Suppose further that the researcher surveys the workers and discovers that most of them conform but are not afraid of being fired (some conform because of a work ethic, some think their own poor work will not be discovered, and some think they are extra lucky). Could the researcher classify this workplace as one coercively controlled to the extent that it would induce all of the workers to form alienated bonds and employ coercive methods of child rearing? By contrast, imagine that a researcher's examination of employer records reveals that poor work is usually handled by reprimand or pay reductions rather than firing, whereas a survey indicates that most of the workers *believe* poor work would result in their being fired. Could this workplace be classified as coercively controlled and be expected to lead to the theoretical outcomes of the theory? Finally, suppose that the records show that poor workers are usually fired and the survey shows that most workers think they will be fired, but the survey also reveals that the workers typically do not perceive that their own conformity is motivated by fear of job loss, perhaps thinking they are motivated by loyalty and commitment. Could the researcher classify this as a coercively controlled workplace?

Colvin and Pauly's theory is also weak in not specifying or recognizing conditions under which it is more or less likely to be operative. Does the process work differently for those of different sexes, races, places of residence, or age? The theory does not say, but evidence suggests that female children are less likely than male children to be reared coercively, even among families with the head of the household in Fraction I of the working class. What is to be expected in families in which the mother works in a normatively controlled environment and the father works in a coercively controlled one? In short, even if the theory were basically correct, it could yield only imprecise and incomplete explanations.

Power Control Theory. A second narrowly focused integration emphasizing power and control is the "power control theory" of John Hagan (1989). Although the explanatory elements of power control theory are similar to Colvin and Pauly's, the two formulations aim to explain different things. Whereas Colvin and Pauly focused on serious, patterned delinquency, Hagan's effort was designed to explain *differences* between males and females in "common delinquency"—minor theft, vandalism, and physical aggression. Although his formulation can be abstractly conceived to imply a theory about this phenomenon, as stated, it is primarily an explanation of a historical trend.

Merging ideas from Dahrendorf's analysis of social class, Weber's arguments about the connection between capitalism and patriarchy, and social control and deterrence theories, Hagan links work relations, family relations, child rearing, and delinquency as they have occurred in advanced industrial societies. He contends that industrial capitalism resulted in the emergence of a unique kind of patriarchy. As production was separated from the family context, males were placed in positions of dominance in the outside world and females were relegated to the home. As a result, females became responsible for rearing and controlling children and were required to "reproduce" the same type of dominance relationships. This caused them to devote disproportionate attention to controlling daughters, and the pervasive presence of the mother led to greater identification of the females with the mothers than of the males with the mothers or fathers. The main consequence of this, presumably, is that females developed less orientation toward risk taking, and since common delinquency is a product of risk taking, they thereby became less likely to engage in common delinquency than males.

Over time, many women entered the workforce and some acquired authority equal to their spouses. By virtue of this, they became less subordinate in family relations and less likely to assume the main responsibility for child rearing and control. Daughters in such families became more like sons in risk-taking propensity, leading to more equal probabilities of common delinquency. Sex differences in rates of common delinquency, then, are depicted as a function of the patterns of dominance between the parents, which in turn reflect their positions in the productive labor force.

Despite his concrete, descriptive approach, it is clear that Hagan intended to formulate a more abstract theory. He refers to it as a theory, and he weaves back and forth from specific historical context to more general principles. However, to appreciate the argument in general theoretical terms, it has to be enlarged like this: Parental work relations affect power distribution in the family, which is reflected in responsibility for child rearing and control. Whoever is employed outside the home is more likely to dominate, and when both are employed, the one with the greater "authority" in the workplace is likely to dominate. Power relationships between spouses, in turn, determine who is charged with training and controlling children, with the subordinate spouse being relegated the child-rearing task. This power-differentiated social control produces differences between male and female children in risk preference and propensity toward risk taking because the child of the same gender as the controller is more constrained and more likely to identify with the source of control than is the child with a different gender, resulting in less willingness to take risks. Since common forms of delinquency are said to be products of risk taking, children with genders different from the controller are likely to be more delinquent. However, as workplace authority of spouses becomes more similar, child rearing becomes less differentiated and risk preferences between male and female children tend to equalize, reducing gender differences in common delinquency.

Specific application of this general formulation to the case of industrial capitalism, in which males first dominated the work environment with women at home tending children, yields the Hagan analysis. In that specific instance, females were more often the controllers of children, and daughters were simultaneously more controlled and more "identified" with the controller. But if this formulation actually has general implications, it should follow that in families with a female head and a male caregiver-controller, sons should be less delinquent than daughters. This type of family is rare in contemporary society, but if trends toward female equality in the workplace continue, it should become more common over time, and the gap between male and female delinquency rates should narrow or disappear, at least for "common" or nonserious delinquency. Moreover, if the formulation is truly general, societies in which females dominate the workplace (whatever the nature of work might be, and assuming that such societies might exist) should be characterized by greater rates of common delinquency among females than males.

Hagan's "integrated" analysis is better than simple theories, inventions, and elaborations of simple theories. Since it uses ideas from many sources and it recognizes dependence on the contributions of others, it escapes the arrogance and defensiveness of invention. In addition, it yields deeper explanation than many theoretical endeavors because it sets forth a chain of causal linkages from the world of work to the home to child rearing to social-psychological orientations of children. Moreover, it implies (but does not explicitly state) certain contingencies for the process: industrial-capitalist economies, societies in which child rearing and control are relegated to individual family contexts, and societies in which industrial capitalist development has been preceded by cultural patterns of male dominance or patriarchy (dictating initial male dominance in industrial production).

Despite these improvements, however, power control theory has technical weaknesses, is extremely narrow in range and focus, and leaves out too much to provide a satisfying explanation. First, the logic of the causal linkages within the theory is so weak that many of its propositions appear to be assertions. For instance, the only reason given for the fundamental idea that dominance in the workplace drives the whole system of causes that eventuate in gender differences in common delinquency is that authority relations in industrial production "occupy so central a place in most people's lives. . . . [that they] . . . often overshadow and determine authority relations in other collective units, including the family" (Hagan 1989:170–171).

To improve the argument, one might infer that differential power of family members is the key to the causal system, not position in industrial production. Power often flows from workforce position, but it can have other sources, as when one or another spouse inherits or controls wealth. Actually, spousal power may be rooted generically in control of resources, with position of authority in the workforce being only one basis for such control.

It is also unclear from Hagan's formulation why a controller of children would more closely control the same-gender child. His argument implies that the child controller more or less automatically embraces the necessity to "reproduce" the social system, which means training the same-gender child to be subordinate and passive. Yet, at the same time, he contends that women, the usual controllers of children (Hagan 1989, chap. 8), are more discontented with their positions than are males, as indicated by the greater number of female suicide attempts. If they are so discontented, why do women still train their daughters to be subordinate by controlling them more intensely than male children? Hagan suggests that many women do not complete their suicide attempts because they are too controlled, so presumably they control their daughters because they are themselves too controlled to change these traditional patterns of child rearing. Does this make sense? The theory simply asserts that males are in positions of authority in the workplace and as a result control females; it does not illuminate why their positions of authority in the workplace can be translated into so much control over spouses that women are unable to avoid training daughters for submission.

Second, though Hagan's theory portrays the link in the causal chain between being controlled and developing a taste for risk taking as more or less self-evident, it is not obvious. Why would being controlled make one less interested in taking risks? Perhaps heavily controlled individuals form habits of "safe" decisionmaking by constant repetition of passive behavior. Another possibility is that controlled people develop attitudes of fear and avoid risk because they anticipate punishment for failing at risky endeavors. However, it is equally plausible that controlled people develop an intense desire to escape that control through risky activity (as implied by Hagan's descriptions of female discontent) and that such desire will override habits of risk avoidance and conformity (see Katz 1988 for such an interpretation).

Even if power control theory did not suffer from incompletely developed causal linkages, and even if it were unquestionably accurate, it still would not fulfill the promise of integration. It is intentionally narrowly focused and as a result does not try to explain deviance or crime generally, nor does it even try to explain delinquency generally. In fact, it does not directly aim to explain "common delinquency." Rather, it explains differences between males and females in rates of common delinquency. Although the argument could be extrapolated to provide a direct explanation of common delinquency (the greater the freedom from control and the weaker the identification with a same-sex controller, the more likely one is to develop a risk-taking orientation, and the stronger the risk-taking orientation, the greater the probability of common delinquency), the range of such an explanation would still be limited.

Furthermore, extrapolation would omit too much to be effective in accounting for common delinquency. Although this theory improves on the simple ones by identifying motivation for common delinquency—orientation toward risk—and by encompassing some forms of constraint on behavior, it ignores opportunity, alternative motivation, and ability. For instance, freedom granted with implied trust often generates responsibility in children (perhaps along with willingness to take risks). Under some conditions that sense of responsibility may be a stronger motivator toward conformity than risk orientation is toward delinquency, just as the absence of opportunity and the inability to commit common delinquency may sometimes intervene.

Despite the relatively greater complexity of power control theory, it is still simplistic in its portrayal because it takes no account of conditions that may affect outcomes. For example, some children are biologically disposed toward aggressive behavior and display it despite the best efforts of parents, particularly mothers, to prevent it—and some of these children are females. The theory also leaves out variables like peer influences, other things learned in the socialization process, and the kinds of provoking circumstances that entice young people to steal, regardless of their usual orientations toward risk. Finally, the theory does not recognize that child-rearing practices for males and females vary by age of the child as well as by the life circumstances of the parents, even within families whose positions vis-à-vis workplace authority remain unchanged. Thus Hagan's work fails to exploit fully the advantages of integration.

General Integrations

Around a Central Reinforcement/Learning Process. Although most of the integrative work in the crime/deviance field has been narrowly focused or confused with empirical model building, some have made attempts to create genuine, adequate integrated theories that apply to all, or at least a wide array of, types of deviance or crime. The best integrations revolve around the reinforcement/learning paradigm central to the utilitarian/deterrence philosophy of classical criminology, behavioral psychology, and rational choice perspectives in economics. The basic postulate of that scheme portrays people as always striving to maximize benefits and rewards while minimizing costs or problems. Thus, individuals will, either through conditioning (past experience of rewards and costs that produce almost automatic or habitual response to anticipated outcomes) or rational calculation (cognitive weighing of potential consequences), respond to stimuli in ways that will benefit them. Presumably, then, to explain any human behavior, one only has to understand the degree to which various things constitute rewards or costs for an individual in various contexts.

Integrations around this basic process have taken one of two forms. In the first type, theorists have tried to show that all existing theories can be subsumed under the reinforcement rubric, that is, that their causal elements can be translated into the language of reinforcement or their causal statements can be shown to imply the reinforcement process. For example, it can be said that anomie theory is really about the ways in which the anticipated rewards of criminal behavior outweigh the potential costs for certain people who lack the means to achieve gratifying goals and who lack internalized moral constraints that would constitute countervailing costs to prevent crime (Wilson and Herrnstein 1985:64). In the second type of integration around the principles of reinforcement/learning, theo-

rists have tried to show how various theories bear on inputs to the reinforcement process. For example, labeling theory has been interpreted as
spelling out one process that leads some individuals to regard criminal
behavior as more rewarding than costly (Akers 1985:69). Either approach
permits full-scale integration, but the adequacy of such integrations depends on whether the reinforcement/learning process is set forth tauto-
logically and on how well the inputs to the process can be specified theoretically. Four different attempts to integrate theories around a
reinforcement/learning process have been advanced.

Glaser. The earliest, and least developed, reinforcement/learning integration is "differential-anticipation" theory by Daniel Glaser (1962, 1978).
He stated that the chances of crime are determined by the consequences
the individual anticipates from the criminal act, meaning that given an
opportunity, any individual will try to commit a crime anytime the expected gratifications exceed the potential costs (Glaser 1978:126). Glaser
then went on to try to show why various things are gratifying or costly to
particular individuals, concluding that "anticipations" about criminal behavior are determined by a person's social bonds, differential learning,
and perceived opportunities.

Glaser did not, however, develop his integration very far. He did not
try to show how social bonds come to influence the reinforcement values
of various acts or how or why people have the bonds that they do.
Similarly, he offered no theoretical account of why and how differential
learning comes into play, nor did he take account of opportunity or attempt to show how individual characteristics and predispositions might
affect anticipations of rewards and costs. Thus, his integration is only a
bare outline of what was to come later.

Akers. A more sophisticated integration around reinforcement is that
by Ronald Akers (1985). Initially working with a colleague, he restated
differential association using the language and principles of reinforcement theory (Burgess and Akers 1966). "Excess of definitions favorable
toward crime" was interpreted to mean differential reinforcement for
criminal behavior, and "definitions" themselves were seen as behavioral
discriminative stimuli. Later, Akers added modeling and vicarious reinforcement to produce what he now calls the theory of social learning. In
various places he has tried to show that social learning theory subsumes
social control, disorganization/anomie, conflict, labeling, and rational
choice theories (Akers 1985, 1989, 1990), either because those other theories assert the same thing as social learning or because they help account
for the inputs to the social learning process.

Wilson and Herrnstein. Still greater sophistication in integrating theories around reinforcement/learning was achieved by Wilson and
Herrnstein (1985) when they introduced three new components. First,
they emphasize that the reinforcement values of different actions are
linked to constitutional factors that may be genetically determined at
birth or to biological processes that become more or less prominent at dif-

ferent points in the life cycle. Among the most important of these are personality traits such as impulsivity that lead individuals to discount potential future negative consequences. Second, the authors stress that reinforcement values of different acts and reactions depend on concepts of equity and justice and the actual distribution of rewards and costs within a given social context. Criminal behavior may seem rewarding to an individual in one context but not in another because there is perceived inequity in one situation but not in the other. Third, their theory recognizes that any given reinforcer may be either of great or of small importance depending on how many other reinforcers are operative for an individual.

These authors think they can subsume everything under this more complex reinforcement/learning process by showing that other theories either imply the same process (with different language) or provide inputs to the reinforcement scheme. In addition, they interpret within the basic reinforcement process the effect of variables suggested by various other theories, as well as those current in the literature but not directly connected to specific theories of deviant behavior. The result is a grand integrative scheme of broad sweep.

Yet, because they devote most of their effort to synthesizing empirical evidence, their integration is adumbrated (it deals only with strain, control, and cultural deviance theories), as are the actual theoretical implications of their argument. Not only are the interlinkages of the variables suggested by other theories not fully developed within the reinforcement process, but Wilson and Herrnstein fail to show in detail how their integrated theory corrects the defects they identify in these existing theories. For example, cultural deviance theory is criticized because it "cannot explain why some persons take their cues from street gangs while others take them from their families and other nondeviant individuals" (1985:65). However, it is not clear how reinforcement theory explains this, either. In a very general sense Wilson and Herrnstein's formulation contends that preference for deviant cues is a product of constitutional factors as they have interacted with various contextual conditions to reinforce (to reward people for taking deviant cues and to punish for taking nondeviant cues) this style of behavior. Without more detail, though, this is no more enlightening than saying that some individuals respond to deviant cues because deviance is more fun and they are freer to pursue it than those who respond to nondeviant cues.

Pearson and Weiner. The most highly developed reinforcement/learning integration is that by Frank Pearson and Neil Weiner (1985). Recognizing that the deviance process involves a number of elements, they specify six that are contained within the basic framework of reinforcement theory. These elements include four internal components: utility demand (motivational intensity), behavioral skill (ability to perform the act), rules of expedience (learned attitudes about maximizing utility), and rules of morality (attitudes about duty and ethical principles). The six basic processual elements also include two external components: signs of favorable opportunity in the situation (discriminative stimuli), and behavioral resources (the wherewithal to accomplish the act in the situation). Behavior itself produces two additional components—utility reception (rewards and punishments) as well as information acquisition (knowledge acquired about various aspects of the situation)—that feed back to affect the future strength of the six primary processual variables. Thus, for a deviant act to occur there must be motivation strong enough to overcome the potential costs, ability to perform the act, and sufficient orientation toward expedience to overcome rules of morality. In addition, the situation must offer an opportunity, and the circumstances of the situation must make the act possible. After deviance occurs, its consequences feed back to reinforce future behavior through the six antecedent factors involved in the initial behavior.

Nonetheless, this is not the whole story since the process operates within social contexts. The nature of the social structure determines the production and distribution of utilities, opportunities, rules of expedience, and sanctioning practices (macrolevel processes). Moreover, individual, microlevel factors influence how these structural variables are interpreted, so behavior is to some extent an interaction between individual level and structural factors as they play upon the eight processual variables identified above.

Pearson and Weiner map 12 different theories into this basic scheme by showing how each bears on the various processes. For example, labeling theory is said to involve utility demand because it provides an account of why some people have intense motivation for deviance, specifies how one comes to have the skill to commit various deviant acts (by forced association with others so labeled), accounts for the absence or loosening of moral standards (by anger and frustration as well as by association with others so labeled), and dwells on feedback from behavior that affects future deviance. Labeling theory, however, does not deal with other variables in the general integrated structure—with differences in attitudes about maximizing utility (rules of expedience) or with variation in favorable opportunities for crime (discriminative stimuli) or in individuals' skills to perform various criminal or deviant acts (behavioral resources).

This framework is more elaborate and detailed than any of the other integrations, making it possible to map most if not all previous theories into one grand scheme around a central reinforcement process. In particular, despite Wilson and Herrnstein's contribution to understanding structural effects through their analysis of equity and contexts of reinforcement, Pearson and Weiner bring in structural variables more extensively, and they segmentalize the deviance process more finely than either Akers or Wilson and Herrnstein. Pearson and Weiner allow structural variables to precede all other variables in the process and to intervene at different points in the process itself, whereas Wilson and Herrnstein give priority to constitutional factors, portraying structural influences as weaker and relevant only later.

Yet Pearson and Weiner do not actually articulate the integrated theory. They note that specific causal relationships need to be drawn with greater specificity, particularly those between social structural and the processual variables, that the integrative structure should be extended upward and downward to include interactions among social structural variables as well as genetic components, and that the framework needs to be translated into an interrelated set of detailed theoretical propositions. Their work, then, stands as a skeleton to which they, or the scholarly community as a whole, must attach flesh. Thus, its statement contains few explanatory examples to guide others in building on their achievement.

Summary on Reinforcement/Learning Theory. Cumulating efforts centering on reinforcement/learning have moved us toward more adequate theory by identifying a workable structure for a broad, comprehensive, deep, and precise integrated theory. When this structure is fully articulated, it may come close to the ideal general theory that I advocate. However, the structure is not yet fully explicated, and the prospect of extensive additional articulation is not good. It is one thing to state that structural conditions, such as unequal distributions of rewards, interact with constitutional factors and family environments in a feedback loop to produce motivations for crime in some individuals (that outweigh potential costs), as well as interacting with skill and opportunity; it is another thing to explain how the structural conditions came about and how, exactly, they interact with situational and constitutional factors to produce reinforcement for criminal behavior as well as opportunity for its commission. Furthermore, since the various theorists disagree about the importance and sequence of some of the variables implicated in an integrated theory around reinforcement/learning, it is clear that such schemes lack compelling theoretical force. Nevertheless, with the exception of Pearson and Weiner, reinforcement integrationists appear to believe they possess the holy grail and are well on their way to slaying the dragon.

A cautionary note, however, should be sounded about integrations around reinforcement/learning; this central causal process may be wrong in important respects. In Chapter 1 I discussed the tautological nature of some versions of this basic process and the fact that proponents tend to use it as a closed philosophical system. If this is true of rational choice, utilitarian, and reinforcement schemes, then integrated theories based on their logic will compound the error. One has to question the logic of reinforcement, at least as a universally operating process. In many instances people do things that do not hold the promise of reward for them, sometimes because circumstances seem to make the behavior appear inevitable and sometimes because they are provoked by forces they do not understand and cannot control. In addition, some people who have been repeatedly rewarded for particular behaviors end up acting contrary, just as some people persist in deviant behavior that has brought them much pain and agony.

Integration Through a Bridging Process. Instead of hooking theories together sequentially, as was done in the mainline delinquency integration, or bringing theories together through their common bearing on a central causal process as the reinforcement/learning theorists have done, John Braithwaite integrated anomie/opportunity, control, subcultural, learning, and labeling theories by linking them through a bridging, or "shunting," process (1989:107) called shaming.

According to the theory, age, gender, marital status, and employment affect how interdependent individuals are with social groups. The greater the interdependency, the greater the likelihood that a person will be subject to shame for misbehavior (informal sanctions). However, the effect of shame depends on whether the shaming process provides an opportunity for the offender later to be readmitted to the group. Shaming that permits this redemption is called reintegrative shaming; shaming with permanent stigma is called disintegrative shaming. Reintegrative shaming discourages future crime directly, and it discourages participation in criminal subcultures that may lead to illegitimate opportunities for crime, or to crime itself. Disintegrative, stigmatizing shaming, on the other hand, encourages criminal subcultural participation and high crime rates. Thus, an individual highly bonded to social groups is less likely to commit crime than one less bonded because of anticipation of potential shaming, and if a bonded person does violate the rules, the frequency and patterning is likely to be less if the shaming is reintegrative rather than stigmatizing.

Thus, the likelihood of crime is dependent on a number of circumstances, all bearing a relationship to each other. Not only does the degree of interdependency and the kind of shaming affect the likelihood of violation and rate of subsequent violation, but the presence or absence of criminal subcultures also plays a part. Whether bonded or not, a person who is merely punished may be somewhat deterred from future misbehavior, provided there is no exposure to a criminal subculture that provides rationalizations, cultural support, and opportunities for deviance. Similarly, a bonded person who is disintegratively shamed will have a lower probability of future violation if there is no exposure to a criminal subculture.

The theory implies nine combinations of interdependency, reaction to crime, and exposure to criminal subcultures that can be ranked in terms of likelihood of initial and recidivist criminal behavior. Those with low interdependency, for whom there is no social reaction (either no punishment for whatever reason or no shaming because such persons cannot be shamed), are most likely to offend and repeat the offense. Violators with low interdependency who are punished and exposed to criminal subcultures are second-most-likely to repeat, and the unbonded who are punished but not exposed to a criminal subculture are the next-most-likely long-term offenders. Following that are individuals with high interdependency who are merely punished (rather than shamed) and are also exposed to criminal subcultures. And so on, to the least-likely repeaters—

those with high interdependency who are reintegratively shamed and not exposed to a criminal subculture.

The theory is still more complicated and richer than this because it blends macro- and microlevel effects. Individuals can be more or less dependent, and the societies or communities of which they are a part can also be more or less communitarian. Communities, or societies, that are high in communitarianism have a high degree of general dependency and a large proportion of their individuals who are interdependent in smaller networks. There is also a reciprocal relationship between micro- and macrosocial solidarity—high communitarianism promotes individual interdependency just as greater individual interdependency affects the degree of communitarianism. The key linkage between the two, however, concerns likely responses to deviant behavior. The higher the communitarianism of a society, the more likely it is to practice shaming rather than mere punishment in its official handling of crime, and the greater the likelihood that it will collectively and informally practice reintegrative rather than disintegrative shaming. A key factor in this is the practice of gossip. When individuals participate in gossip that shames deviants, they learn to anticipate such talk about themselves should they violate the rules, and since communitywide gossip covers more potential deviantness than gossip does in small social groupings, individuals are sensitized to a larger range of rules. By this process individuals develop consciences as well as interdependency.

Braithwaite (1989) goes on to lay out some of the conditions under which the various societal characteristics that affect individually relevant processes (like reintegrative shaming and criminal subcultures) are possible. He explains why criminal subcultural formation is likely only in societies in which legitimate opportunities are systematically blocked for significant segments of the population. He further links communitarianism to urbanization, geographic mobility, and modernization. Moreover, he explicitly sets forth the theoretical bases for the various outcomes that I have previously described, and in most cases they are rich in detail and far more persuasive than they might appear from simple description of the predicted effect.

The theory of shaming is a major contribution because of its original development of the nature and effects of shaming and because it manages to integrate into a coherent whole the causal claims of a large number of theories. The net result is an overarching scheme explaining many forms of deviance (although Braithwaite limits his attention to predatory crime) with substantial depth, comprehensiveness, and precision. In addition, the theory accounts for a number of ancillary intellectual puzzles—especially why crime rates are highest during the late adolescent years and why males have higher crime rates than females. But despite these virtues, the theory is not fully adequate.

First, the internal structure of the theory is not well enough articulated to capture all of the logical possibilities. For instance, subcultural development and participation are postulated to affect the chances of criminal behavior only if disintegrative shaming has occurred. This is unnecessarily limiting since exposure to criminal subcultures logically bears on cases where there is no punishment and on those where reintegrative shaming has occurred. Similarly, the theory fails to show how individual characteristics like impulsivity, intelligence, or self-efficacy might affect the operation of the processes in the theory. Some people will violate rules repeatedly, even with reintegrative shaming, because they impulsively leap at opportunities for criminal expression without fully weighing how their actions might affect themselves or others. In fact, Braithwaite's formulation is silent about how communitarian societies deal with those who repeatedly test group tolerance. In addition, Wilson and Herrnstein's equity ideas would appear to be especially relevant in how people interpret the shaming process.

Second, though the theory is more comprehensive than most, it overemphasizes control while downplaying motivation, includes only a limited treatment of opportunity and ability, and leaves out alternative motivations. Since the focus of the theory is the potential for being shamed, a control mechanism, it is not clear why people would want to violate the rules in the first place. Braithwaite states that blockage of legitimate opportunity can provide an initial motive for crime, suggests that there are some inherent desires for gratification ("tastes") that may impel people, and contends that subcultural normative expectations can drive secondary deviation (1989:103), but he provides no systematic or complete account of primary criminal/deviant motivation. Presumably the only people who might do deviant things are those who are strained or have learned deviant patterns from alternative cultures or those who are driven by pathological desires stemming from biological anomalies or aberrant socialization. Still, if this were so, shaming would have little to do with criminal behavior because the same societies that can effectively shame are also unlikely to have straining social structures, alternative subcultures, or aberrant socialization. Although Braithwaite mentions the importance of opportunities for criminal behavior and hints at ability to commit crime, these factors are not actually worked into the scheme except as they are linked to criminal subcultures.

Third, as with most theories, there is much imprecision. Not only are there numerous unspecified contingencies that might affect the process (such as time discounting and the availability of alternative, but not criminal, subcultures within which a person could seek gratification), but there is only an implicit assumption about the form of the theorized causal effects and scant concern about the causal intervals. Presumably the more reintegrative the shaming, the less crime there is; but it seems logical to imagine that there is a threshold for it to work, or perhaps some flattening of the curve of effects as one approaches saturation. Some shaming, whether integrative or disintegrative, would seem likely to generate resentment, anger, or hostility rather than remorse or repentance. Such an effect could occur near the beginning of the continuum or near the end, but a general monotonic, linear outcome hardly seems likely. Further, Braithwaite suggests that shaming and reintegration must occur more or less simultaneously, one mostly on the covert level, the other on the overt level, but he does not specify the degree of departure from simultaneity within which the process would still be effective. Similarly there is neglect of the time lags between stigmatizing shaming and crime, even when criminal subcultures come into play.

Finally, though the theory is remarkably deep, specifying various causal sequences from the structures of society to individual outcomes, articulating in compelling logic how these effects occur, and calling attention to mutually reinforcing effects on the micro and macro levels, it still fails to grasp many of the reciprocal possibilities (such as that between stigmatization and participation in criminal subcultures), and it does not spell out completely the causal processes (recall the weakness of its account of initial deviance).

Overall, then, the theory of shaming is a brilliant instance of theoretical integration that goes a long way, but not all of the way, toward satisfying the need for adequate general theory.

Conclusion on Integrating Theories

Efforts to improve theory through integration have been somewhat successful, but the products are still not adequate. This is partly due to (1) common misunderstanding of the meaning of general theory, as evidenced by the tendency of some scholars to confuse model building with theory building, (2) the limited objectives of integrationists, who have been more concerned with explaining relatively narrow phenomena (delinquency, serious patterned or predatory crime) than with building a genuinely general theory of crime or deviance, and (3) the lack of attention by theorists to making their products comprehensive, deep, and precise. Limited success has also resulted because theoretical integration has proceeded in a somewhat anomic fashion with no viable framework for synthetic work. In the next section I identify the various implicit blueprints that have guided existing integration efforts, and then I set forth an alternative approach.

Paradigms for Integration

The mainline delinquency integration, integrations around reinforcement/learning, and integration through the bridging process of shaming variously use, in one way or another, three forms of integration, those being structural, conceptual, or assimilative integration.

Structural

In structural integration the theorist links existing theories, or at least their main components, together in sequences, either by conceiving the causal variables in some theories as outcome variables in other theories (what Hirschi, 1979 and 1989, calls end-to-end integration) or by theorizing that under some conditions the causal processes of one theory mesh in particular ways with those of other theories. This second procedure is what Hirschi refers to as side-by-side integration. Structural integration brings to theory building the same rationale used in constructing physical edifices. It employs a building-block strategy by which separate, distinct components like foundations, roofs, walls, and floors are tied together. The final product is distinguishable, but the individual parts are distinct and identifiable.

The mainline delinquency integration mainly employs the end-to-end method, which, since it lacks a compelling theoretical rationale, leads various theorists to link component theories in different sequences. Some decide causal order on the basis of personal preference, some base the order on limited empirical feedback, and still others use arrangements that fulfill technical requirements for modeling.

Braithwaite's bridging integration most clearly illustrates the method of side-by-side integration because he joins various existing theories through the "shunt" of shaming. This works better than the end-to-end method because it provides a firmer basis for the sequencing of the component theories, it allows for conditional outcomes rather than assuming a constant linear effect, and it brings to bear an innovative, perhaps original, theoretical element. Nevertheless, this method is not entirely satisfactory because it encourages omission of essential parts as exemplified by Braithwaite's neglect of motivations for initial deviance and disregard of numerous conditions that likely impinge on the causal processes that he outlines.

Structural integration is a useful mode, but by itself it cannot succeed because existing theories are not sufficient to provide all the necessary components of an adequate general theory, even if they may be completely and cleverly linked together. For example, Braithwaite's theory is weak in accounting for initial deviance because extant theories that might be integrated through the shaming shunt are themselves deficient in explaining initial deviance. Strain theories and subcultural theories identify some motivating forces, but not all, or even most, of them. Reinforcement/learning theories depend on preexisting distributions of potentially reinforcing elements that are not explained within the theory. The theories based on rational choice, like Hirschi's social bonds formulation, assume, rather than account for, motivation. Successful integration must do more than fasten together existing theories.

Conceptual

In conceptual integration a theorist identifies, or possibly invents, a general, abstract causal process that encapsulates preexisting theories in one of two ways. One is by showing that extant theories are saying much the same thing when viewed through the lenses of the abstract process, what Hirschi has referred to as up-and-down integration. The reinforcement/learning integrations depend on such conceptual synthesis.

Although abstract concepts and processes that incorporate more specific, concrete counterparts are useful (see Tittle 1985b, 1989b), general integrations that do no more than reinterpret previous theories through a common causal process will not serve the need. This is because they cannot get beyond the inclusive abstract process they propose in order to explain variations in the inputs with which the central abstraction deals, and the inclusive abstract processes they advance are often sleight-of-hand gimmicks and maybe tautological. Even with care to avoid gimmickry, conceptual integrations often dismiss other theories rather than using them to achieve a more adequate general theory. After all, if the abstract causal process of an integrated theory presupposes a priori everything that other theories propose, then it can only make them redundant. Moreover, without explanation of the variables implicated in an abstract causal process, little can be achieved.

The second way that conceptual integration can be achieved, though it has not been employed in previous attempts to build integrated theory, is by merging existing concepts or processes into larger, abstract concepts or processes (see Tittle 1985b for a hypothetical example). The idea is to find a more inclusive concept or process that represents a merger of prior, clearly differentiated concepts or processes. The end product is a blending of different ideas into a new product. Unlike the up-and-down integration that translates prior arguments into the all-inclusive language of a proprietary process or concept, however, this form of conceptual integration represents a genuine synthesis expressed through a new, emergent concept or process.

This second form of conceptual integration permits disparate-appearing elements to be brought together under the same cognitive umbrella, but no abstraction can encompass enough theoretical elements to suffice alone. Moreover, even very general abstract processes do not operate the same way for all people and in all circumstances. Without some means of accommodating such variation, abstractive encapsulation will quickly flounder.

Assimilative

The third mode of integration also employs an abstract causal process, but it differs in that the process does not consume prior theories, but rather serves as the integrative device permitting other theories to be united. This approach conceives of extant separate theories as accounting for the inputs to the abstract integrative process. The clearest application of this approach is the integration around reinforcement/learning set forth by Pearson and Weiner.

Assimilative integration has a lot to offer the theoretical enterprise, but to the extent that an abstract, central causal process is flawed, the integrated theory that flows from it will be similarly flawed. Such may be the case for reinforcement/learning, which has served as the central element in all of the assimilative integrated theories currently in the literature. Moreover, assimilative theories are inherently focused on the central process, accepting full-blown the theories that supposedly feed into the constituent variables of that process. This encourages neglect of all sorts of interactive relationships and conditional effects that are not directly obvious in the network generated when theories are funneled into the central process, and it diverts attention away from features of adequate theories.

An Alternative Synthetic Approach

Since each of the separate methods used so far in trying to achieve integration is useful but flawed, success will probably depend on effective use of a variety of techniques—integration of integration methods, as it were. I refer to this as synthetic integration. It combines the best features of extant modes in order to build better integrated theory. However, there is more to the synthetic method than merely shoving together structural, conceptual, and assimilative methods of integration.

Effective synthesis involves at least five operations: (1) integrative abstraction, (2) identification or invention of a dominant causal process, (3) explicit specification of the contingencies under which the central causal process operates with greater or lesser force, (4) demonstration of how the strands of existing simple theories feed into the central causal process to capture all relevant causal elements, and (5) attention to precision and depth through articulating how feeding strands explain the elements of the central causal process as well as how the various components of the general theory, including the central causal process and the feeder explanations, interlink to produce various outcomes under various conditions.

The result of these five operations should be a wagon wheel–like edifice with the most abstract statement—the dominant causal process—at the center of the wheel (because it applies to all instances) and other abstract statements located outward from the center along the spokes (because each applies only to specific parts of the more abstract statement at the center), expressed in conditional terms. Still less abstract and more conditional statements fit further out on the spokes toward the rim of the wheel. By this mode, all supposed causal variables and processes having a systematic influence are part of one theory, linked together in a sequential network to feed a central causal process. Any degree of complexity and any number of causal factors can be so accommodated (see Glaser 1980), and the explanatory process can extend as far out as anybody wants to take it.

Abstraction. Since theories (as opposed to explanations) are built of abstract constructs linked by ideas conceptually crystallizing seemingly disparate empirical objects (Tittle 1985b; Willer and Webster 1970), integrations must employ abstract processes that tie together separate, disparate-appearing theoretical components. A synthetically integrated general theory merges existing theories by including their concepts and causal arguments within larger, more abstract concepts and causal arguments, not by grafting them onto a new structure or adopting them in toto. However, such an abstractive process cannot be free-floating and disconnected, nor can it involve cognitive gimmicks that absorb or dismiss existing theories by reinterpreting their arguments, making them appear to be redundant to the abstraction. Therefore, synthetic integration calls for a form of conceptual integration that marshals the strengths of existing theories through abstraction rather than through consumption. Nevertheless, abstraction is essential, which is one reason theoretical integration is different from model building.

   A Central Causal Process. Synthetic integration borrows heavily from the technique of assimilative integration, which links theoretical arguments through a central causal process into which extant theories feed. To serve this purpose, an integrative, central causal process must have some particular features. First, it must be abstract enough to allow input from other theories without absorbing or dismissing them. This is not for the political expedience of diverting criticism and promoting widespread acceptance, nor is it to honor the integrity of existing partial theories. Rather, broad input is desirable because almost every partial theory seems to have something important to offer (compare Turner 1989). Yet synthetic integration does not require complete incorporation of the entire structure of existing theories—that is an impossibility.

   Second, an adequate central causal process must be universally applicable. That is, under the conditions theoretically specified, the process must apply to all people, to all social settings, and to all forms of deviance. In addition, it must state genuine, not tautological, causal principles. In the end, of course, it must be true to the empirical evidence.

   There are at least two forms that such a central causal process can take. One focuses around an inclusive formula representing all causal elements, and with that as a base, it elaborates all theories outward to provide inputs to the terms of the central formula. An integrated theory, for instance, might suggest that *any specific behavior* will occur if X amount of opportunity to perform that behavior is combined with Y degree of ability of the individual to act, and the motivational impulse toward it surpasses, by Z degrees, the forces pushing the person to behave another way and, by Q degrees, the magnitude of restraint (compare Sheley 1983). The theory might also suggest that the *motivation* to do anything, deviant or not, reflects (1) accumulated differential association with social definitions favorable to doing it (Sutherland and Cressey 1978) or the individual's history of reinforcement concerning that behavior (Akers 1985; Wilson and Herrnstein 1985), (2) the way culturally defined means and goals converge for the person (Merton 1968) or the presence of other straining circumstances (Agnew 1992), (3) various biological predispositions (Mednick and Christiansen 1977; Wilson and Herrnstein 1985), (4) interactions among these variables and such things as equity considerations and the reinforcement context (Wilson and Herrnstein 1985), and (5) other elements suggested by prior theory or invented by the theorist. Under various conditions, these factors are postulated to contribute different amounts to motivation.

For any set of conditions, such as a particular kind of deviance for a person of particular demographic characteristics, the theory might indicate that learning will contribute, say, 40 percent to motivation, and strain from noxious stimuli will add 25 percent to the motivation, and so on. Similarly, the theory might contend that the degree of *constraint* faced by someone contemplating this particular deviance is determined by a combination of (1) interdependency with a conventional social group (Braithwaite 1989; Hirschi 1969), (2) fear of legal punishment (Andenaes 1974; Zimring and Hawkins 1973), (3) moral considerations (Parsons 1951; Grasmick and Bursik 1990), (4) particular constitutional factors (Eysenck 1964, 1982; Fishbein 1990; Wilson and Herrnstein 1985), and (5) chemical imbalances in the brain (Jeffery 1990; Podolsky 1955). The theory would also show how these components mesh to restrain any deviance, particularly the one in question, under different conditions. Thus, in the instant case, social interdependency might be theorized to contribute 50 percent to the degree of restraint, fear of the law, 30 percent, and so on.

Similarly, the values of, and effects on and of, other variables in the equation—*competing motives, opportunity,* and *ability*—would be derivable.

The major weakness of a formulary central causal process like the one illustrated is its assumption of additive effects. Since the likelihood of interactive relationships among the five variables—motivation, constraint, opportunity, ability, and alternative motivation—is strong, a transmissive type of central causal process is more likely to capture reality. A transmissive process, like the one used in assimilative efforts around the reinforcement/learning paradigm, channels diverse theoretical streams through a common conduit, but it does not assume additive effects. However, the reinforcement/learning process is prone to gimmickry and tautology and may be flawed in other ways; hence there is a strong need for a new transmissive central causal process to be used in theoretical integration.

Integration around a central process, whether formulary or transmissive, permits and ideally requires theorists to provide intellectual, theoretical rationales for all of the internal linkages and postulates contained in the outward extensions of the basic formula, as the questions *why* and *how* are repeatedly confronted. For instance, one could apply the hypothetical formulary example above to burglary. An integrated theory might be built around a particular personality trait, like interpersonal insecurity, that is portrayed as the main motivator of most forms of deviance, particularly burglary. The theory would contain explanatory arguments about how it works. For instance, interpersonal insecurity might be theorized to cause anxiety about freedom to regulate personal privacy, leading individuals to experience relative deprivation in social interaction—they imagine that others exercise complete control of their own privacy. Because perceptions of relative disadvantage produce psychic discomfort, those experiencing it are motivated to seek relief by violating the privacy of others to equalize what was perceived as greatly unequal personal autonomy (see Agnew 1992; Katz 1988).

By similar exposition employing parts of other theories, an integrative scheme would explain all of the implied interconnections that in the aggregate identify the circumstances where all parts of the central causal statement assume particular values. In addition, the theory would contain the intellectual rationale for explaining how feeders to the main causal process represent outcomes from other causal processes. Degrees of interpersonal insecurity, exposure to various kinds of reinforcement schedules, social interdependency, and so on, must themselves be accounted for through the operation of other variables and processes that have greater or lesser effect, depending on specific given conditions.

Whatever its exact nature, a central causal process is essential for tying together the parts of an integrated theory.

Contingencies. An inclusive theoretical system revolving around a central causal process along the lines described above must pay particular attention to the contingencies under which the central causal process operates with greater or lesser force. All explanatory principles, even those conceived as universally operating, will work better in some circumstances than in others. An essential attribute of adequate theory is precision, which includes specification of the contingencies under which various effects are more or less likely. Integrated theories built around a central causal element, then, must recognize variations or deviations from the main pattern captured in that element, just as any general theory should indicate its own "scope" (Bennett 1980; Cullen 1984; Gibbs 1972b; Walker and Cohen 1985). Effective theories will not emerge without systematic specification of conditional elements, along with explanations of why and how those contingencies intervene.

Spelling Out the Interlinkages. The kind of integrated theoretical system outlined above must also show in detail how various theoretical strands fit together. Specific partial theories should be identified, and the way they mesh with a central causal process or provide inputs to that process must be explained. Ultimately, of course, each of the constituent partial theories must be fully articulated with the integrated structure. However, this must be a collective endeavor. No one theorist can be held accountable for the task; it is simply too large and complicated. Thus Pearson and Weiner (1985) cannot be faulted for failing to fully articulate the integrative structure they set forth, although they can be chided for failing to begin the articulation process. Articulation is the culmination of theoretical integration, but the best that an individual scholar can hope to accomplish is to define the framework within which collective efforts toward general theory can succeed and to illustrate through some articulation how others can help.

Achieving Further Precision and Depth. Finally, a fully adequate integrated theory must attend to the components of precision and depth that have been neglected by present simple, elaborated, and integrated theories. This includes especially the forms of causal relationships, the magnitudes of causal intervals, interactive causal sequences, and intellectually satisfying accounts of why and how things work the way the theory suggests they do. Fully achieving these things requires participation of the entire community of scholars, but individuals trying to specify the framework for integrated theory are obligated to take their schemes far along these trails and, by so doing, point others in the right direction.

Clearly it is not now part of our disciplinary culture to worry about causal intervals or even to answer the questions *why* and *how* in a satisfying way. Most theories contain as much assertion as explanation, and we are to some extent victims of a limiting methodology that encourages emphasis on linear prediction. Without the precision and depth of good theory we are caught in a self-reinforcing trap, thinking it enough to identify variables that seem to "work" without showing how they work or that they may be falsely assumed to work in a linear fashion. In fact, we are even more retrograde than that. Generally speaking, scholars interested in crime and deviance are more interested in statistically significant effects than they are in the magnitude of effects. Although everyone surely recognizes that greater statistical significance simply means that confidence in the presence of a nonchance phenomenon is strengthened, it is nevertheless conventional practice to report three levels of significance and to interpret phenomena statistically significant at a .001 level as somehow more substantively important than those significant at merely .01.

We must get to the point where we can make a large number of *contingent* predictions with enough confidence for our criteria of success to be the number of outcomes in a set that exceed some high level of magnitude. This will be possible only by attending to precision and depth.

General Conclusion

Integrating existing partial theories is essential for developing adequate general theory. However, integrative efforts, though representing substantial advance over simple theories as well as improvement over inventive and elaborative attempts, have not yet fulfilled their promise. The main reasons for this are (1) the absence of a coherent set of guidelines for developing adequate integrated theories, and (2) undue reliance on a unifying causal process that may be flawed.

To help correct these problems, I offer an alternative paradigm for achieving more adequate integrated theory. The "synthetic mode" advocates the simultaneous use of structural, conceptual, and assimilative methods to tie existing theories together through a central causal process. In the remainder of this book, I use the synthetic mode to lay out a framework within which scholars can work to achieve an adequate general theory of deviance. The main feature of that framework is a "new" unifying causal process that I call "control balancing."

5

What Is to Be Explained

Since I am trying to facilitate theoretical development through synthetic integration, an articulated general theory that results will necessarily contain explanations of many things. However, the main feature of the paradigm being advanced is a new central causal process focused on deviant behavior by individuals (which also can be applied to explain rates of deviant behavior in social and political units). Although "control balancing" is only the focal point for a larger emerging general integrated theory, I will nevertheless refer to it as "the theory" in order to communicate efficiently.

The general theory that I hope will emerge around the causal process of control balancing should be inclusive, but the central mechanism itself does not explain why some acts are deviant whereas others are not; rather, it begins with social rules as they exist at a given point in time and in a particular place. However, as will be shown later, the forces encompassed in the causal mechanism actually hinge on the degree to which the acts to be explained are deviant in a particular social context. Therefore, the value of the theory depends in part on the clarity of its explicandum (dependent variable).

The General Meaning of Deviance

There is no generally agreed-upon conceptualization of deviance. Approaches to the problem vary widely (Gibbs 1981:22–39; McCaghy 1985; Thio 1988), but most definitions, in one way or another, convey the idea that deviant acts are inconsistent with standards of acceptable conduct prevailing in a given social group. Two features of deviant behavior make it interesting for discussion: Most members of a group think it is wrong, or there are usually negative reactions to it. Hence, I will define deviance as *any behavior that the majority of a given group regards as unacceptable or that typically evokes a collective response of a negative type*. In this definition, "unacceptable" means disapproved, wrong, shameful, pitiful, inappropriate, bad, abnormal, or loathsome—in short, behavior that a group evaluates negatively. "Majority" means that over one-half of the people in a specified, bounded group regard the behavior as unacceptable. The arbitrariness of this cutoff point is tolerable because the main objective is not to classify behavior as simply deviant or conforming but rather to array it on a continuum from very nondeviant (almost nobody considers it unacceptable) to very deviant (almost everybody in the group considers it unacceptable), with all behavior falling somewhere on the scale. "Collective response of a negative type" implies that the majority of the specified group typically does something to express its displeasure or that the officials who possess coercive power over the group typically respond to the behavior in a way that expresses negative evaluation.

This definition implies that behavior is deviant when the climate of opinion in a group reflects general disapproval of the behavior, even if nothing is typically done collectively in response to the behavior. If most people in Alabama think that photographing a nude person is a bad thing, then that act would be classified as deviant in that state, regardless of anything else. The definition implies that citizens of Alabama need not do anything about nude photography, nor do the police have to arrest anybody for photographing a naked person. However, along with this purely evaluative component of deviance goes an assumption that group disapproval will affect potential deviant actors' thoughts about the consequences of committing the act in question. This assumption makes the definition appropriate for identifying acts to be explained by control balance theory.

The theory contends that the condition of deviantness is essential to the explanation of specific deviant acts because those characterized by "imbalanced control ratios" will, under some conditions, be constrained from committing some kinds of acts by their fear of consequences. The greater the extent to which the members of a group disapprove of a given behavior, the more likely any specific members of that group are to anticipate disadvantageous responses to its commission. This is because individuals and groupings of individuals, especially those likely to be affected by a given behavior, go to a lot of trouble to give the impression that they will do something about objectionable behavior. People talk, gesture, gossip, threaten, and posture, and by those means imply that they will at least express contempt for violators, and possibly more. Individuals who are continuously exposed to these social processes need not see concerted action to fear the consequences of engaging in disapproved behavior. The possibility of informal sanctions is experientially established by exposure to talk, ideas, body language, and so on, as well as through observation of social control and self-help in action.

In this connection it is important to observe that fear of informal consequences is not necessarily contingent on group cohesion or even on individual interdependency with others. To be sure, communally expressed informal sanctions may depend on group cohesion (Braithwaite 1989) and informal sanctions of a condemnatory form (for example, losing the respect of loved ones) may be largely dependent on social bondedness (Hirschi 1969), but even bonded people in disorganized groups, as well as unbonded individuals in tight-knit groups, are likely to fear the reactions of directly offended parties. This fear rests partly on direct perceptions that some potentially offended persons have the strength and means to respond vigorously, but it also rests partly on uncertainty as to the likely response of those offended. After all, unpredictability can be as frightening as knowledge when the potential reactions to violations of social rules or the expectations of individuals are at issue.

Behavior may also be deviant when the members of a group or the officials authorized to act on behalf of the collectivity typically respond in negative ways to it. If the Amish usually shun those who persist in particular violations, then those violations are deviant (Hostetler 1980; see also Kephardt and Zellner 1994). If Kansas City police usually arrest people they discover smoking marijuana, that behavior is deviant in Kansas City, regardless of anything else. Likewise, if marijuana smokers in Kansas City are usually ostracized by most other people in Kansas City, then marijuana smoking is deviant behavior there. Furthermore, some behavior may be deviant in specified groups because popular opinion disapproves of it, implying the likelihood of unpleasant consequences arising from individuals and groups, as well as because there is a collective negative reaction. For instance, most people in Iowa believe that stealing something worth $50 is wrong (Tittle 1980b), and the police in Iowa, like police everywhere in the United States, typically arrest those discovered stealing things worth $50. Hence, stealing something worth $50 is deviant because it is disapproved, implying that lots of people will do things that make life difficult for those who steal (including particularly the victims of theft), but it is deviant also because it elicits a collective reaction.

An act may be deviant by either of two criteria, and perhaps by both, but not necessarily by both. For instance, most citizens of a state may believe that adultery is wrong, but collectively they may do nothing about its occurrence, and the police may rarely or never make an arrest for adultery. Still, adultery would be deviant in that state because people disapprove of it, and as a result there are likely to be unpleasant consequences for adulterers. In another example, police may routinely arrest people for selling alcoholic beverages in a particular state although most citizens of that state may not regard the sale of alcoholic beverages as bad or wrong. Nevertheless, that behavior would still fit the definition of deviance set forth. In many cases, of course, group opinion will match collective response, but there are numerous instances in which the two do not match, such as in gambling, marijuana use, manufacturing dangerous products, and polluting the environment.

Legality and Deviance

Mere illegality is not a reliable guide to the deviantness of some behavior since law does not necessarily reflect public opinion and many laws are never enforced. Indeed, law often expresses the desires and interests of special power groups that are able to mobilize legislative support, sometimes in direct opposition to majority views. Moreover, even when law does embody collective sentiment at the time it is enacted, it may not do so later, and laws are seldom modified in response to changing circumstances. As opinion changes, a statute may become more and more inconsistent with the views of the majority, and sometimes its enforcement becomes lax or completely ignored. If this occurs, the prohibited behavior would not be deviant, although it would continue to be illegal.

Finally, some laws may actually be consistent with public opinion but may not be enforced. Laws prohibiting prostitution in many communities in the United States do express collective disapproval, but only rarely are they enforced, perhaps because the difficulty of controlling prostitution makes it a low priority for police, there are too few resources for enforcement, or the police are in corrupt collusion with the practitioners. In this illustration, the behavior would be deviant because it is generally disapproved of, but the fact of illegality would not be the key determinant. Illegality must be thought of as a variable, which may or may not characterize deviance.

What Is Crime? Conceptualizations of crime are as varied as are conceptualizations of deviance. For my purposes, crimes are those acts that are subject to specified penalties imposed in routinized ways by institutionalized functionaries who are recognized by most members of a given social group as having the power or authority to do so (compare Hoebel 1968:26). Criminal behavior involves the potentiality of receiving a previously specified penalty in a standardized way by somebody who occupies a position especially designated for the purpose of imposing those specified sanctions. For an act to be criminal, the potential sanctions for it must be known in advance by most of those subject to such sanctions, and they must be imposed in a routinized way, that is, they must be of a nature consistent with social rules or expectations of the members of a group, implemented in ways that conform to patterns of expectations shared by the members of the group, and if the system lasts long enough, passed on from generation to generation.

In modern societies most criminal behavior is easily recognized because specific acts are prohibited in written legal statutes, and codified punishments are imposed by functionaries whose main, or sometimes only, job is imposing sanctions; such functionaries include police, court officers, and prison or probation officials. Not all criminal behavior is easily recognized, however, and some behaviors even pose challenges to legal authorities. In fact, one of the purposes of courts is to decide if a given instance of behavior falls within one of the categories prohibited in the law. A good example is pornography.

The law has never been effective in defining pornography, though many laws have prohibited or restricted its production, distribution, and consumption. For instance, if pornography is defined in terms of lewd or vulgar depictions, one has to decide the meaning of lewd and vulgar, two words as imprecise in meaning as pornography itself. If pornography is defined in terms of nudity, the dividing line between artistic presentations of the human body and pornography cannot be made. If pornography is defined in terms of behavior or presentations that shock common sensibilities or defy local standards of decency, one must be able to ascertain what the local standards of decency are.

Moreover, one cannot know for sure that depictions meet particular legal criteria until *after* the behavior has occurred and the judicial process has unfolded. For instance, in Palm Beach County, Florida, in the 1970s certain movies were confiscated by the police on the grounds that they offended prevailing community standards, and the projectionist and theater owner were prosecuted. A jury, however, decided the material was not pornographic. Undaunted, the local prosecutor and law enforcement officials confiscated more films and had another trial, only to have a second jury decide that the material was not pornographic. On the third try, the prosecutor was able to get a jury to judge the film in question to be pornographic. He proclaimed triumphantly that community standards had been upheld. One could question whether any jury reflects community standards, since juries are not chosen by random sample. But even if it were conceded that the third jury's decision established community standards, the person showing those films could not have been certain ahead of time what constituted a violation of the law; after all, it took three different juries to decide this. Therefore, although criminal behavior is *relatively easily* identified in modern societies, determining the criminality of an act is often problematic.

What about nonmodern societies with no written codes? Interestingly enough, such societies often have law, at least if law is conceived the way I have suggested, and the identification of criminal acts is often no more problematic than in modern societies. Consider the Cheyenne Indians (Grinnell 1972; Llewellyn and Hoebel 1941; Hoebel 1968). Although not literate, they had an elaborate system of institutionalized actors and processes for dealing with certain acts that were recognized by the people as deserving specified punishment. The most important law prohibited killing a member of the group. The Cheyenne believed that relationships between the people and the Great Spirit would be undermined if the "sacred arrows" were tainted by an endogenous killing. To anger the Great Spirit would be disastrous, since the Cheyenne depended on the natural environment for subsistence.

Despite this belief, however, an occasional homicide did occur. When a Cheyenne was murdered, any witness was expected to notify the nearest group of fraternally organized hunter-warriors, whose job included acting as a police force. This fraternal group would then take the suspect into custody until the case could be adjudicated by the tribal chiefs. The chiefs would meet, hear the facts, take testimony, weigh extenuating circumstances, and decide what to do with the killer. In essence they would determine for how long to banish the offender, because the recognized punishment was forced separation from the tribe. However, before this sentence was imposed, a messenger was sent back among the people to communicate the sentence tentatively decided upon by the chiefs. The people would discuss the case until some consensus was reached. If the people thought the sentence was too long, the messenger would go back to the chiefs and tell them what the people were thinking, whereupon the chiefs would reconsider. This process continued until a mutually agreeable sentence was arrived at, meaning that a high degree of consensus had been achieved, or at least an acceptable compromise had been forged. At this point the fraternal group would escort the perpetrator, along with things he or she needed for survival, to a place some distance from the tribe. The guilty party would be left to fend for himself or herself alone until the sentence was completed or the individual was able to achieve redemption. Clearly, among the Cheyenne, killing was punishable by institutionalized functionares in a routinized and socially recognized way. Hence it was a crime.

This definition of crime, however, may raise some questions. For instance, universities maintain a cadre of officials standing in readiness to impose specified sanctions on students who violate rules. The imposition of sanctions is routinized (spelled out in university handbooks), and the officials imposing the sanctions occupy positions acknowledged to embody the authority and power to so act. Are university regulations laws? Are their violations instances of crime? My answer would be yes, but in any legal system, there are hierarchies of law. Some legal mechanisms are subordinate to others, so whenever there is conflict between the requirements of one level of legality and those of another, the imperatives of the higher-ranked system prevail. Moreover, hierarchy of law means that some levels of law are restricted, usually in the kinds of sanctions that can be imposed.

In the case of university regulations, penalties are usually restricted to deprivation of privileges associated with university attendance, denial of a degree, blockage of access to university programs, or financial penalties. University officials cannot incarcerate violators or physically harm them; those sanctions are reserved for a higher level of legality. In addition, the rules from higher legal levels, such as state or federal laws, to some extent must prevail in the university. Hence a student who is barred from a university is entitled to "due process." In other words, if the university acts arbitrarily without regard for routinized procedures, the student can probably get reinstated by appeal to a state court of higher law.

Thus, law is more diffusd than most people realize, though it is not always recognized as law or called by that name. Are rules imposed by force, such as those of occupying armies or more powerful surrounding communities against subcultural groups, law? Here the answer is maybe. If the occupying army punishes people in an ad hoc, arbitrary way, for violation of regulations set forth by the military commander, then it is not law, and violations of those regulations are not crimes. They might more appropriately be called "defiant acts." However, if the military commander formulates a set of rules, describes a routinized procedure by which they are to be enforced, specifies the range of penalties to which a violator is subject, and publicizes these plans so that all, or at least most, who are subject to the penalties know of them and understand the process to be used, then violation becomes a crime—provided, of course, that the commander has the power to coerce compliance in case the people do not recognize the occupier's right to enforce the rules.

The same is true of laws formulated by dominant groups and enforced against subcultural or minority groups. Even though the Amish have their own system of laws (Hostetler 1980; Kephardt and Zellner 1994), they are also accountable to laws of the larger society, and the principles of hierarchy apply. As long as Amish law does not usurp the law of the states within which Amish people reside (or federal law) and does not extend into domains prohibited by the larger legal domain, they can operate. The larger legal domain, however, can insist on its mandates because it has coercive power that rests on recognition by most people in the outside society of the right of the institutionalized functionaries to so act.

Criminal and Deviant Behavior. Because criminal behavior is a special category of conduct, it may or may not be deviant. Consider marijuana use. It is a crime in many states to possess marijuana or to use it (using it implies possession, at least temporarily, of course). Still, in many of those states, such as Florida, this law is rarely enforced, and public opinion does not find marijuana smoking unacceptable. In Florida during the 1970s, anybody attending a rock concert would see thousands possessing and smoking marijuana during the performance despite dozens of police officers in the baseball stadium directly observing this behavior. Moreover, though there are no poll data to confirm this, the majority of people in South Florida probably did not regard marijuana smoking as especially bad. Thus marijuana smoking was a crime, but it probably was not deviant.

Similarly, most forms of gambling are illegal in some states. Nonetheless, in many of those same states the law is typically not enforced, and public opinion is tolerant of gambling. Hence it is a crime to gamble, but it is not deviant. Moreover, in other states some forms of gambling are not even illegal. New Jersey has legalized casino gambling, Florida permits gambling on horse and dog racing and on jai alai, and many states have lotteries.

Contrast these cases with others. Chronic overeating and picking one's nose in public are probably regarded by most people in this country as unacceptable, or deviant, but neither is criminal. Negligence by the Exxon Corporation in permitting conditions resulting in the huge oil spill at Valdez, Alaska, in 1989 was regarded by most Americans as wrong, unacceptable, and deviant—yet it was not illegal.

Finally, some acts are both deviant and criminal. Murder is publicly disapproved of and illegal, as are rape, arson, thievery, assault, and many other behaviors. However, criminal and deviant behaviors are not synonymous, deviance is more inclusive than crime, and the designation of acts as criminal involves a political process independent of the deviantness or acceptability of the behavior. Control balance theory aims to explain deviance. To the extent that criminal acts are also deviant, which is often the case, it explains them as well. However, because crime and deviance are not synonymous, control balance theory cannot be characterized as a theory of criminal behavior.

Deviance and Prevalence

Deviance is not determined by prevalence of occurrence. The majority of a given group may actually practice a particular act, or at least at one time or another have committed it, yet still believe that it is wrong, inappropriate, or despicable, and disapproval may carry a probability of unpleasant consequences for committing the act in question. Such a disapproved act would be deviant despite the fact that most people do it or have done it. An example is student cheating. If queried, most students will state that they believe cheating to be wrong. Nevertheless, most students at some time or another during a college career do cheat on exams, and some cheat all the time. Conversely, because something is unusual or atypical does not necessarily mean it is deviant. Few people eat snails, yet it is neither disapproved of nor is there a negative reaction from the majority or from legal representatives when individuals are caught doing it; therefore, snail consumption is not deviant. It is not the number of people doing it that determines a behavior's deviantness; rather, it is how the behavior is evaluated by group members or those in positions to use coercive power.

Deviance and Group Context

Further, and most important, deviance is linked to particular group contexts. No behavior is universally or inherently deviant; it may be deviant in one group but not in another, it may be deviant at one point in time in a particular group but not at another point in time in that same group, and it may be deviant for some within a given group but not for others. Therefore, almost any behavior may be deviant, and almost every behavior is both conforming and deviant. For instance, wearing clothes is conforming behavior in most communities in the United States, but it is deviant in nudist communities. Marijuana use is deviant in many places but it is not deviant in others. Similarly, recreational sex is both conforming and deviant depending upon the normative context. In some communities it is regarded as morally wrong and punishable, but in some modern urban communities recreational sex is quite acceptable. Still, even among people who practice recreational sex or sexual exchange of spouses, participation is deviant for minors. Furthermore, some things are acceptable for men but not for women and vice versa. In the United States, men are allowed to chew tobacco but eyebrows would be raised if women did the same, and women in workplaces are allowed to dress like men traditionally have (in pants), whereas the reputations of working men would be jeopardized if they dressed as women traditionally have (in skirts).

Thus it is misleading to portray specific actions like prostitution, bizarre behaviors usually regarded as the result of mental illness, white-collar crime, or even homicide as inherently deviant. Each may or may not be deviant, depending upon the normative context and the particular factors operative in that situation. True enough, a few behaviors are deviant in such a large number of contexts that initially they may appear to be universally deviant. One illustration is incest. Every society has some form of incest taboo prohibiting sexual relations between close kin. However, who is included in the taboo varies from society to society, although not necessarily along biological lines. Moreover, some societies exempt various categories of people from the taboo. For instance, brother-sister marriage in ancient Egypt was both permitted and encouraged (Bagley 1969; Middleton 1962). Hence, incest prohibitions are nearly universal, but the exact behavior prohibited is not uniform, nor do the norms apply in invariant ways within given societies. The same is true with respect to homicide. Almost every society has some kind of rule prohibiting homicide, but the particular kinds of homicide prohibited or permitted vary widely. U.S. soldiers are permitted to kill, even forced to do so; police officers are sometimes authorized to kill; and executioners are required to commit homicide. Moreover, homicide in self-defense is not deviant. Therefore the act of killing another human being is often not deviant. Indeed, it is probably impossible to identify any specific behavior that is deviant in all societies for all categories of people.

Identifying Deviance

Deviance, then, is limited to acts disapproved of by the majority of a group or that are typically responded to negatively by the majority or by those in positions to use coercive power on behalf of the collectivity. Making precise decisions about deviance requires (1) data about group opinion of the morality or acceptability of behavior, (2) information concerning the rate at which actual sanctions for various behaviors are imposed by authorities, and (3) evidence about the actions of members of the social group in instances when various behaviors have occurred in the recent past. Sometimes all three kinds of data may be required. In specific instances some behaviors may fail to qualify as deviance according to one or another criterion but may still qualify as deviance by at least one of the others. Often only one kind of information will suffice to demonstrate that the behavior is deviant. Unfortunately, none of the three kinds of information is easily available to identify most potential deviant behaviors.

Assessing majority opinion is often difficult and expensive. Collection of meaningful information presupposes identifiable group boundaries. Political boundaries are easy to identify, but it is not always possible to locate the precise social boundaries that separate such entities as the "south" from the "north," Jews from gentiles, Mormons from others, or inner-city neighborhoods from the rest of the city. In addition, general surveys can deal only with a limited number of behaviors, and regularly conducted surveys rarely include deviance items; therefore, special ad hoc surveys are necessary. Finally, since surveys normally sample large, politically defined population units, they do not adequately represent small subunits. A national survey may accurately portray whether the majority of the U.S. population disapproves of abortion, but it will not tell whether the people in Ames, Iowa, or whether Jewish people disapprove of it, since the sample may not include anybody from Ames and will probably include only a few Jews.

In the absence of ad hoc survey information (which can rarely be obtained), one must rely on indirect evidence of the beliefs of group members, which consists of information, such as the results of elections in which candidates have taken stands or been identified with specific kinds of behavior, or the results of local referenda, for example, the one conducted in Dade County, Florida, in 1977. An ordinance guaranteeing equal employment rights for homosexuals was put to popular vote. The election received national attention because of the efforts of Anita Bryant, at the time a popular singer and major advertising figure for Florida orange juice, to defeat the ordinance. Since the measure was soundly defeated, one might conclude that most people in Dade County disapprove of homosexual behavior. Such conclusions must be tentative, however, because all do not vote and results are not direct indicators of disapproval since other issues are usually intertwined in elections.

Other indirect evidence includes newspaper editorials, letters to editors, public speeches or statements by community leaders, or the actions of jurors in particular cases. However, all of these are also problematic indicators because newspaper editors and politicians may not be taking the pulse of the community accurately, people who write letters to newspapers may be unlike those who do not, and jurors certainly cannot be considered a representative segment of the population. Additional circumstantial evidence may help paint a general picture of public opinion. If a population includes a large proportion of young adults, one might reasonably assume more acceptability or nonacceptability of various behaviors because it may be known that, in general, these age groups hold a particular belief about the behaviors in question. Likewise, if the population contains mostly people of one religious or ethnic group, for instance, southerners, Republicans, females, or whatever, general knowledge about typical beliefs may permit interpretation of the local situation.

Finally, common personal experience may suggest that some things are or are not deviant in various locales. For example, few would quarrel with a judgment that interracial dating is deviant behavior in Jackson, Mississippi, even without survey data. Similarly, it is not too difficult to surmise that eating human flesh is disapproved of by most people in every community in the United States because there are many ancillary indicators of this. Indeed, opinions of Americans about eating animals with humanlike qualities are fairly clear. Whereas poultry is readily consumed, few approve of eating cocker spaniels. Still, all in all, ascertaining public beliefs is easier said than done.

Similarly, applying the second part of the definition—collective negative reaction—is also difficult. Newspaper accounts or historical documents can establish whether a community has reacted in the past to instances of particular behaviors, but it cannot tell whether that is a "typical" reaction. Determining whether the reaction is typical requires knowledge of the frequency of occurrence of the behavior that is known to the community or the coercive agents, so as to identify what proportion of instances are actually reacted against. Usually, estimates have to be made from meager data.

Further problems concern subcultures within political entities and subordinate political units within larger arenas. Imagine that the coercive agents for a political entity typically react negatively to a specific behavior, but the majority of a subcultural group or a subordinate political group does not find the behavior objectionable. This is an instance of deviance if the coercive agents are conceived as acting on behalf of or with the coercive power of the collectivity. However, can coercive agents who are not members of the subcultural group act on behalf of the group, and can coercive agents who are members of the subculture but who enforce alien rules (those inconsistent with local standards and formulated by others) be regarded as acting with collective coercive power? More pointedly, does the subculture have any coercive agents?

I contend that coercive agents who do not face organized, forceful opposition are exercising power on behalf of a group even if they are alien to the community. Therefore, despite public acceptability, gambling is deviant in inner-city poverty areas if the police typically harass or arrest people for it. Similarly, if a sectarian religious community within the United States believes in, and practices, polygamy, but law enforcement officers of the particular state where they reside arrest polygamists whenever possible, the behavior is deviant (because the coercive agents of that group are the state police) unless the polygamists resist with organized counterforce.

Such instances make this conceptualization of deviance seem strained, but they point up something crucial. What is deviant is partly a matter of power. Sometimes social rules are foisted upon people, and they are coerced into obedience, or at least an effort is made to coerce obedience. From the point of view of power holders, or the majority of a larger political entity, violations of the rules are deviations, subject to penalty. Inner-city gamblers are sometimes harassed, and, if caught, are subject to punishment on the assumption that evil or sickness motivates violations of the antigambling rules. Yet from the perspective of the inner-city dwellers, the laws may be viewed as unjust, illogical, and stupid, and violation may be thought of as natural behavior. If a definition focuses only on local opinion, the crucial matter of conflicting viewpoints would be glossed over, and the critical consequences for those who follow local standards in defiance of the alien rules would have to be ignored. Therefore what appears as strain in the definition is evidence that it reflects reality, which is itself strained.

A final problem in empirical application concerns situations where there is so much disagreement about behavioral standards and such great capriciousness in reaction to particular instances of behavior that it is meaningless to talk about deviance. Such circumstances prevail in periods of social change when opinions are problematic or in periods of political instability when coercive predominance has not been established. Such situations are best regarded as instances of social disorganization. Deviance is irrelevant because the norms are in the process of being reformulated.

Overall, then, decisions about whether some behavior is or is not deviant will sometimes be somewhat tenuous, and often the judgment will be more speculative than scientific. This does not mean that the study of deviance, or control balance theory, is impossibly imprecise. The categories of behavior with which the theory mainly deals are clearly deviant in most places for most people most of the time. However, those categories are abstractions encompassing a large number of specific acts, some of which may not be deviant. Although the theory explains conformity as well as deviance, the accuracy with which it accounts for the probability and type of behavior depends on the certainty of the behavior's status as deviance or conformity. Hence, one contingency for maximal operation of control balance theory is that behaviors at issue be clearly classifiable as deviant or conforming. Wherever such classification is problematic, the theory will be weak.

Deviance in Control Balance Theory

The theory builds on the notion that constraint on one's freedom or ability to act constitutes the main variable in explaining individual behavior. Various configurations of constraint are postulated as simultaneously motivating and forestalling actions. The theory begins with the fundamental premise of other "control" theories (social bonds, containment, and so on), but it goes beyond them in recognizing that constraints on human behavior must be considered in conjunction with the individual's strength of motivation for deviance. Moreover, the theory contends that control itself, while inhibiting action, is also heavily implicated in generating motivation for deviant behavior. The central premise of the theory contends that the amount of control to which an individual is subject, relative to the amount of control he or she can exercise, determines the probability of deviance occurring as well as the type of deviance likely to occur.

However, because I am primarily interested in developing the causal argument of the theory, I focus on six general types of deviance, taking the contemporary United States as the group context, without paying detailed attention to whether all of the specific acts that might fall within the six categories are deviant by the criteria that have been discussed. Moreover, rather than compiling data to justify or demonstrate the deviance within the six general categories, I make some assumptions about public opinion or collective reactions that bear on the categories. In only one instance is there likely to be any quarrel with those assumptions, and in that case I will later offer a rationale.

Since the theory also explains conformity, albeit with a specific meaning, control balance is a general theory of human behavior. However, since a key explanatory element hinges on the deviantness of various acts, most of the behaviors the theory addresses are in fact deviant, and because the theory is being developed to facilitate integration of extant theories of crime/deviance, I refer to the control balance argument as a theory of deviance.

Seriousness

The theory of control balance explains both the probability of deviant behavior as well as the type of deviance likely to be committed by individuals. In the explanatory scheme it is *crucial that types of deviant behavior be differentiated by seriousness,* but not in terms of one underlying monotonic continuum. Moreover, distinctions among the categories of deviant behavior explained by the theory—predation, exploitation, defiance, plunder, submission, and decadence—hinge on a specific meaning of seriousness.

In the theory, seriousness is the degree to which a deviant act will *actually* activate (1) withholding or granting of things of value to the individual who commits it, (2) imposition or withholding of things unpleasant to that individual, and (3) erection of physical or social barriers to the achievement of that individual's goals by those entities with the capacity for such responses. Note two things about seriousness so conceived.

First, potential activation of controlling responses may involve a moral component, but it does not necessarily rest on moral considerations. Entities that can control may be activated to do so by threat to their interests as well as by feelings that the act is wrong, and some controlling responses may emanate from circumstances or environmental realities that have no consciousness at all. For two miners lost in the mountains, murder is an especially serious act because they need each other to survive, regardless of any moral considerations. The consequences of murder for the survivor are the same even though there is no longer an opposing entity that might have conscious intent to inflict hardship. The seriousness of a deviant act, then, is distinct from its deviantness, which rests on majority ideas about rightness and wrongness or on *possible* activation of social reactions.

Second, seriousness implies activation of controlling responses of several types, not necessarily, or exclusively, sanctions in the usual sense. According to the concept of control being developed, exercising control involves positive or negative actions that block or enhance goal achievement, positive or negative sanctions, and manipulation of things of value to a person. As a result, it is not possible to think of the components of the theory in terms of ordinary considerations about crime, law, and penalties.

Notwithstanding these two considerations, it is necessary to draw on knowledge of public opinion and social sanctions, including patterns of legal sanctions, in judging the likely activation of controlling responses to specific acts and individuals. Otherwise, no predictions could be made about behavior based on considerations of the seriousness of the act, since seriousness would always be an after-the-fact phenomenon. Like judgments about the deviantness of specific acts, judgments about seriousness based on opinion and past patterns of response are imprecise and subject to much error. Nevertheless, such judgments are an important part of the theory.

Categories of Deviance

Predation. In many contemporary societies, most people regard as unacceptable behaviors that involve direct physical violence, manipulation, or property extraction by an individual or group for the benefit of a predator who acts without regard for the desires or the welfare of the individual or group that is the object of the predation. Direct survey data demonstrate the deviantness of some predatory acts, particularly those listed as felonies in the criminal codes. Moreover, many such behaviors are prohibited by laws that are routinely enforced by the police and courts. However, some predatory acts, such as parasitic mooching by a relative, are not legally prohibited, some illegal ones are rarely backed with sanctions, particularly those involving fraudulent manipulation, and there are no survey data to demonstrate the social unacceptability of numerous forms of predation. In such cases, I assume from general cultural themes or from poll data on somewhat similar kinds of acts that they would be judged unacceptable by the majority.

Acts of predation include theft, rape, homicide, robbery, assault, fraud, price gouging by individual entrepreneurs, coercive pimping, and sexual harassment, as well as acts like parental use of guilt to elicit child attention. Note that the general category of predation includes both criminal and noncriminal deviance and may include some predatory acts that are not deviant at all. However, as a category, predation appears to be among the most serious of deviant acts. Most acts of predation are regarded as very wrong morally, and most people, including those with large capacities to emit controlling responses, regard them as threatening even if they are not themselves victims. Of course, if they can, victims are likely to take actions that will be unpleasant for perpetrators. Victims may fight back, seek revenge, try to persuade others to intervene, attempt to humiliate the perpetrators publicly, destroy their reputations, and so forth.

Exploitation. Exploitation involves acts of indirect predation. The individual or group, as exploiter, uses others as intermediaries, or uses structural/organizational arrangements to coerce, manipulate, or extract property from individuals or groups to benefit the exploiter without regard for the desires or welfare of the exploited. Exploitation includes acts such as corporate price-fixing, profiteering from manufacturing processes that endanger workers, influence peddling by political figures, contract killings, and employment of religious injunctions to solicit financial contributions for the personal use of evangelists. In addition, exploitation encompasses ordinary acts of interpersonal, third-party "social control" (Gibbs 1981) when those acts involve coercion, manipulation, or property extraction without regard for the desires or welfare of the exploited.

In contemporary U.S. society, as well as in most societies present or past, most people regard such acts of indirect predation as wrong or bad. However, it is probably true that exploitative acts are regarded as less pejorative than are direct predatory acts and that fewer people regard exploitation as completely unacceptable. Certainly such acts are less likely to be prohibited in the law or typically enforced if included in the criminal statutes, and indicators of the likelihood of controlling responses indicative of seriousness suggest that exploitation is far less serious than many other forms of deviance to be discussed. This is partly because evil and culpability are perceived as proportionate to the directness with which an individual is involved. However, it is also partly because individuals, or groups, in positions from which they can exploit are also able to manipulate public opinion, legal institutions, and the legislative process to make their acts seem less wrong and to forestall legal responses.

Defiance. The third general category of deviance to be explained is defiance. Defiant acts are those in which the individual perpetrator expresses contempt for, or hostility toward, a norm, a set of norms, or to the individual, group, or organization with which that norm is associated. These acts violate normative expectations but are done with concern to avoid inflicting much harm upon the object of hostility, and they are distinguishable by the absence of obvious benefit to the deviant actor. Illustrative acts such as youthful violation of curfews, vandalism, and status restrictions, mocking denigrations of company officials by striking workers, sullenness by a marital partner, exaggerated obedience by employers or students, and political protests are regarded by most people as wrong or unacceptable, often because they challenge accepted authority relationships or because they create inconvenience for others. Thus, acts of defiance against authority are deviant, and they are serious (likely to activate response from those with capacities to control), but less so than acts of predation and probably less so than exploitation.

Another form of defiance is that which represents escape or with-drawal from active participation in a network of social relationships or normative obligations, even if temporary. This includes excessive drug or alcohol use, bohemianism in its various forms, bizarre forms of with-drawal such as use of nonsense language, catatonia, and other behaviors regarded as evidence of mental illness, and suicide (at least in U.S. cul-ture). I contend that escape or withdrawal is a means of expressing dis-taste for a normative system, and that such defiance can take many forms. Most such behaviors have been documented by public opinion polls as being unacceptable, and collective reactions, even in the form of police coercion, are common.

Plunder. The theory also explains plunderous conduct, which is re-garded by most people as especially heinous and deserving of controlling responses. In these acts, individuals or organizations pursue their own ends with little awareness or regard for much else, particularly how their behaviors might affect others. It is not that they consciously victimize; in-stead, their behavior is so aloof that it creates victims as a by-product. Such behavior differs from predatory or exploitative acts in that its perpe-trators have such a poorly developed social consciousness, or conscience, that they do not perceive the suffering or harm caused. Exploiters and predators know they are victimizing others, and they are aware that their benefits cause misfortune for others, but they do not care. Plunderers are not even aware of the effects of their actions.

Among the plunderous acts that control balance theory explains are autocratic behaviors of decadent kings and nobles who destroy peasant fields in fox hunting, massive pollution by giant oil companies with ac-companying price increases to recover costs of cleanup, attempted geno-cide directed against racial or ethnic groups by powerful segments of a population, unrealistic taxes or work requirements imposed by occupy-ing armies or slaveholders, or the arrogant destruction of forests and ani-mals by early explorers.

Decadence. The theory also deals with impulsive acts guided by no consistent or rational life organization, only by the whim of the moment. Decadent acts reflect a search for meaning within a jaded life of undisci-plined excess. Since decadent individuals have no real sense of why they do things, nor any concept of a long-range goal for life, their behavior is erratic, unpredictable, and often irrational. Decadence may include exces-sive or unusual forms of sexual expression such as group sex with chil-dren, cruel debauchery such as humiliating people for entertainment, and nonsensical pleasure seeking or destruction, as in sadistic torture. Such behaviors are regarded by most people everywhere as loathsome, and most of them are in fact prohibited by laws that are typically enforced; hence they are deviant, and among the more serious deviant acts to be considered.

Submission. A fifth form of deviance consists of passive, unthinking, slavish obedience to the expectations, commands, or anticipated desires of others. Examples include: eating slop on command; helping repress others to please power holders; allowing oneself to be physically abused, humiliated, or sexually degraded; or simply conforming to routinized patterns of life without contemplating or questioning whether there is an alternative. Specific examples include: prison or concentration camp inmates who obey all overt and implied orders, even to the point of helping guards abuse them or other inmates; children so cowed by abusive parents that they lose all interest in life; submissive sex partners or abused spouses who protest nothing, no matter how degrading or depraved; and slaves or sharecroppers who demonstrate passive subordination to owners and other authorities. The essence of submission is complete obedience without the ability to imagine an alternative.

Some may question whether submissive behaviors are deviant; indeed, some may regard them as examples of perfect conformity. Remember that deviance is behavior that the majority of a group finds unacceptable or that evokes a collective reaction of a negative type. I contend that in American society, as well as in many other societies, most people regard such behaviors as pitiful, tragic, disgusting—in short, unacceptable—because they indicate that certain essential human qualities, such as freedom of spirit, self-direction, and individualism, have been suppressed. However, it does not follow that submission is a serious deviant act within the meaning of seriousness used here. Indeed, it rarely evokes any controlling responses, and it is hard to imagine that it ever will. For that reason, I classify submission as the least serious of the six deviant acts of concern to control balance theory.

Should the reader still doubt the deviantness of submission, it is important to remember that the theory explains behavior with submissive characteristics, along with the other categories of conduct described above, regardless of whether they strictly fulfill the definitional criteria of deviance. Thus, even if submission were not deviant in a particular society for certain segments of the population, it would nevertheless be explicable within the parameters of the proposed control balance theory. As will become clearer later, unlike the five other categories of behavior, the explanation of submissiveness contained within control balance theory does not depend directly upon its deviantness. Instead, it depends on the deviantness of alternative forms of behavior that a submissive person might contemplate.

The Meaning of Conformity in Control Balance Theory

It will be helpful in understanding the deviantness of submission, and it is crucial to understanding the control balance argument, to grasp the meaning of conformity. Conformity occurs when an individual or organization is aware of, or can contemplate the possibility of, alternative, nonacceptable behavior, yet behaves as the social rules dictate. The key difference between submission and conformity is that the conforming individual can visualize doing differently, should the opportunity present itself, even if this visualization only rarely occurs. The submissive individual, on the other hand, has lost the ability to imagine an alternative; he or she has become resigned to the point where anything else is inconceivable. Hence the behaviors that I call submissive are deviant in some societies or groups because they violate standards of acceptable, or normal, behavior, and in all societies they are distinguishable from the base category of conformity by virtue of the actor's loss of the capacity for imagining alternatives.

General Summary

Control balance theory is designed to explain seven abstract categories of human behavior, or their rates of occurrence in various kinds of social groups. Six of these categories represent different kinds of nonconforming behavior varying in degrees of deviantness, or the extent to which the members of a society find it unacceptable or typically respond collectively to it, as well as in degrees of seriousness, or the likelihood that commission will provoke controlling responses either from victims, random members of the social group, or the group acting in concert. The seventh category encompasses nondeviant, or conforming, behavior. Although most human behavior fits somewhere within these categories, control balance theory mainly explains deviant behavior, partly because one of its key explanatory mechanisms depends on the degree of deviantness of particular behaviors.

The next chapter will explicate the theory more fully, detailing its major concepts and spelling out why and how it explains the various categories of behavior.

6

The Concepts of
Control Balance Theory

Control balance theory accepts the premise of extant control theories (social bonds, containment, and so forth) that constraint on ability to act constitutes the main variable in explaining individual acts of deviance or crime. However, it goes beyond them in recognizing that constraints on human behavior must be considered in conjunction with the individual's strength of motivation to engage in deviance. Moreover, the proposed theory contends that control constitutes an inhibitor of action and that it is also heavily implicated in generating motivation for deviant behavior (compare Brehm 1966; Brehm and Brehm 1981). The central premise of the theory is that the amount of control to which people are subject relative to the amount of control they can exercise affects their general probability of committing some deviant acts as well as the probability that they will commit specific types of deviance. Deviant behavior is interpreted as a device, or maneuver, that helps people escape deficits and extend surpluses of control.

Deviance results from the convergence of four variables: (1) the *predisposition* toward deviant motivation; (2) the situational stimulation of that motivation, which I call *provocation;* (3) the *opportunity* to commit deviance, which is most important in explaining specific kinds of deviance rather than deviance in general, since the opportunity for some kind of deviance is almost always present; and (4) the likelihood that a particular deviant act will activate restraining responses by others, which is called *constraint.* Whether the coming together of these four variables actually produces deviant behavior, however, depends on the nature of their convergence and a number of other conditions. Nevertheless, before this causal process can be portrayed, the concepts must be clarified. Each of the four variables that must converge to produce deviant behavior is made up of two or more component parts.

Control

Although it is not used directly in any of the theory's propositions, the most important concept in control balance theory is "control," because it is implicated in several variables central to the theory's propositions.

Being controlled, or "experiencing" control, means that one's behavioral options are limited because (1) someone else, a group or organization of others, or others generally, can withhold or grant things of value in achieving one's goals or in expressing one's behavioral impulses or motivations; (2) someone else, a group or organization of others, or others generally, can impose or withhold things unpleasant when one is pursuing personal goals; or (3) the arrangement of physical or social "structural" phenomena makes achievement of one's goals difficult. "Exercising control" means that the person, either alone or in organized action, can limit the behavioral options of others or that the person can resist limitations on his or her own behavioral options by (1) withholding or granting things of value to others in trying to achieve their goals, (2) imposing or withholding things unpleasant to others pursuing their goals, or (3) overcoming physical or social structural barriers to the achievement of personal goals.

Control does not imply complete prevention of the expression of behavioral motivations or goal achievements; rather, it implies that full realization of desires or impulses can be curtailed or limited. Control is conceived as a variable; the *degree* to which behavioral expression of impulses or desires can be limited, or curtailed, varies from person to person and from situation to situation. Thus, being controlled, as I use it, is a continuous variable conveying the extent to which expression of one's desires or impulses is potentially *limited* by other people's abilities (whether actually exercised or not) to help, or reward, or hinder, or punish, or by the physical and social arrangements of the world. Further, exercising control is a continuous variable reflecting the degree to which one can limit other people's realization of their goals or can escape limitations on one's own behavioral motivations that stem from the actions of others or from physical or social arrangements.

The term "control" bears some similarity to the familiar concept of "power." Indeed, as Jack Gibbs (1981, 1989) points out, almost all definitions of power imply some connection with control, though few authors clearly define control in relationship to power. Moreover, definitions of power range broadly, with none incorporating all of the elements I have in mind when I use the term "control." In particular, almost all social science definitions of power focus only on social power and hinge on the idea that powerful actors are able to do things or make someone else do things, even when there is resistance. My concept of control incorporates the idea of barriers, or constraints on someone's ability to realize goals that are of a nonsocial as well as a social nature, and it encompasses situations that involve little or no resistance as well as situations in which the constrained party tries to counter or escape from controlling actions or circumstances. In addition, it differs from convention in that control does not necessarily involve conscious intent on the part of the one exercising it. Thus, when a parent feels obligated to answer the cry of a baby, the parent is being constrained or controlled by the baby, even though the idea of parental resistance is foreign to the situation and even though the baby may have no conscious intent of exercising power over the parent. Similarly, a person with access to an automobile is less constrained in movement than someone with no access, even though the idea of resistance and intentional exercise of power are alien.

Because the current concept of control is a little unusual, it is essential that the ideas to be developed in this chapter be considered with this specific meaning in mind. To appreciate the theoretical argument, one must not confuse this notion of control with other conceptualizations of control, power, or social control that have appeared in the literature. Differences between the idea of control as used in the theory being proposed and related social science concepts can best be grasped by comparison. Social scientists have defined control in numerous ways, and there has been little agreement among them or consistency in its empirical use (see Gibbs 1981, 1989). Probably the most fully developed definition is that offered by Gibbs, who defines it in terms of "attempts" at control that are believed by the would-be controller to be likely to produce outcomes he or she finds desirable. Hence, "attempted control is *overt* behavior by a human in the belief that (1) the behavior increases or decreases the probability of some subsequent condition and (2) the increase or decrease is desirable" (1989:24–25).

Gibbs clearly has in mind active, intentional efforts at mastery exercised by people contemplating the outcome of their efforts. He delineates several kinds of control in terms of the objects to be regulated, including inanimate control, biotic control, self-control, various forms of control of others, and numerous specific forms of social control (Gibbs 1989, chap. 3). Being consistent with this, I regard control as potentially exercised by people over inanimate objects, biotic conditions, and structural arrangements, as well as over human actors. Since I am interested in symmetrical features of control in which the individual is conceived as being controlled by those forces as well as being a controller, my usage involves no notion that control must be overt behavior, intentional, or conceived as producing desirable outcomes. After all, how could an inanimate object engage in overt behavior, intend to limit our freedom, or conceive it as desirable to do so? Further, if we extend the earlier example of a controlling infant, we can see that even humans can influence other humans without overt behavior, intent, or conceptions of desirable outcomes. Most parents feel compelled to check on the condition of infants without their crying; indeed, parents generally restrict their own movements when they have responsibility for a baby so that they can monitor the infant's needs without those needs being expressed in actual overt complaint.

A difference between the potential and actual effects of actions or conditions must be recognized. "Limitations" on behavioral options are an empirical condition, though the concept contains a perceptual component. When a person's behavioral options are limited by someone else's ability to withhold or grant things useful for goal achievement, that person (or persons) objectively has the capability of granting or withholding things—the *potential* for action exists. Sometimes a person may perceive that such potentiality exists even when it does not, and the effects may be the same as if domination actually existed. Nevertheless, a distinction must be made between actuality and mistaken perceptions. Further, having the ability to do something is not the same as the probability that such ability will be activated. Thus, in developing the theory, I sometimes refer to "potential controlling responses" to indicate the existence of someone's capability of bringing countervailing control into play, in contrast to the actual activation of controlling capabilities. Here, there is also a difference between the objective likelihood of activation and the perceptions of such likelihood. However, in this case, perception is more important than objective circumstances, for as will be seen, it is the anticipation of controlling responses that helps determine specific outcomes.

Deviant Motivation

The second major concept in the theory is "deviant motivation." In general, motivation refers to the push, reason, impulse, or urge to act. The impetus for deviance has two components—one predispositional, and the other situational. The situational component is the individual's perception or feeling that committing an act regarded by most others as inappropriate or unacceptable might allow that person to alter the balance of control he or she normally exercises relative to that which he or she normally experiences, even if temporarily. The predispositional component of deviant motivation is made up of three interactive parts, two of which are linked with control. The first of the control-linked predispositional parts is a basic *desire for autonomy,* and the second is the person's *control ratio,* which is the amount of control to which the person is subject relative to the amount that he or she can exercise.

Predisposition

Desire for Autonomy. Like a number of psychologists and social psychologists (Adler 1956; Charms 1968; Deci 1975; McClelland 1975; see Burger 1992; Gecas 1989), I contend that a desire for autonomy—escaping control over oneself and exercising more control over the social and physical world than one experiences—is almost universal among humans. This is not to say that the desire for autonomy is innate. Rather, it seems more likely to be rooted in the dependency of infancy and childhood. The helplessness of infants and the necessity for children to obey in exchange for sustenance probably lead them to identify with, and imitate, those on whom they are dependent, thereby creating a desire to manage the conditions of their lives. Yet, at the same time, dependency probably breeds contempt for the condition of being dominated. Thus, as a response to the inherent realities of infant and childhood insufficiency, we all hunger for mastery, and we harbor contempt for being ruled.

Autonomy is the simultaneous exercise of external control and escape from external control over oneself. I maintain that a "need" or desire for autonomy is present in almost all humans, though it may show some variation in magnitude from person to person as a result of the amount, or degree, of dependency experienced in childhood. Yet, after childhood its magnitude is fixed in every individual. Thus, in one sense desire for autonomy can be regarded as a personality trait—a more or less permanent feature of the individual's psychic operation that guides thought and action. However, unlike other personality traits, such as "self-efficacy" (Gecas 1989), desire for autonomy shows only slight variation from person to person.

Several issues concerning my arguments about desire for autonomy are likely to arise. Some will question whether all people possess such a desire. Everybody has known, or heard of, passive or withdrawn people who are seemingly unconcerned about influencing or managing events and things, and critics may cite evidence like that compiled by Burger (1992), whose measurements of "desire for control" distribute people over a wide continuum that includes some very low scores.

I cannot prove the presence of an autonomy drive, but neither can an autonomy desire be disproved, which is why it is an assumption. Neither passivity in some nor the presence of low scorers on Burger's scales constitutes unequivocal evidence against the idea of a fundamental urge for autonomy. Since actual human behavior may reflect physical and social conditions that stifle the expression of innate and learned impulses, obsequence, whether observed in everyday life or documented with hard evidence, is not necessarily a reflection of the absence of a yen for control. Indeed, complete passivity, a state wherein individuals cease to realize they want autonomy, may come about when a person faces overwhelming constraints on behavior (see Burger 1992), as the theory's explanation for "submissive" deviance suggests. How people behave, as well as what they say they want or desire, inevitably reflects some interplay between primary drives or impulses and the social and physical environment. Therefore, neither overt behavior nor self-reports of desires or urges can be taken as direct reliable evidence against the notion that everybody holds some desire for autonomy.

Another reason that evidence like that compiled by Burger, suggesting that some people have little need for freedom, does not contradict the assumption of universal desire for autonomy is that no empirical measures in contemporary social science actually operationalize autonomy as I conceive of it, much less operationalize a need, drive, or push for it. The idea is not simply that people want to subdue their environment. Instead, they desire, first, to escape control, and second, to exercise more control than that to which they are subject; the two in combination constitute a desire for autonomy. Measuring actual autonomy, or an impulse toward it, must be accomplished with relative, not absolute, indicators. Since "desire for control" makes sense only in relationship to the restraint that a person encounters, Burger's (1992:14) indicators of preferences for decision-making jobs, leadership, problem solving, and so on, are one-sided; they do not reflect, in any sense, the regimentation to which people are subject. Hence, his "desirability of control scale," and other scales with the same rationale, though useful for the purposes to which they have been put, cannot reveal anything about the reasonableness of the assumption of a universal desire for autonomy as conceived here, nor can they be used in measuring degrees of such "desire," or other concepts in control balance theory, such as "predisposition toward deviant motivation."

Finally, some who accept the assumption of universal striving for autonomy will challenge the explanation that it stems from identification with power wielders (care providers and other adults) one confronts as a dependent infant or child and from resentment of dependency. No doubt, some will think the autonomy predisposition is genetically determined (see Fishbein 1990; Mednick and Christiansen 1977; Rowe and Osgood 1984; Wilson and Herrnstein 1985), whereas others will interpret it as a product of particular life experience (compare Gottfredson and Hirschi 1990; Sampson and Laub 1993) or of socially determined reinforcement schedules (compare Akers 1985). However, counterarguments about the source of an autonomy desire are not of much import because the validity or plausibility of my explanation for *how* or *why* all people come to have a proclivity for autonomy in no way bears on the validity or plausibility of control balance theory. The theory per se begins with the plausible and useful *assumption* that all people desire to escape control exercised against themselves and to extend their own control. Efforts to account for that which is assumed—the autonomy wish—are completely independent of the theory itself.

Control Ratio. The second control-linked component of a predisposition toward deviant motivation is the manner in which the social structure, reflected in roles, statuses, organizational contacts, and interpersonal interactions, and the physical characteristics of the world impinge on the individual's ability to exercise control relative to his or her experience of control. The proximal outcome of these interlinking components constitutes an individual's "control ratio." For any individual, the control ratio reflects the degree of control that can be exercised relative to the degree of control experienced. Because the control ratio is complex, I want to explicate its features. However, it is important that the reader not become distracted by the details of this digression into the nature of the control ratio. It is important to keep in mind the major contention of control balance theory: An unbalanced control ratio, in combination with a desire for autonomy and fundamental bodily and psychic needs, predisposes an individual to act deviantly. Stated simply, the control ratio, which we are about to examine, plays a large part in generating motivation for deviance. Since everybody wants autonomy, any imbalance in the control ratio will, to some extent, predispose a person toward deviant motivation. However, the extent to which an individual is predisposed toward deviance depends on the magnitude of the desire for autonomy in combination with the control ratio.

By definition, the control ratio is the total amount of control to which an individual is subject relative to the total amount of control that he or she can exercise. Although the control ratio for any person is, in an overall general sense, stable, reflecting that person's social roles, statuses, and characteristics, it also varies from situation to situation as the individual confronts different social and physical entities and as different personal and situational characteristics come into play. Influences on the magnitude of an individual's control ratio, which may be more or less permanent features of the person's roles and statuses or may be purely situational, are called elements.

Individual Elements. An "element" is a feature of the individual, the individual's social relationships, the organizational network of the society, or the physical environment that helps constitute the operative control ratio for that person. Some elements are more or less constant in their effects, and others are dynamic. A constant element is one that almost always produces a particular relative degree of control experienced or exercised for any individual with that element. A dynamic element is one that only sometimes—situationally, irregularly, or episodically—comes into play to affect the control ratio of some individuals. Any individual's *general* control ratio can be described through reference to the constant elements, but for more accurate prediction one must also make adjustments for dynamic factors that determine *situational* control ratios. Some elements are constant, some are dynamic, and some may be both. The descriptions that follow include all three types, but it is indicated when an element is totally constant, when one is totally dynamic, and when one can be both.

1. Group-Linked Elements. Some of the elements constituting one's control ratio are individualistic in the sense that they represent descriptive characteristics of the person. Many such "individualistic" traits, however, are rooted in the social system and only have meaning in relationship to the groups or social networks of which the person is a part.

First, the most important contributors to a person's control ratio are the *roles* played and the *statuses* occupied. Every role implies some control to be exercised, both in a generalized sense and in the specific sense of how the role player is expected to relate to the reciprocal member or members of the role set. The role of parent implies substantial dominance over children, and a modicum of influence over school officials. The role of child implies that parents, school officials, and others who deal with children will exercise substantial control over the child. The role of physician implies substantial control over nurses, patients, and hospital personnel and a modicum of influence on political figures and others who respect the opinions of physicians. People in the role of patient will experience substantial control exercised over them and they will exercise a moderate amount of control in turn over health-care personnel.

In a similar way, the statuses that one occupies imply degrees of control exercised and experienced, regardless of anything else. For example, the status of being female, in addition to implying a set of role relationships vis-à-vis men, other women, and children, also implies some degree of subordination in most societies in the world. Women usually have less ability to control males than males have to control women; women usually even have less capability of controlling other women than do men; and females generally have less ability (in the sense of knowledge, resources, and strength) than men to exercise control over the environment. However, women usually have more capability of controlling children than do men. Racial statuses, as well, usually reflect abilities to control or to be controlled, and most occupational statuses imply something about the ability to rule others or the likelihood of being dominated by others. For instance, most of the time high-status people, by virtue of their jobs as supervisors or decisionmakers or by their access to financial resources, which permit them to manipulate physical and social arrangements, can control as much or more than they are controlled.

Of course, not every role player or status occupant exercises or experiences the control typical for that role or status. Some women exercise more mastery than most men; some minorities escape much of the control that is directed at other members of that minority group; and some low-status people exercise unusual sway, just as some high-status people exercise little. Nevertheless, composites of all the roles and statuses of specific individuals will provide a reasonable indicator of their general control ratios. It is important to note, however, that the general picture of a person's control ratio represented in a composite of personal roles and statuses will be crude. A better, but more difficult, index would accommodate the dynamic variations embedded in role/status configurations. For example, a particular female who usually has little command over males in her interactive environment may have a lot of control over one particular male who is attracted to, or in love with, her. This woman's control ratio is, therefore, more favorable in the presence of that particular male than it is in the presence of other males.

Second, although everyone plays many roles and occupies many statuses, a relatively small number of roles and statuses are so crucial that role/status configurations encompassing them will be fairly accurate reflectors of the overall control ratios of individuals. Since these "crucial" role/status configurations so strongly reflect master statuses indicated by specific demographic variables, one can assume that configurations of those specific *demographic indicators* will yield measures of the generally operative control ratio that are at least minimally correct.

Crucial demographic variables are sex, age, race, ethnicity, marital status, occupation, and wealth. For instance, in the United States, middle- aged, white, Anglo-Saxon, married, wealthy males with managerial occupations probably have the most ability to exercise control and escape control exercised by others. Conversely, those with the greatest deficit of control should exhibit an opposite combination of these crucial demographic characteristics—they should be black, elderly, unmarried, poor females in personal service occupations. Various control ratios could be assumed for individuals with other combinations of the crucial demographic variables.

However, despite the general tendency for configurations of roles and statuses, as reflected in crucial demographic variables, to signify an individual's control ratio, composites of such roles and statuses will constitute an imprecise measure. Not only are there some individual variations in the extent to which demographic variables indicate role/status configurations but even role/status configurations themselves blur a number of other elements that sometimes operate to generate individualized control ratios. These additional elements include both the personal characteristics of individual actors and organizational features.

Third, another important group-linked, individual element of the control ratio is a person's *reputation*. Reputation represents the collective regard or prestige accorded to an individual by the people in a social context, as well as a collectively held configuration of expectations about that person's behavior. Thus a woman known to be loud, aggressive, or troublesome has a reputation that may allow her to exercise more control over those with whom she interacts than another, less obtrusive woman could, even if she had the same role and status configuration. Further, a woman reputed to be gruff may escape regulation experienced by someone else with her general role/status configuration. Of course, such a woman may, in some circumstances, be subject to more control than would another woman with the same role/status configuration, and in some conditions she might be able to exercise less than normal control. Similarly, a male with a passive reputation can usually exercise less control over other people than one regarded as strong and aggressive, even though quiet, passive males sometimes win the confidence of others and dominate more readily than those noted for strength.

Some of the most potent reputations have a neighborhood or community base. Apparently, one of the most important determinants of the control ratio for people in deprived inner-city areas is "rep." Some who otherwise would be subject to a lot more control than they can exercise recognize that a reputation for toughness, violence, revenge, or chaotic unpredictability will change the situation and that a badass reputation will permit them to dominate future social encounters (see Katz 1988). Even so, dangerous reputations can sometimes deprive their holders of respect and of exercising control that others with their role/status configurations would ordinarily enjoy. Reputations that elicit fear may invite closer police attention, and they may spark challenges or resistance among those who would themselves build such reputations.

Reputation is even more important for the control ratios of the relatively few people—politicians, entertainers, sports figures, and so forth—who rely on large public followings. For reasons that are not entirely clear, most people go out of their way to accommodate the needs and desires of famous people, even when they do not like their public persona and even when there is no chance of financial or other tangible reward. Supporters and nonsupporters readily lend their homes and automobiles to governors and senators, surrender their airline seats if asked, and endure without complaint the inconvenience of their political motorcades. Similarly, bellhops, ushers, waiters, police officers, and passersby gladly show extraordinary deference to famous actors, recognized sports figures, and celebrated journalists. This same deference and attention, of course, implies that public figures also may be subject to greater control than others with similar characteristics.

Since an accurate account of control ratios must incorporate the person's general and specific reputations in the social contexts where that person's influence is relevant, role/status configurations, though useful general indicators of control ratios, cannot be fully accurate. Reputation, of course, often stems from patterns of past actual deviant behavior, so prior deviance is an important component of one element of the control ratio.

2. Personally Rooted Elements. Some elements that go into the control ratios for each person are more or less self-contained. Unlike roles and statuses or reputations, they have few linkages to the immediate social group or social network. These individual traits may be products of socialization, genetics, biological functioning, or some combination of the three, but their origins are not particularly relevant here. The important point is that they already exist in the psychic/emotional or physical makeup of the individual at the time that person comes into our range for explanation of deviant behavior.

The concept of *personality* is defined in a multitude of ways by different authors and includes so many potential traits that some of them may be contradictory (Pervin 1985, 1990). Nevertheless, nearly everyone recognizes that individuals exhibit relatively stable patterns of thinking, feeling, and acting that apparently reflect some internal psychic/emotional structure or organization (Caspi and Bem 1990; Caspi et al. 1994; Eysenck 1964; Wilson and Herrnstein 1985). If we know a person well, we can predict with a fair degree of accuracy how that person will react to situations. It is this consistency of reaction that I have in mind when I identify personality as an element influencing an individual's control ratio.

Few dispute that there are personal differences in capability of understanding the world, speed of learning, logical reasoning, capacity for abstract thought, readiness for vicarious empathy, or facility in using their intellects to manipulate (Caspi et al. 1994; Pervin 1990; Wilson and Herrnstein 1985). In addition, some individuals have a high degree of interpersonal skill, usually accompanied by self-confidence, whereas others have little interpersonal skill or confidence. Hence, at least three "person-

ality" traits—intelligence, interpersonal skill, and self-confidence—interact with role/status configurations to alter the control ratios that would
ordinarily be reflected by that role/status combination.

To understand how this works, imagine two individuals with identical
role/status configurations, but with differing intelligence, who are in
similar work situations involving little inherent ability to escape control
from supervisors or other workers with greater seniority. If we strictly
consider their positions, they both ought to suffer serious control deficits.
Yet the person with the superior intelligence may comprehend the social
realities more quickly than the individual with fewer mental capabilities.
The more intelligent person may realize that cultivating the friendship of
a particular boss or laying claim to particular tasks will permit exercise of,
and escape from, more control than the situation ordinarily implies.
Because this same thing is likely to happen in a large number of situations, it follows that the intelligent person will have a somewhat different
overall control ratio than will the less intelligent person.

In a similar way, interpersonal skills and self-confidence can narrow a
given configuration of elements into a control ratio somewhat different
from that which might be expected strictly on the basis of the role/status
configuration. Probably everyone recalls adolescent peers who got away
with a lot more mischief than others did because they were able to charm
parents, teachers, recreational leaders, and so on. They knew how to appear sincere, to be complimentary, to be lovable, and most important,
how to use knowledge they had about adult authorities to their own advantage, either to provoke guilt, generosity, or sympathy. Such individuals have different control ratios than similar adolescents without those interpersonal skills. Similarly, even though most women are cast into
repressed roles, some women, through personal charm, are able to manipulate men for their own benefit and to escape regulations that might
ordinarily be exercised against them. Finally, we know that because of
charisma some business executives and heads of other kinds of formal organizations are able to exercise and escape from even more control than
their positions warrant per se. The presidency of Ronald Reagan compared to the presidency of Jimmy Carter illustrates this as well as anything. With Carter, the "flypaper" president, everything seemed to "stick"
to constrain his movements; with Reagan, the "Teflon" president, nothing
stuck, so he could do just about anything he wanted. Clearly this was not
due to the office of the presidency itself, since both men occupied that office. Rather, it seems to have stemmed from the personal characteristics of
the two men (or at least from media images of those characteristics).

The role/status configuration, then, will not portray the control ratio
accurately for everyone in all contexts because it does not accommodate
personality factors that *can* sometimes make a large difference. Precise
characterizations of individual control ratios require some attention to
traits like intelligence, interpersonal skill, self-confidence, and other personality idiosyncrasies, as they interact with various role/status configu-

rations. I will not attempt to list all such personality characteristics but will leave it to the imaginations of researchers and other consumers of control balance theory to identify other relevant ones that I have not mentioned.

Another personal, dynamic element that sometimes leads to a somewhat different control ratio than might be expected on the basis of the role/status configuration alone is *physical appearance*. Being tall is often politically advantageous for a male because others automatically assume that tall men are authoritative and decisive. In a similar way, in interpersonal interaction, physical strength or an imposing physique sometimes enables a male to escape or exercise control that otherwise would not inhere in the specific role/status configuration. Physical attractiveness can be especially useful for females in altering the control balance that stems from interpersonal heterosexual interaction, since it gives the attractive woman more ability to control males and to escape from male control than unattractive women have in the same situations. At the same time, physical attractiveness can often put a woman at a control disadvantage in occupational or political domains because many people, females as well as males, are likely to attribute shallowness or simple-mindedness to attractive females.

In this connection, it might be noted that physical handicaps can also alter ordinarily expected control ratios of specific role/status configurations. Seriously undersized people are unlikely to have the dominating capability that full-sized people enjoy, even when they have similar role/status configurations. The same is true of people without the use of all their limbs or faculties. Yet, very unattractive or physically malformed individuals may sometimes escape the constraint that might otherwise be forthcoming because others attribute to them supernatural power, wickedness, or pathos. Such is the plight of some homely women who have had to live in isolation because neighbors feared they were witches.

Therefore, like personality, physical appearance must be taken into account to produce the most accurate characterization of an individual's control ratio. It should be emphasized, however, that both personality and physical appearance, which only affect people in some situations, are relatively unimportant compared with role/status configurations. Therefore these personal, dynamic elements will have minimal impact in the general case of predicting outcomes for a large sample, although they might have considerable effect on the accuracy with which control ratios enable us to predict outcomes for specific individuals.

Organizational Elements. More important than the individually rooted elements like personality and physical appearance that episodically affect the individual's control ratio, but probably less important than the relatively constant personal roles and statuses, are "group" or "organizational" elements that sometimes come into play. Whenever an individual is part of some organized group that can act collectively to exercise control on behalf of its members or to help them escape from control, that person's overall control balance will be somewhat different than it would be if he or she operated strictly as an individual occupying a particular role/status configuration, and that person's control ratio in some specific situations will be markedly different. Thus, organizational entities of one kind or another, whether begun or sustained for that purpose, have enormous importance in control relationships.

Almost everybody is organizationally involved, although the degree of such involvement, the strength or solidarity of the organizations, and the ability of the organizations to exercise control or permit their members to escape from their influence vary from individual to individual. Most people are members of families, which can sometimes act collectively on behalf of the individual; many are involved in formal organizations like labor unions, business organizations, legal-aid societies, religious groups, and political units; and some are involved in informal subcultural organizations.

1. Families. It is easy to appreciate that families can exercise control over their members, but families are also organizations sometimes capable of exercising control on behalf of their members. Consider the case of an adolescent female accused by a merchant of having stolen a piece of merchandise from a store. The merchant learns from the youth that her father is a lawyer and that her mother is a regular patron of the store. Rather than calling the police, the businessman calls the father to inform him of the situation. The father assures the merchant that it must be a mistake because his daughter has no reason to steal, and he reminds the merchant that he had better be sure of the facts if he reports this incident to the police. The merchant, aware of the potential damage a lawyer might cause him and cognizant that the profit he makes from the mother's regular purchases far outweighs the youth's theft, apologizes and lets the matter drop. In this case the family has allowed the youth to escape control to which she otherwise would have been subject; indeed, some might say it has even permitted her to exercise some indirect control over the merchant. Thus, because of her family, this adolescent has a different overall control ratio than many other adolescents.

A second example concerns a woman married to a prominent national political figure. Because of her relationship to him, she is often able to command his associates and is taken seriously by political and social groups when she urges action. She finds that businesses want to lend her clothing, transport her, give her gifts, and entertain her, and she finds that she can manipulate social and physical arrangements with little effort or resources of her own. This woman's control ratio is far higher as a spouse in this marital relationship than it would be if she were an independent entity, and it is much higher than if she were part of a less prominent family organization.

As these illustrations show, an individual's overall control ratio must include the control ability that is ordinarily exercised or experienced as a member of a particular kind of family. It must be recognized, however, that the additional control that can be exercised collectively through family organization is often desultory.

2. Interpersonal Relations. In a similar way, controls experienced and exercised by friendship networks are dynamic components of the control ratio. Imagine two lower-status, unmarried, female friends who like to bowl together. On a particular occasion, a rowdy bowler in the adjacent lane tries to force one of the friends to leave the bowling alley so that his daughter can use it for practice. However, as soon as the friend joins the argument, it becomes clear that the rowdy bowler cannot intimidate both adversaries. On another occasion, one of the friends backs into a car and smashes its headlight. The owner of the bashed car insists that the offender, because she does not have the requisite insurance, pay cash on the spot to replace the light or face the prospect of a police call. Having no money, the offender is saved from additional control being exercised against her by calling her friend who soon arrives with the cash. As these examples suggest, the control ratio is sometimes altered by friendship. Each of two friends may exercise and escape from more control than do similar people who face the world as individuals.

Consider also the case of two friendly corporate executives, both of whom would ordinarily have some surplus control. By cooperating, they escape some of the financial constraints that usually bear upon executives, and through their mutual organizational ties they are able to double their abilities to induce others to favor them. The implied threat that business from both firms, rather than just one, will be forthcoming or withheld, or the possible multiplication of capital resources made possible by that friendship, can serve as a potent counter to any potential constraining influences.

3. Formal Organizations. Other organizational networks, formed specifically for particular purposes, have pervasive as well as episodic inputs to the control ratio of the individuals involved with them. Purposive, institutionalized organizations characterize almost all realms of modern human existence. Indeed, some have referred to modern societies as "organizational societies," since practically all human needs are met and satisfied in formal organizations of one kind or another. Modern individuals, if they are to thrive, must learn to relate to, and through, organizations. Everybody must confront business and occupational organizations, often vast and impersonal, through which goods and services are produced and distributed. In addition there are religious, educational, recreational, political, and specialized interest organizations that act on behalf of, and serve the needs of, individuals. All of these formal organizations exercise some control over individuals, but they also can act on behalf of individuals to alter their control ratios vis-à-vis other organizations and individuals. In addition, some of these organizations can, on occasion, be activated on behalf of individuals who are not among their members.

One example concerns labor unions, which represent formally organized efforts to control employers, working conditions, and sometimes markets for goods produced. This control is to be exercised on behalf of the union members themselves to help counter the control that employers have over workers and the conditions of their work. Through collective action, workers can often get employers to do many things that the workers want but that employers would not otherwise do. These include increasing wages and fringe benefits, altering the pace of work in factories, continuing to employ unneeded or unproductive workers, and refusing to hire nonunion workers. Of course, union membership also implies that the workers must now accept additional union-linked controls on their own behavioral options that they would otherwise not have to endure, although such controls are far less than would be required if the workers faced employers as individuals rather than as a segment of a collective organization.

Union membership also has episodic import outside the work situation that may intrude into the control balance process. For instance, imagine two blue-collar workers, alike in all respects except that one is a union worker and the other is not, each of whom has a dispute with a grocery about some spoiled meat. The only control that the nonunion worker can bring to bear is his or her own interpersonal skill at persuasion, a threat not to patronize the store in the future, perhaps some threat of physical violence, or in unusual circumstances the threat of legal recourse—all of which probably will not counter the control the grocer can exercise in withholding the right to patronize the store, to involve the police, or to warn other grocers in the area of this individual's troublesome nature. A union worker, on the other hand, may be able to invoke the potential economic force of other union members who may boycott the store. In addition he or she may call upon the legal-aid resources of the union if need be, and the grocer knows that in unionized areas, local government, which can alter the conditions of his business, may be influenced strongly by union concerns (at least as long as they do not conflict with the corporate entities that employ union workers).

A second example of how membership in a formal organization can affect one's control ratio is the familiar situation of members of the National Rifle Association (NRA). Through their collective efforts they are able to exercise far more control politically than they could as individuals. In fact, for decades this organization has defied public opinion by influencing state and national legislative bodies in opposition to almost any form of gun control. Most politicians fear supporting the popular view because the NRA can mobilize influential political forces almost instantaneously. Just as union membership sometimes makes possible episodic, nonwork-related controls on behalf of the union member, so membership in the NRA sometimes generates "outside" alterations in control that can be exercised by its members. Because of common interests and association in the NRA, individual members often come to have an interpersonal bond that they would not otherwise have. This permits occasional mobilization of NRA associates and friends around personalized issues and problems.

Consider the hypothetical case of a hunter needing storage facilities for business papers while on a hunting trip. By invoking his NRA membership he may find a local soul mate who can help.

As these examples show, affiliation with formal organizations can affect one's overall control ratio, sometimes in unusual ways. It is also true that formal organizations sometimes come into play in episodic ways on behalf of nonmembers to alter predictable outcomes based on the general control ratios of the individuals involved. Nonmembers often benefit from the activities of the American Civil Liberties Union (ACLU), the National Association for the Advancement of Colored People (NAACP), and the Ku Klux Klan (KKK); that is, the control ratio of some nonmember individuals is increased by what these formal organizations do. For instance, an individual restrained by a law may escape that control when the ACLU takes up the case on his or her behalf, even though the individual in question may not even approve of the ACLU, much less have active membership. Individual African Americans may end up with a more favorable control ratio in particular situations because there is an unspoken possibility that the NAACP might take an interest in the case. Individual bigots may in some places and circumstances have more control over minorities because of the implied possibility that recalcitrant minorities may attract the attention of the KKK. The flip side of the coin, of course, is that some legal authorities, some employers, and some individual bigots are less able to exercise control because of the three formal organizations mentioned.

Although organizations like the ACLU, NAACP, and KKK are specifically formed for the purpose of altering the control balance of members and nonmembers, some formal organizations designed to serve only the interests of members occasionally also increase the control ratios of those who are not members. Consider the case of nonunion workers who are able to command higher wages, influence the conditions of their work, and avoid harsh controlling responses from area employers because union contracts in nearby areas have set standards that employers know must be met to avoid the flight of their workers to other areas. Similarly, the independent grocer escapes legislative control along with chain stores when an association of large corporate grocers is able to fight off wage and price regulations.

4. Subcultural Organizations. People with visible identifying traits who interact over a period of time usually end up informally organized to solve common problems or to satisfy widespread needs for companionship, support, or conversation (Fischer 1975, 1982). These organizations are not planned, nor are they conceived by the participants as purposive; they emerge spontaneously, waning or thriving as the immediate need requires. Nonetheless, because of the repeated sharing of common experiences, participants in informal networks often come to embrace distinct ways of viewing the world about them and to develop particular norms, statuses, artifacts, and language that differentiate them from the larger so-

ciety and from other groups. Moreover, these distinguishing traits sometimes pervade the lives of those who share them to the point that they are passed on from one generation to the next. Such subcultures can have substantial effects on the control ratios of individuals involved in them because, through actual or implied collective action, they sometimes permit individuals to exercise much control or escape from control that would not be possible for nonorganized entities with their particular role/status configurations. In addition, subcultural organizations sometimes subject their members to controls that they otherwise would not face (Fine and Kleinman 1979).

Evidence of *peer subcultures* and organizations among socioeconomic status categories, racial or ethnic minorities, adolescents, professional or occupational practitioners, and gender categories abounds (examples: Adler 1985; Brake 1980; Dollard 1957; Jenness 1993; Kephardt and Zellner 1994; Lewis 1961; Miller 1958; Mizrahi 1984; Nardi 1992; Schwendinger and Schwendinger 1985; Sebald 1992; Short and Strodtbeck 1974). Blacks in the American South during the mid-twentieth century, adolescents in the contemporary United States, and pipeline workers I observed in the Southwest during the 1950s illustrate how subcultural organizations can tip the control balance for their individual participants.

Until fairly recently, blacks in the South were exceptionally repressed by a united white majority. They were subject to controls by white employers, merchants, police, landlords, and random whites, and as individuals they had few ways of exercising control back over whites. However, because blacks usually lived in designated parts of towns and cities, they were able to interact around their common needs and problems, the most important one being their oppression at the hands of whites. Out of this grew a black subculture with distinctive norms, language, customs, and ideas. From time to time this subculture could be stirred into collective action to protect individuals from suffering the full force of white oppression. When white creditors or the police came looking for specific individuals, the black community usually united in silence as to their whereabouts, often even denying any knowledge of their existence. When some blacks refused to work for whites under intolerable conditions, the black subcultural community often shared scarce resources. When the demands of white employers were extreme, black workers often collectively dragged their feet, knowing that all of them would not be fired. In a number of ways, then, an informal, black, or African-American, subculture helped change and improve the control ratios of individuals.

A somewhat similar situation prevails with adolescents in the contemporary United States in that young people generally are the objects of far more control than they can exercise. Still, sometimes and in some places, adolescents are able to form an informal subcultural organization capable of acting collectively to divert some of the control exercised over them and to exercise some control back over adults. In many communities youth collectively conceal their activities from the eyes of adults; they share scarce resources like cars, money, and parent-vacated homes; they organize vigilante committees to punish particularly overbearing adults by throwing eggs, mutilating lawns, or destroying curbside mailboxes; and they build a curtain of silence to protect their peers who have offended adults.

The importance of work-related subcultural organizations in changing control balances that ordinarily characterize a particular role/status configuration was first documented in the famous Hawthorn studies, but it has been appreciated by working people themselves as long as there have been work crews. I can add my own young adult experience as a member on a natural gas pipeline crew to the Hawthorn studies. Although we workers were ostensibly heavily controlled by the job supervisors and the owners of the company, we were, in fact, able to exercise a lot of autonomy through our collective subculture. The job was to keep a stretch of the pipeline free of large plant growth so that inspection planes could spot leaks from the air and repair crews could traverse the line. The amount of work or time it took to keep that portion of the pipeline clear, however, was never known to anybody except the work crew itself, which was bound together in a mutually protective subculture. Some days we cleared a couple of miles, other days we sat around the shop reading, talking, or making home barbecue grills with company materials and tools. Yet the crew's official reports always showed a constant daily production of about 1 mile cleared. Higher authorities who inquired would hear stories about how hard we worked, our need for more men and equipment, and the dangerousness of the work. Moreover, any attempts by higher-level supervisors to personally inspect the work operation were easily turned into unpleasant ventures that discouraged future intrusions.

In most realms of human activity, informal peer organizations like the three illustrated above come into play to help determine the operative control ratios of individuals. For that reason, even though the individual's configuration of crucial roles and statuses permits a rough indication of control balance, it will contain many errors. These episodic elements must be taken into account for more accuracy.

The tendency for *institutional subcultures* to arise in institutional settings like prisons, hospitals, and schools is even more pronounced than it is in noninstitutional contexts. This may be due in part to the proximity of institutional inmates, but it is also probably because common problems are so salient in institutions. Whatever the reason, in places where individuals have the least ability to exercise control, tightly knit subcultures are most likely to develop to enable alteration of the control deficits of subordinate individuals.

Several studies have shown that the more repressive the place of incarceration (i.e., where the control arrayed against inmates is maximized, and the control that inmates can exercise in return is minimized), the greater the likelihood of a cohesive inmate subculture (see Tittle 1972).

Such subcultures usually have a set of norms and values emphasizing solidarity against the oppressors, and they impose social controls to help ensure that cohesion is maintained. Among the ways that inmate subcultural organizations help mitigate oppressive control are (1) by using organized networks to subvert the rules designed to restrict the inmates' freedom of movement, autonomy in deciding when and where to satisfy bodily needs, and availability of desired resources, and (2) by constituting the potential for organized resistance in the form of riots, work stoppages, or sit-downs that are dangerous or inconvenient for officials. Most prison authorities make accommodations with inmates in an informal symbiotic relationship within which officials and inmates tacitly agree not to make life too hard on each other if the favor is reciprocated (Cloward 1960; Sykes 1958).

A second example of a subcultural organization that helps soften control discrepancies is the type that grows up among college students. These networks can sometimes make life miserable for professors who are too hard on students (from the students' point of view). In concert, students can embarrass a professor by complaining constantly in public or to the administration, they can refuse to do the work, they can simply stop coming to class (called "blowing it off"), they can be noisy and inattentive, and in the end, they can rate their teachers low on the student evaluations (or if that is not possible, they can undermine reputations by filling personnel files with complaint letters). In addition, almost everywhere, students share information about professors, courses, previous exams, and ways to circumvent administrative regulations.

In short, crucial role/status configurations omit much that is relevant to control balance, and even more extensive role/status configurations including those of student or prison inmate subcultures do not tell the whole story. Simply being a student or an inmate does not necessarily imply subcultural membership and the control that goes with it. Institutional subcultures have to be regarded as dynamic elements that vary situationally.

Finally, many people are interlinked with *specialized subcultures* built around specific, sometimes bizarre interests, and on occasion the collective action implied by those involvements can make role/status configurations somewhat inaccurate as foci for measuring control ratios (see Fischer 1984). Specialized interests include hobbies, like stamp collecting; economic concerns, like grocery customers worried about prices; or recreational activities, like skydiving. In such cases spontaneous organization to protect individuals from outside control or to extend control of the enthusiasts can burst forth. However, the most important specialized subcultures are those oriented around particular forms of deviant behavior. Social scientists have documented subcultures of theft, illicit drug use, white-collar crime, child molestation, homosexuality, bigotry, and deviant sectarian religious practices, among others (for examples, see Gagnon and Simon 1967; Hamm 1993; Jamieson 1994; Kephardt and Zellner 1994;

LaBarre 1969; Levine 1979; Polsky 1967; Sutherland 1937; Wilson and Cox 1983; see also Akers 1985). These deviance-focused subcultures have important effects in generating *contingencies* under which the control balance process operates, which will be discussed later, but they also function as any other subculture does in providing the possibility for collective exercise of, or escape from, control.

For example, through collective efforts to conceal their activities, religious handlers of poisonous snakes (La Barre 1969) protect themselves from the reach of the law that prohibits the practice, as well as from the controlling influences of other community members who disapprove of the practice. They also share resources when outsiders deprive them; they conceal the whereabouts of violators and violations; and they intimidate would-be snoopers who are afraid of the snakes and suspicious of what their handlers might do. Finally, it is even conceivable that on occasion they could boycott local businesses or use snake-handling demonstrations to disrupt activities of legitimate organizations. Of course, involvement with this kind of subculture not only affects one's control vis-à-vis others outside that subculture, but it also subjects one to control from other members of the subculture collectively and personally, and perhaps enables one to exercise some control over other subcultural members as individuals.

Ratios. Since control ratios represent the degree of control exercised relative to the degree experienced, they can be expressed as fractions and arrayed on a continuum with deviations in positive and negative directions from a midpoint. Control ratios can be exactly 1, greater than 1, or less than 1. If a control ratio is unity, or reasonably close to it, experienced and exercised control is balanced. A control ratio above 1 represents a control surplus, and if it is less than 1, the individual has a control deficit.

Although control ratios conceivably can take on an unlimited number of values, small differences are theoretically meaningless. The theory is not concerned with extremely fine gradations among control ratios, at least not at the present state of its development. Rather, it focuses on seven zones on a continuum. The middle zone, encompassing control ratios reasonably close to unity, is called the "balanced" zone. Deviations from the midpoint in the positive direction include three zones representing progressively greater degrees of control surplus: the zone of "minimal" surplus, the zone of "moderate" surplus, and the zone of "maximum" surplus. Similarly, deviations from the midpoint in the negative direction encompass three zones of increasing control deficit: the zone of "marginal" deficit, the zone of "excess" deficit, and the zone of "extreme" deficit.

Although the theoretical effects of control ratios will be specified in terms of these seven zones, I want to make it clear that the effects predicted by control balance theory are not fully discrete. Although the consequences of being in the middle of a particular zone of the control ratio continuum are clearly distinguishable from the consequences of being in the middle of another zone, those differences begin to fade near the edges of the adjacent zones. At the present level of theoretical development, I prefer to regard those as "transition" spaces reflecting somewhat ambiguous possibilities. Later I hope to reduce that ambiguity, but for heuristic reasons the theory will be presented in terms of categories.

Basic Needs. Not only do people possess a fundamental desire for autonomy that interacts with their control ratio to generate propensity toward deviant motivation, but the control ratio also interacts with various primary desires to produce a predisposition toward deviant motivation. These initial impulses include hunger, thirst, sexual need, desire for entertainment or amusement, as well as various activities that gratify fundamental bodily or psychic needs. The likelihood that these urges, or needs, will be blocked is strongly linked to the individual's control ratio; when blocked, they constitute predispositions toward deviant motivation. Although everybody has such desires that potentially propel behavior, their exact form and degree vary from person to person in ways that are sometimes referred to as "tastes."

Summary of Predispositions Toward Deviant Motivation. Predisposition toward deviant motivation has three components: (1) bodily and psychic needs; (2) a basic, universal desire for autonomy, the magnitude of which varies only slightly from person to person; and (3) the control ratio, which varies greatly because it reflects many elements that differ among individuals. Since there is usually little variation from individual to individual in desire for autonomy, and since bodily or psychic needs are seldom severely restricted, for all practical purposes predisposition toward deviant motivation is reflected by the person's control ratio. Therefore, the theory assumes that predisposition toward deviant motivation varies directly with a control imbalance—in either direction from the balanced zone.

Situational Influences on Deviant Motivation

Having a predisposition toward deviant motivation, however, does not necessarily lead to deviant motivation or to deviant behavior. For deviant motivation to emerge, those predisposed toward it by an imbalanced control ratio must comprehend, or perceive, the possibility that deviance will alter their control ratios in an advantageous way. Since the variables that are likely to create a perception that deviance will advantageously alter control ratios are mainly situational, I call them *provocations*. Although some degree of provocation is necessary to activate the causes of deviance, the extent and intensity of situational provocation also represent a contingency under which the causal mechanisms of the theory operate with greater or lesser efficiency. They will be recalled in that capacity and will be discussed further later.

Relevant Features of Provocations. Those predisposed toward deviant motivation may not actually become motivated toward deviance, just as those motivated toward deviance will not necessarily engage in deviant behavior. Thus, although "background" variables are necessary for deviant behavior, they are not sufficient to account for its occurrence or form. Other things have to transpire or be present in the situational "foreground" (compare Birbeck and LaFree 1993).

For deviance to ensue, individuals must become fully conscious of their control ratios and of the possibilities for changing them through the use of deviant behavior. People have a general sense of their control ratios, but most of the time they operate with only secondary awareness of their deficits or surpluses. Everyday life is so routinized that most people rarely contemplate their control ratios. Yet everyone, from time to time, experiences circumstances that bring to mind the balance of control. Moreover, though most people are seldom conscious of what alternatives they might have for altering control balances through deviance, almost everyone encounters situations that make those possibilities come to life.

Provocations—contextual features that cause people to become more keenly cognizant of their control ratios and the possibilities of altering them through deviant behavior—can take the form of specific behaviors by others, such as verbal insults, challenges, or displays of weaknesses. Having one's mother insulted, for instance, is often a verbal provocation that calls the control ratio to mind for young males, as is a racial slur and the questioning of masculinity. On the other end of the control continuum, fawning displays by subordinates, as well as outright refusals to obey, often inspire thoughts about control ratios in the minds of those with surplus control. Provocations may manifest themselves as a special convergence of controlling impingements, such as receiving a pile of bills, getting laid off a job, and having the car break down within a short period of time. In addition, provocations may come in the form of sensual stimuli like seeing food when one is hungry, finding oneself alone with a willing sex partner after having been snubbed by a spouse, or seeing someone flaunt money shortly after one has been denied medical care for monetary reasons. Provocations can stem from direct communications reminding the person of subordination, for example, being told that he or she is not entitled to enter a building, issue an opinion, or enjoy certain perquisites. Provocations may also result from news about organizational changes, such as being notified of governmental action restricting one's favorite recreational activity. All of these circumstances are provoking because they arouse contemplation or thought about the overall state of one's life and they stimulate awareness that some actions can, at least temporarily, help rectify the control imbalance or help extend one's control. Thus, it is on these occasions that the deviance associated with a given control ratio is likely to occur.

Consider juvenile misbehavior. Adolescents are most likely to commit deviance (both defiant and predatory) when they are in the company of their peers, interacting in ways that are not formally organized. Social scientists typically explain this as a product of peer pressure (the individual feels that the others expect him or her to misbehave in order to be accepted). Without discounting that explanation, control balance theory suggests that the group context for most adolescent deviance stems from the enhanced sense of control adolescents feel when they are together, relative to the feelings of having little control when they confront the world as individuals. Peer group support and group action induce deviance because they remind young people of their usual control deficits and because communication within subcultural peer organizations generates awareness that individual control ratios can be altered in a favorable way through collective action.

In other words, adolescent subcultural activities generate acute awareness of repression, and they empower the adolescents to change it, at least temporarily. Peer interaction fosters the notion that sharing responsibility will enable participants to escape some of the controls to which they are usually subject. Interaction among adolescents also helps reduce perceptions of the likelihood of being caught and punished, since the bravado usually accompanying such interaction rests partly on discounted risk. Finally, attempts to rectify an imbalance of control through defiant or predatory acts have more effect when witnessed by peers than when undertaken alone. When peers witness a demonstration of controlling behavior, they will recall it on other occasions, talk to others about it, and perhaps come to respond to the individual in the future in terms of that act. Simply stated, deviance in the company of peers can enhance one's control on that occasion as well as pay actual and vicarious dividends in the future (see Short and Strodtbeck 1974, chap. 8). Thus, although almost all adolescents are repressed, not all commit acts of deviance, and among those who do deviate, the frequency of such behavior varies from individual to individual. Yet when deviance does occur, it usually does so in the context of peer subcultural activity. The fact that not all adolescents commit deviance is, in part, because all adolescents are not accepted in adolescent subcultures and are therefore less likely to encounter situations enhancing awareness of control ratios or offering the hope of successful response to it.

A second example is the exploitative deviance committed by corporate executives who authorize dumping of toxic wastes into rivers after having carefully calculated that those who would be harmed most immediately—farmers and fishers along the river—will not be able to do much about it. Businesspeople do these things when they become aware that they, through the corporate vehicle, enjoy a surplus of control, which can be extended by this means. Of course, in the case of corporate executives, such provocations are probably quite common, since concern with business operations and profits is a continuous, routine activity (which is why exploitation is so common).

Emotions. Provocations call to mind control imbalances and stimulate awareness that deviance can move one toward equipoise mainly by rousing a set of "emotions of subordination," including feelings of humiliation, debasement, degradation, and loss of face (compare Scheff and

Retzinger 1991; Sherman 1993). Such emotions can be experienced by those with surpluses of control as well as by those with deficits. Given the nearly universal desire for autonomy, people with a deficit will obviously suffer such emotions when pointedly reminded of their weaknesses. Those with control surpluses experience "emotions of subordination" when reminded of those surpluses because of anxiety about losing autonomy and because reminders challenge assumptions that superior control obligates others to pay homage. Feelings of belittlement are uncomfortable, so they impel action. Thus, not only are people "hardwired" to seek autonomy, which, under various control ratios, constitutes a propensity for becoming motivated toward deviance, but they are also moved to action by feelings of debasement that stem from provocative situational factors.

Direction of Response. Provocation plays an essential part in deviance by calling attention to the person's control ratio and by stimulating the perception that deviance can help rectify a control imbalance. However, response to provocation is not necessarily directed against the stimulating agent. The point of deviance is to correct an *overall* control imbalance. This can often be accomplished by increasing people's control over individuals and situations not directly involved in the provocations that remind them of the need for, and the means of, deviance. To be sure, there is always considerable pressure to direct corrective action toward objects, events, and people that bring control imbalances to mind, much as ancient kings killed messengers who brought bad news. Nevertheless, deviance is not necessarily focused on provoking agents.

Consider some examples. A bar patron is verbally "put down" by a companion but physically attacks a laughing bystander rather than the person who issued the insult. A woman is fired from her job and goes home to abuse her child instead of stealing from the company or defiantly refusing to leave the premises. A teenager spots a bundle of money on the counter of a bank and is inspired to burglarize a house in the neighborhood but makes no attempt to vandalize the bank. Finally, an individual is refused access to the lavatory in the first-class section of an airplane and says nothing until the driver of the taxi on the way to the hotel makes a wrong turn. Hence, it would be a mistake to look only in the immediate provoking situation for the behavioral expressions activated by provocations.

Variations in How Potential Provocations Are Interpreted. Although provocative characteristics of the immediate context constitute the main stimuli for the perception that deviant behavior will favorably alter one's control ratio, individualized cognitive factors set the parameters within which provocations can operate. For example, perceptions that deviant behavior will favorably alter one's control ratio are not always accurate. Indeed, the anticipated advantage to be gained from deviant behavior often proves disappointing, especially in the long run. Furthermore, what is demeaning to one person may not be humiliating to another. To understand deviant motivation fully, therefore, one must take into account internal psychic factors that vary substantially from individual to individual, such as differences in perceptual acuity, behavioral habits, certain personality characteristics like impulsivity, intellectual and social skills, and values or "tastes" that bear on the likelihood that one will perceive advantage in deviant behavior in particular circumstances. Internal psychic factors also influence the chances that the person will actually resort to deviant behavior after grasping the possibility that it would help to alter the control ratio. However, since these variables bear on the efficiency with which the control balancing process operates rather than constituting essential components of that process, they are treated as contingencies, to be discussed more fully later.

Provocational Calculus. Control balance theory portrays deviant motivation as a product of situational cost-benefit assessments, but this does not imply that potential deviants go through extensive mental calculations to arrive at motivating perceptions. Perceptions of the usefulness of deviant behavior might sometimes be the product of careful thought, but most of the time the person is afforded only a momentary glimpse of what might be. Moreover, the theoretical argument does not imply that deviant motivation is clearly or well-understood by the potential deviant actor. In fact, most of the time humans are only dimly aware of their own perceptions or motivations. In general, thoughts that deviance will modify control ratios are so fleeting that those who act on them often cannot understand later why they committed the resulting acts. Violators are sometimes completely amazed, even embarrassed, about how they viewed the situation at the time of the offense and about what they did.

Structural Foundations of Provocation. Although the beliefs and perceptions that deviant behavior will favorably alter an individual's control ratio and the accompanying emotions of abashment are clearly "within" the person and are influenced by the preexisting psychological makeup of the individual, deviant motivation is depicted in control balance theory mainly as a situationally rooted variable. Something in the immediate social or physical environment draws attention to the control ratio and renders it an acute, salient concern. Such situational provocations represent the interplay between a basic human desire for autonomy, the social structure, and the encounters an individual faces in his or her social roles, statuses, organizational contacts, and interpersonal interactions. Hence, neither a control ratio nor its correlative motivation for deviance is a component of personality, and the theory, though focused on the behavior of individual persons, is basically a sociological theory. The key variables, control ratio and deviant motivation (the perception that deviance will alter the control ratio), are at least structurally or situationally linked, and are perhaps largely determined by structural or situational variables.

Summary of Deviant Motivation

Control balance theory identifies deviant motivation as a key variable for predicting deviant behavior and asserts that it varies from individual to individual and from situation to situation. The degree of deviant motivation a particular person exhibits in a particular circumstance results from a combination of four things. First, deviant motivation reflects basic predispositional desires for autonomy, stemming from variations in degrees of dependency experienced as an infant and child. These desires for autonomy are assumed to vary only slightly from individual to individual. Second, individuals possess some fundamental bodily and psychic desires that, if blocked, predispose them toward deviance. Third, deviant motivation contains a predispositional component called the control ratio, which is the degree of control that one can exercise relative to that which one experiences. The control ratio is itself composed of more or less stable conditions of control embedded in role and status configurations along with dynamic elements that vary episodically and contextually. Finally, deviant motivation, defined as a perception that deviant behavior will advantageously change the control ratio, depends on provocations in specific situations that are interpreted by individuals using varied cognitive and other psychic equipment.

Since the yen for autonomy is only slightly variable, and fundamental "needs" are rarely challenged, predispositions toward deviant motivation are mainly expressed in control ratios. Predispositions do not become actual motivations, however, without being provoked by things in specific situations that cause the person to perceive that deviant behavior at that time will be advantageous in altering the control ratio. The discrete presence or absence of such provocations is conceived as an essential part of the deviance-generating process, but their magnitudes and frequency are portrayed as contingencies for the operation of the control balance process. Though provocations are based on external events and structural realities, they are not entirely objective or concrete since they depend, in part, on perception and interpretation and are usually part and parcel of an emotional reaction.

Constraint

Constraint is a third key concept in control balance theory. Ordinarily constraint implies something similar to "experiencing control," meaning that someone or something can be prevented from doing something, or hindered in the effort to do something, by social or physical barriers or by anticipating some unpleasant social or physical response. In the theory, however, *constraint* refers to the probability, or perceived probability, that potential control will *actually* be exercised. The control ratio indicates the extent to which control efforts can potentially be brought to bear against a person; constraint refers to the actual probability that potentially controlling reactions will be forthcoming. Constraint, then, is a product of three factors: the control ratio, the seriousness of a given act that might activate controls embedded in the control ratio, and the chances that the behavior in question will be discovered by those for whom it is serious (called "risk").

Relativity of Motivation and Constraint

The theory contends that a major variable in explaining deviant behavior is motivation—the perception that deviant behavior will alter a person's control ratio. As will be shown later, the sheer probability of deviance of some kind is mainly a function of motivation, but motivation alone is not enough to account for specific types of deviance. Among other things, the effect of motivation in producing specific types of deviant behavior depends on the relative degree of constraint. An individual with 100 units of behavioral motivation to do a particular thing is not likely to do it if he or she also faces 100 comparable units of constraint, whereas an individual with 10 units of motivation but only 1 unit of constraint has a much better chance of committing the act. Note, however, that it is the relative magnitudes of motivation and constraint that are important and not the absolute magnitude of either, because within the theory, people with 100 units of motivation but subject to 70 equivalent units of constraint are equal to people with 10 units of motivation experiencing 7 equivalent units of constraint, as far as predicting particular deviant acts is concerned.

Risk

A necessary variable affecting the type of deviance likely to be committed (although not the overall chances of some form of deviance) is the probability that a deviant act will instigate countercontrols inhering in the control ratio. The chance of countercontrol activation, however, depends on situational peculiarities as well as the seriousness of the act. Burglary almost always involves some chance of activating control, but that risk is higher when it is done in daylight and in certain sections of towns or cities, and risk is higher if a police car happens to be driving past. Corporate collusion to fix prices is seldom totally free of risk, but it may be more dangerous when particular attorneys general hold office and when particular political parties hold power (Simpson 1987; but see Salinger 1992 for contrary evidence). The same applies to all the various kinds of deviance. Without risk, constraint would become irrelevant, and deviant behavior would be much more likely, which is why risk is an essential component of the explanatory process. However, since the very fact of risk is ubiquitous, the theory's basic explanatory principles take it for granted while focusing on its *magnitude*. When situational risk is greater than or less than average, predictions from the theory will be more or less effective, so the extent of risk is treated as a contingency to be discussed more fully later.

Opportunity

An opportunity to commit a particular kind of deviance is defined as a circumstance where that behavior is possible. Situational features that render deviance possible, of course, vary with the type of deviance in question. An opportunity for predation, for instance, necessarily involves access to a potential victim (or a victim-related object or thing of value) for that particular type of predation and a set of physical realities making the predatory act feasible. A robber must have access to another person with something of value to the predator and must not be diverted by physical barriers; in addition, for eventual triumph, the would-be robber must show superior physical strength, cunning, or weaponry. Theft necessitates access to an object of value with the potential thief having the physical strength or cunning to make off with the object. The requisites for burglary are access to a structure containing something of value to the predator and the means to enter the building and remove the things of value. Rape demands access to another human, usually a female, along with an inequality of physical strength, cunning, or weaponry. People living alone in remote areas rarely come into contact with someone with things of value, much less a potential victim who is inferior in strength, cunning, or weaponry. Similarly, isolated farmers or herders seldom see potential victims of rape, and they rarely approach buildings that might contain valuable commodities or encounter objects to be stolen. Hence opportunities for these predatory acts are much less for such individuals than for residents of densely populated areas.

In a similar way, opportunity to commit exploitative deviance is defined as a set of circumstances involving access to potential victims whose resources or cunning are less than those of the exploiter, at least temporarily, and a convergence of physical arrangements. To manipulate stock prices by creating the image, through a rapid sell-off of stock, that a particular company is on the skids, one must own or control enough shares to create the desired image, the external aspects of the company must appear shaky, and victims must lack the acumen or information to see through the scheme. Such situations occur only occasionally, and they are not equally likely to happen, even to individuals with a minimal surplus of control.

So it is with opportunities for all kinds of deviance. No matter how favorable the motivational and constraint configuration, the actual likelihood of deviance occurring depends on there being an opportunity for it to happen. In addition, however, since opportunity varies episodically with the situation, we must also regard frequency and magnitude of opportunity as important contingencies under which the control balance process operates.

General Summary

The theory of control balance explains deviance as a product of the tension between motivation and constraint when individuals try to rectify imbalances of control. Deviant behavior occurs when several variables come together in a favorable alliance. First, provocative features of a situation activate predispositions toward deviant motivation, generating a perception that deviance will enable the individual to alter a control imbalance; second, an opportunity to deviate exists; and third, the probability that deviance will activate controlling responses is propitious. The chances of deviance, in general, are a product of the magnitude of motivation and opportunity, but the probability of particular kinds of deviance is the result of a complex interplay between motivation, opportunity, and constraint.

The most important concepts in the theory are control, deviant motivation, constraint, and opportunity, but they are meaningful only in reference to a number of additional concepts. Control is defined broadly to incorporate the idea of total ability to limit the behavioral options of others and resist such limitations on one's own behavioral options. Behavior is portrayed as an expression, though modulated and deflected by various circumstances, of an individual's control ratio, or amount of control that can be exercised relative to the control that is experienced. The control ratio, a complicated mix of elements bearing on the interplay of control exercised or experienced, along with a fundamental desire for autonomy and some basic human needs, is described as intersecting in various ways to structure a person's predisposition for deviant motivation. Transformation of those predispositions into actual deviant motivations by provocations (acts or conditions that generate a perception that deviant behavior may alter a control imbalance) represents one condition for the occurrence of deviant behavior, and the presence of opportunity (circumstances making deviance possible) is another. The type of deviance likely to be committed, however, depends on the potential for countercontrol, which is a reflection of the control ratio, the seriousness of the deviance, and risk (the chances of the deviance being discovered by those for whom it is serious).

Even though the underlying ideas of control balance theory have been interwoven into this discussion of concepts on which it is built, the exact causal mechanisms of the theory remain vague at this point. In the following chapter I will explicate those causal mechanisms. In the process I will try to answer the questions *how* and *why* deviance occurs, attempting to do so in such a way that researchers can generate predictions from the premises of the theory.

7

The Causal Process
of Control Balance Theory

The main assertion of control balance theory is that the overall probability of deviance of some kind, as well as the probability of a particular type of deviance, is heavily influenced by the interplay of deviant motivation with constraint. Both deviant motivation and constraint are largely functions of control, meaning whatever amount of control can be exercised relative to the amount to which the person is exposed, as well as the likelihood that potential control actually will be exercised. The process by which these variables converge to produce deviance, however, is complex, and it involves other concepts. Figure 7.1 displays this process.

The Underlying Model

The diagram in Figure 7.1 cannot be interpreted like a conventional causal model; it is offered only as a device for clarifying the arguments being presented. This diagram uses the following notations: (1) the heavy solid arrows indicate strong or predominant influences, the narrow solid arrows represent secondary or lesser inputs, and the broken lines express minor influences; (2) each bracketed number indicates a nexus of converging variables, or concepts; and (3) the pluses and minuses show projected positive and negative influences and the plus-minus combinations indicate that the effect may be positive or negative, depending on the circumstances.

Linkages Among the Variables and Conditions

Beginning in the upper left-hand corner, one will find basic human impulses, with a broken arrow going directly to the ultimate dependent variable, deviance, and a slim solid arrow leading to nexus [1]. Recall that basic human impulses are primary movers of human action that include biological drives as well as social desires. Although many of these, such as the need for food and water, are universal, their magnitude and form vary from person to person, so they can be referred to as "tastes." This

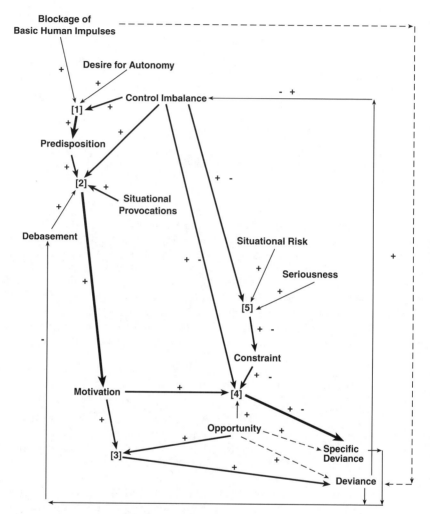

Figure 7.1   Causal Linkages of Control Balance Theory

variable can be defined as whatever an individual recurrently finds important to acquire. These primary urges or needs may have a small direct effect on deviance, indicated by the broken arrow, but their main import stems from their "interaction" with other variables to produce motivation, which is the perception that deviant behavior can change or alter an imbalance of control.

The second concept in the network is desire for autonomy, which is the fundamental yen to escape control over oneself and to extend one's control over the physical and social environment. This characteristic varies only slightly from person to person and as a result can barely be called a variable. However, it is included in the diagram to denote its importance as a necessary condition for the entire causal process underlying control balance theory. Desire for autonomy forms a nexus with control imbalances and basic human impulses to create a predisposition for being motivated toward deviance. That effect is shown by the arrow to [1].

The most important concept is control imbalance, which can be either a deficit or a surplus, as reflected by the control ratio. Control imbalances converge with basic human impulses and desires for autonomy to create a predisposition to become motivated toward deviant behavior. This is indicated by the heavy solid arrow leading to [1]. Control imbalance also constitutes a major force in the overall causal scheme in a number of other ways: (1) through its convergence with situational provocations and feelings of debasement or humiliation in nexus [2] to stimulate actual motivation for deviant behavior, (2) through its "interaction" with motivation, constraint, and opportunity (nexus [4]) to produce specific deviance, and (3) through alliance with situational risk and seriousness (nexus [5]) to make up constraint. Its importance in these interactive outcomes is signified by the moderately heavy solid arrows from it to the bracketed intersections. The underlying theme through which control imbalances are implicated in the production of deviance, and the underlying motif of the theory, is this: Deviance is a device to alter fractional control ratios (those that do not equal 1) and to relieve feelings of humiliation that stem from being reminded of one's unbalanced control ratio. This theme is depicted in the negative thin solid arrows from deviance back to control imbalance and to debasement. These arrows are thin because, even though deviance is undertaken to relieve problems associated with a control imbalance, it usually has only minor consequences for the person's overall control ratio and in most instances the effect on humiliation is only temporary. Sometimes deviance will result in permanent alteration of the control ratio. This can happen in one of two ways. An individual may end up stigmatized or incarcerated, either of which would affect the amount of control that can thereafter be exercised relative to that which is experienced, or, the deviance can be so successful that it has long-range import, such as might happen when an executive acquires millions of dollars through exploitation. These varied possibilities are indicated by the plus and minus signs on the return arrow to control imbalance.

Nexus [1] represents the interplay among basic human impulses, desire for autonomy, and a control imbalance. Typically this involves some blockage of a primary impulse that keys into the fundamental desire for autonomy and plays on an unbalanced control ratio. Thus, three conditions have to come together in a particular alliance for predisposition to emerge. Although basic human impulses may sometimes be strong enough to lead directly to deviance, such impulses alone are usually not enough. Normally, they must be denied, or potentially be subject to denial—a phenomenon that is intimately linked to control imbalances. Deviance, then, almost always starts with an inability by a person with an unbalanced control ratio to satisfy a primary impulse.

The interalliance of primary impulse, desire for autonomy, and a control imbalance in Figure 7.1 is indicated as a bracketed nexus apart from predisposition. This is to make clear that predisposition toward deviant behavior is not a straightforward linear consequence of three variables. Rather, a peculiar "interaction" of the three variables, or conditions, constitutes predisposition. Interaction does not necessarily imply a linear multiplicative effect, or even that the effect of one of the variables is dependent on the value of another. It means, simply, that a minimal degree of all three must exist simultaneously for predisposition to prevail.

Predisposition toward deviant motivation, however, will not produce deviance unless other links in a causal chain are forged. One of those links involves the actual materialization of deviant motivation. Motivation is the outcome of an interactive nexus involving predisposition toward deviant motivation, situational provocations, and feelings of debasement. Typically this interactive convergence comes about when a person with a predisposition toward deviant motivation encounters some circumstance that (1) creates a feeling of abasement or humiliation centering around realization that his or her ability to control is less than it might be, relative to others, and that (2) generates a perception of deviant behavior as a means to alter the source of subordination, the control imbalance, or the effacing emotions stemming from having been reminded of the control imbalance. At this point in the causal network, the three variables are linearly interactive. Whereas predisposition is a necessary condition without degrees of strength, motivation can be expressed in magnitudes. Stronger motivations are more important than weaker ones, and the strength of motivation is a product of the intensity of situational provocation and the degree of debasement experienced, both of which are rooted in the magnitude of control imbalances.

However, even very strong motivation toward deviance is not sufficient to produce deviant behavior. At least one other variable is necessary for the production of deviance, and that variable is opportunity. Deviance cannot occur without social and physical conditions making it possible. Thus, nexus [3] involves the intersection of motivation with opportunity. The theory contends that this nexus is both necessary and sufficient to produce some form of deviance, although knowledge of it alone will not predict a specific type of deviance. The general probability of deviance of some unspecified type is independent of constraint because, given opportunity, motivation can be expressed in any kind of deviance that constraint permits, and constraint always permits some form of deviance, even if it is submission. Hence, the diagram shows nexus [3] leading to deviance but not to specific deviance.

It is important to recognize that the alliance of motivation and opportunity is not a multiplicative interaction. Opportunity is a discrete variable representing a necessary condition for any deviance. An individual's opportunity for deviance can vary in frequency, however, as can his or her frequency of motivation, so that there is a multiplicative interaction between frequency of motivation and frequency of opportunity that enhances the likelihood and frequency of deviance over a given period of time. Moreover, opportunity alone may sometimes, though rarely, lead to deviance without motivation. This possibility is noted by the broken arrows from opportunity to deviance and to specific deviance.

Motivation for deviance leads to specific deviant acts through causal nexus [4], involving the intersection of motivation, opportunity, control imbalance, and constraint. Motivation implies the perception that deviant behavior will alter a control imbalance, and the theory assumes that such perception encompasses a stimulus to employ the most effective deviant behavior for that purpose; potentially, the most effective deviant behaviors for shifting a control ratio are the most serious ones. Opportunity, of course, signifies that the given deviant behavior can possibly occur. Given appropriate motivation and opportunity, the actual odds of a particular form of deviant behavior occurring, however, depend on constraint and the direction of the control imbalance. Constraint is itself the outcome of an interactive causal nexus [5] among control imbalance, seriousness of the potential act, and situational risk. This alliance is cumulative: the greater the magnitude, the greater the constraint. Given some degree of motivation and an opportunity, the magnitude of constraint as well as the direction of the control imbalance will determine the specific deviance: the greater the constraint, the less serious the deviant behavior that is likely to occur. Furthermore, the direction of the control imbalance influences the specific type of deviant act likely to be committed. Imbalance on the deficit side portends repressive-type deviance, whereas control imbalances on the surplus side augur deviances of an autonomous type.

Although the control ratio is implicated several places in the causal network, none of the variables acts alone to produce the predicted outcomes. Thus, even with ample opportunity and favorable individual disposition to commit a particular deviant act, that deviance may not occur if there are no provocations to raise the person's consciousness or if the risk of activating countercontrols is too great. Similarly, even with opportunity and provocation, high risk may intrude to prevent the deviance. The occasions for deviance are those where all of the conditions and variables specified by the theory come together simultaneously, a circumstance that is often unusual for specific individuals with particular control imbalances.

Application

Because the causal process implied by this model is conditional, it cannot be fully evaluated using typical approaches. Conventional methods with standard criteria should yield supportive results, but measuring a few key variables to see if they independently predict deviance will not reveal the richness of the theory. Any of the central causal variables should predict deviant behavior better than chance, but examining the theory in that way underplays more complicated and precise outcomes. Even large absolute associations between any one of the causal variables and deviance will not be particularly meaningful. In deriving and testing highly focused predictions (hypotheses), one must consider the different conditions and variables simultaneously. Overall evaluation of a series of such hypotheses will be far more useful than limited tests of single, general hypotheses about the effects of central variables. Moreover, the efficiency of the theory, and the accuracy of its predictions, depend on contingencies that are not part of the internal structure of the model portrayed in Figure 7.1. Incorporating those contingencies into hypotheses should make predictions still more accurate.

It should also be obvious that variables converging at different points in the causal chains are not independent of earlier variables. For instance, since control imbalance is implicated in four of the five causal intersections, conventional statistical methods requiring independent predictors will not be easily interpreted. Moreover, since a number of the causal linkages are nonlinear, the tools routinely used in research, especially those normally used to estimate causal models, cannot be employed in straightforward fashion to assess the empirical adequacy of this theory. The acid test will not be whether most predictive coefficients can be shown to be statistically significant, or whether an overall interactive network of linear effects proves to be statistically adequate, but will instead be whether, considered as a whole, an interlinked set of quite specific, conditionalized hypotheses, often implying nonlinear effects, provides accurate predictions.

Furthermore, the model is dynamic; all of its parts are intimately linked so that changes in any one proliferate throughout the network. This is especially important since (1) the theory is founded on feedback relationships between deviant behavior and both control imbalances and feelings of debasement, and (2) several of the variables in the theory are situationally volatile. Any "snapshot" test of the model will be less informative than will tests that assess changes through successive iterations and use proximate measures.

Finally, the theory must be applied in different ways to account for different aspects of deviant behavior. It explains the probability of deviance of unspecified form in a different way than it explains particular kinds of deviance. Furthermore, to explain the frequency of deviance, the components of the theory must be applied in yet another way. Before explicating exactly how the theory does these things, I want to make it clear that this discussion of the complexity of the theory, and the resulting difficulties involved in application and testing, should in no way be interpreted as an effort to escape empirical accountability or as an attempt to render the theory nonfalsifiable. As I will show later, numerous hypotheses can be derived from the theory and tested empirically, a multitude of hypotheses constituting coherent "sets" can be evaluated empirically, and there are even ways to assess the fit of the overall model to the real world. Results from any or all of these approaches could challenge the theory, and a collection of such nonsupportive outcomes would ultimately doom it. At this point, I am simply trying to show that the theory is capable of generating uncommonly sophisticated applications and that really meaningful tests of it will key into that complexity.

Probabilities of Deviance

The theory implies that an individual's general probability of engaging in some form of deviance is mainly a reflection of that individual's motivation toward deviance. Opportunity for deviance to occur is an essential component of any deviant act, but opportunity for *some* kind of deviance is almost always present. Further, since motivation for deviance is largely a reflection of the person's control ratio, the probability of deviance, in some form, is a function of control ratios. However, these probabilities form a U-curve with respect to the control ratio. They are lowest when the control to which an individual is subject is balanced by the control he or she can exercise, and they are at maximum when the control ratio is most imbalanced, in either direction, that is, deviance is most likely when there are large deficits of control as well as when there are large surpluses.

Although the probability of deviance in general is chiefly a direct expression of motivation toward deviance, the actual commission of deviant behavior is not a mechanical manifestation of preexisting, background variables. Rather, deviant behavior stems from a proximate causal process involving several situational variables. First, the actor must be motivated toward deviance. This motivation comes from a combination of predispositions toward motivation and immediate circumstances that generate awareness of the control ratio and perceptions that deviance will help change the balance of control. Second, there must be opportunity to commit the act; opportunity is completely situational. Third, except for submissive deviance, the chances of countercontrol must not be overwhelming. Potential countercontrol is partly predetermined—by the control ratio and by the seriousness of the act—but it also reflects the situational component of risk.

Control Deficits

A person with a control deficit is predisposed toward "repressive" forms of deviance—predatory, defiant, or submissive—and the greater the magnitude of the control deficit, the greater the total chances of one or another of these deviances. First and foremost, the greater the control deficit, the greater the chances that predatory and defiant forms of deviance will help rectify the imbalance. Second, the effects of impulses toward deviance that stem from desire for autonomy and from pursuit of ordinary goals are to a large extent absorbed and reflected in the control ratio. Third, although provocations that might activate propensities toward deviant motivation are situationally variable and perceptions of their potentialities are affected by individual differences, the import of control ratios is so great that even with situational provocations varying widely, gross probabilities of deficit-generated deviance can be predicted. Fourth, constraints that might counter motivations toward deviance mainly affect the type of deviance likely to be expressed rather than the likelihood that any deviance at all will occur. This is because constraint usually causes deviantly motivated people to choose less serious forms rather than to refrain from deviance altogether.

Consider an example. Everyone has numerous primary goals, perhaps including acquisition of food and shelter, sexual gratification, group acceptance, prestige, entertainment, and so forth. Since the chances of achieving those goals are strongly influenced by control ratios, people with control deficits are sometimes doubly motivated toward deviant behavior: They are motivated by blockage of the primary goal that results from their relative control disadvantage, and they are further motivated by the debasement inherent in a control deficit. Hungry people want to get food, but the greater their control deficits, the less their capacity for soliciting, buying, or demanding it. Furthermore, if hungry people cannot get food that is readily available to others, they will feel even more acutely disadvantaged. If, in addition, they are told directly that the food is only for those who are already enjoying it in abundance, they will feel hunger and disadvantage, and they will feel demeaned, insulted, or otherwise humiliated. Most such victims quickly recognize that stealing can potentially relieve their hunger—that is, it will achieve their initial goal— and at the same time it will help them conquer their feelings of abasement or ridicule, which at this point may be even more important than hunger. In addition to becoming motivated to steal, they will in all likelihood also want to slug the person, perhaps a grocer or restaurant worker, who withholds food or dispenses verbal humiliation. Hurting a grocer or restaurant manager would help balance the unfavorable control ratio implicated in this hypothetical situation because it would put the attacker in charge, at least for the moment. Assault or theft dramatically shifts the terms of control, thereby allowing those with a control deficit to overcome their feeling of debasement.

Thus the hungry individual in the example above is doubly motivated to steal because theft would permit him or her to achieve an initial *and* a situationally generated goal. Successful theft would satisfy the physiological need for sustenance, but equally important, since people are rarely actually starving, it would overcome the circumstances, at least temporarily, of denigration. Theft, therefore, is attractive in part because it affords some control over those who ordinarily control the potential thief. Hence, the person may be motivated toward theft or assault by the dynamics of the situation even when the deviant acts hold little promise of satisfying hunger. Thus, the theory takes for granted that people are propelled toward various gratifying acts, but it contends that these primary "pushes" will not lead to predatory, defiant, or submissive deviant motivation or behavior unless they are blocked, and the likelihood of blockage is closely linked to the individual's control deficit. Moreover, the blockage itself enhances potential motivation toward deviance because it keys into the desire for autonomy in a way that generates feelings of debasement or humiliation.

Although much deficit-generated deviance involves double motivation like that described above, humiliation associated with control deficits often motivates deviance even when no initial, basic need is obvious. Most of us have been in situations where someone has made us acutely aware of our relative control deficit, even when we were not actively pursuing any focused goals, but rather were doing nothing, or basically minding our own business in a nondirective sort of way. An example would be adolescents sitting around a shopping mall when a security guard approaches and tells them to leave. Even though their initial goal of resting or "goofing off" is not a particularly powerful motivator even when blocked, the action of the guard, especially if delivered in a demeaning tone, will nevertheless create a strong motivation toward acts that the youths did not previously contemplate. They want to get back at that person to show that they cannot be pushed around. In other words, they feel the urge to balance the scales of control. It may occur to them that they ought to steal something just to spite the security guard and those the guard represents or to demonstrate that they cannot be humiliated with impunity. They may also momentarily contemplate an assault. Surely most people in such circumstances will want to protest verbally, call names, defy the guard's admonition by challenging authority, or in the final analysis pretend to obey but drag their feet as a way of signifying they are not totally subordinate. The point is that the main motivation toward deviance occurs in the acute realization that one's control is less than that of others. Sometimes this motivation reinforces other motives, which are in most instances linked to the control ratio as well, but it may stand more or less alone and still exert strong influence on the probability of deviance.

Indeed, lest the hunger example cause the theory to be misinterpreted as an emphasis on material deprivations, it should be noted that the main focus of control balance theory in explaining repressive deviance is on the deprivations of control and the feelings of being "put down" that accompany comparatively rare material blockages and the more frequent blockage of trivial impulses or that often stand alone without any apparent barriers to goal achievement. Initial "ordinary needs" are of comparatively little import. Hence, the theory is consistent with the observation that much property crime is not linked to real material deprivation (Cameron 1964; Cohen 1955; Curran 1984; Hepburn 1984) and that most acts of violence follow trivial insults rather than serious affronts (Katz 1988; Luckenbill 1977, 1984). Control deficits sensitize people to environmental reminders of their subordinate positions regardless of, or in addition to, the usually operative motivators of action. It is the realization of relative weakness of potential control that constitutes the chief motive for deviant behavior.

Of course, a person with a serious control deficit faces the possibility of controlling reactions from others who might be affected by efforts to rectify a control imbalance through deviant acts. The greater the potentiality that the deviant acts will inconvenience, hurt, or threaten the social positions of those against whom they might be directed (the more serious the act), the greater the chances that controlling responses will be activated. Thus, individuals with a control deficit are both highly motivated and highly constrained. However, constraint is act-specific. Therefore, when a person highly motivated toward a serious form of deviance faces the possibility of massive controlling responses, that person will usually forgo that particular expression for fear of activating the potential controlling responses reflected in the control ratio and in the type of deviance being contemplated. Nevertheless, such individuals will still be motivated toward deviance, and if they can, they will fall back on a less serious form of deviant expression. Hence, deficit control ratios will always be positively linked to the total chances of committing predatory, defiant, or submissive deviance.

Control Surpluses

As explained above, predisposition toward predatory and defiant forms of deviance flowers into actual motivation when specific situations stimulate a person to recognize that deviance is a possibility and that it holds the promise of rectifying the control imbalance. The theory also contends that control "surpluses" reflecting ability to exercise more control than that to which one is subject will express themselves in "autonomous" forms of deviance—exploitative, plunderous, or decadent. Consequently, the greater the control surplus, the greater the chances of some form of autonomous deviance. This is so because (1) autonomous deviance is most likely to permit the fullest extension of control for those who already have a surplus, (2) the effects of the universal desire to escape controls on oneself and to extend one's control over others, as well as the pursuit of ordinary goals of life, are absorbed and expressed in the control surplus, (3) the effects of the control surplus are so important that they overshadow other variables, and (4) countercontrols mainly affect the type of deviance rather than the simple probability of some form of deviance occurring.

Consider again the case of hunger, but this time imagine people with control surpluses for whom severe hunger is extremely unlikely. If food is available, they can get it, and they will seldom encounter any negative reactions from grocers or restaurant workers that would humiliate or demean them. However, if resistance should appear, they can call on their resources to overcome it. Normally, however, even without activating their potential controlling abilities, individuals with a surplus of control will witness others going to extraordinary ends to accommodate the needs of people like themselves with control surpluses. However, given the fundamental drive toward autonomy, which in this case involves a desire to extend control as far as possible, the actions that a grocery clerk or restaurant worker willingly takes to provide food for the person with superior control actually motivate deviance on the part of the superior controller. They do this by spurring the superior's awareness that deviance will further enhance his or her control advantage.

Imagine a famous, wealthy, or powerful woman entering a restaurant and nobody noticing or doing anything more to accommodate her than they would for an ordinary customer. She will feel slighted and suddenly become aware that she has not gotten the deference she deserves. Then she will be inspired to use some of the control at her disposal, by offering an advance tip, or bribe, demanding to see the manager, or using sharp words to remind the restaurant personnel of their responsibilities toward her. If there is resistance, she is likely to become motivated to use deviance to extend her control; she may contemplate threatening to have the host fired (exploitation) or storming to her favorite table and ordering anybody in the way to move out (plunder).

Suppose, on the other hand, that restaurant workers immediately recognize her and rush up to take her coat and escort her to a desirable table. Since this is expected and routine, no motivation toward deviance would be generated. However, suppose that in addition to this ordinary special attention, the restaurant host led this woman into the dining room, ostensibly pushing aside someone else in order to acquire the most desirable table for her. Since this extra deference is unusual, it also would provoke an awareness in the woman of her superior control, and it would generate motivation to use deviance to extend that control even further. The famous customer might then contemplate telling the host to order all the customers in the room to leave (exploitation) or demand that the chef drop everything and immediately prepare her a special dish (plunder).

Hence, there is double motivation in the case of a control surplus just as in the case of a control deficit—the motivation generated by blockage of the goal of obtaining food (hunger) and additional motivation generated by the realization that the controller's dominance can be extended. As with control deficits, surpluses themselves may create a motive toward deviance even in the absence of a specific, focused goal like hunger. Those with surplus control often find others seeking ways to please them even when the controllers exhibit no visible specific goal. A superior does not need to be hungry in order to induce those with less control to offer food. Control is, therefore, often exercised without direct intent simply because the potential for superior control evokes ameliorative reactions.

When control is successfully exercised, whether in response to resistance or without direct intent, it generates awareness of potential further extension, and if that potential extension involves exploitation, plunder, or decadence it constitutes deviant motivation. In the example being considered here, provocation comes from the willing acquiescence of those who possess the food. Regardless of its source, however, deviant motivation stimulates efforts to extend control as far as possible. The limit to extending control is the point at which effective resistance is encountered, which, of course, is linked to the seriousness of the deviance. Even in the face of potentially effective countercontrolling responses, those motivated to use deviance for extending control surpluses will not usually give up but instead will resort to a less serious form of autonomous deviance.

One implication of all of this is that people with control surpluses usually do not feel grateful for things, whether they are in need or not at the time and regardless of whether there is resistance to their acquisition. Instead, awareness of superior ability to control leads them to think that others should acquiesce, and they usually imply, or directly say this, to those with inferior control. This generates feelings of humiliation among those with inferior control. When situations allow those with relatively less control to perceive the potentiality of deviance for rectifying the control imbalance generating those feelings, repressive deviance is likely. Therefore, to some extent deviance is reciprocal. Efforts to extend control surpluses are likely to lead to efforts to overcome control deficits.

This process is evident in the restaurant example. The wealthy woman assumes superior service and food to be her right. Privileges have made her insensitive to the feelings of subordinates, and by extending her control she humiliates the restaurant workers, thereby generating awareness on their part that deviance would rectify the control imbalances under which they suffer. As a result they may contemplate spitting in her food or defecating in her car (defiance) or perhaps stealing her purse or slugging her (predation). In like manner, supervisors often lose sensitivity to the feelings of their workers and begin to perceive obedience to supervisory commands as their right. In conveying this, the line between work directives and degradation becomes blurred. The likely result is that the workers will become motivated toward defiance (as in work slowdowns) or predation (such as stealing company property) for alleviating the control imbalance that always existed but came into acute focus with the overbearing actions of the work supervisor.

Summary of the General Probabilities of Deviance

The theory contends that the principal determinant of the *probability* of deviance of some kind occurring is the strength of motivation to correct a control imbalance or to extend a control surplus. Since the strength of motivation is so closely linked to individual control ratios, the likelihood of deviance is a function of the magnitude of the ratio of control exercised to control experienced, beginning from a point of balance (a ratio of 1) and extending in both negative and positive directions. The lower the control ratio, measured in a negative direction from unity, or the greater the ratio, measured in a positive direction from unity, the greater the chances of some form of deviance being committed.

These effects are portrayed in Figure 7.2 by the upwardly ascending lines as one moves outward from the center along a continuum indicating the magnitude of the control ratio. The probability of deviance in the balanced

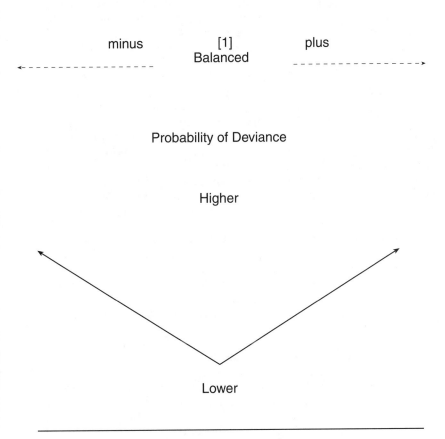

Ratio of Control Exercised to Experienced

minus [1] plus
Balanced

Probability of Deviance

Higher

Lower

Figure 7.2   Continuum of Control Balance and Types of Deviance

zone (where the control ratio is close to 1) is very low, but it rises steadily as one proceeds along the continuum toward the ends on each side.

Types of Deviance

Basic Assumptions

Control balance theory asserts that various imbalances of control determine the type of deviance likely to be committed. Explanation of the type of deviance involves an additional variable not implicated in the explanation of the general probability of deviance. Whereas the probability of some act of deviance being committed depends on the strength of motivation for deviance that stems mainly from the degree to which control abilities or capacities are unbalanced, the likelihood that particular forms of deviance will be committed depends jointly upon the total volume of control that can possibly be brought into play and the probability that potential control from other entities will actually be used. The chances of actual use of potential control depend on the seriousness of the act that might be committed.

To understand how motivation and constraint intersect to influence the chances of deviant behavior of a given type occurring, we must recognize three simple assumptions. First, everybody is motivated to do some things, either because of primary needs or because of socially generated desires. Second, some of what any given person wants to do is objectionable to or disadvantageous to others, or it is difficult to do, given physical and social circumstances. Third, if what an individual wants to do is troublesome to others and those others are in a position to do so, they will limit the extent to which the things can be done. A corollary of this third assumption is that if the things that an individual wants to do are difficult, given the physical and social circumstances, that individual's options are limited (he or she is controlled) by the "structural" and physical arrangements. Since no individual is capable of totally preventing others from limiting his or her options and since everyone will at some time desire to do things that are impossible or difficult in the physical and social environment, everyone is subject to some control, that is, everyone's behavioral options are limited by potential actions of others or by the physical and social structure.

At the same time, everyone has some capacity to limit the options of others. Even seemingly helpless infants can exercise control over adults, especially their parents, by making disruptive noises. Those within earshot of such noises, whether parents or not, will almost inevitably have to make some adjustment. They may attend to the infant's needs, leave, put in earplugs, ask someone else to do something about it, learn to ignore the noise, abuse or kill the baby, and so on. Hence, without any conscious awareness of its ability, a screaming infant can control others.

Similarly, the lowest-status slave can limit the options of his or her master (as well as the options of other slaves) by working slowly, displaying insolence, or ultimately, by committing suicide. Each of these patterns has some effect on options available to the slave owner. The owner might punish or reward a slow-moving slave to induce faster work, try to persuade the slave to do better, threaten to punish others if the slave does not improve, try to get other slaves to influence the recalcitrant one, ignore the situation and accept the loss of income that the slave's labor would otherwise produce, and so forth. An insolent slave can be handled in similar ways, or ignored, but even passive acceptance requires some effort by the owner. If the slave commits suicide, the owner has to take a financial loss, make arrangements for replacement or change the expectations of those benefitting from that slave's labor, and attend to the details of disposing of the body and personal effects.

Although everyone can potentially control and is potentially controlled, the relative balance of those potentialities differs from individual to individual. Those differences are expressed in control ratios, which predict the general probability of some form of deviance. However, to understand the likelihood of specific types of deviance, we must focus on the chances that particular deviant acts will actually activate potential countercontrol. The massiveness of potential control that can come from other entities depends upon the magnitude of the imbalance of control abilities and capacities (the individual's control ratio), whereas the likelihood that potential control will actually be used depends on the seriousness of the act.

For instance, even though people may be subject to large deficits of control (by definition, abilities or capacities), they are not likely to experience the actual exercise of that controlling potential unless they do something serious. Some acts by individuals with a control deficit will almost certainly inspire use of controlling capacities or abilities by other social entities, but different acts will inspire use of those capacities only rarely. Very serious acts (those regarded as the most unacceptable, consequential, or threatening to those with capacities of control over the individual) will have a high probability of provoking the controlling responses inherent in the individual's control ratio; less serious acts are less likely to provoke the full use of controlling abilities.

Whether those motivated toward deviance actually commit specific deviant acts depends to a large extent on the chances, or perceived chances, that those acts will activate countercontrolling responses. The acts that are most appealing to people with control imbalances are usually also those most likely to activate the potential countercontrols implied by the control ratio. Individual behavior, then, represents a trade-off between motivation and constraint. Ironically, the higher the motivation for deviance, the more the most effective (for rectifying a control deficit or extending a control surplus) potential deviant acts are to create problems for others (i.e., they are serious acts) and the greater the likelihood that the acts will provoke countercontrol. The actual chance of a specific form of deviance occurring, then, is a reflection of the relative strengths of motivation and constraint.

Clearly, I am claiming that individual behavior is influenced by the likelihood and magnitude of anticipated controls (sanctions, limitations on future conduct, and so on), that is, that people's actions can be, and typically are, curtailed, partially curtailed, or channelled into alternative behaviors by anticipation of the likely controlling responses of others. If a specific type of deviance that an individual is likely to commit in an effort to alter his or her control balance is perceived as highly likely to evoke strong controlling reactions by others, the individual will be deterred from that act, and if strongly motivated, will turn to a type of deviant behavior perceived as less likely to evoke potential controlling responses.

Some will find this argument surprising in view of the inconsistency and weakness of evidence in support of the "deterrence doctrine" (Burkett and Ward 1993; Decker et al. 1993; Grasmick and Bursik 1990; Williams and Hawkins 1986). I hold to it for several reasons. First, the idea that constraint affects human behavior is imminently logical. Indeed, it is difficult to imagine how people could be totally unaffected by potentially punishing, limiting, or unpleasant responses from other entities (Meehl 1971). Furthermore, in the theory, constraint is systematically intertwined with a coherent network of processes so that the logic of the whole supports the logic of the separate parts.

Second, evidence about deterrence is not necessarily relevant to the general idea of constraint because much of it concerns only one source of potential control—formal operation of the law—and only direct punishment. The concept of constraint is far broader than this, encompassing a range of informal interpersonal, organizational, and structural sources, as well as a variety of different kinds of constraining elements. Hence, the bulk of deterrence research is tangential to the fundamental ideas of control balance theory. The most relevant extant deterrence research, although it too is narrowly focused (on interpersonal elements), has been consistent and fairly strong in support of the idea that individual perceptions of informal negative reactions from significant others affect individual behavior (Paternoster 1987; Tittle 1980a).

Nevertheless, the effects of constraint as conceived in this theory have never been investigated. To ascertain if constraint works as portrayed, researchers must investigate a broader range of informal controlling reactions (not necessarily sanctions in the basic sense). In addition, they will have to measure constraint in terms of the potential deviant acts that might be committed (which will be interlinked to variations in control ratios) relative to those actually committed. Constraint (or deterrence) should not express itself in straightforward variations in rates or probabilities of crime or deviance, or even in the probabilities or rates of specific offenses. Rather, its effects will be seen in choices of one form of deviance over another, varying among individuals depending on their control ratios and differing with the seriousness of the acts in question in specific contexts.

The Mechanics of Cause

Control imbalances on the deficit side imply that as the strength of motivation increases, the ability of others to exercise countercontrol also increases, but this is only one aspect of potential countercontrol. Another aspect of potential constraining response depends on the seriousness of the act in question. Since any control deficit provokes a desire to rectify the situation, all individuals with a control deficit are prone toward motivation for behaviors perceived as maximally effective for overcoming those deficits. However, such behaviors are also the ones regarded by others as most dangerous or threatening, that is, individuals with a control deficit will want to commit serious acts of deviance.

When people's overall control deficits are small, they will be able to contemplate committing serious deviant acts without excessive fear that controlling responses will be marshaled in response. Although such acts have a high probability of provoking some kind of controlling response, the abilities and capacities of others to control are not enough greater than the individual's to fully curtail the behavior. Hence, relatively small control deficits imply some probability of serious acts of deviance being committed, though most such acts will be deterred. As a result, those "marginal individuals" with relatively small negative control imbalances have low probabilities of deviance in general, but when they do commit deviance it is likely to be predatory in form. This is due to a complicated convergence of motivation and constraint. Those with marginal control deficits have less motivation for deviant solutions than those with moderate or extreme deficits, but they, like all people with control deficits, are mainly interested in predation because it is the most effective potential device for rectifying negative control imbalances. Yet, because it is serious and stimulates countercontrol, predation is rarely used. Those most likely to employ predatory behavior in the face of greater potential counterresponses are actually the ones who suffer the least control deficit, that is, those with marginal, rather than moderate or extreme, control deficits. This is because the amount of control that can be brought to bear against a marginal individual, relative to the control that can be returned, is not great enough to discourage all predation.

As the magnitude of the control deficit increases, however, and individuals become more motivated to commit serious deviance, they are less able to imagine that such behavior will escape controlling responses from others. Hence, as the control deficit increases, people search for less serious means to help rectify the imbalance of control because less serious acts have less chance of provoking the full weight of steadily increasing potential control responses from other entities. In short, as the magnitude of a control deficit increases, the probability of some form of deviance goes up, but the seriousness of the likely behavioral response decreases. Further, since predatory deviance is regarded by most social entities as more serious than defiant acts, predation corresponds with small control deficits, and defiant acts of deviance correspond with larger control deficits. In other words, those who commit defiance would commit predation, but their control deficits are too large to allow much chance of escaping counterresponses from those with more control. However, given their relatively high motivation toward deviance, they resort to defiance as a less effective but safer ploy. Since submissive deviance is regarded as even less serious, or threatening, than either predation or defiance, it is associated with overwhelming control deficits. "Extreme" persons—those with large control deficits—are highly motivated toward deviance and would employ predation or defiance if they could. Since those forms of deviance are more likely than submission to provoke counterresponses, and by virtue of their large control deficits, extreme individuals are in the weakest position to escape countercontrolling responses. In fact, they are in such weak positions that they cannot even contemplate the possibility of an alternative.

The same processes are at work on the surplus side of the control continuum. Although people with the ability to exercise more control than they experience are motivated to extend their control as far as possible, the chances of provoking controlling responses from other social entities serve as a check. Hence, the probability of deviance of some kind varies directly with the magnitude of the control surplus, but the seriousness of the deviance likely to be committed varies directly with the magnitude of the control imbalance, rather than inversely, as it does on the deficit side. With slight surpluses of control, individuals, or social entities, can only commit less serious deviant acts to extend their control because of the possibility of provoking controlling responses from other social entities, but as the control imbalance gets larger, those with surpluses of control can anticipate less and less likelihood of generating controlling responses from others. Hence, the seriousness of the deviance likely to be committed varies directly with the extent of control surplus the individual or social entity enjoys.

Manifestations

These effects can be illustrated with two overlapping continua and their corresponding types of deviance (Figure 7.3). One continuum reflects a continuous variable representing *lesser* ability to control relative to being controlled, or repression. The second reflects *greater* ability to exercise control relative to being controlled, or autonomy. These two continuous variables extend in opposite directions on the same underlying continuum, running from extreme repression on one end (the same as extreme lack of autonomy) to maximum autonomy on the other end (the same as maximum absence of repression). As already noted, autonomy and repression can be conceived as specific to particular domains of activity as well as being overarching. For instance, an individual's autonomy can be conceived of in a total sense, encompassing amounts of control experienced relative to that exercised, in all realms of human activity, or it can be conceptualized in terms of a specific domain of concern. Hence, some individuals may have medium autonomy in most realms of life, although they may have a control deficit in a particular domain such as sexual expression. Others may be repressed in terms of the totality of human activity, but nevertheless be autonomous in some sphere such as religion.

Repressive Deviance. The center of the continuum represents balance—approximately equal amounts of autonomy and repression. In that zone we expect conformity (conscious recognition of the rules with stud-

Overlapping Continua

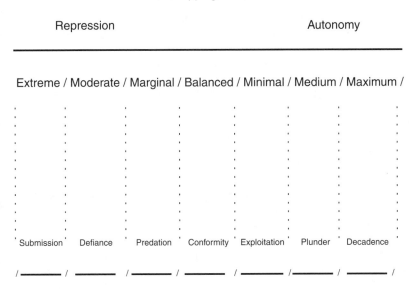

Figure 7.3 Continua Representing Variation is Control Ratio and Predicted Forms of Deviance Associated with Position on those Continua

ied obedience). People in other zones of the continuum are liable to commit one or another form of deviance. Consider the three zones of increasing repression (decreasing degrees of autonomy). The first one-third of that part of the continuum is a marginal zone. There people are subjected to somewhat more control than they themselves exercise, but they are not so controlled that they have no freedom of action. They have some likelihood of becoming motivated to overcome their control deficit by taking things from others or by directly forcing others to do what they want. The predisposition for this motive stems from the residual, universal disgust at being controlled, as intensified by a current situation in which individuals are subject to more control than they exercise. Because the deviance that would most effectively rectify the control imbalance is also most likely to activate countercontrolling responses, the chances of curtailment of the potential deviance are high. Nevertheless, the imbalance of control is small enough for people in this situation to sometimes be able to imagine that they can escape control from others. Such people have a low probability of deviance generally, but they are also the ones most likely to commit predation. Predation includes such things as theft, assault, rape, or homicide, as well as any behavior in which one person directly preys upon another person or entity, such as when a mother invokes guilt in her children to gain their attention.

The second, or moderate, zone of repression contains people with modest control imbalances, and it is likely to generate defiant behavior. These people have a stronger predisposition to be motivated toward using deviance as a device that might enable them to overcome their control deficits than people with slight control deficits do, but at the same time the control to which they are subject permits them less freedom. Their relatively larger control deficit renders too great the cost of serious acts that might otherwise help rectify the imbalance. As a result, moderately repressed persons have a relatively high probability of some deviance, but they will not commit predation very often. Instead, they are liable to engage in deviant acts of protest against the sources of the control deficit they experience, or they will less dramatically register their frustration by withdrawing from participation. Defiant acts allow people to escape unfavorable control without running the risk that the full force of countercontrol will be brought down on them. The result is deviance like defiance of parental and legal curfews and other status offenses among adolescents, mocking denigrations of power holders by student rebels or striking workers, sullen obedience by children, or exaggerated overconformity by employers or students. Occupying an extremely repressed position may also lead to escape behaviors like alcoholism, drug abuse, suicide, family desertion, mental illness, or countercultural involvement.

The extreme zone of repression (the last one-third of the continuum) is associated with submissive deviance. The very large deficits of control characteristic of individuals here lead to extremely strong predispositions for motivation toward using deviance to help rectify their situations. Yet, such people are so disadvantaged that almost any deviant behavior can activate strong counterresponses. Hence, potential predatory and defiant acts are curtailed, or deterred, and in most instances, extremely repressed people are left having to accept subordination. Repetitious subjugation dulls the human spirit and erodes cognitive creativity. The result is a high probability of slavish submission without the ability to imagine alternatives.

Autonomous Deviance. There are also three zones on the autonomous end of the continuum. The first is that of minimal autonomy. Here individuals exercise slightly more control than that to which they are subject. Their motivation to deviance stems from the desire to extend their own control, which is inspired by blockage of basic human impulses and situational provocations, including circumstances where the control they already have is successfully implemented. Nevertheless, because they cannot totally escape control by others, they are restrained from direct acts of deviance that would activate such countercontrolling responses directed against themselves as individuals. Instead, they use exploitation, which involves indirect predation, as a safer means of expanding control, that is, they use their controlling positions to arrange things so that other persons or organizational units accomplish acts that enhance their control.

Such persons may mandate price-fixing (if they are corporate executives) or shakedown schemes (if they are gang leaders who can induce neighborhood gangs to sell protection to local merchants). They might also profiteer through influence peddling (legislators taking bribes to vote on legislation favorable to the briber), buy off, or injure adversarial entities (famous actors making financial settlements with complainants to escape bad publicity or athletes hiring someone to injure their competitors). Furthermore, they might use third parties to extract money or dignity from victims (estranged wives creating provocative situations between their husbands and other women to yield evidence for more favorable divorce settlements or pimps living off the earnings of prostitutes who have tricked their clients). Finally, those with minimal surplus of control are liable to contract with others to bring about the punishment or death of a troublesome person (organized crime figures having an uncooperative judge pistol-whipped or business partners using soldiers of fortune to eliminate troublesome associates).

The second zone on the positive end of the continuum is that of medium autonomy. Those with such control imbalances can exercise considerably more control than they experience, that is, they are relatively free of being controlled at the same time that they can control others. By observing that others generally concede to their anticipated needs and wants, individuals with medium autonomy come to perceive that there is relatively little to restrain their actions, and repeated success produces insensitivity to the absence of autonomy among those whom they can control. The freer people are from control, the less appreciation they have for the condition of others; control corrupts its wielders because they cannot relate to subordination through recent personal experience. Characteristic forms of deviance are really selfish acts—forms of plunder—that include things like environmental pollution inflicted by imperialist countries whose leaders are in search of scarce resources in underdeveloped countries, programs of massive destruction of forests or rivers for the personal gain of corporate owners or executives, unrealistic taxes or work programs imposed by autocratic rulers, enslavement of natives by invading forces for the benefit of military commanders, pillage of communities by hoods doing the bidding of crime bosses, pogroms through which political or military leaders try to exterminate whole categories of people they find undesirable (as in the Hitler-imposed holocaust or the devastation of Native Americans by any number of people during the frontier expansion in the history of this country), and acts of tyrants like Jim Jones, who ordered the suicide of hundreds of his People's Temple followers (Hall 1987). Those occupying this medium zone of autonomy are simply indifferent to the needs of others or to their potential responses.

The maximum zone of autonomy includes those with very large control surpluses. Occupants enjoy almost total freedom to exercise control over others and to act as the mood strikes without concern for countercontrol. Even more than those with medium control surpluses, individuals here are stimulated, by the slightest provocation and by the very success of previous intended or unintended extensions, to increase their already substantial control advantages. Very few people find themselves in this situation, but those who do have a high probability of committing bizarre and jaded acts. They become bored by the ordinary in life, turning to the unusual and the atypical to find meaning. Classic examples are autocratic rulers like Nero, who fiddled while Rome burned, and a few eccentric billionaires like Howard Hughes and perhaps Michael Jackson, whose publicly known lifestyles and tastes border on the macabre. If those with medium control surpluses are insensitive, individuals with maximum control surpluses are completely oblivious to the potential of countercontrol as well as to the effects of their actions on others. The resulting patterns of behavior can best be called decadent.

Summary of the Causes of the Types of Deviance

People may become motivated toward deviance when their control ratios are unbalanced. The type of deviance they are likely to commit is a product of the magnitude of the imbalance and the seriousness of the acts that would potentially change it in their favor. The theory contends that slight control deficits, though implying relatively small motivation toward deviance, nevertheless lead to predation when deviance actually occurs. Slight control surpluses, on the other hand, produce exploitative behavior on the comparatively rare occasions when deviance is committed. This is because motivation toward deviance stimulates an urge to use the most serious forms of deviance to escape control deficits or to extend control surpluses, whereas potential countercontrolling reactions dictate that only those with relative freedom from control will be able to employ the most serious forms of deviance for their own advantage. Thus, only those with small deficits can entertain the possibility of actually using predation, and only those with small surpluses are restrained from pursuing the most serious forms of control extension—plunder and decadence—and turn instead to exploitation.

By the same mechanisms, those with moderate control deficits have more motivation toward deviance and want to use the most serious methods, but they are more restrained than those with slight control deficits, just as those with medium control surpluses are motivated toward decadence but are constrained to commit plunder. Continuing this logic, those with extreme control deficits are liable to be submissive, just as those with maximum control surpluses are highly likely to fall into decadence.

General Summary of the Control Balancing Process

The theory contends that deviant behavior is undertaken mainly to alter the deviant's control ratio, even if temporarily. Deviance serves a specific purpose for the individual who commits it, and this purpose is not necessarily obvious or ostensibly connected with the form of deviance. The first-person account of criminal activity by Nathan McCall, whose book *Makes Me Wanna Holler* was excerpted in *Newsweek* (McCall 1994a) prior to its publication (McCall 1994b), serves to illustrate the point. McCall describes his feeling the first time he burgled a house: "As I rifled through those people's most private possessions, I felt a peculiar power over them, even though we'd never met" (1994a:46). Later he "graduated" to stickups, and the satisfaction that this provided was clearly not the increase in income or the ease of the job. Rather, it was the exhilaration associated with a shift in control.

> Sticking up gave me a rush that I never got from B&Es. There was an almost magical transformation in my relationship with the rest of the world when I drew that gun on folks. I always marveled at how the toughest cats whimpered and begged for their lives when I stuck the barrel into their faces. Adults who ordinarily would have commanded my respect were forced to follow my orders like obedient kids (1994a:47).

When McCall ended up actually shooting someone, he felt even more control. "I walked toward Plaz, looked into his eyes and saw something I had never seen in him before. Gone was the fierceness that made him so intimidating all those years. In its place was shock. And fear. It was more like terror. In that moment, I felt like God. I felt so good and powerful that I wanted to do it again" (1994a:49).

From the premise that deviance serves to alter relative distributions of control, the theory reasons that motivation to commit acts of deviance will vary with the relative amount of control a person has, whereas the expression of deviant motivations in actual behavior is influenced by the amount of countercontrol that can be expected, along with the probability that it will be activated. Thus, the theory explains both the probability and type of deviance as consequences of the amount of control exercised relative to the control suffered (along with other activating variables like generation of deviant motivation, opportunity, and constraint). When the two are balanced, people generally conform. When the two are unbalanced, the probability of deviance increases directly with the degree of imbalance or by the distances from the center of the continuum in both directions, as portrayed in Figures 7.2 and 7.3. From the center, which represents a ratio of 1 as the balance of control varies along the repressive end of the continuum, there is increasing probability of deviance generally, although the seriousness (type) of likely deviance decreases. In like manner, as the degree of imbalance increases in movement from 1 on the surplus side of the continuum out to the end, the probability and the seriousness (type) correspondingly increase.

The chance of deviant behavior of some kind is mainly a function of motivation toward deviance, which increases with the degree of an individual's control imbalance and other situational provocations (though opportunity must also be present). This is because a fundamental urge for escaping and extending control interacts with the relative potentialities for control embedded in the immediate and general statuses, roles, and experiences of the individual. The type of deviance likely, however, is a function of motivation and possible countercontrol, both of which are linked to the control ratio (but not totally determined by them). An additional factor in explaining the type of deviance, however, is the seriousness of the potential act, which reflects the likelihood that the behavior will activate countercontrolling responses. Motivated individuals contemplate the most effective deviance for overcoming a control deficit or for extending a control surplus, but their actual behaviors reflect a hydraulic relationship between motivation and potential countercontrolling responses (assuming opportunity). The net effect of this is (1) a positive relationship between the magnitude of a control deficit and the likelihood of some deviance, but an inverse relationship between the magnitude of a control deficit and the seriousness of the deviance that does occur; and (2) a positive relationship between the magnitude of a control surplus and the likelihood of some deviance, as well as a positive relationship between the magnitude of a control surplus and the seriousness of the deviance that emerges.

Levels of Potential Applicability

Control balance theory attempts to explain the general probability of some kind of deviance as well as the probability of specific forms of deviance through a causal chain composed of background and foreground variables, most of which do not have fixed values. For expository purposes, this theory has been portrayed as if it were concerned only with the deviant event, but it also applies to interlinking networks, or structures, of events in ways relevant to perennial issues in the field. Such applications concern (1) *prevalence,* or the probability that people with various degrees of the variables in the theory will commit deviance or specific deviant acts within some time span (such as a lifetime or during the adolescent period); (2) *incidence,* or the frequency with which individuals characterized by various degrees of the variables in the theory commit deviance or specific deviant acts within specified temporal frames; (3) *the developmental issue,* or variations in probabilities or frequencies of deviance or specific deviant acts over the life course of individuals; and (4) *the comparative question,* or differences in probabilities or frequencies of deviance or specific deviant acts for groups or categories of individuals reflected in demographic or political distinctions at given points in time or over various time spans.

Prevalence

From the arguments presented in this chapter, it should be clear that people differ in their simple probabilities of deviance, whether the deviance is general or of specific types, as they differ in the intensity of exposure to the combination of causal conditions set forth. Some never experience the conditions likely to lead to deviance, others at some point or another experience the propitious combination of those conditions but only in slight degree, and still others encounter the predictive alliance with much intensity. For example, some people have control ratios near unity, and as a result, they lack the most important condition predictive of deviance. Some have imbalanced control ratios but never simultaneously experience deviant motivation and an opportunity for deviance. Some have control imbalances, become motivated toward deviance in the presence of opportunity, but never deviate in the specific way the theory suggests people with such control imbalances will, because constraint does not permit it. There are other people, however, who have slight control imbalances and develop small degrees of motivation in the presence of opportunity but encounter large degrees of constraint. They end up with a small probability of committing deviance in general as well as small probabilities of committing any specific kinds of deviance. A few people, of course, have control imbalances, develop strong motivation on occasion when there is opportunity, and face relatively little constraint. The probability of their committing deviance is high, and the probability of their committing specific deviant acts commensurate with their control imbalances is great.

The prevalence of deviance, or the chances that some individuals relative to others will commit deviance, are, therefore, a function of the likelihood that the necessary variables specified in the theory converge with sufficient strength. Higher probabilities of deviance are associated with greater magnitude of the appropriate variables and with the completeness with which these variables interact in the unique combinations specified by the theory.

Incidence

The theory also explains and predicts the frequency of deviance among those who have crossed a threshold of probability for committing it or committing specific forms of it. Those most frequently exposed to the minimal conditions for the production of deviance, over some specified time span, will most frequently commit deviant acts. Since the theory has probabilistic premises, it follows that no person has an absolute certainty of committing deviance even when the conditions for it are maximal. However, a person repeatedly exposed to propitious conditions will more likely deviate than a person only rarely exposed to the right combination of variables, and the more frequently a person experiences favorable circumstances, the more often that person will deviate.

There is more to the frequency question than simple probability, however. Deviance itself, once committed, has a causal effect on the chances that future deviance will occur, particularly if prior deviance is successful, which it often will be, at least in the sense of temporarily but favorably altering a control imbalance. This is because (1) successful prior deviance is remembered and helps spark motivation for further deviance, (2) prior deviance affects how one assesses risk, which is implicated in constraint, and (3) repeated deviance can produce habits of nonconformity that serve as a favorable contingency for the full operation of the causal process. Hence, deviance feeds back on the causal variables that produce it in the first place, normally with a net cumulative effect. The more deviance one commits, the more one is likely to commit, unless the control ratio underlying it changes. Of course, deviance may itself produce permanent changes in the general control ratio if, for example, a person is stigmatized or incarcerated because of it.

The Developmental Question

The principles of control balance theory may also be applied to questions about differential probability and frequency of deviance during different stages of the life cycle, because the variables in the theory are more likely to converge with greater degrees of intensity during some parts of the life cycle. Indeed, the key variable of the theory—the control ratio—is highly dependent on life-cycle stages because people typically gain more ability to control as well as to escape control as they move from childhood to adulthood, and they typically lose both as they enter into old age. The intricate and complicated way that this plays out will be discussed more fully in a later chapter when the theory is fitted to existing empirical facts, but for now it is sufficient to note the intimate linkage of the variables with structural reflections of life-course statuses.

Some of the central variables, like situational risk and feelings of debasement, as well as a number of contingencies for the full operation of the theory, are altered by experience and wax or wane throughout the life cycle. No doubt some aspects of those variables or contingencies are preset by biological inheritance and early childhood training, thereby encoding some long-range stability in patterns of behavior, but the theory is basically dynamic. It assumes that its central variables change in various ways with changes in circumstances and situations and over the life course, and it also assumes that those changes are expressed in different probabilities of deviant behavior. In addition, it provides an explanation, based on the principles of cumulativity, for patterns of deviance that actually turn out to be stable.

The Comparative Question

Societies and Other Organizations. Previous examples illustrate the operation of control balancing for individuals because that is the theory's primary aim. Nevertheless, it can also be applied at the macrolevel if we think in terms of rates of deviance rather than individual probabilities, and if we assume that such rates are an aggregate function of individual motivations and behaviors. This assumption is not accepted by all social scientists, but if it is granted, some interesting implications of the control balancing argument follow.

Specifically, societies vary in average control ratios because such ratios represent complex combinations of roles and status, access to resources, and so on, that are incorporated within the larger social structure. In some societies most individuals and other social entities are balanced midway between repression and autonomy. In such balanced societies, probably very democratic ones with social institutions arrayed to sustain mutually controlling checks and balances, *rates* of deviance should be low.

Marginally repressive societies, which have slightly more average control experienced relative to that exercised, should have relatively low rates of crime and deviance, although the primary form of deviance that does occur will be predation. Those societies in which the people generally experience considerably more control directed at them than they return (moderately repressive societies) should be characterized by fairly high rates of deviance, primarily of a defiant form. Finally, some societies will have populations in which the average amount of control directed against them relative to that returnable is overwhelming. In such extremely repressive societies there should be a high degree of submissiveness.

Similarly, societies might fit at various positions on the autonomous end of the control ratio continuum. Minimally autonomous societies in which the average degree of control exercised slightly exceeds that suffered should have low rates of deviance, but the deviance that does occur should be mainly of the exploitative type. Societies in which the average level of control exercised exceeds by a considerable amount that experienced should have high rates of deviance, and it should be mostly of a plunderous form. Finally, societies in which the average control exercised overwhelmingly exceeds the average experienced, that is, maximally autonomous societies, should have very high rates of deviance, and it should appear mostly as decadence.

This assumes, of course, that other variables like opportunity have corresponding average values in the various types of societies. Such assumptions are hard to sustain, and some of the logical possibilities of types of societies are almost impossible to imagine, particularly since control ratios imply some reciprocity of social control. It is difficult, for example, to visualize a society in which the average control exercised by individuals or other social entities overwhelmingly exceeds that experienced. Nevertheless, depending on how "average" is conceived, various types of societies might be imagined, and perhaps found in reality. For instance, if the average control exercised is based on the total volume of control possible by social entities, a few entities with enormous control possibilities could create an average "surplus" control. Yet this kind of society would likely have high rates of plunder or decadent behavior as well as a high rate of defiance and submissiveness. On the other hand, if average is the control balance of the typical person, it might be rare for a society to have greater average control exercised than experienced, though imbalance in the other direction is feasible. In estimating average control ratios one should remember that the theory is concerned with all kinds of control, not just that exercised by and against other humans; furthermore, even some control in a given society might be directed against people in other societies. Thus, a society highly advanced technologically might have an overall surplus of control because of the average ability of its citizens to control the physical world or because of the collectivity's capacity for international dominance.

Similar logic makes the theory relevant to nonsocietal groups, particularly formal organizations like corporate entities. Conceivably, any organization can be characterized in terms of the average control ratio among its members, and if so, the rates of various kinds of deviance should be predictable following the theoretical argument outlined earlier.

A Related Application. The theory also applies to relationships between rulers and subjects in societies or other organizational networks. Subjects should be somewhere on the repressive end of the continuum, and the rulers should fall somewhere on the autonomy end. In societies in which the rulers are relatively restrained by the citizens and the citizens are relatively free, both should generally conform. However, when the citizens have slightly less control than the rulers, high rates of predation among the citizens and high rates of exploitation among the rulers should prevail. Similarly, if rulers have much more control than the ruled do, only modest rates of deviance by citizens should result, and it should be mainly in the form of defiance, whereas medium amounts of deviance by the rulers, mainly plunder, should occur. Finally, where rulers have overwhelming control, one would expect high rates of decadence among the rulers matched by high rates of submissiveness among the citizens.

Demographic Categories. One of the most important comparative questions concerns differences in rates of deviance between and among aggregates demarcated by demographic identifiers. These identifiers include sex, race, religious affiliation, place of residence, and socioeconomic status. Again, the principles of control balance theory apply if one thinks in terms of aggregates and conceptualizes the dependent variable as rates of deviance. The average control ratio, and the average likelihood of encountering various relevant situational variables, may vary by demographic category. To explain demographic differences, one must theorize, or empirically establish, that the relevant control balance variables, in the aggregate, differ in ways relevant to the theory, and one should then spell out the implications.

For example, to explain sex differences in rates of deviance, one would show, or assume, that males and females typically differ in one or more of the variables of the theory and then follow through the logic of the argument from that point. Thus, if the sexes typically differ in their control ratios, in the likelihood of encountering situational provocations that demean, in opportunities for deviance, in constraints on their behaviors, or in one or more of the contingencies for the efficient operation of the theory, then this should produce differences in rates of deviance in general and in rates of particular kinds of deviance, depending on the actual average control ratios. The explanatory principles of the theory show why a typical difference in one or more of these variables produces a difference in rate of deviance.

In a later chapter, I will go through this process to show how the theory accounts for known differences among demographic categories in rates of crime/delinquency, which are the closest systematic indicators of rates of deviance that we have. My objective at the moment, however, is to show that the theory has wide applicability to the issues that engage most students of deviance, and that it is accountable in all of those domains.

General Summary

Control balance theory portrays the probability of deviance as a function of the ratio of control exercised to that experienced, and it stipulates the type of deviance likely to be committed as a joint function of the magnitude of one's control imbalance and the seriousness of potential deviant acts. The magnitude of a control imbalance is directly related to the probability of deviance of some kind. However, the seriousness of specific types of potential deviant behavior varies inversely with the magnitude of a control deficit and directly with the magnitude of a control surplus. Thus, a small control deficit portends predatory deviance, one of the most serious types, and whenever an individual enjoys a large control surplus, the chances of decadence are greatest. Moderate control deficits signify enhanced chances for defiance and whenever medium control surpluses prevail, chances of plunder are increased. Finally, with large control deficits, submissive deviance is likely, whereas those with small control surpluses will most likely exploit.

Although the probability and type of deviance are functions of control ratios and constraints, they are not straightforward consequences of those variables, nor are their effects necessarily linear. The theory implies an underlying causal process that begins with a predisposition toward deviant motivation, which is an interactive outcome of a control imbalance, a basic human desire for autonomy, and usually some blockage of a primary human impulse. Predispositions are translated into actual motivation when they converge with situational provocations, which are closely linked to feelings of degradation, to generate a perception that deviant behavior can favorably alter the control imbalance or relieve humiliation. The magnitude of motivation toward deviance, in combination with the presence of opportunity, predicts the general probability of deviance. The chances of a specific form of deviance occurring, however, stem from an alliance of the original control imbalance, the presence of motivation and opportunity, and constraint. Constraint is a convergent product of a control imbalance, the seriousness of a potential act, and situational risk. The entire process is conceived as both dynamic (the values of the variables are situationally volatile) and reciprocal (deviance feeds back to alter some of its own causes).

In this theory, the control ratio is conceived as a generalized characteristic of the individual's configuration of roles, statuses, social relationships, and accommodations to the physical and organizational world. Unfortunately, the overall control ratio is difficult to measure because it includes many different elements that operate in a variety of situations. Still, even crude measurement will produce fairly good results because the bulk of the control ratio is embodied in a circumscribed set of roles and statuses.

Control balancing theory explains prevalence of general and specific deviance among individuals, the frequency of deviance for given time spans, variations in prevalence and incidence over the life course, and differences among societies, organizations, and demographic categories in rates of deviance. It makes no assertions, however, about absolute probabilities or frequencies of deviance for any ratio of control, for any individual, or for any group or category. In addition, although control imbalance is postulated as the primary factor accounting for most deviance, the theory does not contend that everybody with a particular control balance will inevitably engage in the prescribed deviant behavior. There will be instances where the control ratio suggests low likelihood of deviance that does not occur; there will be instances where the actual control ratio suggests a high likelihood of deviance that does not occur; and there will be instances where individuals commit types of deviances not predicted by their control ratios or fail to commit types of deviance that are predicted by their control ratios. In part, this is because the causal forces implicated in the theory operate with greater or lesser force under various conditions or contingencies. The nature and effects of those contingencies are discussed in the following chapter.

8

Contingencies for the
Central Causal Process

Although an individual's control ratio strongly influences both the probability of deviance and the type of deviance likely to be committed, this effect does not occur with the same strength or likelihood in all circumstances. Contingencies impinge on, and alter, the "ordinary" operation of the control balancing process.

The Nature of Contingencies

A contingency is defined as: any aspect of an individual; social relationships; organizational structures; or the physical environment that influences how completely or strongly the control balancing process operates. A hypothetical example from the medical field will show the nature of contingencies and will highlight the importance of recognizing and accommodating contingencies when specifying causal effects implied by a theory.

Suppose a medical scientist formulates a theory containing the hypothesis that drug X will cure or alleviate a disease. A researcher then contrives an experiment to test the hypothesis. Following normal procedure (double-blind administration and measurement, and neutralization of all intervening conditions), the researcher randomly assigns a batch of 500 diseased people to two groups. The experimental group is administered drug X, while the control group is given a placebo. After an appropriate time lag, severity of the disease in each experimental subject is ascertained. It is found that 50 percent of the experimental group has recovered completely, and 20 percent more have realized significant improvements. At the same time, only 20 percent of the control group have overcome the disease, and only 10 percent more have enjoyed some improvement. Scientists would conclude from this that drug X probably have a causal influence on the demise of the disease, and if the findings were repeated in other experiments, this would justify therapeutic use of the drug as well as confirm the theory that led the researchers to their interest in it.

Even though the overall effect of the drug is clear, however, it is nevertheless the case that not all members of the experimental group recovered completely and some did not improve at all, whereas 30 percent of the control group either recovered or improved without the drug. The remaining task is to understand why it worked for some and not others. Suppose a researcher, on a hunch, entertains the notion that body weight influences how effectively the drug works. The researcher examines the records and determines that most of the successful participants in the experimental group weighed less than 150 pounds, most of those who improved but did not recover weighed between 150 and 200 pounds, and most of those who saw no improvement weighed over 200 pounds. This suggests that body weight is a contingency for the causal effect of drug X; it generally works, but it works most effectively for lighter people.

Of course, a careful researcher would not stop there, but would probably devise another experiment to test this contingent notion. The second series of experiments might begin with three different weight-categories of sufferers. Within each category, the subjects would be assigned randomly to control and experimental groups, and the conditions of the previous experiment would be repeated. Now suppose that in the lowest weight-category, 90 percent of the experimental group recovered and 5 percent improved, while the rate of recovery in the control group remained about the same as in the original experiment (20 percent recovery and 10 percent improvement). Imagine that only a small minority in each of the other two experimental groups recovered, although 60 percent of those in the middle weight-category and 20 percent of those in the high weight-category improved—while the rates of recovery and improvement in the control groups remained at about what they had been in the initial experiment. Under these circumstances, and again assuming replication in a variety of circumstances, the researchers could infer causal effects for drug X, but they could feel fairly confident that it worked better for low-weight people.

Careful researchers would not even stop there, however, for they would want to know why there was an interaction between the drug and body weight, and this would inspire still further theory and research. Ultimately, they might learn the reasons for the interaction, but even without that understanding the potency of drug X would still be dependent on the contingency of body weight. Even more important, by taking account of body weight, and other possible interactants, medical scientists would have greater confidence in drug X and especially in the theory that led to its development or application than they would by assuming its effects to be universal and invariant.

This will become clearer if one thinks about the conclusions that might have been reached had the original experiment inadvertently been conducted on a sample with an excess of heavy people. Instead of finding effectiveness rates of 70 percent (50 percent recovery, 20 percent improvement), the researchers would have found the experimental group benefitting no more than the control group. Without some theoretical reason for attention to body weight, the scientists might never have hit upon the idea of examining the effect of the drug within weight-categories. As a result, the theory that suggested that drug X would have a causal effect on the disease would have been rejected, and a good theory might have died without ever receiving a fair test.

No causal effect of any kind, especially those implied by control balance theory, ever operates the same way under all conceivable conditions. Yet, a good theory will not use the reality of contingencies as an escape from the discipline of empirical accountability; instead it will show how, when, and why the contingencies come into play. Such specification will not only improve the theory's credibility, but it will make empirical tests more feasible. In the example described above, if the theory that led to drug X had specifically indicated an interaction with body weight, the scientists could have devised an appropriate series of experiments in the beginning rather than having to rely on situational inspiration. Moreover, if the theoretical reasons for the expected interaction had been clear, researchers would have had a basis for imagining other potential contingencies not specifically incorporated in the theoretical statement, and they would have been spared the inefficiency of trial-and-error investigation.

As desirable as it is for a theoretical statement to demarcate contingencies, it is not always possible for a theorist to identify every possible one. No theory can emerge full-blown from a given set of causal arguments; there must always be continuous feedback with empirical evidence. Therefore, though I try to "conditionalize" control balance theory, no claims for exhaustiveness are made. My main objective at this point is to identify enough contingencies for reasonable empirical tests to be conducted and to ensure that the theory will not be rejected because of a wrongful assumption that it asserts effects that are invariant in all circumstances.

A contingency may affect the operation of a central causal process in one of several ways. First, as the magnitude of the contingent variable increases or decreases, the effect of the main causal variable may increase or decrease. This linear interactive effect is like the effect of drug X under the contingency of body weight in the medical example. As body weight decreased, the effect of drug X increased.

Second, as the contingent variable changes values, the effect of the main causal variable may show some nonlinear effect—perhaps increasing, then decreasing, and finally increasing again, or maybe decreasing, then showing no effect through several values of the contingent variable, and then increasing. All of these possibilities are nonlinear interactive effects. The potential effect of ferritin levels in the bodies of patients in the medical experiment may illustrate the point. Drug X might combat the disease without any interference from ferritin as long as the ferritin level was fairly low. However, with moderate amounts of ferritin, drug X might cease to work altogether. With high levels of ferritin, an individual's body might undergo some metabolic adaptations that once again would permit drug X to operate.

Third, when the effects of the central causal variable are confined entirely to a particular magnitude of the contingent variable, this is a focused contingency. In the medical example, drug X might reduce the disease among low-weight people and have no effects whatsoever for others.

Because of such variations, contingency statements are much less useful—sometimes they are actually misleading—when they fail to state the exact nature of their effects on the operation of the main causal variable or process. I will therefore try to provide details needed for maximum effectiveness.

Contingency statements make a theory more precise and believable, but their main practical purpose is to guide the formulation of research hypotheses and ensure the integrity of empirical tests. This practical purpose can be served in two ways. First, researchers can treat contingent effects as "noise" to be neutralized while ascertaining the effects of the main causal variables. In experiments, this might involve initial sampling to ensure little variation in the bothersome variable prior to random assignment. In survey research, it might involve measurement of the "contaminating" variable to permit statistical control of its effect in a predictive equation.

Second, researchers can directly test contingent predictions. If a theory suggests body weight as a positive linear contingency for the effect of drug X, researchers can examine variations in the effects of the drug for different values of the contingent variable. This could be done using experimental contrivances in which body weight and receipt of the drug are manipulated or by the conventional survey method in which a multiplicative interaction term, involving natural variations in consumption of the drug multiplied by body weight, is used to predict the presence or severity of the disease.

Of these approaches, testing exact contingent hypotheses is far more desirable because the alternative of "controlling" or neutralizing the effects of contingencies can produce false conclusions. Consider again the hypothetical medical experiment. Imagine that body weight actually exercised a focused contingent influence on the effect of drug X—the drug ameliorated the disease only among those with low weight. If patients' weights were held constant or neutralized, say by preselecting equal numbers of subjects with different body weights to be randomly assigned to experimental and control groups or by measuring body weight and statistically removing its effect in analysis of survey data, one might incorrectly conclude that the drug has no effect, although its effect is actually quite strong under specific circumstances. Direct testing of contingent effects minimizes this possibility and permits more sophisticated assessment of the theory. However, direct tests require precise contingent statements, a virtue lacking in most deviance theories.

Control balance theory is a contingent theory, and it must be tested with that feature in mind. Although a control balancing process is proposed as the main causal mechanism accounting for deviant behavior, the effects of its variables are not free of other influences. Indeed, I believe that the key to developing an adequate general theory lies in linking the control balancing process with a large number of additional variables, most of which are implicated in existing theories of deviance; this is one form of theoretical integration. The first step toward an integrated theory, then, is to identify the main contingencies for control balancing and to state how and why they influence the central causal effects.

Personal Contingencies

Perception

Probably the most important contingency affecting the extent to which control imbalances produce the deviant outcomes suggested by the theory is perceptual accuracy. People do not always see the world around them as it actually is. Sometimes they lack appropriate information to judge reality correctly, and at other times they simply misperceive or misinterpret information to which they are exposed.

Inaccurate perception is particularly evident in risk assessment (Cherniak 1986; Nisbett and Ross 1980). This is of prime importance because the theory's predictions of the type of deviance likely to be committed hinge on the individual's assessment of the likelihood that potential control will actually be activated. However, people often behave irrationally by misapplying probabilities of dangerous or costly outcomes of risky behaviors to themselves. Even when provided with correct base-rate information (the actual probability of an event occurring), many ignore it in favor of simplified heuristics, idiosyncratic or irrelevant information, or the recency of personal experience they or their acquaintances have had in similar situations.

In view of this human tendency to perceive reality incorrectly, an individual's actual control ratio may sometimes be far less relevant than the control ratio that he or she thinks is operating, and perception of the likelihood of potential controlling responses may sometimes be more relevant than the true seriousness of a given act. If an actual control ratio favors a particular kind of deviance, some individuals may misperceive the situation and end up behaving as if they had a different control ratio.

Imagine a middle-aged male with a supervisory position that grants him the right and capability of commanding a large number of workers. He is married, has four children, and exercises considerable sway over his wife, and to some extent, over his children. He has a relatively high income, so he exercises much control over the environment. His intelligence and charisma permit him to exercise more interpersonal dominance than that to which he is subject. In concrete terms, this individual appears to be somewhat autonomous. According to the control balance argument, he has some probability of committing exploitative or, possibly, plunderous deviance. Nonetheless, imagine that this man, for whatever reason, begins to believe that he is losing control, or that he has much less of it than he actually does (some might call this anxiety or mental illness). He begins to think that his occupational subordinates do not respect him or pay as much attention to his orders as they should; that his wife is leading her own life independent of his opinion or desires; that his job is in jeopardy or that inflation is eating away at his financial ability to manipulate the environment; and that people do not seem to take him seriously. As a result he comes to *perceive* that he is being controlled by external forces and that he, in turn, has little mastery. Because of these perceptions, this individual is, in his own mind, marginally or moderately repressed rather than minimally or moderately autonomous. As a result, he may commit some form of defiant or predatory deviance despite the reality of an autonomous control ratio that would predict something else. In this case, one would make incorrect predictions about behavior unless perceptual deviations are taken into account.

Imagine further that this man, who perceives himself to be marginally or moderately repressed although he is in reality minimally autonomous, also seriously misperceives the likelihood that some of those who he imagines can exercise control against him will, in fact, bring those regulations into play. Suppose, for instance, that he perceives the chances of his being arrested for an act of predation as extremely high (a misperception), and he perceives that as a result of such arrest, his having committed an act of predation would become known to his family, friends, associates, and employer. Imagine also that he perceives that all of these important people in his life, having learned of his deviance because of the arrest, would totally reject him as an unworthy human being. Because of these perceptions, at least the first of which is false, the man probably will curtail potential predatory or defiant acts of deviance. Thus, he commits neither the acts signified by the reality of his control ratio nor those suggested by his initial misperceptions of the control imbalance. He would represent, on two counts, a contradiction to expectations based solely on the actual control ratio. Instead of committing exploitation, as would be expected, he conforms. His conformity in this illustration involves motivation, by misperception of the control imbalance, to commit predation, but he is deterred from predatory acts by still further misperceptions of the actual probability that the restraining abilities and capacities of others will be activated.

As these examples suggest, the more accurate the perception of the actual control ratio and other aspects of the control balancing process, the better the theory will work. The best way to deal with the contingency of perception is to measure how accurately subjects perceive the reality of their control ratios and the seriousness of various deviant acts they might employ in their efforts to overcome a control deficit or to extend a control surplus and then to examine the effects of the variables with perception controlled or for subgroups representing degrees of accuracy of perception. The more accurately the person perceives the control ratio and the seriousness of various deviant acts, the more fully the effects implied by the theory will unfold.

Some might initially object to this approach, contending that the theory should be applied strictly at the perceptual level. It might be reasoned that since people act on the basis of their perceptions, it does not matter whether individuals correctly or incorrectly perceive, as long as their perceptions of their control ratios and the likelihood of countercontrolling responses can be measured. Unfortunately, however, using the individual's perceptions of the relevant variables would not necessarily produce correct predictions, even if the theory were flawless. This is partly because there are additional contingencies that may be operating, which we will examine later, and partly because human behavior is not totally driven by perceptions.

Behavior is sometimes checked, or constrained, despite perceptions to the contrary. Imagine, for example, a person who perceives that he or she is experiencing a marginal deficit of control and tries to overcome that deficit by a predatory act, only to find that he or she lacks the strength or emotional makeup to carry it out. Consider another individual who, perceiving that he or she is only marginally repressed, contemplates an act of predation, but in the nick of time, peers, or the police, show up to prevent the deviance. Finally, think of the organizational executive who imagines that he or she has the ability to fire someone but finds that a morass of bureaucratic rules make it practically impossible to accomplish the act.

Actual behavior does not simply reflect perceptions of reality; Peter Pan notwithstanding, one cannot fly by faith. To be sure, tracing the effects of perceptions of the variables in the theory might sometimes lead to better predictions than can be accomplished using concrete variables, and analyzing perceptual and objective indicators in combination might produce still better results. After all, two of the theory's variables are inherently perceptual. Motivation for deviance hinges on a situational perception that deviance will be useful for altering one's control ratio, and before motivation can lead to deviance, a person must perceive that the potential countercontrol will not be forthcoming. Therefore, using perceptual variables for testing the theory may be useful as long as perception is recognized as epiphenomenal to the key causal forces specified by the theory, which are social structural facts.

In contending that tangible things matter more than perceptions of those things, I assume that *most* people discern control-relevant factors with at least a reasonable degree of accuracy. Even research demonstrating common misperception reports that under some conditions factual probabilities are perceived and applied with considerable soundness, and that within normal, individually relevant contexts, a crude but workable correspondence between reality and cognitive appreciation of it prevails (Bar-Hillel 1990; Jungermann 1983). Research may ultimately demonstrate this for most of the domains covered by control balance theory, but until the intricacies of the perception-reality relationship are worked out empirically or theoretically, it is probably best to approach the problem as I have suggested.

Moral Commitments

During early socialization most people incorporate ideas about right and wrong behavior into their patterns of thought and feelings. When moral imperatives are so ingrained that one feels emotionally uncomfortable committing, or even contemplating, wrongful acts, they have been "internalized," and emotional discomfort from contemplating, or after actually committing, morally prohibited acts is called "guilt." Because internalized ethical standards can provoke or inhibit behavior and can influence the way other variables operate in an individual's life (Etzioni 1988; Grasmick and Bursik 1990, 1993; Grasmick and Green 1980; Tittle 1980a), conduct may sometimes be inconsistent with predictions based on straightforward principles of control balance theory.

An example will illustrate this. Adolescents in the United States are subject to control by parents, other adults, school officials, the police, future employers, the government, the social and physical environment, and other adolescents. They, in turn, can usually exercise substantial influence over other adolescents and their parents, and through subcultural organization, they can sway school officials, but they have only limited mastery of the rest of the world. The control ratio of most adolescents, therefore, reflects moderate repression (the middle zone of the repressive end of the continuum), and as a result we would expect any individual adolescent to have at least a modest likelihood of defiance. Suppose, however, that an adolescent has been trained by his or her parents, and perhaps through association with a religious group, to regard acts of defiance, at least against legitimate authority or legitimate social arrangements (as well as many other acts of deviance), as morally unacceptable. Because of that personal ethic, this young person is stricken with strong feelings of guilt anytime he or she thinks about acts of defiance such as vandalism, curfew violations, or drug use. It might be said that this individual's conscience signals that there will be an emotional penalty if he or she commits wrongful acts, or even seriously contemplates doing them. Consequently, this adolescent may defy no rules or authority despite strong motivation to do so and despite realization that controlling responses in reaction to such deviance are unlikely.

Internalized values, then, constitute a second contingency under which control balance theory has greater or lesser force. In other words, if there are no personal moral imperatives, the predictions of the theory will be more accurate than if moral inhibitions do exist. This does not mean, however, that morality is more important than control ratios or that the control balancing process will not explain deviance independently of internalized values. After all, no person is completely diverted from all deviance by moral standards, and the strength of ethical barriers against any particular deviance varies from individual to individual. Moreover, even the strongest moral convictions do not always block deviance. Indeed, dealing with persistent guilt stemming from behavior committed in violation of personal moral codes is a recurrent human problem that makes much work for psychiatrists and clinical psychologists (Kaufman 1989). Nevertheless, explanation and prognosis from control balancing will be stronger when moral commitments are controlled or otherwise taken into account.

The contingent effects of moral sentiment are not straightforward or linearly interactive. Among those with minimal control deficits—those people who are most likely to resort to predation in efforts to rectify their situations—strong moral inhibitions will decrease the chances of actual predatory behavior. Weak moral constraints, however, will not increase the chances of actual predatory behavior over what would be expected for those with average morality. This follows from the logic that small control deficits are likely to produce predatory motivation because predation is the most effective potential device for balancing control. Those with small control deficits are more likely than others to resort to predation because they can reasonably imagine escaping from countercontrolling responses. Since ethical inhibition plays no direct part in the central causal process, its absence can have no effect on the outcome. Modest to strong moral restraint, however, can intervene to disrupt the central causal process. Therefore, moral commitment represents a focused contingency for the theory.

Habits

Habits represent a third contingency that helps account for behavioral outcomes incongruent with expectations based exclusively on control balance considerations. Every person routinizes repetitive actions. As a result much human behavior is patterned and habitual, involving action undertaken automatically without forethought or critical reflection. The more often an individual does a particular thing in a specific way, the more proficient that person becomes at it, the more comfortable the person feels in doing it, and the easier it is to do it without thinking. For instance, people living in the United States routinely eat with a fork, don clothing before leaving their houses, drive on the right-hand side of the road, kiss spouses, greet friends and associates, offer a handshake to new acquaintances, and refrain from most forms of deviance. Habits are conditioned responses; they involve no moral considerations that might invoke guilt. Rather, the hallmark of habit is a feeling of awkwardness if the individual behaves in an unaccustomed way.

Most people are generally habituated to conformity. As a result they often continue to fulfill normative expectations despite their own specific motivations for deviance in various situations. Occasionally, however, people form habits of committing particular forms of deviance. Thus, habits can cause behavior to depart from that which is predicted by control balance. The case of a university president arrested for making obscene phone calls represents one example of how habit can condition the causal effects of the control balancing process. This man grew up with a sharp sense of being extremely repressed (Hammer 1990). In response to that control imbalance he began a regular pattern of defiance. One form of defiance he particularly favored was obscene phone calls, which he habitually made over many years, but he also managed to become educated and to succeed at the tasks set before him. By and by, he ascended to the presidency of the university where he was employed at the time of his arrest. In that position his control ratio might have been described as one with at least minimal autonomy (although we do not know much about the other realms of his existence that would affect his overall control ratio). Yet the habit of making obscene phone calls did not leave him, despite a change in control ratio.

It is not enough to recognize that habit makes a difference, however. We must consider the exact directions that such effects might take. Before pondering this, it should be noted that much habitual behavior stems from original acts of deviance or conformity that were generated previously by the control balancing process. Since general control ratios may change over time and situational control ratios are sometimes quite variable, the effects of a specific control ratio at a given point in time may be conditioned by the outcome of another control ratio at a different point in time. Thus, there is often temporal reciprocity of the variables in the theory that helps account for continuous patterns of behavior over the life course.

Whatever the basis of habits, they affect control balancing in linearly interactive ways. The stronger the habit of a particular kind of deviant behavior, the greater the likelihood that the conditions for that kind of deviance will result in the predicted outcome; and the stronger the habit of conformity, the less likely that conditions for a particular kind of deviance will eventuate in its manifestation. For example, although all people with marginal control deficits who become motivated for predation and who encounter opportunities to commit predatory acts stand a better chance of preying than others, they differ among themselves in the actual chances of predation. Those chances vary in inverse proportion to habits of conformity or conversely in direct proportion to their habits of predatory deviance.

Personality

Earlier, the influence of personality traits, particularly intelligence, interpersonal skill, and self-confidence in accounting for variations in control ratios among individuals with similar role/status configurations, was discussed. In those passages, personality characteristics were treated as component parts, called elements, of the control ratio. Here, I want to illustrate how personality traits can be contingencies for the central causal process by sometimes intruding to alter expected behavioral outcomes without necessarily affecting the operative control ratio. In portraying personality as a contingency for control balancing, intelligence and self-confidence will again be used as illustrations, but impulsivity will be substituted for the previously discussed characteristic of interpersonal skill.

Impulsivity. Some people are normally deliberate and reflective, cautious in response, and rational in contemplating the consequences of their actions (see Gottfredson and Hirschi 1990; Wilson and Herrnstein 1985), whereas others tend to act without thinking or reviewing the ramifications of situations and without weighing the potential consequences of their behaviors (Caspi et al. 1994). How might impulsivity intrude into the control balance process? Suppose there are two individuals with similar control ratios, both subject to considerably more control than they can exercise. According to the theory, and disregarding for the moment other contingencies, they should both have equal probabilities of committing some deviance, and the deviance most likely to be chosen is defiance. However, imagine that one of these individuals is rather impulsive, and the other is more circumspect. The chances of the spontaneous individual actually committing some form of defiance are somewhat higher than they are for the contemplative person because the spontaneous one has an inner drive that propels him or her to seize immediately any opportunity for balancing the scale of control, without much concern for the potential controlling reactions of others, whereas the less spontaneous person will take the time to think about reactions that various behaviors might provoke.

The contingent effects of impulsivity will be linearly interactive across most of the control balance range, but they will display a slight reversal of effect on the extreme repressive end, producing an inverted J-curve of deviance probability for that half of the continuum. Impetuosity induces one to stretch the bounds of constraint, which, within most zones of the continuum, will lead to greater chances of committing specified deviances. In the extreme repressive zone, however, impulsivity will delay the onset of submissiveness. Recall that submissive behavior results when the control ratio is so out of balance that the person cannot reasonably contemplate escaping countercontrolling responses should he or she try to use deviance to help rectify the situation. Since nondeliberative people have difficulty reflecting on the future, they may dare the limits of overwhelming constraint long after others have submitted. Still, the result will not be a complete change in direction of effect because repeated confrontation of massive constraint tends to dull the imagination, eroding the capacity to visualize that deviance could alter the control ratio. This process bears directly on deviant motivation, which is the situational perception that committing prohibited or threatening acts will be useful for balancing the actor's control ratio. Without such motivation, impulsivity becomes irrelevant since it implies unrestrained pursuit of gratifying actions. If gratifying deeds cannot even be contemplated, there can be no quest for relief.

Intelligence. There is little question that intelligence conditions the control balancing process. Imagine two individuals, each with a slight deficit of control, who, according to control balance tenets unmitigated by consideration of contingencies, are equally likely to commit acts of predation. Suppose, however, that one of those individuals is extremely intelligent, whereas the other has less than average wit. The more discerning person may comprehend the ramifications of situations more quickly and accurately than the one with less acumen and probably will be more likely to foresee alternative possibilities. The less intelligent person may fail to appreciate that controlling reactions will be activated if he or she uses the most immediate and effective coping strategy (i.e., that there is a high likelihood of some controlling response from others if he or she engages in an act of predation). Moreover, the nimble individual may quickly figure out a strategy to manipulate someone else into committing acts of predation on his or her behalf (i.e., he or she may employ a form of exploitative behavior despite the repressive nature of his or her overall control ratio).

The general form of the interactive effect of intelligence as a contingency is difficult to state, however. Although intelligent people probably grasp the likelihood of countercontrolling responses more fully and refrain from deviance for that reason, they may also be more capable of performing the deviant act in a way that will minimize the chances that controlling responses will be activated, and recognizing this, will be more likely to commit the deviance in question. More astute people may have the ability to alter control imbalances with incongruent forms of deviance, such as using exploitation, which is normally a tool of those with control surpluses, to modify control deficits, but there is no basis for predicting the alternatives that an active imagination might invent. Until empirical research identifies patterns by which intelligence affects control balancing, mental abilities must be measured and their impacts statistically neutralized.

Self-Confidence. Self-confidence—or feeling optimistic or lucky, or perhaps having a sense of self-efficacy—is the tendency to believe that advantageous things are likely to happen, either when one attempts to make them happen or simply by chance. An optimistic person more often challenges oppositional control than a pessimistic individual, and small opportunities are more likely to stimulate deviance among optimists than among pessimists.

Consider two elderly women with no jobs, no children, abusive husbands, and few financial resources, who nevertheless differ in beliefs about their own efficacy. Both suffer from extreme control deficits and both are potentially subject to despair and submissiveness. The one with a weak sense of self-potency may become submissive, losing the ability to imagine any alternative. The other, though in the same boat, may refuse to concede the hopelessness of the situation and as a result may continue to visualize defiant behaviors that would allow her to rectify her control imbalance.

The contingent effect of optimism is similar to that of impulsivity—linearly interactive across most of the control balance range but with a delay of effect on the extreme repressive end. Optimism permits the individual to discount potential limitations inherent in the control ratio, thereby increasing the chances of particular forms of deviance within zones of the continuum of control ratios. However, it also counters the despair typically characterizing those with extreme control deficits and induces them to seek relief through defiance despite the prospect of overwhelming countercontrol.

Other Personality Characteristics. There is no doubt that other personality traits are contingencies for the full operation of the control balancing process. Those mentioned illustrate how personality can intrude to strengthen or weaken the force of the control balance effects. It will be left to other theorists or to empirical researchers to identify and show the contingent influences of additional personality features.

Ability

As Sutherland reminded us years ago, some kinds of crime cannot be successfully undertaken by just anyone who might be motivated to attempt them, even if the opportunity exists, because some criminal acts require special skills (Sutherland 1937). He had in mind crimes like picking pockets, safecracking, embezzlement, or corporate price-fixing, but many deviant behaviors require basic abilities, if not specialized skills, not possessed by everyone. Successful assault often presupposes superior physical strength, burglary sometimes demands agility, and mass sniper killings depend on knowledge of weapons. Similarly, many kinds of exploitation (for example, manipulation of stock prices through takeover bids) are based on specialized knowledge of organizational functioning, and some defiant behavior (particularly political protest) rests on the ability to organize rallies and demonstrations. Hence, even when motivation to commit deviance is present and the magnitude and likelihood of counterresponses are favorable to deviance, behavior predicted by the theory sometimes cannot occur because the person lacks the aptitude for it.

Consider an adolescent on a deserted street with an unattended automobile. Given the absence of observers, the likelihood is minimal of provoking countercontrolling responses if he takes it for a joyride. Since his status places him in a moderately repressed condition, there is a predisposition for deviance that will help rectify his control deficit. The happenstance of encountering an unguarded, though keyless, auto stimulates the perception that his control imbalance can be rectified. Knowing that deviant conduct will activate forces of control, he turns to defiance because it permits some rectification of the control imbalance without jeopardizing the meager control that he can exercise. "Borrowing" the car for a joyride fills the bill, particularly since the probability of being caught appears to be slight. Imagine, however, that this adolescent did not know how to hot-wire, so he could not start the car. Under such circumstances, joyriding probably would not occur—certainly it would not occur without the help of someone else.

Another hypothetical example will demonstrate a different way in which the ability to commit a deviant act might enter into the control balancing process. A second adolescent boy is also motivated to commit some form of defiant behavior. However, this adolescent has learned how to use his computer to make long-distance calls without his parents' home phone being billed. Moreover, he has become so adept with the computer that this predation of the phone company is unlikely to activate the restraints that other forms of predation, or even of defiance, might. As a result this boy commits computer fraud, a form of predation, rather than the defiance that might otherwise be predicted.

As these examples suggest, control balancing operates more completely when the predictive variables and the individual's ability to commit the designated forms of deviance match. The contingent effects of ability to commit various acts of deviance are linearly interactive. The greater the ability, the more effective the theory will be in its predictions, and the lower the ability, the less effectively the causal process will unfold.

It is important to remember that contingencies modulate the full effect of the control balancing process; they do not have important independent causal effects on deviant outcomes, nor do they represent necessary conditions for the causal impact of control balancing variables. The control balancing process will not have *maximum* power unless capability for the deviance is taken into account, but the general validity of the argument is not dependent totally on the competence of individuals to commit predicted deviance. After all, some people try to do things they do not know how to do, some learn on the spot how to commit various acts of deviance, and some pursue their goals by enlisting the help of more skillful accomplices. Thus, as with the other contingencies already discussed, even if aptitude for deviance is left to vary freely, the theory should still produce far more correct than false predictions.

Alternative Motivation

The theory embraces an assumption that the major force in human behavior is a desire to escape control over oneself and to extend control over other people, objects, and circumstances. As this desire interacts with the realities of control impinging on the individual, motivations toward various kinds of deviance are generated. However, motivations toward nondeviant behavior also play a part in human conduct. Most people desire sexual gratification, almost all want to eat and drink, many yearn to reproduce, and everybody wants to stay warm or cold as the occasion may require. Most of the time those motivations are realized in nondeviant ways. Sometimes, of course, the resulting activities are deviant; and insofar as they are unacceptable, we can interpret their manifestations within the control balance schema. For instance, sexual gratification may be a basic biological need for most people, but sometimes it is a mechanism for manipulating and controlling others or a medium through which others regulate and channel us, and certainly it may be undertaken in ways and in situations judged inappropriate by a majority.

Thus, motivations for deviance sometimes compete with motivations for nondeviant behavior, and the presence and strength of these alternative motivations can be regarded as contingencies under which the causal processes of the control balance theory operate. Imagine a man with a slight surplus of control who, according to the theory, has some probability of exploiting others. However, suppose he loves a woman with whom he experiences frequent and highly satisfying sexual encounters and that the desire to spend time with her is so strong that it outweighs his compulsion to extend control over others. Although the woman's appeal represents a form of control over the man (incorporated in his overall control ratio), he still has a control surplus. Yet the desire to be with her still represents an alternative motivation that may disrupt the usual operation of his favorably unbalanced control ratio.

Sometimes, then, people are driven by alternative motives so strong that the ordinary operation of the control balancing process is deflected. However, such cases will not be numerous, nor will alternative motivations prevail in all situations even for those with extremely strong ancillary motives. Nevertheless, the theory will be more effective when there is no overarching, extremely intense, optional motive, that is, the contingent effect of alternative motivation is linearly interactive in a negative direction.

Prior Deviance

Experience with particular deviant behaviors constitutes a final individualistic contingency. A history of deviance operates to some extent like a habit, though one may have a history of deviance without habit. Habit is a behavioral pattern requiring no forethought. Specific behaviors rooted in habit are usually emitted with considerable frequency by the individual, and because deviance is episodic by its very nature, people are more likely to form habits of conformity than of deviance. As a result, most deviance, particularly serious forms, is not habitual. Yet when deviance has been employed with success, the odds that it will be used again are greater than its initial probability of use.

There are several reasons for this. Imagining deviant ways to manage a control imbalance, whether in surplus or deficit, requires at least mimimum ingenuity. Experience, however, reduces the need for creativity.

Prior deviance is easily remembered, so those who have committed it previously are more likely to think of repeating it, especially if its previous use proved successful. More important, a person who has already deviated can more easily appreciate the illusory nature of much potential control. Prior to initial deviance, people often have unrealistic fears about what will happen. Only after behaving in socially unacceptable ways do violators learn that the anticipated consequences of their acts may be exaggerated. Most of the time nothing happens, and certainly the consequences are fewer and less severe than the uninitiated imagine. Thus, without a history of deviance, individuals are more constrained by fear of potential countercontrolling responses, whereas experienced deviants have often broken the "shell of illusion" that constrains most of us and thus more readily resort to deviance.

This phenomenon has been documented in research on the deterrent effects of formal sanctions. Experienced law violators typically estimate much lower probabilities of possible apprehension and punishment than do naive subjects (Horney and Marshall 1992). Offenders presumably learn by experience that the chances of legal reaction are slim, and some longitudinal data actually show that people reduce assessments of risk after challenging the law and suffering only benign consequences. In fact, "experiential effects" are now thought to account for the negative correlations between perceived sanction possibilities and criminal behavior that were previously regarded as evidence of deterrence (Paternoster et al. 1983; Saltzman et al. 1982).

Experiential effects may counter most of the controls to which people are subject. Indeed, one of the main supports for social order may be "pluralistic ignorance," a shared misconception that things will be regarded as more serious than they usually turn out to be. Since only relatively few people actually challenge those assumptions and discover their illusory nature, most people continue to be constrained by anticipated reaction. Moreover, when the number of people breaking rules begins to grow, for whatever reason, it activates an upward spiral of violation as they share their newfound knowledge that social control is overrated. Thus, without denying that violators may sometimes discover actual reaction to their deviance to be as bad, or worse, than they imagined, the oft-observed ability of prior deviance to predict subsequent deviance is due, at least in part, to experiential neutralization of the potential controls inherent in the control ratio. Repeated acts of deviant behavior, therefore, are reciprocally linked in a developmental pattern.

An illustration may make clear how prior deviance conditions the control balancing process. Imagine two professional men, each with a slight surplus of control, who both perceive they can extend their control by sexually harassing females under their supervision. One of these men has a history of such harassment and knows from experience that very little will happen, even if the women complain to higher authorities or file lawsuits. Moreover, he remembers that this previous harassment "worked," in the sense of providing at least temporary satisfaction for his autonomy need. He therefore knows that even if countercontrolling responses are activated—women complain, warn other women to avoid him, or sue—harassment may still turn out to be a successful maneuver, and he is not restrained by potential countercontrolling responses. The other man, however, having never harassed an employee, is tortured by fear that other people will find out and withdraw their respect, that he will be disciplined or fired by superiors, that he will perhaps be sued, or worst of all, that the woman might insult his masculinity and convey that attribution to others. In addition, he can only imagine, not remember, that exploitation provides the satisfaction sought by those trying to extend their mastery. Under the same conditions, the first man is more likely than the second to engage in this particular form of exploitation because it has paid off for him in the past.

Prior successful deviance, then, has a positive and linearly interactive contingent effect on the control balance process. The greater the prior success with a particular form of deviance, the more it will be used again under the conditions specified by the theory. An important stipulation, however, is that the prior history of deviance must have been successful. Unsuccessful prior deviance has the opposite effect in that it reduces, in a negatively linear fashion, the force of control balancing in producing specified outcomes. Overall, then, the contingent effect of prior deviance is curvilinear, depending on the success of results.

In this contingency, the meaning of "success" must be understood theoretically, not as it is used in everyday life. In the theory, success (in the use of deviance) has two components. The main objective of, or reason for, deviance is to relieve feelings of debasement that accompany control imbalances. A deviant act can accomplish that purpose, at least temporarily, even if some of the consequences that follow are extremely costly. Recall the nationally publicized case of a graduate student of mathematics who killed his teacher because the professor allegedly belittled the student for lack of creativity. The killer, convicted and sentenced to a long prison term, later came up for a routine parole hearing but undermined his own chances by declaring he would slay his teacher again if possible. This homicide was an immensely satisfying act despite the fact that the perpetrator paid with his freedom. Indeed, he continued to maintain that the professor deserved death. In his analysis of cold-blooded murder, Katz (1988) describes killers who did not even believe that the victims deserved their fates. Indeed, their very innocence made the bizarre and vicious murders all the more gratifying as ritualistic statements of total dominance. Although most instances are not this extreme or clear-cut, successful deviance must be interpreted from the subjective point of view of the perpetrator. The question asked should be Did it work for him or her, and not strictly, Did he or she get away without paying a price.

The second component of successful deviance concerns the extent to which that deviant behavior actually activated the countercontrolling responses implied by the individual's control ratio. As noted before, much deviance simply does not have the consequences that many fear or that are prescribed. Yet the individual's interpretation is of major importance in assessing actual costs. Some deviants misconstrue countercontrolling responses, just as some gamblers discount their losses. Criminals, for instance, sometimes think of their apprehensions and convictions as flukes, and rather than concluding that crime does not pay, they conclude that they came so close to getting away with it—but for a minor error or happenstance—that it will pay the next time.

Thus, even though the exact contingent effects of prior deviance depend on its success, most previous deviance will turn out to have been successful—because of psychic satisfactions, escape from potential countercontrolling responses embedded in the control ratio, discount of those responses when they did occur, or some combination of these. Nevertheless, some prior deviance does fail and for the person who has experienced more failure than success, the direction of contingent effects will be reversed.

Summary on Personal Contingencies

Among the contingent variables for the control balancing process are seven that are individualistic in the sense that they are linked with internal psychic and emotional traits. They include perceptual tendencies, internalized moral precepts, habits, personality characteristics, ability to commit various kinds of deviance, overarching alternative motivations, and memories associated with prior deviance. Control balance theory itself makes no attempt to explain these individualistic characteristics, although an integrated general theory built around the central causal process of control balancing will draw on other theories to account for these contingent variables. There is no doubt that individualistic features stem partly from socialization, genetic or biological characteristics, and the interaction of these two, as well as from other processes reflecting qualities of the social structure, all of which have been the objects of explanation by existing theories. For now, their sources are not at issue; the issue is only their potentiality for intruding into the operation of the control balancing process to produce some incongruencies in empirical outcomes.

Although individual characteristics may, under particular circumstances and in specific ways, alter outcomes stipulated by the nuclear variables of the theory, they are not conceived as primary causal forces that compete with control balance in explaining and predicting deviance. Rather, even if these individualistic contingencies are ignored and allowed to vary freely, control balance theory should still permit great accuracy in predicting the probability and type of deviance. The control balancing process is postulated to be like a river whose main current inexorably flows toward its ultimate destination, though that current will vary in strength as its tributaries, streams, and backwashes fluctuate in activity.

Organizational Contingencies

Although some organizational affiliations constitute elements of the control ratio itself, other organizational arrangements represent contingencies for the control balancing mechanism, and some are both elements and contingencies. The most important are subcultural organizations oriented around specific forms of deviance.

Consider users of illegal drugs such as marijuana. In the theoretical scheme, consumption of prohibited drugs is a form of defiant behavior stemming from moderate control deficits. However, because illegal drug use typically brings people into contact with a subcultural group allied at least in distributional networks, they stand a good chance of becoming regular members of, or participants in, that subculture. Once an individual is part of a drug-oriented subculture, that person's motivation for the drug use is transformed and enhanced. Initial drug use is undertaken to overcome a control deficit, but continued use and subcultural involvement produce additional motivations. They include an inclination to please other subcultural members (itself linked to the context-specific control ratio) and the constructed or inherent pleasure provided by the drug. "Transformed" motivation can then alter operation of the normal control balance process.

Contemplate two people with similar control deficits in the defiance-generating range. Marijuana use is, for both, a potentially viable means for overcoming this control deficit. Suppose, however, that one of these individuals first uses marijuana in company with representatives of the marijuana subculture and eventually becomes a full participant in that group, whereas the other initially tries the drug in another context. The subculturally exposed person may cultivate a strong ancillary drive for future use that merges with the original propensity for overcoming control deficits as well as with the enhanced motivation from success in having managed the original control deficit through defiant drug use. These three allied forces provide a much stronger push toward drug use than did the initial causal factors. The individual unexposed to a drug subculture, on the other hand, will continue to pattern his or her behavior in response to the initial penchant for escaping control and perhaps to some extent to the physiological satisfaction produced by the drug. Together they will provide strong motivation for continued use, particularly if the earlier use proved successful in its original purpose, but the overall push toward repeated drug use by the second person will be quite a bit less than for the first. If this contingency were not taken into account, equal probabilities of future marijuana use would be predicted, but far more marijuana use by the subculturally involved individual would actually occur.

Moreover, marijuana subcultural participants may learn things from co-smokers that increase their potential for other forms of deviance to solve control deficits (Goode 1970). There are several reasons for this.

First, a subcultural smoker encounters collective rationalizations for use, and since all deviance shares common characteristics associated with social unacceptability, justifications for marijuana use to some extent generalize to other kinds of deviance. Second, since all lawbreakers share some kinship in being the objects of social control, they are likely to have some degree of social contact, particularly through overlapping subcultural memberships. As a result, subcultural smokers more frequently observe other types of deviants who have escaped countercontrols. Third, with the collective strength of the subculture, an individual has greater potential for escaping countercontrol, which can come into play in facilitating other forms of deviance. In a number of ways, then, involvement in a marijuana-using subculture can increase the chances of deviance that might not be expected from straightforward control balancing.

This is generally true of all deviant subcultures (Agnew 1995; Esbensen and Huizinga 1993; Fischer 1984; Hagan 1991; Kephardt and Zellner 1994; Sebald 1992; Thornberry et al. 1994). Because the activities of these subcultures are regarded as unacceptable by the larger population and are routinely reacted to by authorities, individuals involved in them become aware of their distinctness as lawbreakers. Therefore, they develop general rationales for rule breaking that make it seem like the thing to do. In addition, no matter what the deviance, subcultural members feel pressure to do it to gain the approval of their peers or to avoid rejection. Hence, participation in any deviant subculture generates ancillary motivations to repeat that deviance and to engage in other forms.

For these reasons, the accuracy of predictions from the theory will depend on the extent to which individuals are involved in deviant subcultures; the greater the involvement, the more distorted are the predictions of the theory. In most cases this distortion will be toward increasing the chances of all forms of deviance, and it will push the probabilities of most forms of deviance beyond the zones in which they would normally be confined. For example, if the probability of predation is 10 percent for an individual not involved in a predatory subculture, the probability may be 50 percent for a similar person who is involved in such a subculture. Although the chance that a person who is usually likely to commit predation will actually commit exploitation is normally small, it might become larger if the person, through subcultural contact and instruction, has learned ways to exploit.

Situational Contingencies

Although control balance theory predicts the probability and type of deviance, asserting that the odds of some form of deviance as well as the type of deviance likely to occur vary with the degree to which control is imbalanced in either direction from a central zone, it does not imply that an individual with a particular degree and type of control imbalance will necessarily, or frequently, commit the deviance in question. The actual likelihood and frequency of deviance, given an individual's general probability of committing a specific type of deviance, based on that individual's particular control imbalance, are influenced by three sets of factors. One includes things that bring about episodic, temporary alterations in the control ratio. A general control imbalance for any person reflects all forms of control, all role/status configurations, and other elements, but that general ratio of control will not be constant throughout the life cycle, the year, or even the hour. As the individual moves from one social and environmental situation to another, the controls exercised and experienced will also change. Some of these temporary variations may be quite dramatic, as individuals move from domestic to business contexts or from organizational to interpersonal encounters. Because a control deficit in one situation can be balanced by a surplus of control in another situation, an individual's general probability of deviance is closely connected with his or her overall degree of control imbalance, but there are variations that upset universalistic predictions.

Some of those variations are due to the contingencies being discussed. However, these contingencies presuppose a propitious arrangement of the variables in the basic causal sequence of the theory. If those variables do not converge in the ways specified, control imbalances will not eventuate in deviance. Furthermore, a causal alliance of the central variables of the control balancing process may be more or less favorable, depending on the degrees to which the essential variables exist in given situations. Three of the key variables in the causal chain—opportunity, risk, and provocation—are largely contextual, and they have both a discrete and a continuous character. They may or may not be present at all in given circumstances, and that presence or absence is crucial to the basic causal network because without them deviance cannot occur or will take unspecified forms. Even when they are present they may vary in strength, and that variation affects the extent to which the theory operates with greater or lesser efficiency.

Opportunity

Opportunity to commit a particular kind of deviance is a circumstance in which that behavior is possible, that is, the means for its occurrence are at hand. Deviance cannot occur without opportunity, so it is an essential component of the causal process by which control imbalances are translated into deviant acts. Yet, some opportunities are better, or more frequent, than others, and some opportunities barely qualify, whereas others are "golden." Moreover, even minimal opportunities may appear with greater or lesser frequency. Other things being equal, the greater (the fuller and more frequent) the opportunities for deviance appropriate to the particular control ratio, the better the theory will work. This is a clear-cut, linearly interactive contingency.

Consider the hypothetical case of two married individuals, each with all of the relevant conditions to expect adultery. Imagine that one of them is left alone in an inviting situation with an attractive coworker who makes it clear that a sexual encounter would be welcome, whereas the other is left alone with someone who might be interested in a tryst but who is unattractive, and although the situation would permit a sexual encounter, it is not ideal. Clearly, the first is more likely to stray than the second because, even though the causal mechanisms for extramarital sex are present for both, there are differences in the "quality" of opportunities. Similarly, the fact that the first individual encounters an opportunity almost daily, whereas the second individual rarely experiences such favorable circumstances, implies that the causal forces of the theory will work better for one person than the other.

Risk

Given an otherwise favorable array of circumstances, including opportunity, one variable affecting the type of deviance likely to be committed (though not the overall probability of deviance) is constraint. It is made up of the control ratio, the seriousness of a deviant act (implying the amount of countercontrol that potentially can be activated), and risk, which is the probability that the act will be discovered and acted on. Although a minimum of risk is necessary for constraint, and is, therefore, a component of the basic causal process determining the type of deviance likely to occur, the magnitude and frequency of risk are variables heavily dependent on situational peculiarities.

Many things affect the odds that a potential act will be observed by those who might activate countercontrol, and once observed, the chances that the potential act will result in apprehension or action against the offender. These include the number of people around, their attitudes about the deviance, the evidence that might be brought to bear, the presence or absence of control agents or devices for surveillance, the time of day, the physical location and characteristics of the locale, and a host of other things. Moreover, people differ in the frequency with which they encounter highly risky or less risky opportunities. Thus, risk is individually and situationally variable, and in most instances those variations affect how well the process specified by control balance theory operates.

Imagine two potential burglars. One is known by the police and the residents of a neighborhood as a potential threat to property, but the other enjoys relative anonymity. As a result, the risk connected with a local burglary is greater for the first individual than the second, and all other things being equal, the chances of its occurring are less even though the main theoretical conditions for the occurrence of burglary may be present in both cases.

With a similar array of control balancing variables, then, the likelihood of deviance is contingent on the magnitude and frequency of risk inherent in situations and lifestyles, as they bear on specific forms of deviance.

When situational risk is large or small, predictions from the theory will be correspondingly more or less effective, in a linearly interactive fashion.

Provocations

A third situational contingency is the degree to which individuals are made acutely conscious of their control ratios and of the possibilities for changing them through the use of deviant behavior. Recall that provocation is an essential part of the control balancing process—with rare exception, deviance does not occur without it. However, provocation is also a contingency; its intensity and frequency are conditions that influence the extent to which the control balancing process unfolds with greater or lesser force. The greater the provocation, the greater the chances of deviance specified by a particular control ratio, and the weaker the provocation, the lower the chances. Thus provocation is a linearly interactive contingency for the control balancing process.

A common pattern of familial violence illustrates this (Goode 1974; Pagelow 1981; Walker 1979). When a spouse or lover kills a mate, usually it is not a surprise. These killings are preceded by histories of conflict, often involving humiliation, or at least perceived degradation, of one by the other. The conflict usually climaxes with a final ultimate insult when one or the other party is discovered to have taken a lover, claims to have taken such a lover, or threatens to do so. Sometimes these final insults involve verbal denigration of the lovemaking skill or physical attributes of the mate. Yet, most couples experience some conflict, and most people at one time or another degrade their partners.

What is the difference between those marital relationships that end in violence (predation) and those that do not? The answer provided by the theory is twofold. On the one hand, it suggests that they differ in probabilities of violence because the individuals have different control ratios along with different convergences of the variables relevant to control balancing. On the other hand, even those conflicts involving a convergence of control balancing variables favorable toward violence, including provocation, differ in the intensity and frequency of provocation, thereby providing different chances of the predicted outcomes. Those couples with more intense, or more frequent, provocations for creating motivations for deviance to correct a control imbalance will have the greatest chance of acting out the expected predatory deviance.

Multiple Contingencies

So far the contingencies under which the control balance theory operates with greater or lesser force have been discussed as separate and distinct properties. It should be recognized, however, that two or more of these contingencies may combine to affect the theoretical process, that is, contingencies may interact to constitute second-order contingencies.

Consider, for example, an individual with strong moral commitments but weak self-control for whom control balancing variables converge to suggest a particular kind of deviant response. Ordinarily, strong moral commitments will make the theoretical outcomes less likely, whereas weak self-control will make them more likely. If these two contingencies are of equal strength, they will cancel each other so that no contingent effect can be observed. If one is stronger than the other, then a small contingent effect in the direction suggested by the stronger of the two is likely, but since it is not known whether moral sentiment is more important than self-control, this contingent effect cannot be specified more precisely.

In contrast, imagine that an individual otherwise characterized by a convergence of variables favoring a particular deviant outcome has strong moral feelings about that particular type of deviance as well as strong self-control. Since both of these contingent variables are linearly interactive with the control balance process, we would expect their own interaction to affect the process even more acutely than either would alone. Thus, with other things being equal, the predicted outcomes for the individual with moral feelings and strong self-control should be much less than for individuals with either weak moral feelings or weak self-control, or both. In this connection, interacting situational contingencies should be of special import, particularly as they mesh with prior deviance. An individual with strong or frequent opportunities, intense and frequent provocation, recurring exposure to low-risk situations, and a history of having resorted to deviance should have a far greater chance of committing the deviance under consideration than someone with some other combination of the situational variables and prior deviance, assuming that both individuals are characterized by a favorable interconnection of other theoretical variables.

Since there are many contingencies, and each may interact with others in various ways to affect the control balancing process, specifying exact outcomes can be exceptionally complicated. Nevertheless, if the theory is to be given its due, these contingencies must be taken into account singly, in combination, and in interactive alliances. Still, even without such specific application, the theory stands accountable; it should predict the general probability of deviance, as well as specific types of deviance, somewhat better than chance. When the interconnections of the entire theoretical model are accommodated in the ways specified in Chapter 7, an overall set of specific predictions will be demonstrable, and most should prove accurate far beyond chance. When the network of specific predictions is further refined by taking into account the contingencies discussed in this chapter, the outcomes should be even better.

General Summary

Control balance theory holds that there is a fundamental desire or need in human behavior to escape controls that limit one's own options and to extend one's own control, and this sometimes intermeshes with social arrangements to produce a motive for deviant behavior when the ratio of control that can be exercised relative to control experienced is not equal to 1. Given opportunity, this motive expresses itself in actual deviance of some type in reverse proportion to its magnitude, and it expresses itself in specific forms of deviance, depending on constraint. Constraint is a function of the seriousness of the deviance, the degree to which control is imbalanced, and the risk involved in a given situation. The theory assumes that the interplay of the control ratio with the blockage of basic human impulses and the fundamental desire for autonomy affects the predisposition for being motivated to engage in deviant behavior. Such predispositions are activated into actual motivation when situational provocations, especially ones that produce feelings of belittlement, come into operation. The theory alleges that consideration of the control balancing process, taking into account the multitude of elements that go into the overall control ratio, as well as the variables just mentioned, will permit explanation and prediction of both the probability of deviance and the type of deviance likely to be expressed.

However, the theory does not project absolute probabilities; rather, it revolves around relative probabilities of various kinds of deviance. Empirical digressions from theoretically ideal outcomes are postulated and attributed to a number of contingencies under which the control balance process operates with greater or lesser force. Some of those contingencies are personal, some are organizational, and some are situational. The empirical accuracy of the theory depends upon the extent to which these contingencies are taken into account. Three methods of accommodating contingencies can be used in empirical application of the theory. One is to measure and control the effects of the contingent variables by neutralizing them, that is, through statistical procedures to remove their effects. The second method is to examine the effects of the control balance process within subsamples of individuals that differ with respect to the specific contingent variables. The third, and most desirable, approach is to spell out and test highly refined hypotheses that incorporate the interactive effects of the contingencies.

9

Compatibility of the Theory with Evidence

A person's control ratio is complicated because it represents a composite of many specific control relationships reflected in a variety of roles and statuses, groups, organizational structures, and social situations. Since the control ratio is a concept unique to control balance theory, it obviously has not been measured before. Nevertheless, an estimate of a person's general control ratio may be obtained by simultaneous consideration of the major, or crucial, roles the person plays and the main statuses he or she occupies. Such estimates are extremely crude, however, because central roles and statuses reflect only a portion of the control relationships embodied in all of the roles and statuses of the individual and because they omit control relationships embedded in situational social relations and structural arrangements. Moreover, estimating overall control ratios from roles and statuses requires two dubious assumptions: that specific roles and statuses always imply (1) particular amounts of control exercised and experienced and (2) the same control relationships for everybody with those roles and occupying those statuses. Indirect estimates from stable roles and statuses, therefore, cannot yield very good measures of individuals' control ratios. Truly adequate measures must be based on direct indicators of experienced and exercised control in all of the various domains in which control is conceivable, and such indicators must tap general as well as situational variations.

Indicators of Comprehensive Control Ratios

Since there are no measures of control ratios and other concepts specific to control balance theory, extant data directly bearing on its propositions cannot be evaluated. In addition, there are few systematic data about the probability and types of deviance as they vary by *combinations* of roles and statuses, so it is impossible to show the theory's potential by relating estimates of the overall control ratio, based on a combination of the crucial roles and statuses, to probabilities and likelihoods of various kinds of deviance. Indeed, the only reasonably agreed-upon "facts" about deviance concern simple, single-variable demographic distributions of rates of crime and delinquency, which only obliquely represent the deviance categories central to control balance theory. Until data specifically tailored to this theory can be collected, I will have to rely on indirect, ancillary information to show that the theory is compatible with empirical reality.

Single-variable patterns of common criminal/delinquent behavior reflected in "known" rates will be considered first. Although such rates are imperfect reflectors of the actual patterns of these criminal and delinquent acts (Kempf 1990; MacKenzie et al. 1990; O'Brien 1985), only partially mirror the full range of crimes and delinquent acts, and hardly correspond at all with the larger domain of deviance to which the control balance argument is addressed, the theory should at least be consistent with them.

Single-Variable Demographic Variations in Crime and Delinquency

Some demographic patterns of criminal/delinquent behavior seem reasonably well established, though there is still heated debate about their exact nature. I will not try to demonstrate the validity of the patterns to be described, nor will I go into details and technical permutations, because to do so would involve a major scholarly effort detracting from the immediate objective. Instead, I will simply state my interpretation of what current information seems to show and then stand in readiness to reapply the theory if one or another of those interpretations is later shown to be incorrect.

The evidence seems to indicate the following about the demographic distribution of crime and delinquency in the United States: First, except for a few offenses, males commit more crime/delinquency than females (Elliott 1994; Gottfredson and Hirschi 1990:144–149; Nagel and Hagan 1983; Smith and Visher 1980; Steffensmeier and Streifel 1991; Sutherland et al. 1992; Warren 1981; Wilson and Herrnstein 1985:104–115), but the magnitude of the male-female difference varies inversely with age (Farrington 1986; Sutherland et al. 1992:161; Tittle 1980a:81–86) and size of place (Sutherland et al. 1992:161; Tittle 1980a:85) and is greater among whites than among minority groups (Elliott 1994; Sutherland et al. 1992:160; Tittle 1980a:84). In addition, most evidence shows the magnitude of the difference to be greater for serious and violent offenses than for other delicts (Stark and McEvoy 1970; Steffensmeier and Streifel 1991; Sutherland et al. 1992), though some data contradict this (Tittle 1980a:83).

Second, youth engage in more street crimes and moralistic deviance than do older people, although adults commit more violence and middle-aged people commit more professional-occupational deviance and white-collar crime than do younger people (Empey and Stafford 1991; Hirschi and Gottfredson 1983; Steffensmeier et al. 1989b; Sutherland et al. 1992:152; Tittle and Ward 1993).

Third, disadvantaged minority group members seem to commit more street crime, particularly of a serious nature, than do dominant group members (Elliott 1994; Elliott and Ageton 1980; Hindelang 1978, 1981; Hindelang et al. 1979; Wolfgang et al. 1972), although the opposite pattern obviously holds for professional-occupational deviance and white-collar crime.

Fourth, single, unattached people commit more crime and deviance than do married or otherwise socially attached people (Sampson and Laub 1993), and fifth, urban dwellers are more inclined toward crime and deviance than are residents of smaller places (Archer and Gartner 1984; Clinard and Meier 1992:326–327; Fischer 1984; Tittle 1989c).

Sixth, the likelihood of crime/delinquency being committed by people of differing socioeconomic statuses is controversial, with only weak and sporadic, though greater than chance, evidence of an inverse relationship (see Tittle and Meier 1990).

In the following sections control balance theory is applied to these "facts" to assess the compatibility of the theory with existing evidence.

Gender

Differences in Control Ratios. In considering whether the theory is consistent with "known" gender differences in deviance, it is important to stress that available evidence about gender and deviance covers only some types of deviance relevant to the theory. In particular, submission, an extremely important type of deviance dealt with by control balance theory, especially in that it differentiates between males and females, is not usually regarded as deviant by most scholars attempting to measure deviance or compile data concerning gender differences in rates of deviance. Only recently have there been attempts to collect any systematic data about submission, and only a few forms have been studied. Examples of submissive deviance receiving some attention, but rarely mentioned in discussions of gender differences in deviance, are (1) capitulation to, and apparent cooperation by wives and girlfriends in, repeated instances of personal abuse by their lovers or spouses (Giles-Sims 1983; Pagelow 1981; Walker 1979), (2) passive acceptance of sexual harassment in employment, made all the more dramatic by the comparatively rare instances of complaint that have been widely publicized (Anderson 1993), and (3) prostitution in compliance to the demands of pimps (Hall and Adelman 1972). Gender-specific data about some types of defiance (such as vandalism and illegal drug use or abuse of legal drugs) are also available (Anderson 1993; Ferrence 1980a, 1980b; Wilsnack et al. 1984), but other types of defiance (such as withholding sex in a marital relationship or refusal to dress in "gender-appropriate" ways) are neglected by data collectors. The evidence documenting greater male than female deviance, therefore, primarily concerns "ordinary" crimes of predation, a few forms of defiant deviance, and some types of exploitative deviance that are usually referred to as "white-collar crime" (Daly 1989). In addition, historical accounts of jaded rulers suggest that most forms of plunderous and decadent deviance are more likely among males than females.

Control balance theory, however, is acutely sensitive to specific types of deviance. Its power and accuracy cannot be appreciated without considering the panorama of ways that an individual might violate social expectations. As we will see, although the theory explains why males are more likely to commit predatory and all forms of autonomous deviance (the "facts" documented by extant data), it suggests that measurement of other kinds of deviance not currently addressed in any systematic data collection would show male-female differences to be somewhat divergent from the pattern revealed by existing data. Moreover, the principles of the theory suggest that gender differences in specific forms of deviance can be expected to change as current social trends unfold more completely.

Why are there male-female differences in deviance? Control balance theory explains the greater deviance of males suggested by presently available data for the United States and other modern societies mainly as a product of variations in control ratios. Most objective observers acknowledge that female status is ranked lower than male status, that the normative female role is subordinate to the normative male role, and that gender roles influence the distribution of individuals in occupational, political, and social positions that permit the exercise of control and the expression of personal autonomy (Messerschmidt 1986; Schur 1984). Since organizational positions directly reflect capacities for exercising or escaping control, and because social statuses and roles indirectly do so, most females are "repressed" (as opposed to "autonomous") to one degree or another, that is, they have control deficits.

As a result, the largest proportion of females should be in the extreme repressive zone of the control balance continuum (see Figure 9.1), where they have a high probability of committing some form of deviance, most likely of the submissive variety. A lesser, but still notable, proportion should fall in the zone of moderate repression, where they have a smaller probability of committing deviance but have a high probability that the deviance they commit will be of the defiant form. The proportion of women falling in each zone from the left side of the continuum to the right should decline steadily. Consequently, the third-highest concentration of females should be in the marginal zone of repression, where the probability of deviance is small but likely to be of the predatory type when it does occur. The fourth-highest proportion of women should be in the balanced zone, where conformity is the mode. Each successive zone on the autonomy end of the continuum, where the probability of autonomous deviance increases monotonically, contains a smaller proportion of all females, with the maximum zone of autonomy encompassing only a tiny proportion of all females.

The zones of the control balance continuum are demarcated with vertical lines in Figure 9.1, and the characteristic deviances for the zones are noted at the bottom of the columns representing those zones. The darkened space in the upper panel represents the relative proportion of fe-

FEMALES

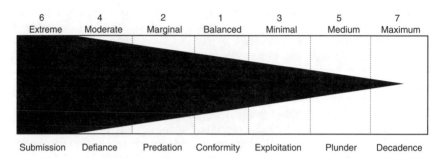

MALES

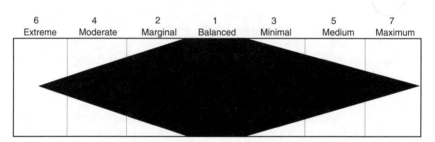

Figure 9.1   Female and Male Concentration in the Various Zones of the Control Balance Continuum

males in each zone. The declining proportion of females in each successive zone from the left to the right of the continuum is portrayed by the narrowing of the darkened space. This figure depicts expectations based on speculative reasoning because hard, direct data concerning control ratios do not exist, nor are there systematic data concerning the potential for exercising or escaping control inherent in statuses and roles. Morever, even though the control ratio is the most important factor in understanding deviance, other variables are involved, and they may reflect systematic differences between males and females that get translated into gender differences in probabilities and types of deviance. The focus here is on the control ratio as it bears on male-female differences in rates of deviance.

The lower panel in Figure 9.1 portrays the likely proportion of males in each zone of the control balance continuum. Because of the advantages males enjoy in having a higher-status role that is normatively more desirable and that helps distribute them in occupational, political, organizational, and social positions with greater potential for exercising control

FEMALES AND MALES

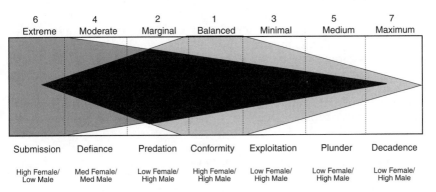

Figure 9.2   The Relative Ratio of Female to Male Concentration in the Various Zones of the Control Balance Continuum

and expressing personal autonomy, the largest proportion of males should fall in the balanced zone of the continuum, where they are characterized as conformists. Males with unbalanced control ratios are concentrated in decreasing proportion as one moves out from the central zone of the continuum in both directions. Thus the second-highest concentrations of males are in the marginal zone of repression or the minimal zone of autonomy, where their probabilities of deviance are low but where either predatory or exploitative types are expected when violation does occur. The third-highest concentrations are in the moderate zone of repression and the medium zone of autonomy, where deviance has a modest probability of occurring and where the likely type is defiance and plunder, respectively. Finally, the smallest concentrations of males are in the extreme zone of repression and the maximum zone of autonomy, where the probabilities of submission and decadence are high. As with females in the upper panel of Figure 9.1, the relative proportion of males in each category is depicted by the darkened space in the lower panel of the figure. The largest space is in the middle of the continuum and progressively declines from zone to zone outward from the center to each end of the continuum.

Superimposing the male distribution over the female distribution (Figure 9.2) shows how the relative proportion of the sexes in each zone compares. There is an excess of males in the areas designated by slanted hatchmarks. And an excess of females in the areas designated by squares. Females are far more concentrated in the extreme repression zone than males, and are about equally, or perhaps a little more, concentrated in the moderate zone of repression. In all other zones of the continuum, however, males are more concentrated than females. Therefore, females should have far higher rates of submissive deviance and slightly higher or about equal rates of defiant deviance, but they should have lower relative rates of all other forms of deviance, including predation and the autonomous forms of deviance. Moreover, they should conform *less* than males.

Whether males, relative to females, have higher general rates of deviance depends on the absolute numbers and age distributions of males and females in the various zones of the continuum and on the interaction of those absolute numbers with the probabilities of deviance in each of the categories. Since those absolute numbers and age distributions are not currently known, it is impossible to derive explicit hypotheses. However, the proportion of males would appear to exceed the proportion of females in four of the deviance-generating categories, whereas the proportion of females would appear to exceed the proportion of males in only two deviance-generating categories, so there should be an overall higher rate of male deviance. However, this is complicated by the fact that females predominate in the zone of the continuum indicative of the highest probability of repressive deviance and males predominate in categories with higher probabilities of autonomous deviance. Therefore, it is more meaningful to make gender comparisons within zones of the continuum, at least until systematic data appropriate to the theory are collected.

Two aspects of the above discussion may trouble some readers because they seem to contradict what "everybody knows." The first one is the suggestion that a larger proportion of males than females conform. Since much literature indicates that females violate fewer rules, this might seem to cast the whole control balance argument into doubt. Recall, however, that deviance and conformity are defined in specific ways that are meaningful within the parameters of the theory. In particular, conformity and submission are different. Conformity occurs when the individual can realistically visualize alternative forms of behavior but nevertheless chooses to obey social expectations. Submission occurs when the individual completely and passively obeys the rules without contemplation or imagination of alternatives. Hence, much behavior usually regarded as conforming is actually submissive. If deviance meant only violation of codified rules, it would be clear that males commit more deviance. The theory, however, concerns violations of social rules, and it suggests that because of the unfavorable control ratios of females, they will be particularly prone to submissive deviance but less prone to conformity.

A second aspect of the gender and deviance discussion that may appear to contradict evidence is the suggestion that females exhibit about the same amount of, or perhaps more, defiant deviance than males. Remember that systematic data about defiance is quite limited, usually including only things like nonmarital sex, illegal drug use, vandalism, truancy, running away, curfew violations, and suicide, while ignoring many forms of defiance that may be much more characteristic of females, such as withholding sexual response or access, pouting or crying, slowdowns or deliberately faulty performance in household or occupational work, less than maximum effort in child care, excessive use of prescription or over-the-counter drugs, and "acting-out" behaviors that are often interpreted as manifestations of mental illness. Moreover, male-female differences for specific types of defiance for which systematic data have been collected (sometimes referred to as peccadillos in criticisms of self-report studies) are small, at best (Smart 1979; Smith and Visher 1980). In view of this, the theory's portrayal of gender differences in deviance appears compatible with "commonsense" information. Moreover, when sufficient appropriate data are available, they should provide empirical support for the patterns described above, even for those that might now appear to be aberrant.

It is important, however, to specify exactly how the theory explains the distributions of males and females in the various zones of the control balance continuum. Those distributions rest on general patterns of differential control exercised along gender lines. Most men are subject to some control from other men, organizational arrangements, environmental constraints, and to a lesser extent from women and children, but most men in turn exercise considerable control over the environment, substantial control over women (especially in a collective sense), and some control over children. Thus in general, the control deficit that some men experience comes mainly from other men and from organizational arrangements. However, the potentially greater deficits they might experience are somewhat compensated for by the increased control most men have over women and children. Therefore, the control ratio for many men is close to 1, that is, the control they exercise is reasonably well balanced by the control they experience. Yet, a fairly large proportion of males do have control deficits because they suffer a larger than usual deficit resulting from control by other men, they have little or no control over the environment or organizations, and they have very limited control over women or children. A significant minority of males can be characterized as having a surplus of control because they can control other men, women, and children, as well as organizations and the physical environment.

Since most females suffer serious deficits from control exercised by men collectively, from organizational arrangements, and from the environment, they might appear to be extremely repressed and likely to commit submissive deviance. There are, however, some compensating controls. The dispersion of females over the entire continuum, portrayed in Figure 9.1, is partly due to the role of women in dealing with children, partly because of their potential ability to control men in the sexual realm, partly from the skills and abilities of many individual females in modern societies that enable them to escape some repression or to exercise control they might not otherwise have, and partly due to the collective organization of women in modern societies.

The traditional linkage of females with children is a major factor affecting their control ratios. In all societies, almost any woman can claim a role giving her control over children, either her own or those she attends to as teacher, nursemaid, preschool supervisor, or baby-sitter. Collectively, the greater the number of children, the greater the possibility of control by females. Thus, regardless of the political and social subordination of females to males and regardless of how disadvantaged females might be in controlling environmental factors, most have a means of reducing a potentially greater control imbalance. Of course, this alleviating mechanism has become less available in modern societies with the decline in the number of children (Petersen 1969; Wattenberg 1987).

Second, many women can mute potential control imbalances by manipulating males through sexual attraction, even without actual physical contact. Male eagerness to please women whom they perceive as potential, or even fantasized, sex objects is well known. Although the potentiality for manipulating males varies with the perceived attractiveness of the individual female, the overall number of females relative to males (Guttentag and Secord 1983), and other factors, it nevertheless remains an important source of control.

Third, although women have been generally repressed throughout history, some strong, resourceful females have always managed to overcome those circumstances. In modern societies where women have greater opportunity for education and the exercise of talent, the abilities and skills of larger numbers of individual women are being expressed.

Finally, despite centuries of subordination and isolation, women in modern societies are organizing themselves to promote their interests in opposition to male-dominated structural and political arrangements. Despite their generally subordinate statuses, modern females vary greatly in their control ratios, and some number of women can be found in all the zones of the control balance continuum.

Since modernization's effects on the likelihood of female deviance have been controversial (Smart 1979; Steffensmeier 1978; Steffensmeier and Cobb 1981; Steffensmeier et al. 1989a; Steffensmeier and Streifel 1991), it is important to contemplate that issue from the point of view of control balance theory. In dispute are changes in rates of female crime and whether females are "catching up" with males. Scholars claim that in response to modernization and political organization (the women's movement) the roles and freedoms of males and females are becoming more similar. As a result, female rates of crime are said to be growing, eventually to equal those of males (Adler 1975; Simon 1975). Evidence in support of this contention includes a documented increase in absolute rates of female crime and delinquency (Merlo 1995), but the argument turns mainly on evidence of relatively higher *rates of increase* in female than male crime.

The counterargument suggests that even though female crime has been growing, increases are mainly in "soft" (nonpredatory) forms of crime. Moreover, an appearance of ballooning female crime is an illusion created by focusing on rates of increase that are biased by low base figures (Steffensmeier 1978; Steffensmeier and Cobb 1981). Thus a group that commits 10 crimes in one year but commits 20 crimes the next (10 additional crimes) registers a 100 percent increase, whereas a group that commits 100 crimes in one year but 150 the next (50 additional crimes) registers only a 50 percent increase. It appears that the first group is gaining on the second group because the rate of increase is 50 percent greater (100 percent versus 50 percent), but actually the first group is committing only 20 percent as many additional crimes as the second group (10 additional crimes versus 50).

The theory suggests that both sides of the dispute are correct. Female rates of "serious" crimes increase with modernization because many females shift from the category of extreme deficit of control toward the right side of the control balance continuum. However, that trend also produces increases among females in rates of defiant (or "soft" crime), and it simultaneously raises rates of predatory and defiant crime among males because their previously favorable control ratios are shifting toward the left side of the continuum with erosion of their control over women. The net effect is an increase in female crimes of all types, but the overall rate of female crime relative to male crime will probably not change much. This apparent contradiction is due to the fact that the same forces that affect female crime rates also affect those of males, although in different ways, and to the fact that the rate of female deviance relative to male deviance depends upon the proportion of each gender distributed over the various control balance zones.

Distributions of the genders across the control balance continuum change with alterations in the number of children in a population, the number of males relative to females, and the level of technological advancement, all of which are interlinked and differentially operative in complex ways. As a society modernizes, the control balances of males and females shift in the direction of increasing predatory and defiant deviance for both, but especially for females. The major stimuli for these changes are (1) declines in fertility resulting from increased contraceptive knowledge and use and from abortion, (2) growth in female labor-force participation, and (3) decreases in mortality (all rooted in advanced technology) (Keyfitz 1982; Retherford 1975; Weeks 1981).

Reducing fertility has two important effects on differential control ratios. First, lower fertility, coupled with declining mortality, causes the sex ratio (males relative to females) to decrease. This is because without modernization, the high sex ratio at birth (it is currently about 105 in modern societies and is probably higher in simple societies) in conjunction with high fertility (children born per woman) produces a young population dominated by males. This condition tends to prevail despite higher mortality of males at all ages because, without modernization, life expectancy is too short to allow that mortality difference to balance the sex ratio. With modernization, however, fertility tends to decline, and life expectancy tends to increase (Petersen 1969; Thomlinson 1965). As a result, high fertility, which increases the proportion of the population that is male and young in simple societies, is reduced drastically, and longer life expectancy permits higher male mortality (at all ages from conception to late age) to equalize the sex ratio in the late twenties and to distort it drastically in favor of females in later ages.

Drawing on the insights of Marcia Guttentag and Paul Secord (1983), one can project that a high sex ratio (more males than females), characteristic of nonmodern societies, creates competition among males for sexual partners. This gives individual females considerable leverage to control and manipulate males interpersonally through sexual attraction. As the sex ratio declines (females become more numerous relative to males) with modernization, however, so does the ability of females to achieve a more favorable control balance through manipulation of males by sexual attraction (this argument assumes that homosexuality due to genetic influence is equally distributed across both genders; to the extent that homosexuality is socially produced, constituting a form of defiant deviance, the theory provides an explanation for differing rates among genders and other social and demographic categories that draws on the same sex-ratio logic). At the same time, lower fertility associated with advanced technologically oriented societies decreases the control that women can exercise over children. Thus, if this were the whole story, modernization would tend to redistribute females further toward the repression end of the continuum than they are in simple societies, creating higher rates of female deviance of the submissive and defiant types.

However, there is a counterimpetus in modern societies, also linked to changing sex ratios (Guttentag and Secord 1983). As women become more numerous relative to men, they gain the ability, and develop the desire, to organize politically and to express individualism in conduct, both of which permit escape from male-dominated interpersonal control as well as exercise of collective control against organizations and males. In addition, as modern technology removes the necessity for physical strength in most work and relieves the burden of childbearing, females become more occupationally dispersed, independent, and capable of overcoming environmental constraints, that is, their abilities to control and to escape control move closer to those of males. This is expressed as a reduction in the control deficit females would otherwise experience, thereby dispersing them toward the right of the control balance continuum. This leads to increases among females in the kinds of deviance that were previously the province of males (especially predatory and autonomy-associated deviance), as well as to an increase in conformity.

Hence, reductions in control of children and in interpersonal control of males that result from modernization pull women toward the repressive end of the control continuum where more submissive and defiant deviance (that would register as reductions in "nonserious criminal behavior") is expected. Alternatively, greater participation in the labor force and expanding political control push females toward the autonomous end of the control continuum where more predatory and autonomous-associated deviance (that would register as increases in rates of "serious" and white-collar crime) would be expected. Still, even with this countertrend occurring, modernization should produce long-term increases among females in the types of deviance previously almost the exclusive domain of males, and it should decrease types of deviance previously dominated by females, particularly submissiveness. This is because equalization of political and organizational control is, in the long run, a more potent influence on control ratios than is decline in control over children and in interpersonal control over men. The processes that are increasing female crime rates, however, are likely to unfold slowly because changes in status and political organization in response to a favorable sex ratio take a long time, particularly to reach the point where female exercise of, and escape from, control is sufficient to overcome the loss of control due to declining numbers of children and to shrinking ability to manipulate males interpersonally.

Achieving control parity with males will also be slow for females because modernization modifies the usual dispersion of males across the control continuum, thereby affecting their normal rates of particular kinds of deviance. Since part of the control ratio for males depends upon their control relationships with females, technological and other changes affecting the ability of women to exercise control over males or to escape control from males also affect the control ratios of males. Declining fertility, for instance, which ultimately affects the sex ratio and reduces female ability to exercise control over children and over males interpersonally but which leads to greater political and organizational control by females, simultaneously increases interpersonal, sexually driven control by males over females while reducing males' collective organizational and political control of females. Since organizational and political control are generally more important components of control ratios than interpersonal control, modernization results in shifts of substantial numbers of men leftward toward the repression end of the control balance continuum. This, of course, reduces male conformity and increases predatory and defiant deviance. So, modernization enhances female defiance, predation, and autonomy-associated deviance as well as conformity while at the same time increasing male predation and defiance and decreasing male conformity and autonomy-associated deviance. Thus despite absolute increases in female predation and defiance in modern societies, there has also been an absolute increase in male predation and defiance. Therefore the *relative* rates of the two have not changed much (Steffensmeier and Cobb 1981; Steffensmeier and Streifel 1991).

Furthermore, the deviance (or crime) rates of males and females probably will never match. Correspondence cannot occur unless males and females are fully equal socially (especially including equality in dealing with children and each other), organizationally, politically, and in the ability to control the environment. Since such equality depends at least in part on an equal sex ratio, which is, in turn, tied in with fertility and differential mortality rates, the prospects for it are extremely remote. Because differential mortality apparently is at least partially biological (Retherford 1975), it is hard to imagine that fertility rates and sex ratios, even if the sex ratios at conception or birth became medically manipulable, could ever be fine-tuned and coordinated with rates of mortality enough to generate equal sex ratios across the various age categories or even for a whole population. Despite ideology and the potency of organization, gender inequality in some form and degree, with corresponding differences in rates and types of deviance, may always persist because demographic forces lie outside the reach of human control.

The relative distribution of males and females in the various control balance zones (and their likely relative rates of various kinds of deviance) not only varies historically in the same society but also varies across societies. Women in the contemporary United States, for example, are more widely dispersed over the control continuum than are women in Third World countries, and they are far more likely to commit predatory and autonomous types of deviance as well as to conform than Third World women. At the same time, Third World women are far more likely to commit submissive acts than are women in the United States (though much submission in Third World countries may not be deviant).

Differences in Other Variables in the Causal Chain. In the theory, the control ratio is implicated in a number of ways in the causal processes affecting the probability and type of deviance, and for that reason the control ratio is the most important variable in accounting for gender differences in crime or deviance. Nevertheless, differences between the genders in other variables in the causal scheme are also relevant for explaining male-female differences. Recall that in addition to a control imbalance, the causal scheme involves predisposition toward being motivated for deviance, actual motivation, opportunity, and constraint and that all of these except opportunity are produced by interconnections of other variables, including situational provocation, debasement, situational risk, seriousness of potential deviant acts, and constraint. Since all of the main variables except opportunity are partly products of the control ratio, which has already been shown to be highly likely to show gender differentiation, it follows that they reflect gender differentiation that could produce differences between males and females in the probability and type of deviance. In addition, there are probably gender differences in opportunity, situational provocations, and debasement, which are not directly linked to the control ratio but which could affect male-female differences in deviance.

Cultural patterns of interaction and social structure typically restrict the number of contexts within which females operate during any given time period to a much greater extent than they do males. As a result, females encounter fewer opportunities for many kinds of deviance, particularly those associated with the autonomous end of the control continuum and predation, although females may confront more opportunities for defiance or submission. This accounts for some gender differences in deviance. Patterns of offense among females who actually engage in deviance are consistent with this reasoning. Female predation is almost always against the children and husbands (or boyfriends) who populate their domains, whereas defiant behavior by females is usually directed against narrow normative domains (those governing styles of dress, personal autonomy, or conventional modes of behavior) or interactional networks (such as the family), rather than against large institutional structures (such as the government, corporate economic relationships, or religious organizations). Differences in opportunity, therefore, appear to contribute to gender differences in deviance, though differences in control ratios seem far more important.

Variations in situational provocations as well as in debasement probably also contribute to gender differences in deviance. Males more frequently encounter situations reminding them of their control ratios than do females, and males are more prone to feel "putdown" by such reminders. This might seem counterintuitive since female roles and statuses are more subordinating and social and other restrictions women suffer might seem inherently humiliating. Being provoked, however, is partly a matter of simple probability. Frequency of movement through situations of any kind increases the chances that some of them will be provoking. Males have more experiences of all types, including those that might stimulate awareness of relative control imbalances. Furthermore, tendencies for humiliation are linked to self-definition, anticipations, beliefs, and personality traits like self-confidence. Expecting deference will cause a person to feel demeaned by an insult or an unintended slight that is ignored by those who have accepted subordinate status. Since females are often socialized to accept an inferior or passive role, they are less easily humiliated by actions or circumstances that produce acute distress among males.

Furthermore, male interactions always feature more jockeying and challenging for dominance, especially physical dominance and especially among late adolescents and young adults. The reasons are not established, though many believe it is linked to testosterone (Booth and Osgood 1993). In my view, masculine struggles for dominance represent efforts to escape or extend control, particularly in the face of deprivation. The reason such "tests" of strength prevail among males and not females, who generally are more deprived, may be due, in part, to two things.

Traditionally, and to some extent continuing into the present, the male role was defined by active subjugation of the forces of nature and protection of his domain, including the females under his influence. The female role was defined by nurturance and manipulation of the products produced by the male's subjugating activities. These role distinctions made sense in primitive environments because they meshed with the superior physical strength of males and the relative confinement and dependency of females handicapped by childbearing and nursing. Even though these differentiations have become less rational with advancing technology, some have been perpetuated, though they have been more diluted with each iteration, as the cultural heritage has been transmitted through inter-

generational socialization. Because of these role distinctions ideally calling for dominance, males are more concerned about their relative control
ratios. Consequently, they suffer much anxiety about whether they are
living up to expectations, and uncertainty stimulates tests. Recurring
challenges within male culture (Luckenbill 1977, 1984) produce more potentially demeaning situational provocations than are faced by females
(Sanders 1981; Short and Strodtbeck 1974).

A second relevant male-female difference is the greater freedom of
males to move among social domains. They see and meet more people,
and their associational networks are broader than those of females, whose
activities are more circumscribed and whose territories are less extensive.
This creates more challenges and more potentially provoking situations
for males because challenges often settle, at least for a while, the issues
that produced them. New encounters hold uncertainties about dominance that often stimulate new challenges. Once dominance is established
and has been certified through successful handling of "tests," the dominant individual is less likely to be challenged by the same parties. New
interactants, however, re-create uncertainty and stimulate provocation.

Because roles prescribe male conquest and defense and lead to tests for
dominance made more frequent by the fluidity of social contacts, males
often face conditions likely to generate deviant motivation, which enhances gender differences in deviant behavior. Moreover, these processes
are accentuated under conditions of material deprivation. Being without
resources, as adolescents, especially inner-city ones, and prisoners are, often stimulates cooperation to elicit the maximum possible gain from an
environment, as illustrated by subcultural organization. However, at the
same time it spurs masculine competition for dominance. Male adolescent gangs, losing athletic teams, prison inmate groups, underpaid work
crews, and military units in especially difficult circumstances are almost
always arenas for struggles of dominance. Under depriving circumstances, many males feel inadequate because they cannot display the
fruits of subjugating activities called for by the male role. This incites
competition for scarce symbols of masculine achievement. Sometimes, of
course, the need for cooperation is so compelling that tests of dominance
take a back seat to organized attack on the real or perceived sources of deprivation. This happens when an "enemy" or "depriver"—usually someone or something that embodies the masculine ideal of dominance—is
easily identifiable and close at hand. Military units and individual soldiers vie unless engagement with the external enemy is imminent or in
process. Prison and other institutional inmates contest intramurally except when they must confront their keepers as a collectivity (such as in a
lockdown or other mass restriction). By contrast, deprived adolescents,
even in gangs, can rarely identify external enemies, so they resort to turf
wars and internecine conflict.

Since gender differences in deviance are in part due to more frequent
and intense provocations among males, changing roles and statuses of fe-

males that expose them to more of these kinds of situations should ultimately lead to a narrowing of overall gender differences in deviance. This
is confirmed by observing contemporary groups in which male and female
roles are closer, such as among blacks in the United States, that suggest
smaller gender differences in rates and types of deviance than elsewhere.

Differences in Contingent Variables. Although the main explanation
for gender differences in deviance involves the control ratio, other variables in the causal chain through which the control ratio affects deviance
also play some part. In addition, variations in contingencies influence
male-female differences in rates and kinds of deviance. To the extent that
some contingencies are more prominent in one gender than the other,
there should also be some differences in actual deviance.

Whereas some contingencies probably vary only among individuals
(for example, personality variables and perception), others probably
show general sex differences. For example, prior deviance and organizational contingencies seem particularly characteristic of males. For reasons
already specified, the control balancing process produces more deviance
among those who have previously engaged in successful deviance; males
commit more nonsubmissive and nondefiant deviance than females; and
males begin deviating sooner. Therefore males are more likely to experience the recidivist effects of prior deviance. As time goes on, prior deviance grows more powerful in its contingent consequences for males.
The end result is greater gender difference in deviance than otherwise
would exist.

The same applies to organizational contingencies. Since males are freer
at all ages to associate with others, they have more chance than females of
becoming enmeshed in organizational networks encouraging deviant
mechanisms for changing control ratios or discounting the fear of potential countercontrolling responses. As a result, the control balancing
process is more likely to lead to deviance among males than among females—at least the kind of deviance that attracts the attention of officials—even when other variables in the process are more or less equal.

Age

Variations in Control Ratios. Although some aspects of the age-crime relationship are controversial, the main facts are unchallenged. However,
whether they correspond with age-deviance patterns predicted by the
theory cannot be fully ascertained for the same reasons that the theory's
predictions about the gender-deviance relationship could not be tested.
There are no adequate measures of the relevant variables, and applying
crude, indirect measures requires numerous dubious assumptions.
Nevertheless, the theory should account for, or at least be consistent with,
the apparent facts about age and crime: (1) Defiant and predatory crime is
concentrated among those in the late teen years, (2) the likelihood of
predatory and defiant forms of crime declines steadily from its peak years

in the late teens or early twenties, and (3) white-collar and occupational crime are concentrated among the middle-aged.

Since youth have the highest rates of predatory and defiant crime, most young people must have control deficits if the theory is to fit the facts. I contend that they do. Because American and other postindustrial youth undergo long periods of training in specialized educational institutions before they can assume occupational, marital, parental, and political roles (Sebald 1992), they are necessarily dependent and disadvantaged in control relationships. Young people are generally controlled by adults, organizations, the political structure, the environment, and their peers, but they, in turn, can control only each other and selected adults. As a consequence of this, young people suffer serious control deficits, just as the theory requires. Nevertheless, at first glance it might appear that the theory is wrong, since the above considerations suggest that young people are almost totally concentrated in the moderate and extreme zones on the repressive end of the control continuum, where the characteristic forms of deviance to be expected are defiance and submission. Yet, although the data on crime confirm a large volume of defiance among young people (Empey and Stafford 1991:95–100), they also indicate much predation and conformity, contradicting the expected predominance of submission.

This apparent inconsistency stems from a conception of the control ratios of youth based strictly on their individual roles and statuses. Adolescents do not always confront the world as individuals, however. Rather, there is a strong tendency, enhanced by modern warehouse education and recreation, as well as by proximal residential patterns in urban centers, for young people to organize themselves into subcultural groupings (Agnew 1995; Hagan 1991; Schwendinger and Schwendinger 1985; Sebald 1992). These subcultural organizations enable adolescents to escape adult control, especially by school authorities and parents, and in some instances help them exercise control over the environment and adults. Adolescent subcultural organizations range from loosely structured friendship groups through modestly cohesive clique networks to tightly organized juvenile gangs. Although not all youth alliances are strong, any degree of organization shifts young people from concentration on the repressive left end of the control continuum toward the center. Thus, because of affiliation with subcultural organizations, the location on the control continuum for many young people is in the moderate zone rather than in the extreme zone; by the same token, some youth who as individuals would be in the moderate zone actually have control ratios placing them in the marginal zone, where the control they experience begins to exceed only slightly that which they exercise. The net effect of subcultural organization among youth is to disperse them more widely over the control continuum.

Being dispersed across the three repressive zones of the control continuum, but being especially concentrated in the moderate zone, youth are theoretically candidates for fairly high rates of deviance (relative to adults), especially of the defiant type (much of which is regarded as delinquent behavior). Youthful defiance includes such things as disobeying authorities and parents, perpetrating vandalism, exhibiting surliness, engaging in sexual escapades, and indulging in various kinds of drug usage. The deviance of some youth, especially that committed by those who have managed to organize themselves into gangs, is mainly predatory, including various forms of theft and violence (which is registered in the statistics as criminal behavior). With some assumptions about the control ratios of youth, then, the theory produces predictions consistent with what is known about delinquency and crime among young people.

The theory is also compatible with two other accepted facts about delinquency, namely, that (1) most delinquency occurs in company with other young people (Erickson and Jensen 1977; Sarnecki 1986; Stafford 1984; Zimring 1981), and (2) individual adolescents usually do not specialize in one or another type of delinquency (Farrington et al. 1988; Paternoster and Tittle 1990). The group context of delinquency is easily explained by control balancing. When alone, most young people suffer serious deficits of control, that is, without the support and cooperation of peers, most adolescents have control imbalances of extreme repression. This gives them a high probability of submission, a form of deviance not generally regarded as delinquent by adults. With peers, however, adolescents are more widely dispersed along the continuum toward the center, that is, peer support enables them to escape the repression they would otherwise suffer as youthful individuals. Cooperation among peers renders youth particularly prone to defiant forms of deviance, and some become candidates for predatory deviance. Hence, the circumstances that alter the "otherwise operative" control ratios of youth, pushing them into greater likelihood of the kind of deviance counted as criminal or delinquent, are those in which delinquency has been demonstrated to occur most often—in company with peers. Remember also that provocations for deviance emerge in situations reminding people of their usual control ratios and that make them acutely aware of means to alter them. Peer group association is one circumstance that has that provocative ability.

The pattern taken by young people in committing many different types of delinquency also makes sense within the theory. Teenagers are marked by insecurity about their position in life, which stems from inconsistent definitions of role, position, rights, and responsibilities. Adolescence is a status defined by ambiguity; expectations of child and adult behaviors are mixed and invoked almost arbitrarily by adults. Sometimes teens are given responsibilities with a good deal of autonomy; at other times they are denied even the smallest freedom, with the change from one set of expectations to the other being frequent and abrupt. The control ratios for young people, therefore, are not nearly as fixed as they are for adults. Most youth literally slide back and forth, daily or even hourly, from one repressive zone of the control balance continuum to another.

Since the probability and type of deviance are largely reflections of the individual's control ratio, youth commit a variety of different kinds of deviance rather than just one type, which would be characteristic of individuals with more stable control ratios.

With adulthood comes greater ability to exercise control relative to being controlled. Labor-force participation yields increasing control over the environment and weakens control by others, especially parents and school authorities. Marriage and full community participation produce control of women by males and control of children by females. With increasing seniority there is incremental gain in occupationally linked control, leading to more balanced control ratios and less deviance.

For men, this gain in control exercised and the decline in control experienced continue until late middle age when they face retirement, loss of physical strength, and declining income. With adulthood, most men move into zones of the control continuum where they are inclined to conform or become likely to commit autonomous kinds of deviant behavior, such as occupational or white-collar crime. With increasing age, there is a steady decline in predatory crime and delinquent behavior among males, with a corresponding increase in the rate of exploitative, contemptuous, and decadent deviance. A particularly noticeable rise in exploitative deviance occurs as males acquire political, economic, or professional control that exceeds the control to which they are exposed. Ultimately, however, old age erodes this favorable control ratio, as men reach retirement age and their incomes decline. This shifts many back toward the left of the continuum, often to the moderate zone where their behavior begins to resemble that of adolescents, but sometimes they shift dramatically to the extreme repressive zone where they become highly submissive.

Growth in autonomy with the achievement of adulthood is seldom as great for females since the vast majority of them never assume political, economic, or professional roles that afford more favorable control relationships, and many quickly exchange the subordination of youth for subordination in marriage. Although adulthood produces some gains in autonomy for females—mainly through increases in interpersonal control of males and children and in expanded control of economic resources—these gains typically continue only to early middle age when women face declining sexual attractiveness, fewer child care opportunities, and reduced sources of economic support. In early adulthood most females move into the zones of the control balance continuum signifying conformity, though many continue to have control ratios implying a fairly high probability of engaging in noncriminal deviance, such as submissiveness or defiance, committed by those who are bound by traditional housewife roles. A few move into autonomous zones through their career achievements. In middle age, and considerably sooner than for males, the control ratios of females begin to shift back toward the repressive end of the continuum. The result is increasing submissiveness and defiance among post-middle-aged females.

Thus, with some assumptions about control ratios implied by age and gender, accounts from control balance theory appear consistent with life-cycle variations in deviance. The analysis, however, may not be convincing to some who might reason that the theory's logic requires most aged people, at least during the transition from active adult to aged status, to engage in more predation and defiance than do middle-aged people. With advanced age, people (at least in modern societies) begin to lose control because of changes in occupational positions (especially men), loss of control of children and members of the opposite sex (especially by women), and decline in environmental control due to eroding physical strength and health and reductions in income (characteristic of both genders), while they become more susceptible to being controlled by organizations, younger adults, and the environment. This transitional shifting of older people back toward the left of the control continuum makes them prone to commit types of deviance not characteristic of adults in their active years. For those previously in the balanced zone (conformists), the immediate shift would be to the marginal zone, and then with passing time into the moderate, and finally into the extreme repressive zone, generating higher rates of predatory and defiant deviance along the way. This, of course, seems to contradict much empirical evidence suggesting that aged people commit little crime and that the relationship between age and many forms of predatory deviance is monotonically downward from the early twenties on.

Two additional considerations, however, support the theory. First, much evidence shows that older people engage in a lot more defiant and predatory deviance than police data reflect. Research using private security police records reveals astounding amounts of shoplifting (Curran 1984), and other data show much insurance fraud (forms of predation) as well as other forms of minor crime among those in their later years (Alston 1986; Wilbanks and Kim 1984). In addition, the aged display high rates of suicide, alcoholism, and bizarre behavior usually thought to be indicative of mental illness (Gottheil 1985; Lester and Tallmer 1994; Turner 1992), and common observation suggests that aged people readily defy the social conventions of ordinary courtesy, such as grocery checkout, elevator, and public transport etiquette. Remember that the theory is about deviance generally, not about criminal behavior specifically.

Second, the transition from active community and economic participant (with the means to avoid control deficits) to dependent (where few resources of physical strength, occupational and political position, and economic means can be marshaled) is very rapid for most males. Once a man retires from active employment, he loses much ability to control and to escape control and almost immediately finds himself with a substantial discrepancy between the control he experiences and the control he exercises, that is, most find themselves in the moderate or extreme repressive zones, having entirely bypassed, or having spent only a short time in, the marginal zone. Others, who during middle age had surplus control ratios, move quickly into balanced zones, and a few move into the marginally repressive zone. Aged males, therefore, are concentrated mainly in the defiant or submissive zones, with smaller proportions in the marginal and balanced zones. As a result, older males exhibit fairly high rates of defiant or submissive deviance, far exceeding the rates of these types of deviance among active adult males in late middle age, when occupational, social, and political roles produce control that balances or exceeds the control to which they are exposed. In particular, these men turn to alcoholism, drug dependency, disrespect for established institutions, and discourtesy. For those males who are quite old, the theory predicts a huge control deficit that produces slavish obedience for a large number of them, no matter where they previously were on the control balance continuum. Changes in male control ratios that accompany aging also produce some increase in ordinary predatory deviance that gets registered as crime (usually shoplifting or fraud). Thus control balance expectations are consistent with evidence of age-linked declines in all crime except physically nondemanding property offenses, and with evidence of dramatic increases in defiant acts as well as submission, that accompany advancing age.

The transition for adult females to less active age-categories is not nearly as dramatic or rapid as for males, though it usually transpires at younger ages. Women lose their attractiveness and special role as supervisors of children much more slowly than men lose their occupational and political positions, although females may lose their economic means quickly through death of the spouse or divorce (though some, of course, gain economic resources through these same events). However, since a greater number of active adult females than males fall toward the left of the control continuum, female transition to old age is a slow, incremental shifting toward still more repressed control imbalances. Thus, most females in the autonomous zones, where they are likely to commit exploitative deviance, shift to the balanced zone, where deviance is unlikely. In turn, many females previously in the balanced zone move to the marginal zone, replacing some there who then slide down to the moderate zone, where they replace many who then move to the extreme repressive zone, where submissiveness is likely. Since there is greater absolute movement to the far left of the continuum than to positions in the center or shallow left of center, the overall effect is continuous decline in female crime rates with advancing age. There is also a correspondence between aging and increasing rates of defying social conventions, of suicide, and of "mental illness."

In addition to the ability of the theory to account for the general relationship between age and crime as well as the less widely recognized relationship between deviance and age, it has the potential for resolving issues about some aspects of age and crime. Three provocative but testable assertions set forth by Hirschi and Gottfredson (1983) represent the main foci of emerging debate. They contend that (1) the commonly observed age-crime curve is invariant across time, societies, and types of crime, (2) the relationship between age and crime is inexplicable with any nonbiological variables currently available to criminologists, and (3) the causes of crime are the same for all ages and age-categories. Although research addressing these hypotheses is accumulating, the ideas remain controversial and challenging.

The assertion that the age-crime relationship is invariant cannot be resolved until all agree on the meaning of "invariant." If it is taken to mean that the age-crime pattern is identical in all respects in all societies, in all historical epochs, and for all types of crime, it is clearly wrong (Greenberg 1985; Steffensmeier et al. 1989b). Even Hirschi and Gottfredson report evidence of this kind of variance. However, if "invariant" is liberally interpreted to imply a generally similar form of relationship, then the assertion appears to be correct. Hirschi and Gottfredson's major critics appear to concede this point when they report that "by being selective one could produce comparisons that would support an argument of either invariance . . . or variance" (Steffensmeier et al. 1989b:829).

Since an age-crime relationship cannot be absolutely invariant in the strict sense, the general form of the age-crime relationship would seem to be the issue. The logic of control balancing supports that Hirschi and Gottfredson assertion but only as it applies to those particular forms of predatory and defiant deviance that are likely to be registered as *crime.* The theory suggests that the picture for exploitative, plunderous, and decadent deviance, some of which is registered as white-collar crime, will be quite different. Moreover, the theory points to the possibility that the usual age-crime pattern, as it applies to the aged, might well vary from society to society, depending upon how older people are situated in different cultures. The "invariant" pattern of criminal behavior, however, stems from the idea that youth always commit more predatory and defiant crime/deviance than adults, and adult propensities toward those types of crime/deviance always decline with age. This is because the very notion of youth implies that young people must be trained for adulthood and guided in their development (translation: They must be controlled, but they must not be stifled to the point where they cannot mature into adulthood). Therefore young people always experience some deficit of control but they never experience a wide enough deficit to generate only submissive deviance. By the same token, adulthood always implies more favorable control ratios that reduce predatory and defiant deviance.

Can an age-crime relationship be explained with nonbiological variables? Control balance theory uses sociological variables, and its explanation of the age-crime relationship has already been presented. In addition, it points to a more precise but complex age variation in kinds of deviance not usually covered in criminal statistics. Of course, empirical confirmation of the theory's position and of its specifications of other age variations must wait for data that measure control ratios directly and provide more comprehensive information about deviant acts of various kinds.

Since the theory is meant to be general (to explain deviance for all individuals regardless of age and other characteristics), it obviously supports Hirschi and Gottfredson's contention that the causes of crime (and deviance) are the same for all ages. The main variable (or variables) explaining the probability of criminal behavior among youth (the control ratio) also explains the probability of criminal behavior among adults and the aged. The chief variable influencing the type of deviance likely to be committed by youth (chances of evoking countercontrol) also influences the type of deviance likely to be committed by adults and aged people. Moreover, the causal processes and the variables they imply operate in the same way for all ages. However, this does not imply that the actual values of the variables are the same for all ages. Indeed, it is age variation in the magnitude of the variables that accounts for the age-deviance relationship.

Variations in Other Variables in the Causal Chain. Differences among age categories in the probability and types of deviance are linked most closely to categorical variations in control ratios, though other variables in the theory's causal chain are also important. Situational provocations, debasement, opportunity, and risk all vary by age in ways that could influence age variations in deviance.

In particular, adolescents and young adults more frequently than adults encounter situations reminding them of their disadvantageous control relationships, creating feelings of humiliation. This is due partly to the more active lifestyle of young people, who traverse a wider field of social contact in search of excitement and potential sex partners or mates. However, it is also partly because youthful cohorts contain a larger proportion of males, and male-female roles are closer in younger cohorts. The fact that there is a greater proportion of males in younger cohorts, especially since there is more deprivation among youth than adults in contemporary society, means that the youth population as a whole will spawn regular contests of dominance. The greater similarity of gender roles in younger cohorts means that many modern females practice behaviors described earlier as pertaining to males, especially the tendency toward contests of dominance exacerbated by the relative deprivation that characterizes all youth in postindustrial societies. All young people commonly antagonize each other by teasing, daring, putting down, insulting, and challenging status and courage. The remnants of childhood dependency frequently intrude into later encounters with parents, relatives, and neighbors to provoke and demean in ways that adults have long forgotten. Furthermore, with the exception of opportunities for autonomous types of deviance, young people's lifestyles expose them more frequently to opportunities for deviance and to reduced situational risk.

Variations in Contingent Variables. Not only do people of various ages differ in control ratios and other variables important to the control balancing process in ways that would produce the age-deviance relationships described earlier, but there are also important age differences in contingencies that would lead in the same direction. Certainly there are age differences that affect the ability to commit deviance, as well as involvement in various organizations that might promote or discourage it. Youth are physically better equipped for much predatory deviance, whereas middle-aged people are usually more capable of exploitation and other autonomous deviance; the aged are less able to do either. Furthermore, patterns of organizational affiliation follow clear age progressions. Youth are more involved in informal subculturally organized affiliations that encourage deviance, whereas adults are more enmeshed in formal organizations such as professional, civic, and religious groups that help discourage it.

Race

Differences in Control Ratios. Blacks and other minorities appear to commit more ordinary criminal behavior, predatory deviance, and defiant types of deviance than do whites, but much less white-collar or elite deviance. The theory explains this as a product of the inferior social and political status of blacks and other minorities. They are subject to much control from whites but in turn can exercise control only over other minorities. In addition, lacking access to economic resources, minorities have less control over the environment than do whites. As individuals, minorities suffer substantial deficits of control that imply the probability of submissive or defiant forms of deviance.

However, in the United States, blacks and other minorities are cast into proximal residential arrangements by custom, prejudice, and economics, and they are subject to much social degradation. Because of such conditions, minorities are inspired to form subcultural organizations that distinguish them from whites and that permit them to overcome some of the oppression to which they would otherwise be subject. The fact of organization, then, enables many blacks and other minorities to move themselves toward the center of the control balance continuum. For some, this means movement from the extreme zone into the moderate zone, although for others it means movement from the moderate into the marginal zone. Hence, partly because of subcultural organization, a sizable proportion of blacks or other minorities in the contemporary United States find themselves suffering only a small or modest deficit of control, which leads toward predatory or defiant forms of deviance.

In addition, the control differences that generally characterize males vis-à-vis females and youth vis-à-vis adults operate for minorities but in ways reflecting variations in fertility, mortality, and sexual power of the minorities. Because disadvantaged people have higher fertility than do whites, as a group they are much younger. Therefore, the control ratio patterns for youth apply proportionately more to blacks and other disadvantaged minorities than to whites, inflating defiant and predatory rates of deviance among minorities. Moreover, although the sex ratios for minorities are more unbalanced in favor of males in the early years, higher mortality, especially among males, shifts the sex ratio sooner in favor of females and ultimately results in a lower overall sex ratio among blacks and other disadvantaged minorities than among whites. As a result, minority males quickly gain interpersonal control over females, enabling them to shift toward the right side of the control continuum into the zones where they are prone to commit defiant and predatory deviance. At the same time, since childbearing among minority females begins sooner and ultimately results in greater lifetime fertility, they more quickly move out of the extreme repressive zone of the control continuum (where submission is expected) into the zones where defiance and predation are more likely. Furthermore, adulthood for minority males and females involves less gain in control or in the ability to escape control than it does for whites, thereby reducing the chances that minority individuals will have control surpluses. Therefore, according to the principles of the theory, as applied in recognition of demographic and social realities, minority people are more likely than whites to resort to crime and delinquency at all ages, and those criminal/delinquent acts are more likely to be of the predatory type than are the delicts of whites.

These processes are highlighted by changes in black control ratios during the past 200 years. Black slaves had extreme, or at best moderate, control deficits and either submitted or engaged in defiant forms of deviance. With emancipation, their deficits narrowed, leading to greater degrees of defiance and predation. However, because of social and political inferiority and lesser ability to control the environment, blacks continue to suffer serious deficits of control, ameliorated mainly by subcultural organization, control of females by males, and control of children by females. Yet the control deficit of blacks today is less than it was 50 years ago and a lot less than it was 100 years ago. This is reflected in an upsurge of predation and defiance and a decline in submission. As the social and political status of blacks improves even further, there should be continuing high levels of predation and defiance as individual blacks move from the left side of the continuum toward the balanced zone. Ironically, elevation of a subordinate group initially increases its rates of the more visible forms of deviance, even accelerating those rates as the formerly subordinate group approaches equality with the dominant group (compare LaFree et al. 1992). Small control deficits create predation, whereas large ones lead to submission.

The differences between whites and minorities in white-collar and elite deviance are also linked to the subordinate social status of minorities. Having surplus control is unusual for anybody, regardless of race. However, because minorities have little control over whites and because their limited resources prevent control over the environment, only a tiny proportion of minorities occupy positions on the autonomy end of the control continuum (mainly famous athletes or entertainers). Hence, it is extremely unusual to find decadence and plunder among minorities, and it is even rare to find minorities engaging in exploitative deviance, especially of the white-collar crime type. As minorities' social status relative to whites improves, the number of minorities with a surplus of control will presumably increase, and the near monopoly on autonomous forms of deviance by whites will weaken.

Differences in Other Variables in the Causal Chain. Other variables in the control balancing causal chain most likely to differ by racial group in ways that might help account for the greater rates of "ordinary" crime and deviance among minorities and the greater rates of "white-collar" crime among whites include situational provocations, debasement, situational risk, and opportunity. The most important of these is situational provocation. Just as the lifestyles of males (relative to females) expose them to more situations that bring to mind in a belittling manner their control ratios, so minorities more frequently than whites encounter demeaning circumstances stimulating awareness of control ratios, which usually are in deficit. This is due mainly to three factors.

First, since many whites believe that blacks, as well as other minorities, are inherently inferior, minority individuals frequently find themselves the object of degrading remarks and insulting actions that accentuate their disadvantageous control relationships. Indeed, even without overt affronts, discrimination or perceived discrimination is provocative and demeaning.

Second, economic disadvantage leads to demeaning provocation. Males are especially prone to provocation when not fulfilling the ideal masculine role prescribing conquest and defense, and in modern society masculinity rests heavily on steady, well-paid employment. Such employment is in short supply for minority males, especially since their average age is lower than that of white males. The result is an even stronger pattern of provocational testing within minority male subcultures than among whites.

The third condition contributing to the greater likelihood of provocation among minorities is the proximity of male-female roles. Probably because of differential employment possibilities over many generations, minority, especially black, females are often heads of households and the prime wage earners. Furthermore, they assume many of the responsibilities for dominance that traditionally fell to men. Like many males, they are deprived of the means to fully achieve those purposes, and they are weakly organized to confront the sources of their deprivation. In that position, minority females are probably subject to many of the same dynamics characteristic of male subcultures—considerable competition marked by interpersonal tests and challenges. Thus, minority males as well as minority females confront more provoking situations that are demeaning than do whites, and these differences may help account for greater rates of crime among them.

Disadvantaged minorities also differ from whites in opportunities for various kinds of deviance. Given their social positions, minorities have far fewer chances to commit autonomous types of deviance (usually white-collar crime or deviance), since those delicts generally require an individual to be in a position of authority or to be in control of substantial resources.

Differences in Contingent Variables. Prior deviance and organizational relationships represent two contingent variables that affect how the theory accounts for racial differences in probability and type of deviance. It has already been shown that deviance itself impinges on the other variables in the causal process to increase the chances of future deviance. Since minority individuals more often initially resort to predatory and defiant deviance and less often engage in autonomous forms of deviance than do whites, they are more likely to face new situations with a history of prior defiance and predation and are less likely to have a pattern of autonomous types of deviance. At any point in time, then, a minority person's possibility of expressing repressive deviance is exaggerated, which translates into greater chances of exhibiting repetitious patterns of it, just as whites have an enhanced likelihood of autonomous types of deviance that transpose into larger possibilities of repetitious patterns.

Perhaps of equal weight is the apparent greater proneness of minorities to become involved in criminal or deviant subcultures (Katz 1988) that enhance motivations for deviance as well as help divert or influence misperceptions of potential constraint. Minorities may be more involved with deviant subcultures because they are generally confined in concentrated, crowded residential patterns that promote street activity and in places where neighborhoods are too "disorganized" to control the development and promotion of deviance. They may also be drawn to subcultures because they afford a supportive and protective network for activities that displease those who can make their lives as individuals even more miserable. In any case, the greater the involvement in deviant subcultures, the greater the effects of control balancing variables that bear on racial differences, and there is reason to think that minorities score higher than whites on this contingent variable.

Marital and Parental Status

Variations in Control Ratios. Unattached people apparently are more prone to deviance, particularly of the predatory or defiant types, than are married individuals, those with children at home, and those socially obligated in other ways (Hirschi 1969; Sampson and Laub 1993). Of course, much of this difference is due to age. Since marriage, along with childbearing and child rearing and the accompanying attachment to family and the community that goes with it, usually occurs after the teen period, the explanations concerning age also help account for differences in deviance among the differentially attached. Nevertheless, even after controlling for age, a greater social obligation, or social bondedness, seems to inhibit predatory and defiant deviance (Hirschi 1969; Sampson and Laub 1993; Tittle 1980a).

For the theory to be consistent with the facts about deviance and social attachment, most unattached people must have control ratios that reflect small to moderate deficits, that is, unobligated individuals generally should be in the marginal or moderate zones of the control continuum. Initially it might seem that such people would be in the balanced zone or perhaps even in the minimal zone of autonomy where they would conform or, at most, be likely candidates for exploitative forms of deviance because of their ability to escape a lot of the control to which more bonded people are subject. It is certainly true that they avoid the control that comes from responsibility for families, because without familial obligations, individuals are freer to leave jobs, to refuse to work for prevailing wages, to avoid confining participation in community institutions and the constraints that implies, and they are able to avoid the control that comes from accountability to, and for, spouses and children.

This, however, is more than compensated for by the superior potential that attached people have for exercising control. Most unbonded males exercise much less control over females, particularly over one specific female, than do many married men, and unattached females have relatively little control over children compared with married females. Moreover, because people who are unconstrained by social entanglements and family obligations are generally distrusted, they are less likely to acquire responsible positions in occupational and political structures and in community affairs that would enable them to exercise control over others. Even the unattached attribute less reliability to unbonded individuals than to those linked into obligating social networks. Furthermore, despite the capacity of unmarried or unattached people to escape some controls, they are subjected to greater surveillance and more extensive institutionalized controls in the various social circles within, and through, which they move. Unfocused distrust by others is one cost of freedom.

Variations in Other Variables in the Causal Chain. In addition to probable differences in control ratios that might account for the greater likelihood of predatory and defiant deviance among those who lack familial entanglements, the unattached probably also experience differences in some of the other variables in the control balance causal network. Since the lifestyles of the unmarried or unattached often involve wider movement, more diverse interactional dynamics, and exposure to more unconventional settings, they more often face provocative situations with the potential for humiliation. They also encounter more opportunities for predatory and defiant deviance but fewer opportunities for autonomous deviance, and to some extent they suffer more situational risk than the attached because of the suspiciousness that others, including the police, have of those who escape the bonds of marriage and active parenthood.

Variations in Contingent Variables. An additional increment of differences between the bonded and unbonded in patterns of deviance is probably due to variations in contingencies, the most important of which is prior deviance. To the extent that being unattached affects one's control ratio and other variables in the causal chain, it will increase the chances of particular kinds of deviance generally, particularly among those who remain unbonded over a long period of time. The longer one has been unbonded, the more likely is a history of prior deviance. Since prior deviance increases the chances that additional deviance will be used to fight an imbalance of control, unattached people more often recidivate. Since the net effect is cumulative, those lacking familial ties deviate more.

Urbanness

Differences in Control Ratios. Most kinds of deviance, particularly predatory and defiant forms, vary directly with the size of place (although it is not clear that *increases* in size lead to increases in rates of deviance, that the relationship between violence and size of place follows a straight linear path, or that suburbs fit neatly into the size-deviance gradient) (Archer and Gartner 1984; Fischer 1984; Tittle 1989a; Tittle and Stafford 1991). Part of this effect is compositional, resulting from the differences between places of differing sizes in age, sex, race, marital or parental status, and other demographic factors (Gans 1962; Kasarda and Janowitz 1974; Sampson 1988; Tittle 1989a) that bear on the likelihood of criminal/deviant behavior in ways consistent with the theory. Some of it may also stem from greater subcultural development in urban areas that results from density and from what Claude Fischer (1975) calls "critical mass" (Bursik and Grasmick 1993; Fischer 1982; Tittle 1989a). However, crime and deviance seem to vary directly with the relative size of place, independently of population composition and subcultures (Fischer 1982; Tittle 1989c).

The variation in crime/deviance (and other variables) that remains after demographic composition and subcultural processes are discounted is usually assumed to indicate a distinctive lifestyle in urban places that Louis Wirth ([1938] 1969) called "urbanism." Control balance theory explains this urban effect as a reflection of control deficits that most urban dwellers experience relative to residents of smaller places. Although city dwellers escape a lot of social control through their anonymity and mobility (Tittle 1989a; Tittle and Paternoster 1988), they simultaneously lose the capacity to exercise many controls, and they become objects of more environmental control than do residents of other types of places. Weakened ability to exercise control over others, in combination with the additional environmental subjection that urbanites suffer, outweighs the freedom from social control made possible by anonymity and mobility. As a result, urbanites are at a relative control disadvantage that implies greater likelihood of predation and defiance.

This argument, of course, contradicts the typical view that urban living provides great freedom, but the "liberation" view is based on a narrow "social control" focus. Since the proportion of total interaction time that city residents spend with strangers is large, they escape many potential sanctions, particularly those exercised on an interpersonal level. However, living in settlements with large populations also deprives people of some liberties, and it diminishes their ability to exercise certain kinds of control.

First, urbanites are (1) restricted in capacity of movement, by traffic and the press of other people; (2) incapable of providing for their personal subsistence needs—water, electricity, clothing, fuel, and food—being totally dependent on organizational entities; and (3) unable to claim behavioral options because of their potential effects on others, an inherent feature of the interdependency of city life. Thus, others constrain movement, specialization makes accession to the requirements of organization necessary, and interdependence prohibits expression of everyday impulses. For example, despite the "tolerance" supposedly pervading cities (Abrahamson and Carter 1986; Wilson 1985; see Tittle 1989a, footnote 1, for additional citations), people cannot spit on the sidewalk, burn down their own houses, protect their property, play stereos loudly, or build structures the way they want because such actions impinge on the welfare and safety of others.

Second, because of greater labor-force participation and economic independence, urban females are not as subordinate to males. They are much less subject to male control, and they are far less likely to produce large numbers of children. The net effect is a general relative (1) loss of control by urban males over females, reducing their overall control ratios relative to males in other types of places, and (2) loss of control over children by urban females, also increasing their overall control deficits.

Thus, despite the illusion that urban dwellers are more autonomous, they are, in fact, somewhat more repressed. The net loss due to reductions of control over the environment and weakened gender-linked control (males over females and females over children) exceeds the gains that urbanites enjoy from expanded anonymity and mobility. Therefore, cities have higher rates of defiant and predatory deviance because a larger proportion of their populations fall in the marginal and moderate zones on the repressive end of the control balance continuum.

Furthermore, cities also contain more people on the autonomous end of the control balance continuum, where exploitative, plunderous, and decadent deviance is generated. This is because institutionalized economic, political, and other forms of power are centered in urban areas. Most individuals exercising more control than they experience are highly placed in the power systems of the economy, the government, or other institutions, and since the headquarters of those power systems are usually in places of population concentration, autonomous individuals are mainly urbanites. Thus, cities exhibit higher rates of all forms of autonomous deviance.

Differences in Other Variables in the Causal Chain. Urbanites also score higher on all of the key variables in the control balancing causal chain. Their motivations for deviance are stronger because urban life presents more situations that remind them of control imbalances and that are humiliating, their opportunities for all types of deviance are magnified, and the constraints inhibiting deviance are muted.

Consider, first, how urban living presents provocative situations. Not only does the diversity of interaction contexts and the anxiety of dealing with unfamiliar interactants breed deliberate challenges and tests, but the frustrations inherent in traffic tie-ups and the delays in gratification of basic needs rooted in population size make for constant and humbling awareness of one's control disadvantage. As a result, urbanites are more frequently motivated toward deviance as a solution to their control imbalances.

In addition, since cities have heterogeneous, dynamic populations, and urban centers make available all sorts of products and services, opportunities for deviance are rife. Furthermore, given anonymity, self-centeredness, and weak overall community organization, the likelihood of getting caught for deviance is less and the seriousness of various deviant acts is diminished. The result is weakened constraint for a large number of urban people in comparison to those in other types of settlements.

Differences in Contingent Variables. Finally, urbanites differ from other people in some of the contingent variables, the most obvious of which is prior deviance. Urban lifestyles and the circumstances of city living contribute to an enlarged probability of initial deviance, and for the reasons noted before, deviance tends to escalate into patterned expression. Thus, urbanites have greater chances of committing deviance in the first place as well as greater chances of repeating those acts.

Urbanites also differ in moral commitments and in the chances of being involved in subcultures that are oriented around deviance or that encourage deviance. Since the conditions of urban life tend to undermine religious training, to expose youth to contradictory messages about right and wrong, to encourage tolerance, and to elevate expediency relative to moral values (see Tittle 1989a), city dwellers generally have fewer internalized moral precepts to mute the operation of the control balancing variables. Moreover, urbanites more readily seem to form deviant subcultures (Fischer 1975, 1982; Tittle 1989c) of most types (an exception may be subcultures of violence; see Tittle 1989c and Fischer 1995) that alter control ratios and serve as contingencies that encourage greater deviance by intensifying the control balancing process.

Socioeconomic Status

Variations in Control Ratios. The relationship between socioeconomic status (SES) and crime/deviance has been of interest to social scientists for a long time and is a source of great controversy (see Tittle 1983). Empirical evidence seems to indicate a strong positive association between SES and the kind of crime/deviance committed in connection with a high-status occupation or social position, particularly "white-collar crime," occupational violations, and governmental deviance. The relationship for other forms of deviance and crime, however, is not so clear. Although there is a strong tradition in social science of assuming a negative association between SES and ordinary street crime or other forms of deviance, or at least to attribute a disproportionate share of them to those at the very lowest point on the status continuum (the "underclass"), the evidence has been contradictory and subject to differing interpretations (Braithwaite 1981; Clelland and Carter 1980; Kleck 1982; Nettler 1978, 1985; Stark 1979; Tittle

1985a; Tittle et al. 1978, 1979, 1982; Tittle and Villemez 1978). Recent reviews suggest no pervasive or strong relationship between SES and ordinary crime/deviance, although the likelihood of finding a negative relationship under some circumstances does appear to exceed chance (Farnworth et al. 1994; Tittle and Meier 1990, 1991). The problem for control balance theory, then, is to account for the positive relationship between SES and white-collar or professional deviance and to explain why the relationship between SES and predatory and defiant deviance is problematic.

The positive association between SES and elite deviance is easily explained since elite deviance depends on the violator's being in a particular social position. One cannot fix prices without holding a position of authority with a business organization offering products or services for sale. One cannot manipulate legislation for private gain without being in a position of political power or having large financial resources. One cannot engage in unprofessional conduct without being a professional. High-status people are situated so that they *can* deviate, whereas low-status people could not commit those kinds of deviance even if they wanted to. Designating someone as an elite, a professional, or a power holder is simply another way of saying that the person is autonomous and quite likely has a surplus of control.

In control balance theory, the main factor causing elites, professionals, and power holders to deviate, as well as the main factor accounting for the form elite deviance takes, is the degree to which the control these people exercise exceeds the control they experience. Autonomous people are motivated to extend their own control. The extent to which they can extend their control, however, is limited by the control to which they are subject. Most high-status people differ from others in being able to extend their control beyond that which they experience, but most of them cannot extend their control very far because even they are subject to constraints, some of which inhere specifically in the high-status positions they occupy. There are legal, political, and social restrictions on government functionaries, corporate executives, professional practitioners, and even on medieval kings. Thus, those who commit acts of white-collar crime and elite deviance fall mainly in the minimal zone of autonomy with a slight surplus of control. A few, of course, can exercise quite a bit more control than that to which they are subject and are in the medium or maximum zones. High-status people, then, have varying chances of committing exploitative or plunderous deviance, depending on their exact control ratios. Since those of lower SES almost never have surplus control implying possible exploitation or plunder, the positive relationship between SES and elite deviance is obvious.

This does not mean, of course, that all high-status people are autonomous or commit elite deviance; after all, only a minority occupy powerful positions in the governmental, commercial, institutional, or professional realms. Indeed, most high-status people fall in the balanced zone of the continuum, and some are repressed. Being of higher SES, as usually measured, does not guarantee that a person's overall control balance will show a surplus, particularly not if the person is female or young. For that reason, a minority of higher-status people do commit predatory, defiant, and even submissive deviance. The controversy, however, is not about whether people of high status ever commit ordinary crime and deviance, rather, it is about whether occupants of lower socio-economic statuses are especially likely to commit acts of ordinary criminal predation and defiance; therefore, a negative relationship between SES and these types of deviance sometimes emerges but does not prevail.

In applying the theory to this issue, several countervailing effects have to be recognized. On the one hand, lower-status people are heavily controlled. They lack the economic resources, and often the knowledge, to control the environment; they either have no jobs or low-paying ones that trap them in occupational positions where they are subject to much control; they have little political power and few organizational apparatuses to improve their ability to exercise control; and they are closely watched and constrained by police. In addition, because of higher fertility and lower life expectancy, a larger proportion of them are in the adolescent or young adult categories; as such, they are mainly objects of control and have few compensating abilities to control others or the environment. All of these conditions point toward extreme repression that results in submissive, not defiant or predatory, behavior. Hence, one reason research has failed to confirm the widely accepted assumption that lower-status people commit much more ordinary deviance than higher-status people may be that the conditions of extremely low SES generate mostly submissive behaviors not usually thought of, or recorded, as deviance.

On the other hand, with few exceptions (Thomlinson 1965) people of lower SES have more children and higher mortality at all ages (Haines 1979; Petersen 1969; Weeks 1981). Partly because of higher fertility, lower-status females get less education. Since opportunities for higher-level positions go mainly to women with advanced skills, those of lower status have remained more subject to male control than have higher status women. Moreover, despite the higher sex ratio among lower-status people of young ages, produced by high fertility, the overall sex ratio of the lower-status population is low because mortality among lower-status males is so great. The especially weak position of lower-status females (relative to higher-status females) combined with the scarcity of lower-status males permits the males to exercise unusual control over the females. By means of this, lower-status males move themselves closer to the center of the control continuum away from the extreme repressive position. At the same time, however, lower-status females move from the extreme repressive position toward the balanced zone by virtue of their greater ability to control children, which stems from higher fertility and their more traditional social statuses.

Furthermore, because of residential proximity and the necessity for "self-help" and close alliances, lower-status people often form subcultures that favorably alter their control ratios. For many of these people, these two "recovery mechanisms"—gender-linked interpersonal structures and subcultures—are enough to overcome some of the control deficit of lower social status, allowing them to end up in the balanced zone, where conformity is most likely. Not all, however, enjoy the advantages of these recovery mechanisms, particularly not both of them simultaneously. Although most lower-status people can exercise (or escape) some control through subcultural organization and most lower-status women can dominate children, the option of controlling women, though generally more available to lower-status rather than higher-status men, nevertheless varies among disadvantaged males, with some men lacking the necessary personal qualities. Hence, for some lower-status individuals, especially some males, the recovery mechanisms by which most others advance themselves toward the center of the continuum only move them from the extreme zone to the moderate or marginal zones of repression, where predatory and defiant deviance is produced.

Thus, some conditions of their lower status push people toward submission or toward conformity, and other conditions pull control ratios toward the zones where defiance and predation are expected. This is one reason for the absence of clear-cut, stable differences between the socioeconomic statuses in recorded probabilities of predatory or defiant forms of deviance. Hence, combining the principles of the theory, at least as they bear on the control ratio, with some assumptions and observations about the conditions of life for those of lower SES produces explanations consistent with the evidence on the relationship between SES and "ordinary" crime and deviance. Of course, without more precise information about control ratios in specific circumstances, it is impossible to predict the relative likelihood of occurrence of defiant and predatory deviance in lower-status and high-status people. The best that can be said, from theoretical considerations alone, is that a minority of people in both statuses should engage in those acts, which is what the evidence seems to indicate. A positive relation between SES and white-collar or other forms of exploitative or plunderous deviance is much more certain. According to the principles of the theory as they concern control ratios, those deviances should be almost exclusively the province of those with high status, and few would deny that this is the case.

Variations in Other Variables in the Causal Chain. Other variables in the causal chain also imply complicated countereffects producing episodic differences among the socioeconomic statuses in predatory and defiant deviance, as well as greater autonomous deviance by those of higher SES. One such variable is situational provocation. Although those of lower SES probably encounter many more potentially degrading situations reminding them of their control disadvantages, lower-status individuals are less likely to regard those situations in this light than are people of higher SES because provocation and debasement depend somewhat on expectations. It is mainly when someone is challenged about things ordinarily taken for granted that belittlement results. Since higher-status people expect to exercise more control, they are especially distressed when that expectation is not realized. Overall, then, the greater number of potential provocations among people with lower SES is probably balanced by the greater intensity of provocations encountered by those of higher SES.

Those of different socioeconomic statuses differ in opportunities for various kinds of deviance in ways consistent with actual differences in behavior. Higher-status people clearly have much more opportunity for exploitative and plunderous deviance. Lower-status people generally have more opportunity for some kinds of predatory or defiant deviance, such as illegal gambling and drug use, though opportunities for other types of predatory and defiant deviance, such as assault and direct theft, are probably equal.

Variations in constraint also run in countervailing directions. Those of lower SES face much situational risk in committing predatory and defiant deviance because more of their behavior is exposed to public view and the police are deployed to react to them. However, higher-status people are more vulnerable to informal sanctions and are more closely allied with conventional groups that might eventually discover misbehavior and withhold respect.

Because of all these compensating mechanisms, those with varying socioeconomic statuses do not differ much in overall propensity toward defiant and predatory deviance, though because of opportunities, they have substantially different chances of committing exploitative or plunderous deviance. This matches the conclusion reached from considering the socioeconomically linked effects of control ratios, and it is what the evidence suggests—those of lower SES sometimes, but not consistently, commit more defiance and predation, whereas those of higher SES consistently commit more exploitation and plunder.

Variations in Contingent Variables. Variations by SES in contingencies affecting the efficiency of the control balancing process appear to be minimal. Nevertheless, to the extent that the variables already discussed result in some tendency for those of lower SES to exceed those of higher SES in repressive types of deviance, that tendency will be magnified by the effects of prior deviance. The result is an incrementally greater chance that those of lower SES repeatedly resort to defiant and predatory deviance. Since there is a consistent, clear-cut propensity for people with higher SES to commit more exploitation and plunder, and since prior deviance has a magnifying effect on future conduct, those of higher SES are inclined toward recidivism in autonomous forms of deviance.

In addition, the conditions of lower SES existence make it more likely that lower-status people will be involved in criminal or deviant subcultures that encourage defiant or predatory deviance. Those conditions include residential crowding and community organization too weak to keep deviant activities out, both of which influence exposure to deviant role models and the possibility of subcultural participation (see Bursik and Grasmick 1993). Those of higher SES are more likely to observe role models who participate in, and encourage affiliation with, subcultures that enhance the chances of autonomous forms of deviance, particularly corporate or white-collar crime.

To the extent that involvement in deviant or criminal subcultures intensifies the force of the control balancing process, patterns of predatory and defiant deviance should be more evident among those of lower SES, whereas patterns of exploitative and plunderous deviance should be apparent among those of higher SES. However, since contingencies are not the primary causes of deviance and operate simply as conditions that modify the full operation of the control balancing process, they do not have much additional effect beyond that produced by the other variables in the causal chain.

Direct Tests

Since applying the logic of the theory to explain and predict patterns of deviance that are manifest in differences among categories of various demographic variables yields results consistent with the evidence, it can be said that the theory accounts for the "facts" of deviance as they are currently known. Moreover, in some instances the theory foreshadows empirical patterns still to be documented. Thus, it seems to merit further attention.

Nevertheless, any judgment about the adequacy of control balance theory is premature. First, the facts about deviance are not established. Systematic information concerning all forms of deviance to which the theory applies simply do not exist, and even when systematic data are available on some of the relevant forms of deviance, those data are sometimes themselves subject to controversial interpretations. Second, in applying the theory to variations in deviance among demographic categories, it is necessary to speculate about how people vary with respect to most of the relevant variables because there are no actual measurements of the central variables of the theory. Since some of these speculations, or assumptions, may be wrong, the theory may not be as good as it appears to be in the expositions set forth above. For these reasons, my case in favor of the theory must be regarded as tentative.

Problems in Attempting Direct Tests

Firmer judgment about the empirical credibility of the theory must wait for tests with more precise and directly applicable data, which existing data sets do not permit. One of the major predictions of the theory is that imbalance of control in either direction from the midcontinuum, or balanced zone, predicts the likelihood of deviance of some unspecified type. To conduct a direct test of this hypothesis, one would need to measure the control ratios of individuals in a sample as well as the incidence of a large number of different kinds of deviance, and then ascertain if the control ratios were directly related to the overall likelihood of committing deviance. However, few surveys have collected data permitting even a gross measure of respondents' overall control ratios. In addition, most surveys do not attempt to measure deviance at all, much less the kinds of deviance crucial to the theory. For example, the General Social Survey, one of the most popular sources of social science data (Stark 1989:117), asks only about criminal victimization and attitudes about deviance rather than about deviance committed by the individual. At best, a few surveys contain information about predation and defiance. None, however, has systematic data about submission, exploitation, plunder, or decadence. Furthermore, even for those acts of predation and defiance that have been investigated, measures typically focus on only a few forms—those that constitute criminal violations or those that are usually taken as indications of juvenile delinquency. Such limited information precludes conclusions about the extent to which individuals have committed at least some deviance among the variety of possibilities of different kinds of deviance, even if it were possible to measure control ratios.

Similar problems preclude tests of the second general hypothesis concerning the effect of the magnitude of control imbalances on the likelihood of committing particular kinds of deviance. Theoretically, for example, those with a minimum control deficit have the highest probability of committing predation, those with a moderate deficit have the highest likelihood of committing defiance, and those with an extreme deficit are most likely to submit. Although a researcher conceivably needs data only about the commission of two instances of deviance adjacent on the deficit side of the continuum, such as one form of predation and one form of defiance, or one form of defiance and one form of submission, to conduct at least a partial test, measures of control ratios are also needed.

It is clear, then, that good tests must wait for more appropriate data. There are simply none now available that permit direct measurement of the control ratios of individual persons that take into account a variety of settings in which they operate. Gathering appropriate data is feasible, but it will be expensive and time-consuming, and given the current dearth of research funding, it is unlikely to be financially supported—certainly not until the promise of the theory has been thoroughly established.

Requirements for Better Direct Tests

Specificity of Hypotheses. Empirical assessment of any theory rests, first of all, on the derivation of appropriate hypotheses. Tests of hypotheses not intimately linked to a theory will say little or nothing about it. Indeed, improperly drawn hypotheses can produce false assessment, sometimes leading to unjustified rejection and at other times producing an illusion of support. Fortunately, deriving appropriate testable hypotheses from control balance theory should not be difficult because the theory is comprehensive, having been designed to apply to all individuals, in all situations, and for all social units. However, since the theory is complicated, the most appropriate hypotheses should be specific, ultimately even incorporating the various contingencies postulated as influencing how effectively the processes of the theory operate.

Initially, however, it is appropriate to be less specific, as long as the criteria of success are adjusted accordingly. For instance, the theory makes eight broad assertions about the behavior of individuals or social units:

(1) The probability of deviance of some kind varies directly with the magnitude of control imbalances; (2) whenever control is balanced, there is a high probability of conformity; (3) whenever control is marginally imbalanced on the deficit side, there is a small probability of deviance, but the likelihood is high that the deviance will be of the predatory type; (4) whenever control is moderately imbalanced on the deficit side, there is a modest probability of deviance of some type, but the chances are good that it will be of the defiant type; (5) whenever control is excessively imbalanced on the deficit side, there is a strong probability of deviance, and there is a high probability that the deviance that does occur will be of the submissive type; (6) whenever control is minimally imbalanced on the surplus side, there is a small probability of deviance, but a high probability that the deviance will be exploitative; (7) whenever control is moderately imbalanced on the surplus side, there is a medium probability of deviance, but a high likelihood that it will be of the plunderous type; and (8) whenever control is extremely imbalanced on the surplus side, there is a high probability of deviance and a high probability that it will be decadent.

In testing these general hypotheses, one must recognize that really strong relationships are not to be expected. One reason for this is the current inexactness of demarcations between the zones on the continuum. For instance, the precise point where the marginal zone ends and the moderate zone begins is problematic. Until those cutting points are specified empirically or theoretically, a task to be deferred, there will be error in predicting types of deviance. In addition, general hypotheses do not reflect the complexity implicit in the underlying causal chain through which the control ratio has its effects. They simply express in gross terms outcomes that ought to emerge as the control ratio interacts with other variables in the causal chain. Although the control ratio is extremely important, it is one part of the whole. Its effects are not only modulated and transformed by other variables in the causal chain, including provocations, motivation, opportunity, situational risk, and constraint, but the completeness of this process can be somewhat affected by a number of contingencies. Hence, tests of the general predictions (hypotheses) stated above cannot produce exact outcomes.

More precise hypotheses are better. Consider four examples: (1) The probability of deviant behavior of a particular type varies directly with the degree to which deviant motivation exceeds constraint for that behavior; (2) deviant behavior of a particular type varies directly with the degree to which deviant motivation is matched by opportunity for that deviance; (3) the probability of deviance of any unspecified form varies directly with the interaction between motivation and opportunity for that deviance; (4) the probability of deviant behavior of a specific form varies directly with the frequency of demeaning situational provocations, provided that opportunity is present and constraint is weaker than motivation. Each hypothesis is logically derived from the processes in the causal chain, and because they are more focused, empirical evidence concerning them should be stronger than for the general hypotheses stated before, that is, predictive coefficients should be large enough so that statistical significance becomes irrelevant.

One reason for expecting large predictive coefficients in testing specific hypotheses is the omnipresence of the control ratio, which directly or indirectly affects, or is embedded in, all of the variables. Since the control ratio is theoretically implicated in this way, researchers must first develop a measure of it and then use that measure as a component of the indexes of all the other variables. This strategy will trouble many scholars who have become sensitive (overly so, in my opinion) to multicollinearity. They will worry that incorporating measures of the control ratio directly into the measures of other variables in the causal chain creates artificial interdependence leading to biased estimates of the effects. The danger, as some see it, is a set of built-in relationships masquerading as real effects.

However, keying measures of other variables to those of the control ratio when testing specific, focused hypotheses is not only appropriate but is necessary, and the results will not be artificial or false but will accurately reflect reality because the interlinkages of the control ratio with the other variables is inherent, as shown by Figure 7.1. The conventional approach to testing the exemplified hypotheses would dictate that independent measures of all variables be constructed and then the control ratio be held constant while examining the effects of the other variables. To rule out the influence of the control ratio in this way, however, denies the causal structure that the theory asserts is the underlying basis of human behavior. Holding the control ratio constant permits only partial effects to emerge—those due to the different variables as they operate apart from, and independent of, the control ratio. Therefore, in testing specific, focused hypotheses extracted from the overall causal chain, it is preferable to implicate the control ratio in the measurement of all variables when it is theoretically implicated.

This recommendation is not intended to guarantee the success of the theory by making falsification difficult. Indeed, I endorse very demanding criteria of success in testing specific, focused hypotheses from control balance theory. Predictive coefficients must be so strong that they cannot be due to correspondence in measurement. If care is taken to create appropriate indexes along the lines to be suggested and results of that magnitude are not found, the theory will be cast in doubt, and I will be the first to acknowledge it.

Aside from the multiple influences of the control ratio, there are other reasons to expect better predictive outcomes when testing specific, focused hypotheses than when testing the general hypotheses identified at the beginning of this section. These narrower, more precise hypotheses key into the conditional operation of the specific causal variables in ways that general hypotheses cannot. General hypotheses ignore a lot, pay no attention to countereffects, and conceal the possibility that effects occur under some conditions but not others; they simply assert that despite all of these things, particular overall consequences are expected. More specific hypotheses attempt to identify detailed effects, and to the extent that they do that accurately (as the theory signifies), they should be far more accurate. Hence, as direct testing of the theory progresses from general to focused hypotheses, predictive capability should increase in accuracy.

A still better approach, however, is to specify and estimate an overall causal model that captures the processes depicted in Figure 7.1. That diagram portrays the control ratio in various interlinkages with other variables, as well as interlinkages of the other variables with each other. Since the underlying causal structure does not imply the kind of patterns usually dealt with in conventional causal modeling, it cannot be handled in standard ways. Figure 7.1, remember, is simply a visual aid to show what is happening in the production of deviant behavior. It contains some components, or "variables," that actually vary little from person to person or from situation to situation; it incorporates nonlinear relationships; and some of the variables represent thresholds or ceilings for the operation of other variables. Given the limitations of current statistical technology, probably the best approach would be to decompose the causal effects of control balancing variables into a series of nested causal models, perhaps employing specific and sometimes unusual estimation procedures for each of the submodels. If some of the advantages of the best contemporary estimation procedures could be brought to bear in estimating these nested submodels—particularly those procedures allowing for correlated measurement error, reciprocal effects, and complex causal structures— one should expect quite strong results, and those results should be free of any suspicion of artificial interdependence.

Finally, tests of even more specific hypotheses than those stated above, or evaluations of sets of focused hypotheses expressed in more complicated models than implied by Figure 7.1, should produce still more accurate outcomes. An advanced level of specificity can be achieved by deriving predictive statements or causal models that are qualified by the contingencies discussed in Chapter 8. If a theoretical effect, or relationship, is sensitive to conditional influences and those contingencies are not taken into account in tests, the results will be imperfect. If they are taken into account, however, predictive results should be extremely good.

There is another sense in which differences between general and specific hypotheses are relevant. All that was said above concerns distinctions between abstract hypotheses that apply to general relationships and their effects and those concrete, focused hypotheses that apply to narrower, more precise connections among variables. Distinctions based on realms, or domains, of activity are also important. Every person moves within many contexts, and within each of those contexts there are specific, characteristic ways of deviating. For example, most people are simultaneously participants in family or domestic contexts, work contexts, local and national political contexts, religious contexts, recreational contexts, interpersonal friendship contexts, local communities, whole societies, the economy, and various physical environments. In each of those realms there are characteristic control ratios, motivations, opportunities, and constraints, as well as distinct forms of predation, defiance, submission, exploitation, plunder, and decadence. The narrower the application to one of these given domains, or realms of activity, the more precise hypotheses concerning the causal mechanisms leading to characteristic ways of expressing deviance can be. Thus, whereas the abstract hypotheses discussed before concern, say, the causes of exploitation of some kind, or suggest the likely probability of, say, defiance of some kind, domain-specific hypotheses might concern the causes of workplace treachery (a particular instance of exploitation) or the probability of student vandalism of school property (a particular instance of defiance).

Measuring the Variables. In addition to good hypotheses, direct tests of the theory will require appropriate measurement of the variables. The first step is to focus on the correct units of analysis. Since the theory can be applied at various levels from individuals to whole societies, the focus of measurement must match the application. If the theory is applied to whole societies, ecological measures should be employed, which means that *rates* of deviance will serve as the final dependent variables. For practical reasons, particularly cost, ecological measures of most of the variables probably cannot be obtained by aggregating individual indicators. Therefore, ecological-level testing may require clever indirect indicators, based on what is learned from research about individuals. For instance, if direct measures of the control ratio for individuals confirm that the control ratios can be predicted reasonably well from key roles and statuses, then the relative proportions of people with such roles and statuses can be taken as indirect measures of the overall control ratios of entire populations. It may be possible to find useful ecological indicators without prior research about individuals, but they will inevitably be weak. For example, the number of autos in a geographic area might be taken to indicate opportunity for auto theft, but this assumes that every auto constitutes an opportunity for theft by one or more individuals and that everybody has an opportunity to steal them. Neither assumption is strong.

Therefore, ecological applications should probably wait until sufficient data about individuals are available for inferences to identify appropriate ecological indicators. Moreover, though the theory can be applied at various levels of generality, it is mainly for deviant behavior of individuals. The primary task for research, then, is to develop measures of variables for individuals, the most important of which is the control ratio.

Measures of individuals' control ratios must recognize that each person has a general, global control ratio that expresses the total control experienced and exercised that flows from all situations and domains. Each person also operates within several specific domains and therefore has a series of particular control ratios that apply within those domains.

Although a control ratio in one domain often spills over into other domains, discrepancies from domain to domain are still possible. For example, a man may have a control surplus in the domestic realm but a control deficit in the work environment, a youth may have a control deficit in the society as a whole but have a surplus in the recreational domain, and a woman may have a control surplus in the realm of interpersonal relationships but a control deficit with respect to the physical environment. Finally, there is some episodic or situational variation in any individual's general or domain-specific control ratios.

Ideally, multiple measures of the control ratio will be developed to accommodate these various realms, but the most important measure is of the overall, general control ratio. However, since a general measure will reflect and summarize all of the control ratios in more limited domains and time spans, efficiency dictates that the specifically focused ratios be derived first and then combined to create the general measure. Four methods for initially obtaining indicators of relative control in specific domains seem feasible.

One is the general perceptual method. Samples of individuals can be given a description or definition of control and asked to estimate on a questionnaire rating sheet the degree of control they can exercise over specific others, objects, and circumstances as well as the degree of control specific others, objects, and circumstances exercise over them. For example, in the domestic realm a person might rate on a 10-point continuum, anchored on one end with the words "total control" and on the other end "no control whatsoever," the amount of control he or she can exercise over each of the following: spouse, each child, other members of the household, pets, the environment (such as being able to control heat, cold, plant growth, availability of food, and cleanliness), his or her own body (such as avoiding or regulating illness, fatigue, or appearance), and others, such as neighbors, solicitors, and repair persons, and the degree of control each of these persons, objects, or circumstances has over him or her. The specifically matched rating can then be divided and the resulting ratios averaged, or the specific ratings could be totaled and then divided to produce one overall ratio.

Another method would use the same objects but instead of the respondents' rating the amount of control exercised and experienced, they would be asked to report the actual outcome the last time there was an encounter involving the various objects or sources of control. For example, in the domestic realm, a respondent could be asked to recall the last time he or she interacted with the spouse about food. Perhaps the respondent is a woman, and she recalls the last interaction as having occurred that morning at breakfast. She then describes what transpired—perhaps her husband entered the kitchen first and prepared her a pot of tea and started breakfast. She then arrived, completed making and serving the breakfast, and asked to see the paper, only to have her husband refuse to surrender it. They argued, and finally, he relinquished a portion. They ate the food, he rose, said goodbye, and left for work.

An interviewer could then raise questions about each part of the interaction to elicit factual reports of control. Thus, the interviewer might ask
if the wife influences who goes to the kitchen first, and if she says yes, the
interviewer asks her how that occurs. The questioner would then ask if
the husband could get the wife to go to the kitchen first and if so, how.
Based on the answers, the interviewer (or later, a coder) would judge the
relative control of the wife vis-à-vis the husband concerning responsibility for first kitchen work. The same procedure could be applied to beginning the breakfast, completing the breakfast, access to the newspaper, and
so on. The various ratios for the different duties, activities, and desires
could then be averaged to reflect the control of the wife (respondent) relative to the husband in the zone of food preparation and consumption.
This would then be repeated for other types of activity with the husband,
such as sex, home repair, or purchases, and all of these ratios could be averaged to obtain an overall estimate of the control ratio of the wife relative to the husband. A similar procedure could be employed for other objects and sources of control in the domestic realm, such as children or
neighbors, and for various zones of activity to create a ratio of control for
the wife relative to them. Finally, all of these average ratios for different
objects and sources of control could be averaged to estimate the woman's
overall control ratio in the domestic realm.

A third approach would use vignettes in which respondents are asked
to imagine themselves as actors in scenarios encompassing likely actual
situations where one confronts various objects and sources of control, and
to judge likely outcomes. In the domestic realm, there might be a series of
vignettes portraying a person trying to accomplish something requiring
control over a specific object and source, such as a husband or child, the
physical environment, a solicitor, and so forth. In each instance, the respondent judges on a 10-point continuum the likelihood of success, and
the greater the estimated success, the greater the relative control. An average across the scenarios would then represent the overall domestic control ratio of the respondent.

Finally, simulations could be devised. One might prepare a computer
game in which a subject whose control ratio is to be measured pursues
various modes of action vis-à-vis the different objects and sources of control. The subject would be instructed to act as he or she normally does
with respect to the person or situation being confronted and to imagine
that the object and source will react in a normal manner. The objective
would be to see how much force the subject exerts against various objects
and sources, as well as the degree of force by the simulated objects and
sources necessary to get the subject to capitulate to attempts at control.
This will yield an average for control exercised relative to that to which
the person is subject that presumably reflects habitual patterns by which
control ratios are experienced in the subject's life.

Each of these methods has weaknesses and rests on assumptions that
may not be correct. Hence, the indexes they yield, like all measurements
in social science, are imperfect. Moreover, even before they could be em-

ployed, much refinement would be necessary. Nevertheless, these seem like sensible starting points for measuring the control ratio in specific domains in order to test control balance hypotheses about deviance within, and pertaining to, those domains. These initial measures of control ratios in specific domains can also serve as beginning indicators to be combined to create a global index of the general control ratio for individuals. These methods also seem applicable to measurement of other variables in the theory as they apply to specific domains or realms, the results of which can then be combined across realms for general measures.

Consider, for example, provocation, which is anything that acutely reminds a person of his or her control imbalance. Various realms of activity, along with objects and sources of potential provocation, could be identified, and respondents could be asked to rate the likelihood, and intensity, of being made aware of their relative control when confronting each of them. Average scores could be combined across types of encounters and for different objects and sources to generate estimates of provocation. In a similar way, interviews concerning outcomes of actual encounters, projections of probable action in vignettes, and observations of simulated encounters could all be used to create specific and general measures of provocation.

Although the variables of the theory can legitimately be measured with different degrees of comprehensiveness, it is most appropriate to employ variables measured at comparable levels. Thus, a measure of the total control imbalance, given particular values of other variables also measured as totals across all domains, should predict overall probabilities of some form of deviance, regardless of the realm, just as it should predict the likelihood of particular deviances in any specific realm. However, domain-specific measures of the control ratio should predict only within that domain. If a person's specific control ratio in the interpersonal, sexual realm is measured, provocations, opportunity, and the various forms of deviance should be measured for that realm as well. Thus conformity will mean conformity to the prevailing norms concerning interpersonal sexual conduct, and predatory deviance will refer to behaviors such as taking sexual pleasure without giving it in return, making superficial seductions through false promises, and committing outright rape. Within the interpersonal sexual realm, defiance will refer to extramarital and premarital sex when norms prohibit it, homosexual behavior, out-of-context flirtatiousness, and activities like swinging. The same would apply to other domains.

A limited test of the general hypotheses identified at the beginning of this section, then, could make use of any sample of individuals and any realm of control. The first step requires estimating and expressing in common units the actual or perceived total control that each individual in the sample exercises and the total control to which he or she is exposed in that realm, calculating the ratio of the two, and distributing the cases along the control balance continuum. The second step involves measuring the extent to which each individual has committed or is likely to commit various forms of deviance in that realm. The third step matches the categories of control balance to the measures of types of deviance to ascertain whether the predictions are correct. Additional tests would do this for a variety of realms, perhaps finally encompassing all domains.

Criteria of Success. Appropriate criteria for judging the theory vary with the level of abstraction, the precision of the hypotheses, and the narrowness of the domain under consideration. On the most abstract, general level the usual standards involving nonchance relationships are suitable, but for more precise, focused hypotheses mere statistical significance should be secondary to strong prediction. These criteria, however, must be employed with due regard for correct derivation of hypotheses and measurement accuracy. Hypotheses have to reflect well the theoretical premises' logical implications. In addition, more stringent hypotheses should take account of conditions and contingencies as specified by the theory. Finally, it is more appropriate to examine sets of hypotheses linked to each other than to test single, isolated hypotheses.

Even with good hypotheses, strong results cannot be anticipated without satisfactory measurement of the concepts, which almost certainly cannot be accomplished without new data collected specifically for that purpose. Indeed, until good measurement is achieved, the theory should probably be judged favorably if *collections* of specific, focused hypotheses, which are logically interlinked, show correct directions of effect and overall statistical significance. As better measurement becomes possible, the standards of success can shift to the magnitude of effects, and if the theory ultimately is to be judged adequate, predicted effects will have to be confirmed with a high degree of accuracy.

Research has a dual purpose—to evaluate a theory at a given point of development and to provide a basis for altering and improving it. Therefore, whereas the current statement of control balance theory invites and requires empirical testing to confirm its worth, this specific formulation should not be regarded as a finished product to be accepted or rejected in its entirety. If initial results are favorable, scholars should use empirical evidence acquired in tests, along with that obtained in exploratory research designed to fill in knowledge gaps, to amend the theory. In this way, future statements of the theory will be collective achievements.

The current version of the theory is meant to be a beginning; actually, as will be shown in the next chapter, it is really a merging of preexisting work, constituting at best a change in approach. As such, it cries out for modification. Some changes may represent creative theoretical infusions or corrections of logical errors, others will be based on empirical evidence compiled from tests of hypotheses designed to judge the theory's current worth, and additional refinements may flow from exploratory research to fill in gaps in the theoretical development. Some of those gaps will be identified in the final chapter, and others will become obvious as scholars begin to apply the theory. The need for research to establish exact demarcations between the zones of the control ratio continuum as well as to explore the precise impact of different conditional and contingent variables has already been mentioned.

Lest my openness to modification be misunderstood as a maneuver to avoid empirical accountability, I want to make it clear that the present version of the theory must be tested empirically, and if a *collection* of appropriate tests indicate that it is off base, it should be abandoned. Nevertheless, caution against premature rejection is warranted. If initial testing shows it to be generally on track, additional research and theoretical effort should be expended specifically for emendation. I hope that this will be one of the rare instances in which the scholarly community departs from the typical procedure whereby researchers repeatedly test original versions of theories as if they were immutable entities to be embraced or relinquished. Provided that this theory passes first muster, at least some of the additional research should furnish profitable feedback that leads to revision and amelioration.

General Conclusion

Without data collected with control balance variables specifically in mind, it is impossible to conduct direct tests of the theory. Moreover, the theory concerns types of deviance that make sense only within its own parameters. Systematic data about deviance simultaneously interpretable within the theory and part of the usual domain of acts included within the field of crime or deviance are limited to only a few types, and there is controversy about some of the distributions of deviance for which there are systematic data. Therefore, it is difficult even to apply the premises of the theory to "known patterns" to ascertain with confidence its "face validity." Nevertheless, the theory seems to make sense of demographic distributions of the "facts," at least in the imperfect form that we understand them. This suggests that the theory is worth further consideration.

Although the first step in additional examination will undoubtedly involve logical criticism and application of extant empirical information, evaluation will also require direct empirical tests. The criteria for such tests include appropriate derivation of hypotheses, multitiered standards of acceptance, and most important of all, good measurement of the concepts. The credibility of the theory rests on empirical results from direct tests, but it should be regarded as a theory in evolution rather than as a final, take-it-or-leave-it product. Therefore, provided initial results are promising, an invitation is extended for scholars to participate in building a better theory by using empirical information and results from exploratory research to amend and improve the current and succeeding formulations.

10

Integration and Critique

The explanatory principles of control balance have been explicated and shown to be consistent with the known facts about crime and deviance. The task now is to show more explicitly how this formulation synthesizes other theories and to assess its adequacy according to the criteria set forth in Chapter 2.

In Chapter 4, a blueprint for developing more adequate general theory through integrating parts of the collective theoretical repertoire was presented. This method of synthetic integration involves five operations: abstraction, or conceptual integration; identification or invention of a unifying central causal process; specification of the contingencies regulating its operation; linking existing theories to the variables and contingencies; and articulating how the various components of the synthetic theory mesh to produce various outcomes under particular conditions. Much attention has already been devoted to some of these operations. Existing theoretical ideas were conceptually integrated to create the main abstract concept—the control ratio; a central causal process, called control balancing, was described; contingencies under which the causal process operates with greater or lesser force were identified; and different issues in the study of crime and deviance, oriented around prevalence, incidence, development, and comparisons among various categories and social units, were addressed to show how the components of the theory come together to produce different outcomes under various conditions.

Two tasks remain. The first is to identify more systematically the theoretical or conceptual strands incorporated in the control ratio and to show how existing theories feed into the control balancing process through their explanations of the values of contingent variables and the linkages in the causal chain underlying the theoretical argument. The second task is to turn a critical eye on my own efforts. Since synthetic integration aims to produce general theory with adequate breadth, comprehensiveness, depth, and precision, and since it mandates paying explicit attention to these matters, an honest appraisal of how well that has been done is important. Theories must be built collectively, and success requires integration as well as constructive criticism. Above all, theorists must not become committed to their products or overly defensive about them. To that end, then, I try to apply the standards of adequacy set forth in Chapter 2 to control balance theory.

Integration

Conceptual Abstraction: The Control Ratio

The main concept in control balance theory is the control ratio. This concept is directly implicated in four of five interactive convergences important in the control balancing process, and it is indirectly implicated in the other one (see Chapter 7). The control ratio has a crucial direct impact on predisposition for deviant motivation, on deviant motivation itself, on constraint, and on the probability of the actual expression of specific forms of deviance. In addition, it indirectly, though essentially, affects the probability of deviance generally.

Control ratio, however, is not a free-floating, original concept. It is an abstraction that blends and summarizes a number of concepts implied or explicitly stated in other theories of crime, deviance, or human behavior. Identifying the sources of this concept will show it to be a product of conceptual amalgamation, the first operation in synthetic integration.

First, the control ratio idea owes much to Gibbs (1981, 1989, 1994). I have been inspired by his demonstration of the omnipresence of the idea of control in sociological writings, which, of course, include most of the theoretical reasoning and conceptual apparatus of scholarship in the crime/deviance area. It is evident, however, that Gibbs has not gone far enough. Although he does an admirable job of translating sociological thought into the language of control, he does not actually show that the central notion in sociology is control, only that it *could become* the key concept if sociologists were to reorient their thinking and alter their language (Gibbs 1989). Moreover, his theory of control does not rely on conceptual abstraction, nor does it involve a central causal mechanism that explains why individuals do things, especially not why they engage in deviant behavior. Rather, he is concerned with reciprocal relationships among control attempts and perceived control capacity as they are manifested in societal conditions like the amount of scientific activity and the division of labor (Gibbs 1994). My efforts, therefore, were propelled by what Gibbs's work implies rather than by what he claims or achieves. Control can, and probably should, serve as a central organizing principle for sociology, or at least for the sociology of crime and deviance. However, for this to happen, it is clear that a control-related abstraction has to be derived to play upon, but also to transcend, extant notions of the influence of control in human relationships and organizations. The control ratio is a candidate for that synthesizing concept.

A second component of the control ratio is the idea that discrepancies between two contending forces produce tension. Relativity of influences and equilibrium, or balance, assumes that comfort requires equality of the two forces. Without balance, or relative equality of the contrasting components, an organism or social entity experiences pressure (or strain) that can only be relieved by action directed toward equilibration. Thus the impetus for behavior is a desire to relieve the discomfort produced by the relative imbalance of two antithetical forces.

Several classic theories feature discrepancies between contending elements. In most, potential for action is expressed as a ratio reflecting the numerical relationship of the two contrasting variables. One of these "ratio" arguments undergirds the eighteenth-century utilitarian philosophy that spawned modern thinking about deterrence, rational choice, and social learning. Utilitarians, particularly Jeremy Bentham and Cesare Beccaria, contended that the potential pain (cost) relative to the potential pleasure (reward) associated with a contemplated action determines the outcome (Plamenatz 1958). Thus, the greater the surplus benefit of a criminal act, the greater the probability of its occurrence, and the greater the surplus cost, the lower the probability. According to economic theory and its cousins, utility (the relationship of benefit to cost) affects deviant and conforming behavior, but it is especially salient for socially unacceptable conduct.

Sutherland's differential association theory is also oriented around a relativity, or equilibrium, principle. He theorized that the cause of criminal behavior is the ratio of favorable to unfavorable definitions of (messages about) criminal behavior to which the individual has been exposed, weighted by certain characteristics of the definitions (messages), that is, their intensity, priority, source, and repetition. He used the term "excess" to refer to any ratio of favorable to unfavorable definitions of crime larger than 1 and implied that the greater the excess, the greater the chances of criminal behavior (Tittle et al. 1986). Although his theory has usually been interpreted as explaining criminal behavior in terms of the strength of motivation to commit crime, it is also possible to conceive of constraints on behavior as unfavorable definitions of criminal behavior.

A third classic theory emphasizing contending forces is Merton's anomie formulation. Although his presentation is inconsistent and muddled (see Chapter 3), it seems to imply that the motivation for deviance is to be found in an individual's perception of the discrepancy between culturally prescribed goals and available, socially acceptable means to achieve those goals. Moreover, his theory seems to imply that the type of deviance likely to occur depends on the nature of the discrepancy between the goals and the means. Merton did not speak of the *degrees* of goal acceptance or of *degrees* of availability or acceptance of means, but his schema does suggest an underlying concept reflecting the relative values of two dichotomized variables—the acceptance or rejection of culturally prescribed goals, and the acceptability (availability) or nonacceptability (nonavailability) of culturally approved means for achieving culturally prescribed goals.

There are also several contemporary theoretical statements that make use of a relativity notion. First, there are variations of learning theory, which express the basic notions of Sutherland's differential association in more sophisticated and elaborate form. These include Akers's (1985) social learning formulation and Wilson and Herrnstein's theory (1985), both of which draw on principles of behaviorism that have a long history in the field of psychology. A second equilibrium like formulation is Austin Turk's conflict argument (1969), which maintains that relative degrees of power of contending groups determine whether their behaviors will be criminalized (made illegal) and sanctioned. Turk implicitly assumes that power differences generate tension for action both by those with superior power and by those who are subordinate. A final example is found in social exchange theory, which rests on the idea that people seek balance, or reciprocity, in their social exchanges with other people (Blau 1964; Homans 1961; see also the general discussion in Alexander 1987, chap. 11) because imbalances cause feelings of discomfort or awkwardness (see also Tallman and Gray 1990; Gray and Tallman 1984).

Ideas about the import of power, social influence, and prestige on the ability to predict behavior provide a third impetus for the control ratio. Numerous explanations of behavioral differences among individuals, demographic categories, and social groups assume that those with superior social positions will conform to rules, whereas subordinates will deviate (see Tittle 1983). Although the evidence for that hypothesis is weak or contradictory (see Chapter 8), many scholars refuse to relinquish the idea that "social class" influences conformity (Goode 1994:333; Hagan 1992, 1994). I have expended a lot of intellectual effort trying to understand why this notion—that status or material deprivation will generate or predict deviance—has such intuitive appeal. There are plenty of plausible possibilities, including ideological biases, cognitive commitments stemming from professional socialization, ignorance of the evidence, and selective perception, but some scholars might be confusing particular aspects of social status, or some phenomenon akin to social status, with socioeconomic status itself (see Tittle and Meier 1990). After all, social status is a complex, composite concept encompassing a number of parts or dimensions. As such, it only imperfectly reflects its component elements, and those constituent parts might vary independently of the overarching concept of which they are a part. With that possibility in mind, I began to reexamine class- or status-linked explanations to try to identify what that constituent part might be.

Rethinking theories about social status, in the context of Gibbs's discussion of control and with cognizance of the recurrence of the equilibration idea discussed above, led to the control ratio concept. First, it became clear that the social-class argument rests mainly on the idea that lower status implies some kind of deprivation that motivates deviance. The usual treatment assumes deprivation to be of a material form and the result to be frustration, anger, or self-depreciation. These emotions, in turn, are usually hypothesized to cause irrational, uncontrolled behavior resulting in violence or other impulsive conduct, or to cause calculated behavior aimed at changing the material conditions that produce frustration, anger, or self-depreciation (compare Agnew 1992). This putative process, however, can be linked to something besides material deprivation, as Agnew notes, and it can be activated by deprivation of something that is more abstract than social status, which transcends and is only imperfectly related to it.

I came to believe that deprivation of control is that transcendent component. If social status can relieve potential deprivation of material goods, it does so through its implication for control. Further, if material deprivation produces negative emotions, it probably does so because it implies absence of control. Moreover, control, though linked to social status, also varies independently of it. Following this line of reasoning and taking a cue from arguments about relative deprivation, it also became clear that control as an absolute entity is meaningless; it is salient only in a relative sense. What matters is the amount of control that one exercises relative to the amount of control that one experiences—a variable that again bears only an imperfect relationship to social class or SES. Furthermore, if the causal element is one of equilibration, even relative control cannot be conceived of as having a linear effect on deviance.

Thus, the control ratio captures and reflects the meaningful aspects of social class or social status while permitting correction of the explanatory mistakes underlying arguments about socioeconomic status and deviance. Among those explanatory errors are associating deviance with measures of absolute status rather than with proportional, or relative, measures based on a constituted element of social class; assuming linear effects (but see Hirschi 1972); and positing material deprivation as a first-order, almost exclusive, activator of deviance. Because of these advantages, control balance theory brings some order to the chaos that has fueled the social class–crime debate. Indeed, I am now of the opinion that the concept of social class, or socioeconomic status, per se, is outmoded and of practically no value; the important causal elements buried within it are better expressed in terms of the control ratio (compare Wright 1979).

Control balance theory, then, starts with a central concept representing an abstract weave of three fundamental sets of ideas embedded in existing theories: the centrality of control to human behavior, as demonstrated by Gibbs; the necessity of considering ratios of important variables, as shown by numerous theories; and the import of relative control, or autonomy, suggested by numerous arguments about social class and crime/deviance. Such abstraction constitutes one of the essential operations necessary for building general theories through the technique of synthetic integration.

The Causal Mechanism

Beginning with the concept of a control ratio, the theory adds an underlying causal principle—that deviant behavior is undertaken to accomplish something for the person who commits it. Deviance is conceived as a device employed by individuals to try to alter a control imbalance. A control imbalance, under various prescribed conditions, then "motivates" an effort to correct an unfavorable one or to extend one that is favorable. Sometimes that motivation eventuates in deviant behavior, depending on the likelihood that deviance will activate countercontrols, and the type of deviance likely to be emitted reflects the nature of the control imbalance. Portraying deviance as a "functional" mechanism is not new since most theories of deviance do this, although the exact nature of the functionality proposed by other theories departs considerably from that used in this theory. There are, however, at least three theories about deviance that actually propose a functional argument quite close to the one encompassed within control balance theory.

Before those two theories are discussed, the meaning of "functional" must be clarified. Unfortunately, "functional explanation" has a pejorative connotation for many who associate it with a form of analysis practiced by some leading sociologists during the 1950s and early 1960s. Such analysis was based on an equilibration principle that conceived of societies as finely honed, integrated systems of parts. Some "functional" theorists assumed that societies achieved internal structural and cultural interdependency through an evolutionary process that proved that whatever social arrangements happened to prevail at a given time were in place because they had contributed to the survival of the social group. Thus, all features of contemporary societies were theorized to exist because they were functional in promoting the continuity of the society or because they once served a useful purpose and continued to exist because insufficient time had transpired for the evolutionary process to show their maladaptivity.

So-called functional theory or analysis, therefore, explained why a structural feature existed, or why recurrent behavior patterns occur, by specifying some "useful" purpose (for societal continuity) they might have, no matter how remote or obscure. Once a plausible function was identified, the behavior pattern or structure was said to be explained. Moreover, it was assumed that any disturbance in a social system, such as social disruption or excess deviance, would provoke accommodation in other parts of the social system to reestablish equilibrium. The result was often tautological and simplistic explanations that had difficulty accounting for social change. Moreover, this type of functional theory often found itself a handmaiden of conservative ideologues who wished to argue that social arrangements, which worked to their advantage, were inherently beneficial to society. It is hardly surprising that this type of functional analysis was soundly criticized on logical and ideological grounds (Gross 1959; Pfohl 1994; van den Berghe 1973).

Despite this history and the disrepute that the term "functional" has acquired among social scientists, functionality has retained an important place in explanations of individual behavior, and though rarely recognized, it has earned a place of respect among students of deviance in particular. Indeed, with the possible exception of some psychological, biological, and learning theories, most efforts to explain an individual's deviant behavior incorporate functional assumptions, for example, that deviance "works" for people in various circumstances, and they involve functional explanations, for instance, that the benefits of deviance to the potential deviant are important in explaining its occurrence. Social control theory and its stepchild, self-control theory, contend that all people are inherently motivated to satisfy their desires, needs, or wants and unless prevented from doing so, they will gratify themselves in ways that are deviant or criminal. Deviance and crime, then, are advantageous modes of behavior for those individuals who commit them; they satisfy preexisting tastes or needs of the deviator. Of course, these control theories aim to explain why some people refrain from gratifying their desires through deviance, and in that quest focus on things that prevent gratification. Nevertheless, a crucial assumption of those theories is a functional one; without it, the theoretical restraints would be meaningless.

Similarly, utilitarian/deterrence theory posits that deviance and crime are functional. Since all human behavior presumably represents a calculus to maximize benefit and minimize cost, crime must result because, under particular circumstances, it is beneficial, or pleasurable; it is functional for the person. Marxian conflict theory, of course, sees crime as a means of survival (for subordinates) and as a means of competitive advantage for capitalists. Routine activities theory assumes the existence of potential predators motivated to offend. Although it does not specify the nature of that motivation, it leaves the clear impression that predation is beneficial to the offender—he or she gains something of material value. Certainly anomie theory, and its offshoots, including Agnew's general strain theory, posit that crime/deviance is useful in various ways to the person who commits it and that this usefulness is an important component of its explanation.

The central causal mechanism of control balance theory, then, draws on a rich tradition, at least as far as the form of its argument goes. However, it attempts to integrate three particular theories by abstracting their underlying causal mechanisms. One of them is "transcendence" theory (Katz 1988). Katz repeatedly enunciates two underlying ideas. One is that deviance is motivated by a desire to escape from something undesirable. Sometimes the undesirable condition is portrayed as chaos, sometimes as humiliation, sometimes as rationality, and sometimes simply as external control. The second prominent idea is that deviance, in whatever form it manifests itself, allows the person to go beyond mere escape; deviance permits the person to triumph or transcend. Even though Katz never uses this language and never clearly says this, the latent argument seems to be that deviant behavior is attractive because it puts the person in control.

A cold-blooded murderer tries to control the chaos in his life by making a bold statement of his unspeakably evil nature, and through the intricate details of his crime, demonstrates ultimate control of the immediate situation, rendering his will, no matter how bizarre, on the victims and the context of the crime. A man who commits righteous slaughter by killing his adulterous wife wishes to overcome not only the loss of control over his wife and his own destiny that her betrayal has produced but also to overcome his loss of control in the larger community implied by the denigration of his status, which is connected to his perceived sense that others have learned of his own humiliation. Killing the suitor, and perhaps the wife, puts him back in charge, particularly if he can convince himself he is acting on behalf of the community, upholding sacred values. Street-elite behavior seems to be a clear example of deviance designed to escape control imposed by the social world and to permit its practitioners to impose their own controls. Creating an aura of unpredictability and violence—an awesome presence—allows a person to call the shots. Finally, sneaky thrill seekers would not have to be sneaky if they were free of controls by others. Their deviance permits defiance of externally imposed constraints and allows them to order their own lives.

My interpretation, which attempts to see all of the episodes described by Katz as of one cloth, is probably contrary to Katz's intent since he unashamedly eschews general explanations. Katz's claim to be describing each type of situation as it would be seen through the eyes of the deviant, his attempt to understand what a person is doing when he or she commits deviance, and the peculiar language applied to different situations imply that the naturalistic contexts he dissects are unique. Yet, they seem to me all similar in some fundamental respects. All appear to involve efforts to escape control exercised by others or dictated by circumstances, and they all seem to express efforts to impose control back over proximate people and circumstances. Further, the deviant behavior so generated appears to involve a duality of effect. The escape, or assertion of autonomy, is accomplished by triumphant redirection of control. This mirrors my own observations of deviant behavior of various kinds, and it is that process I have tried to capture in the control balancing argument.

A second functionally oriented theory that is abstractly incorporated in the central causal mechanism is that of Turk (1969). He spells out the complexity of the process by which power groups negotiate their positions and express themselves in view of strategic considerations of the power of others. Various moves by contending, or potentially contending, parties involve deviant behavior, declarations of the behavior of other groups as criminal, efforts to control that criminal behavior, and maneuvers to shift power. Underlying the whole process seems to be an effort by subordinates to deflect or escape the control of those with more power, along with an effort on the part of those with some power already to extend control further. Thus Turk's ideas reflect the notion that deviance, whether perpetrated by individuals or organized social units, is a coping strategy for managing imbalances of control.

Although Turk's theory is about social groups rather than individuals and is played out in a political arena rather than on the interpersonal or individual level, a similar conflict process seems to be operative at the microlevel (see in particular the discussion of aleatory risk by Short and Strodbeck 1974). Control balance theory attempts to project the conflict process that Turk identifies into the behavior field of individual actors. It focuses on relative degree of control exercised and suffered (including a wide range of controls, not simply social power) by individuals, with group affiliations and social statuses as backdrops. The theory attempts to spell out the probability and type of deviance (rather than criminalization and sanctioning) as consequences of relative degrees of control.

A final specific theory that fuels the abstract central causal process is a psychologically rooted one called "reactance" theory (Brehm 1966; Brehm and Brehm 1981). According to it, people are stimulated to violate rules, rebel, or act in opposing ways when denied some freedom they perceive that they have. When confronted with authority or when told they cannot do something, people try to restore their perceived loss of freedom. This sometimes implies behavior opposite to what one is told, and sometimes it implies violation of norms. The underlying assumption is that everybody has an inherent impulse for autonomy that is provoked by constraint. However, not all denial of freedom results in deviant or oppositional behavior. The theory, as elaborated in light of research evidence, specifies the conditions under which different kinds of reactions, including submissive behavior, will result from various kinds of deprivation of freedom (Brehm and Brehm 1981). Since I do not apply reactance theory per se to the problem of deviant behavior, it will not be described in detail. My objective is to call attention to the fact that the central causal mechanism of control balance theory represents an abstraction of reactance theory's fundamental idea that constraints on behavior generate a motivation to gain control, and that much behavior, in this case deviant behavior, is a functional device to deal with an absence of control. Control balancing also incorporates the relativity of reactance theory. Jack Brehm calibrates the likely behavioral effect of deprivation of freedom on the basis of the extent to which the person perceives he or she possesses the freedom in question, just as control balance theory projects various probabilities of deviance in general and probabilities of specific forms of deviance on the basis of the control ratio.

The central causal process of the theory, then, abstractly expresses the general idea, embedded in many theories, that deviance serves the deviator and that this function is important to the explanation of the deviant behavior. More important, it expresses in abstract form the underlying causal mechanisms of three specific theories: Katz's transcendence theory, Turk's conflict theory, and Brehm's reactance theory. In that sense the control balance formulation is an integrated theory. It is an integrated theory in others ways as well. Control balancing involves a more complicated causal process than is implied by the mere idea that a control imbalance is linked to the probability of deviance and the type of deviance likely to occur.

In Chapter 7, I tried to show that several variables must interact and converge in particular ways for deviance to occur. Although the basic notion that individuals commit acts of deviance to overcome or extend control imbalances is crucial and although the control ratio is implicated heavily at a number of points in the causal chain, it is also clear that other variables are involved. These include situational provocations, debasement, motivation for deviance, opportunity, and constraint, which itself is implicated with risk and seriousness. In all of these interconnections, the theory owes much to other theories. None of the concepts are original, and in each instance, there are existing theories that help explain or predict the magnitude of the values that each of those variables might assume in a given case. Spelling out how these extant theories produce specific values of the variables in the control balancing process represents another form of integration.

This book contains no fully detailed account of how various specific theories might be brought to bear to account for the values of specific variables in the control balancing process, so the theory is not completely integrated. Such articulation could be done, however, if space permitted, though each nexus of the control balancing process probably calls for some theoretical integration of its own. It is not enough, for example, to show that several different theories offer an explanation of the degree of constraint that a person feels, with the implication that any one will do to account for the value of that variable in a given instance. The magnitude of constraint that a person experiences is itself a serious theoretical problem that necessitates some abstract combination of causal processes implied by the different theories that deal with such matters. The point is that theory building—which inherently involves theoretical integration—is an ongoing task. To claim that a formulation is an integrated theory should never be taken to imply that it is complete. Further development and further integration are always needed. That is a collective endeavor to be undertaken by the community of scholars, not a task for one person.

Contingencies and Integration

No causal process works exactly the same way and to the same degree in all circumstances. Contingencies always set the parameters within which causal effects operate, and they affect the force and completeness with which effects unfold. Several contingencies that bear on the control balancing process were previously identified, and the specified values of those contingent variables within which control balancing presumably operates with least and most effectiveness were specified. The theory itself, however, involves no explicit attempt to account for the contingent variables themselves or to predict the values they would actually take in specific situations, for specific individuals, or for categories of individuals. Instead, control balance theory begins with the contingent variables as they exist (accepts them as givens) and adapts the predicted outcomes accordingly.

To integrate the theory fully, one would have to provide explanations for these givens, and such explanations would necessitate explicit articulation of the influences of other theories or theory fragments. In each instance, such a merger would require additional integration. The explanatory principles of other theories, therefore, are integral parts of control balance theory to the extent that they account for, or at least provide clues about, the particular values that contingencies for control balancing might assume.

The appropriate descriptive imagery is of a wagon wheel. The control balancing process represents the hub, whereas the processes of other theories and theory fragments represent either spokes of the wheel or reinforcing braces at various points that connect two or more of the spokes at various distances from the center. These spokes and reinforcing braces provide the inputs that account for variation in the variables of interest to the theory, including the contingent variables. For example, one of the personal contingencies for the operation of control balance theory is morality. Since the effects of a control imbalance are muted when moral feelings directed against a given type of behavior are strong, it is important to know when moral objections are likely to be high. There is no doubt that the particular style of child rearing employed by the parents, the personalities of the parents, their moral commitments, the number and ages of siblings, the characteristics of the community, the economic situation of the family, the models of behavior representing various moral options, the hereditary or biological makeup of the individual, and other things all influence internalized moral sentiments. Hence all theories showing how these various influences affect moral development are essential parts of a completely integrated theory built around the principle of control balancing.

It is clear, therefore, that the theory, all by itself, will not provide complete explanation, even if it ultimately proves totally correct. A fully integrated theory must furnish the means to explain and predict the strength of numerous contingent variables, as well as its main variables. In other words, the central causal mechanism, which is general (and thus applies to all cases), must depend on input that is specific enough to account for the actual observed values of the variables that are part of the control balance process and that impinge on it as contingencies. Since many theories and specific explanations already attempt to account for the variables that presumably influence the central causal mechanism directly or as contingencies, they can be brought into an integrated theory as input mechanisms.

Critique

Three mandates inspired this work. The most important contends that the goal of students of deviance should be to build general theories. The second maintains that the most effective method for achieving general theory is synthetic integration. The third is that theories, whether developed through synthetic integration or by some other means, should generate adequate explanations of the phenomena to which they are addressed. Adequacy is defined, and judged, according to four criteria—breadth, comprehensiveness, precision, and depth. It has been my intent to go beyond mere preachment by actually doing the things I contend should and must be done. I have employed the method of synthetic integration to develop a general theory, and it has been presented for the reader's consideration. I now invite evaluation of those efforts, particularly in terms of the criteria that were set forth in Chapter 2 and by which the adequacy of existing theories was assessed.

Control balance theory is clearly deficient in a number of ways when judged by those principles. The following pages will detail some of those shortcomings in order to speed the process of collective theory building, assuming that the community of scholars will find this theory interesting enough and initially promising enough to warrant attention. If some of its weaknesses can be identified now, conference time, journal space, classroom discussions, and interpersonal conversations can be devoted to those deficiencies that are not so readily recognizable, and more energy can be devoted to actually clarifying the problematic areas to be identified.

Some may wonder why I do not just correct the deficiencies instead of pointing them out. The answer is simple: In some instances I am not able to, so I am pleading for help, and in other instances, I am working on improvements but delaying publication usurps an essential scientific process. Theories should be cumulative, and they should be products of the collective effort of the entire community of scholars. Since any person's part in the theoretical enterprise is limited, it would be arrogant to think that the whole job of developing general theory should wait for my complete contribution. Control balance theory, to the level that it is now developed, is designed to provide a vehicle for collective effort to unfold.

Breadth

Good theory explains a wide range of instances of its dependent variable—if possible, all instances. Since control balance is about deviant behavior, mainly about individual manifestations but also about rates of deviance for aggregates, it should explain all forms of deviant behavior. The dependent variables encompassed within the scheme, as described in Chapter 5, include six categories of deviance, three being associated with control deficits and the other three, with control surpluses. Almost all forms of deviance are incorporated within the categories of predation, defiance, submission, exploitation, plunder, and decadence, and to the extent that the theory satisfactorily explains those categories of deviance, it has great breadth.

There are some obvious problems, however. First, it is not always clear whether a specific act qualifies as deviance within the scheme. The definitions and assumptions implied by the general definition of deviance and by the specific categories of deviance often require information about the behavior that is lacking. For example, predation is defined as having two components. One of those components is behavior by an actor who directly employs physical violence, manipulation, or property extraction.

This part is reasonably easy to apply, though deciding what is violent, or what is property, or even what is manipulation is always subject to some imprecision. The second component, however, is more problematic because it involves a quality of the act, the social definition of the behavior prevailing in the social context, or perhaps the state of mind of the actor. To qualify as predation, the direct behaviors noted above must be undertaken with no regard for the effects on the objects of the predatory acts, that is, the desires or the welfare of the individual or group that is the object of the predation must be of little concern to the predator. Predation is fundamentally a selfish act, undertaken to benefit the predator by altering a control imbalance. However, without intimate knowledge of the thoughts and feelings of the actors in specific situations where deviance occurs or might occur, how can one know that the perpetrator of violence, manipulation, or property extraction does it with insensitivity toward the victim? Moreover, one might ask, is it not possible that a robber might feel sorry for his victim and perhaps treat the individual gently? Maybe some robbers would take only one-half of a victim's money out of concern for his or her ability to survive. Do these concerns make the act of robbery any less predatory, and do they render such forms of robbery inexplicable by the theory?

Certainly it cannot always be known whether an act or possible act of violence, manipulation, or property extraction involves insensitivity to the suffering of the victim; an inference is necessary, and inferences can sometimes be wrong. In that sense, then, some acts of deviance that might seem like predation may escape classification as predation and fall outside the purview of the theory. Nevertheless, I contend that most predatorylike acts will be classifiable, especially by focusing on features of the central act. For example, even if a rapist feels enough sympathy for his victim to wear a condom, makes an effort to see that she is relatively comfortable, and closes a door to shield her children, the rape itself is a violation of her wishes and is contrary to her welfare. In other words, the rape is undertaken without regard for the interests of the victim concerning that particular act, even though the rapist showed some concern for the victim through adjustment of ancillary aspects of the encounter. Similarly, the robber who takes only one-half of a victim's money nevertheless disregards the wishes of that person by stealing the person's property.

Nevertheless, since all of the deviance categories that are of concern to the theory embody ambiguities similar to those just discussed, it is clear that the definitions of the concepts in the theory, particularly those having to do with the things to be explained, are problematic and that the breadth of the theory may suffer because of it. Perhaps this problem can be overcome, or maybe others can provide better guidelines for the categories of deviance to be explained by the theory. When that is done the theory may become broader than it now appears to be.

Requiring that an act must be regarded as unacceptable by the majority of people in a social group or in the social context in order to qualify as deviance (and thereby be subject to explanation by the theory) can also cause problems. Ascertaining the nonacceptability of behavior and appreciating the relative nature of that attribution are not always easy, and they open the door for misclassification and a weakening of breadth. Nevertheless, inferring social acceptability, though difficult, is possible in most cases. Even without survey data, most can agree that the physical violence exhibited by participants in an athletic contest does not usually qualify as predatory deviance, both because it involves some sensitivity on the part of the perpetrators for the welfare of the objects of the violence (there are rules of the game and ethics of sportsmanship) and because most people in the places where such contests occur find such violence acceptable. It is usually clear when, on occasion, the regulated violence of athletic engagement is transformed into predatory deviance. A "fight" on the football field is distinguishable from a tackle or a block, and "dirty" tactics are both different from normal athletic violence and widely recognized as such.

Second, even when a given act qualifies as deviance by its social unacceptability, it cannot always be unambiguously placed into one or another of the six categories of deviance implied by the theory. Prostitution, for instance, may be a form of predation, but it could also be a manifestation of defiance. It usually involves manipulation of the client by the prostitute and an extraction of property (the fee) without concern for the welfare of the customer. Still, some women prostitute themselves to defy rules of conventionality or to show contempt for parental expectations. Similarly, some adolescent acts of theft represent defiance as well as predation. Moreover, it is not always easy to ascertain if theft, coercion, or manipulation is directly committed by a given individual, which would qualify it as predation, or whether it is done through intermediaries, which would make it exploitation. If an employee makes a fraudulent business deal, following the guidelines of a company policy, is that employee a predator or an agent of exploitation acting on behalf of the company owners or directors? Clearly such ambiguities must be resolved if the theory is to have maximum usefulness and breadth.

Comprehensiveness

To answer the questions *why* and *how* fully an adequate theory must incorporate many causal forces, ideally all possible ones. At a minimum, this would entail an accommodation of various motivating factors, those things that constitute constraints on behavior, alternative motivations that may divert behavior away from deviance, opportunity to commit deviance, and capacities to actually accomplish various deviant acts in question. Control balance attempts to be comprehensive in this sense.

It identifies a motivator for deviance—the perception that a given deviant act can alter a control imbalance. This motivator is conceived as an abstract representation of the motivating elements in many other theories, and it is regarded as being itself a product of specific activators, including a predisposition toward deviance, situational provocations, and a sense of debasement. Furthermore, control balance theory recognizes the important conditioning effects of other motivating forces that influence the extent to which the causal processes that it emphasizes unfold with greater or lesser force, including various forms of motivation for alternative, nondeviant behaviors. The theory also brings in constraint as a major influence on the likelihood and type of deviance that is likely to be manifested, and it portrays constraint and motivation in relative relationship to each other. Furthermore, constraint is depicted as an outcome of other causal factors, such as situational risk and the seriousness of the act, which are central to the situation, as well as others that represent contingencies. Moreover, the theory explicitly introduces opportunity into its causal framework, allows for other causal forces to affect opportunity, and specifies that ability to perform the deviance operates as a contingency.

Despite this, the theory may not be comprehensive enough. In one sense it has concealed or muted the potential operation of some causal variables rather than fully incorporating them. Consider the potential effects of an impulse to achieve a meaningful self-identity or self-esteem (Kaplan 1975, 1980; Scheff et al. 1989) that a number of theories tout. Currently, the theory allows this causal force to operate only in a latent, ancillary fashion through its possible influence on whether various provocations produce debasement, or allows it as a general contingent variable for the operation of the overall control balancing process. In reality, of course, this variable might be a powerful independent motivator of deviance, and what control balance theory abstractly portrays as an effort to alter a control imbalance may be an effort to restore a damaged self. Hence, some might argue that control balance theory dilutes the effect of self-enhancement rather than bringing it into a comprehensive causal scheme. Certainly, the possible influence of self-enhancement is left unarticulated, and in that sense its power may be concealed or subordinated to the causal forces postulated by the theory.

This same criticism would apply to any number of other variables or potential causal forces. For example, self-control, the prime variable in Gottfredson and Hirschi's general theory, has only a secondary place, and not a fully articulated one at that, in control balance theory. It implicitly operates as a contingency for the full expression of the control balancing process, but it is not explicitly brought into the formulation. Those with high self-control may be less likely to act on their motivations toward deviance, may show greater appreciation for constraints, and perhaps may display more propensity toward defiance, submissiveness, and exploitativeness than others with similar control imbalances, regardless of the degree of their control imbalances. This is a contingent role, however, and the theory treats it as such. Critics will probably object to this, claiming that control balance theory has relegated what they regard as a central variable to the periphery. To them, using the periphery for contingent elements does not create comprehensiveness but instead is a cover for downgrading a competing theory (or a theoretical variable).

This positioning of variables is a potential weakness. The theory tries to allow for all possible causal forces, but sometimes it does so subtly, and in the process it ranks and orders variables. In addition, the theory may not actually accommodate all possible causal forces. Something that will not fit in the current formulation may have been overlooked. Identifying such variables and altering the theory to accommodate them stand as a crucial mission for the larger community of scholars. Moreover, whether the subtlety with which many variables are handled leads to neglect or greater utility and whether the ranking and ordering among variables suggested by existing theories is sensible or arbitrary remains to be seen. It depends largely, but not entirely, on empirical research. There is still much that can be accomplished with theoretical input from others.

Precision

A key feature of good theory that most existing formulations lack is precision. Precision encompasses three things: specification of the contingencies under which the causal processes operate with greater or lesser force, projection of the form of the causal relationships the theory predicts, and delineation of the time intervals between the theory's causal variables and effects. In developing control balance theory I have tried to improve on the theoretical efforts of others by paying special attention to precision.

Chapter 8 is devoted to identifying contingencies and projecting how the different values of each affect the causal processes in the central theory. The central causal process, as well as contingent effects, are described with attention to the form of the effects. The main argument in particular implies nonlinearity, since the overall probability of deviance theoretically increases with the magnitude of a control imbalance in either direction from the balanced zone, though the probability of specific forms of deviance is specified as fixed within zones of the control continuum. Moreover, the effects of many of the variables in the causal chain to which a control imbalance contributes at several points are spelled out, and many of those effects are predicted to be linear. The final feature of precision reflected in the theory is specification of the length of the causal intervals implied by the various effects. The main effects, involving the generation of deviant motivation and its expression in deviant behavior, take place with a short lag—almost instantaneously, in fact. Other effects, such as those involving the control ratio as it impinges on predisposition for deviant motivation, constraint, and actual deviant motivation, unfold over longer time periods, sometimes years.

Despite my intent, however, the theory does not fulfill ideal standards of precision. For one thing, contingencies other than those identified probably affect the control balancing process. Other scholars may be able to say what they are, and research may reveal some that are unexpected. A more important deficiency is my failure to spell out exactly the way in which various contingent variables will affect the control balancing process. Since the theory simultaneously deals with potential movement from one possible form of deviance to another and with the overall probability of deviance of some kind, it is extremely complicated to figure out how contingencies will affect the process. Imagine, for example, an individual, with a control ratio of a magnitude ordinarily suggesting predation, who becomes motivated to deviance in a situation where constraint is relatively weak. If this individual has strong moral feelings, he or she should display less likelihood of predation than if he or she has weak morality. Still, what about the overall probability of deviance? Would moral individuals be likely to engage in one of the less serious forms of deviance, which would not ordinarily be expected from their control ratios, thereby increasing their overall chances of deviance, or would they simply suppress the motivation toward any deviance? I simply have not been able to work out the predictions theoretically, and this is the case with many of the contingencies. In fact, in a number of instances, the best that I can say is that the identified contingent variable will affect the operation of the causal processes somehow, with no clear specification of exactly how.

Moreover, although the theory tries to be specific in identifying the form of its causal effects, this is only partially achieved. Once one gets beyond the main relationships linked to the control ratio, imprecision intrudes. In many instances the form of the causal effects is simply not addressed; in other instances, the form is implied to be linear when it actually may be of some other form. This is complicated by the expectation that most of the effects specified by the theory involve interactive nexuses in which some of the interacting variables may have linear effects within some ranges of another variable but nonlinear ones in other ranges. The fact is, all of these causal forms have not been teased out theoretically. It will have to be done with the help of others who might be interested in working on these issues, or it might have to be left to empirical research.

The greatest precision-related failure of the theory, however, concerns the length of the causal lags. It is clearly not detailed enough on this point. One problem is that the control ratio, so critical at so many points in the proposed causal chain, is not a fixed quantity. It is true that the general control ratio, influenced by one's major roles, statuses, and positions, is more or less stable. However, even the general control ratio varies from situation to situation, and certainly the control ratio within specific domains is highly variable across domains. The effects of the general control ratio are long-term—but I do not know how long that term is, since other situational variables must come into play in the short term for the effects of a control imbalance to be realized. All of those causal intervals have not been figured out, nor has the length of the interval during which the reciprocal effects of deviance itself feed back to debasement and to the control ratio. Unfortunately, this has been left for others and for empirical feedback.

Depth

The final feature of good theory, depth, concerns the extent to which a given formulation answers the questions *why* and *how* systematically and exhaustively. To do this a theory must provide the details on how its variables produce the outcomes it predicts, it must explicitly situate its variables within a larger causal process in which they are understood as part of a dynamic sequence of interacting events or effects eventuating in the outcomes of interest, and such dynamic sequences of effects must recognize potential reciprocal effects. Control balance theory strives for depth by detailing a causal chain involving five causal nexuses of interacting variables that under certain conditions produce deviance in general and under specified conditions produce particular forms of deviance. It also tries to show how and why things work the way they do, with particular focus on the counterbalancing influences of motivation and potential constraint.

As formulated here, however, the theory does not completely situate its causal process within a full dynamic sequence of events or effects. Like many other theories, it ends up taking many things for granted, treating them as givens. In one sense, it cuts into an underlying causal chain at midpoint, though it stretches to the background in accounting for predispositions toward deviance. I like to think, however, that the theory provides all of the essential elements for the unspecified dynamic sequences to be traced out fully. More telling, perhaps, is the fact that the control balance formulation does not show in detail the nature of the interactions involved in the causal syndromes that form the model underlying the theory. Moreover, some people will not be satisfied with the explanations provided by the theory. Some will find them incomplete; some will find the whole scheme incomprehensible, particularly since it departs from the standard linear model, and others will find it sparse in essential details.

One area in which missing detail is obvious concerns the transition zones between areas where the probability of one type of deviance, such as predation, merges into the probability of another type of deviance, such as defiance. The theory does not identify the exact point along the control ratio continuum at which the chances for defiance begin to exceed the chances for predation. It only specifies that about the first one-third of the continuum of repression will be the zone of predation. In reality, it may turn out to be only one-fourth of that continuum, or maybe it will actually be 40 or 50 percent. Regretfully, this can only be worked out with the help of empirical evidence.

General Summary and Conclusion

In developing control balance theory, I have employed the technique of synthetic integration, which involves conceptual integration through abstraction of ideas from existing theories, further bringing the components of extant work together through a central causal process and through specification of the contingencies that affect the operation of the theory. Such synthesis also involves articulation of how the components of such a theory combine to cause various effects. In this chapter, the details of how synthetic integration was employed have been spelled out, and the way that the resulting theory incorporates elements of existing theories or theory fragments has been described. I conceive of the theory as a continuation, or a temporary culmination, of the collective efforts of crime/deviance scholars who have gone before, and in this chapter, I have tried to demonstrate that.

Since theoretical work is best pursued as a collective activity, control balance theory should be no more than an intellectual bridge for further advancement. The need for modification is already clear. In developing the theory to this point, I was attentive to the criteria of adequacy set forth in Chapter 2 which I used to evaluate prior theories in the crime/deviance area. In thus assessing the adequacy of my own efforts by those standards, it is clear that much remains to be done, and my belief that theory building must be a community endeavor is confirmed. Although control balance appears to be more adequate than most theories in that it simultaneously expresses great breadth, much comprehensiveness, unusual precision, and considerable depth, it does not ideally fulfill these criteria. Improvement will depend on long-term feedback and modification stemming from critical review and input by the scholarly community and from empirical evidence. I hope that others will regard the theory as worthy of such attention and will accept my invitation to use it as a vehicle for trying to achieve a fully adequate general theory.

References

Abrahamson, Mark, and Valerie J. Carter. 1986. "Tolerance, Urbanism and Region." *American Sociological Review* 51:287–294.

Adler, Alfred. 1956. *The Individual Psychology of Alfred Adler.* Edited and annotated by Heinz L. Ansbacher and Rowena R. Ansbacher. New York: Basic Books.

Adler, Freda. 1975. *Sisters in Crime: The Rise of the New Female Criminal.* New York: McGraw-Hill.

Adler, Freda, and William S. Lauter, eds. 1994. *The Legacy of Anomie Theory.* New Brunswick, N.J.: Transaction Publishers.

Adler, Peter A. 1985. *Wheeling and Dealing: An Ethnography of an Upper-Level Drug Dealing and Smuggling Community.* New York: Harper and Row.

Agnew, Robert. 1985. "A Revised Strain Theory of Delinquency." *Social Forces* 64:151–167.

———. 1992. "Foundation for a General Strain Theory of Crime and Delinquency." *Criminology* 30:47–87.

———. 1995. "Strain and Subcultural Theories of Criminality." Pp. 305–326 in *Criminology,* 2d ed., edited by Joseph F. Sheley. New York: Wadsworth.

Akers, Ronald L. 1985. *Deviant Behavior: A Social Learning Approach.* 3d ed. Belmont, Calif.: Wadsworth.

———. 1989. "A Social Behaviorist's Perspective on Integration of Theories of Crime and Deviance." Pp. 23–36 in *Theoretical Integration in the Study of Deviance and Crime: Problems and Prospects,* edited by Steven F. Messner, Marvin D. Krohn, and Allen E. Liska. Albany: State University of New York Press.

———. 1990. "Rational Choice, Deterrence, and Social Learning in Criminology." *Journal of Criminal Law and Criminology* 81:653–676.

Alexander, Jeffrey C. 1987. *Twenty Lectures: Sociological Theory Since World War II.* New York: Columbia University Press.

Alston, Letitia T. 1986. *Crime and Older Americans.* Springfield, Ill.: Charles C. Thomas.

Andenaes, Johannes. 1974. *Punishment and Deterrence.* Ann Arbor: University of Michigan Press.

Anderson, Margaret L. 1993. *Thinking About Women.* 3d ed. New York: Macmillan.

Andrews, D. A., and James Bonata. 1994. *The Psychology of Criminal Conduct.* Cincinnati: Anderson Publishing Co.

Archer, Dane, and Rosemary Gartner. 1984. *Violence and Crime in Cross-National Perspective.* New Haven: Yale University Press.

Arneklev, Bruce J., Harold G. Grasmick, Charles R. Tittle, and Robert J. Bursik, Jr. 1993. "Low Self-Control and Imprudent Behavior." *Journal of Quantitative Criminology* 9:225–247.

Bachman, Ronet, Raymond Paternoster, and Sally Ward. 1992. "The Rationality of Sexual Offending: Testing a Deterrence/Rational Choice Conception of Sexual Assault." *Law and Society Review* 26:343–372.

Bagley, Christopher. 1969. "Incest Behavior and Incest Taboo." *Social Problems* 16:505–519.

Bagley, Kate, and Alida V. Merlo. 1995. "Controlling Women's Bodies." pp. 135–153 in *Women, Law, and Social Control,* edited by Alida V. Merlo and Joycelyn M. Pollock. Boston: Allyn and Bacon.

Bar-Hillel, Maya. 1990. "Back to Base Rates." Pp. 200–216 in *Insights in Decision Making,* edited by Robin Hogarth. Chicago: University of Chicago Press.

Becker, Gary. 1968. "Crime and Punishment: An Economic Approach." *Journal of Political Economy* 76:169–217.

Becker, Howard S. 1963. *Outsiders: Studies in the Sociology of Deviance.* New York: The Free Press.

Becker, Howard, and Harry Elmer Barnes. 1961. *Social Thought from Lore to Science.* 3 vols. New York: Dover.

Bennett, Richard B. 1980. "Constructing Cross-Cultural Theories in Criminology: Application of the Generative Approach." *Criminology* 80:607–629.

Berk, Richard A., Alec Campbell, Ruth Klap, and Bruce Western. 1992. "The Deterrent Effect of Arrest in Incidents of Domestic Violence: A Bayesian Analysis of Four Field Experiments." *American Sociological Review* 57:698–708.

Birbeck, Christopher, and Gary LaFree. 1993. "The Situational Analysis of Crime and Deviance." Pp. 113–137 in *Annual Review of Sociology,* edited by Judith Blake and John Hagan. Palo Alto, Calif.: Annual Reviews.

Blau, Peter. 1964. *Exchange and Power in Social Life.* New York: The Free Press.

Bohm, Robert M. 1982. "Radical Criminology: An Explication." *Criminology* 19:565–589.

Bonger, Wilhelm Adrian. 1916. *Criminality and Economic Conditions.* Boston: Little, Brown.

Booth, Alan, and D. Wayne Osgood. 1993. "The Influence of Testosterone on Deviance in Adulthood: Assessing and Explaining the Relationship." *Criminology* 31:93–117.

Braithwaite, John. 1981. "The Myth of Social Class and Criminality Reconsidered." *American Sociological Review* 46:36–57.

———. 1989. *Crime, Shame and Reintegration.* New York: Cambridge University Press.

Braithwaite, Richard B. 1960. *Scientific Explanation.* New York: Harper and Row.

Brake, Mike. 1980. *The Sociology of Youth Culture and Youth Subcultures: Sex and Drugs and Rock 'n' Roll.* London: Routledge and Kegan Paul.

Brehm, Jack W. 1966. *A Theory of Psychological Reactance.* New York: Academic Press.

Brehm, Sharon S., and Jack W. Brehm. 1981. *Psychological Reactance: A Theory of Freedom and Control.* New York: Academic Press.

Buckner, H. Taylor. 1971. *Deviance, Reality, and Change.* New York: Random House.

Burger, Jerry M. 1992. *Desire for Control: Personality, Social, and Clinical Perspectives.* New York: Plenum Press.

Burgess, Robert L., and Ronald L. Akers. 1966. "A Differential Association-Reinforcement Theory of Criminal Behavior." *Social Problems* 14:128–147.

Burkett, Steven R., and David A. Ward. 1993. "A Note on Perceptual Deterrence, Religiously Based Moral Condemnation, and Social Control." *Criminology* 31:119–134.

Bursik, Robert J., Jr., and Harold G. Grasmick. 1993. *Neighborhoods and Crime: The Dimensions of Effective Community Control.* New York: Lexington Books.

Cameron, Mary Owen. 1964. *The Booster and the Snitch.* New York: The Free Press.

Caspi, Avshalom, and Daryl L. Bem. 1990. "Personality Continuity and Change Across the Life Course." Pp. 549–575 in *Handbook of Personality: Theory and Research*, edited by Lawrence A. Pervin. New York: Guilford.

Caspi, Avshalom, Terrie E. Moffitt, Phil A. Silva, Magda Stouthamer-Loeber, Robert F. Krueger, and Pamela S. Schmutte. 1994. "Are Some People Crime-Prone? Replications of the Personality-Crime Relationship Across Countries, Genders, Races, and Methods." *Criminology* 32:163–195.

Chambliss, William J. 1967. "Types of Deviance and the Effectiveness of Legal Sanctions." *Wisconsin Law Review* (Summer):703–719.

Chambliss, William J., and Robert B. Seidman. 1971. *Law, Order, and Power.* Reading, Mass.: Addison-Wesley.

Charms, Richard De. 1968. *Personal Causation: The Internal Affective Determinants of Behavior.* New York: Academic Press.

Cherniak, Christopher. 1986. *Minimal Rationality.* Cambridge, Mass.: MIT Press.

Clelland, Donald, and Timothy J. Carter. 1980. "The New Myth of Class and Crime." *Criminology* 18:319–336.

Clinard, Marshall B. 1964a. "The Theoretical Implications of Anomie and Deviant Behavior." Pp. 1–56 in *Anomie and Deviant Behavior*, edited by Marshall B. Clinard. New York: The Free Press of Glencoe.

Clinard, Marshall B., ed. 1964b. *Anomie and Deviant Behavior: A Discussion and Critique.* New York: The Free Press of Glencoe.

Clinard, Marshall B., and Robert F. Meier. 1992. *Sociology of Deviant Behavior.* 8th ed. New York: Holt, Rinehart and Winston.

Cloward, Richard A. 1959. "Illegitimate Means, Anomie, and Deviant Behavior." *American Sociological Review* 24:164–176.

———. 1960. "Social Control in the Prison." In *Theoretical Studies in Social Organization of the Prison*, ed. Richard A. Cloward et al. New York: Social Science Research Council, pamphlet no. 15.

Cloward, Richard A., and Lloyd E. Ohlin. 1960. *Delinquency and Opportunity: A Theory of Delinquent Gangs.* New York: The Free Press.

Cohen, Albert K. 1955. *Delinquent Boys: The Culture of the Gang.* New York: The Free Press.

———. 1959. "The Study of Social Disorganization and Deviant Behavior." Pp. 461–508 in *Sociology Today*, edited by Robert K. Merton, Leonard Broom, and Leonard S. Cottrell, Jr. New York: Basic Books.

Cohen, Lawrence E., and Marcus Felson. 1979. "Social Change and Crime Rate Trends: A Routine Activity Approach." *American Sociological Review* 44:588–608.

Colvin, Mark, and John Pauly. 1983. "A Critique of Criminology: Toward an Integrated Structural-Marxist Theory of Delinquency Production." *American Journal of Sociology* 89:513–551.

Conger, Rand D. 1976. "Social Control and Social Learning Models of Delinquent Behavior: A Synthesis." *Criminology* 14:17–40.

Cornish, Derek B., and Ronald V. Clarke, eds. 1986. *The Reasoning Criminal.* New York: Springer-Verlag.

Cressey, Donald R. 1953. *Other People's Money.* New York: The Free Press.

Cullen, Francis T. 1984. *Rethinking Crime and Deviance Theory.* Totowa, N.J.: Rowman and Allanheld.

Curran, Debra A. 1984. "Characteristics of the Elderly Shoplifter and the Effect of Sanctions on Recidivism." Pp. 123–141 in *Elderly Criminals*, edited by William Wilbanks and Paul K. H. Kim. Lanham, Md.: University Press of America.

Daly, Kathleen. 1989. "Gender and Varieties of White-Collar Crime." *Criminology* 27:769–794.

Deci, Edward L. 1975. *Intrinsic Motivation.* New York: Plenum.

Decker, Scott, Richard Wright, and Robert Logie. 1993. "Perceptual Deterrence Among Active Residential Burglars: A Research Note." *Criminology* 31:135–147.

Dollard, John. 1957. *Caste and Class in a Southern Town.* Reprint, Garden City, N.Y.: Doubleday Anchor Books.

Dubin, Robert. 1959. "Deviant Behavior and Social Structure: Continuities in Social Theory." *American Sociological Review* 24:147–164.

Durkheim, Emile. [1897] 1951. *Suicide, A Study in Sociology.* Translated by John A. Spaulding and George Simpson, edited with an introduction by George Simpson. Reprint, Glencoe, N.Y.: The Free Press.

Edwards, Willie J. 1992. "Predicting Juvenile Delinquency: A Review of Correlates and a Confirmation by Recent Research Based on an Integrated Model." *Justice Quarterly* 9:553–583.

Elliott, Delbert S. 1985. "The Assumption That Theories Can Be Combined with Increased Explanatory Power: Theoretical Integrations." Pp. 123–149 in *Theoretical Methods in Criminology,* edited by Robert F. Meier. Beverly Hills, Calif.: Sage.

_____. 1994. "Serious Violent Offenders: Onset, Developmental Course, and Termination." *Criminology* 32:1–21.

Elliott, Delbert S., and Suzanne S. Ageton. 1980. "Reconciling Race and Class Differences in Self-Reported and Official Estimates of Delinquency." *American Sociological Review* 45:95–110.

Elliott, Delbert S., Suzanne S. Ageton, and Rachelle J. Canter. 1979. "An Integrated Theoretical Perspective on Delinquent Behavior." *Criminology* 16:3–27.

Elliott, Delbert S., David Huizinga, and Suzanne S. Ageton. 1985. *Explaining Delinquency and Drug Use.* Beverly Hills, Calif.: Sage.

_____. 1989. *Multiple Problem Youth: Delinquency, Substance Use, and Mental Health Problems.* New York: Springer-Verlag.

Empey, Lamar T., and Mark C. Stafford. 1991. *American Delinquency: Its Meaning and Construction.* 3d ed. Belmont, Calif.: Wadsworth.

Erickson, Maynard L., and Gary F. Jensen. 1977. "Delinquency Is Still Group Behavior: Toward Revitalizing the Group Premise in the Sociology of Deviance." *Journal of Criminal Law and Criminology* 68:262–273.

Erikson, Kai T. 1962. "Notes on the Sociology of Deviance." *Social Problems* 9:307–314.

Esbensen, Finn-Aage, and David Huizinga. 1993. "Gangs, Drugs, and Delinquency in a Survey of Urban Youth." *Criminology* 31:565–587.

Etzioni, Amitai. 1970. "Compliance Theory." Pp. 103–126 in *The Sociology of Organizations,* edited by Oscar Grusky and George A. Miller. New York: The Free Press.

_____. 1983. "Rainmakers in the University: Economists Keep Their Variables Vague." *Chronicle of Higher Education* 27 (March 16):72.

_____. 1988. *The Moral Dimension: Towards a New Economics.* New York: The Free Press.

Eysenck, Hans J. 1964. *Crime and Personality.* New York: Houghton Mifflin.

_____. 1982. "Development of a Theory." Pp. 1–38 in *Personality, Genetics, and Behavior,* edited by Charles D. Spielberger. New York: Praeger.

Eysenck, Hans J., and Gisli H. Gudjonsson. 1989. *The Causes and Cures of Criminality.* New York: Plenum Press.

Farnworth, Margaret, Terence P. Thornberry, Marvin D. Krohn, and Alan J. Lizotte. 1994. "Measurement in the Study of Class and Delinquency: Integrating Theory and Research." *Journal of Research in Crime and Delinquency* 31:32–61.

Farrington, David. 1986. "Age and Crime." Pp. 189–250 in *Crime and Justice: An Annual Review of Research*, edited by Michael Tonry and Norval Morris. Chicago: University of Chicago Press.

Farrington, David P., Howard N. Snyder, and Terence A. Finnegan. 1988. "Specialization in Juvenile Court Careers." *Criminology* 26:461–485.

Felson, Marcus. 1986. "Linking Criminal Choices, Routine Activities, Informal Control, and Criminal Outcomes." Pp. 119–128 in *The Reasoning Criminal*, edited by Derek B. Cornish and Ronald V. Clarke. New York: Springer-Verlag.

Ferrence, Roberta. 1980a. "Sex Differences in the Prevalence of Problem Drinking." Pp. 69–114 in *Alcohol and Drug Problems in Women*, edited by Orina Kalant. New York: Plenum Publishers.

_____. 1980b. "Sex Differences in Psychoactive Drug Use." Pp. 125–201 in *Alcohol and Drug Problems in Women*, edited by Orina Kalant. New York: Plenum Publishers.

Fine, Gary Alan, and Sherryl Kleinman. 1979. "Rethinking Subculture: An Interactionist Analysis." *American Journal of Sociology* 85:1–20.

Finestone, Harold. 1957. "Cats, Kicks, and Color." *Social Problems* 5:3–13.

Fischer, Claude S. 1975. "Toward a Subcultural Theory of Urbanism." *American Journal of Sociology* 80:1319–1341.

_____. 1982. *To Dwell Among Friends: Personal Networks in Town and City*. Chicago: University of Chicago Press.

_____. 1984. *The Urban Experience*. 2d ed. New York: Harcourt Brace Jovanovich.

_____. 1995. "The Subcultural Theory of Urbanism: A Twentieth-Year Assessment." *American Journal of Sociology* 101: (forthcoming).

Fishbein, Diana H. 1990. "Biological Perspectives in Criminology." *Criminology* 28:27–72.

Freese, Lee. 1972. "Cumulative Sociological Knowledge." *American Sociological Review* 37:472–482.

Gagnon, John H., and William Simon, eds. 1967. *Sexual Deviance*. New York: Harper and Row.

Gans, Herbert. 1962. "Urbanism and Suburbanism as Ways of Life: A Reevaluation of Definitions." Pp. 625–648 in *Human Behavior and Social Processes*, edited by Arnold M. Rose. Boston: Houghton Mifflin.

Gecas, Viktor. 1989. "The Social Psychology of Self-Efficacy." Pp. 291–316 in *Annual Review of Sociology*, edited by W. Richard Scott and Judith Blake. Palo Alto, Calif.: Annual Reviews.

Gibbs, Jack P. 1966. "Conceptions of Deviant Behavior: The Old and the New." *Pacific Sociological Review* 9:9–14.

_____. 1972a. "Issues in Defining Deviant Behavior." Pp. 39–68 in *Theoretical Perspectives on Deviance*, edited by Richard A. Scott and Jack D. Douglas. New York: Basic Books.

_____. 1972b. *Sociological Theory Construction*. Hinsdale, Ill.: Dryden.

_____. 1975. *Crime, Punishment, and Deterrence*. New York: Elsevier Scientific.

_____. 1981. *Norms, Deviance, and Social Control*. New York: Elsevier Scientific.

_____. 1989. *Control: Sociology's Central Notion*. Urbana: University of Illinois Press.

_____. 1994. *A Theory About Control*. Boulder: Westview Press.

Giles-Sims, Jean. 1983. *Wife Battering: A Systems Theory Approach.* New York: Guilford.

Glaser, Barney, and Anselm Strauss. 1967. *The Discovery of Grounded Theory.* Chicago: Aldine.

Glaser, Daniel. 1962. "The Differential Association Theory of Crime." In *Human Behavior and Social Processes,* edited by Arnold Rose. Boston: Houghton Mifflin.

————. 1978. *Crime in Our Changing Society.* New York: Holt, Rinehart and Winston.

————. 1980. "The Interplay of Theory, Issues, Policy, and Data." Pp. 123–142 in *Handbook of Criminal Justice Evaluation,* edited by Malcolm W. Klein and Katherine S. Teilman. Beverly Hills, Calif.: Sage.

Glueck, Sheldon, and Eleanor Glueck. 1950. *Unraveling Juvenile Delinquency.* New York: The Commonwealth Fund.

Goode, Erich. 1970. *The Marijuana Smokers.* New York: Basic Books.

————. 1994. *Deviant Behavior.* 4th ed. Englewood Cliffs, N.J.: Prentice-Hall.

Goode, William J. 1974. "Force and Violence in the Family." Pp. 25–43 in *Violence in the Family,* edited by Suzeanne K. Steinmetz and Murray A. Straus. New York: Dodd, Mead and Company.

Gottfredson, Michael R., and Travis Hirschi. 1990. *A General Theory of Crime.* Stanford: Stanford University Press.

Gottheil, Edward, ed. 1985. *The Combined Problems of Alcoholism, Drug Addiction and Aging.* Springfield, Ill.: Charles C. Thomas.

Gove, Walter R., ed. 1975. *The Labelling of Deviance: Evaluating a Perspective.* New York: John Wiley.

————. 1980. *The Labelling of Deviance: Evaluating a Perspective.* 2d ed. Beverly Hills, Calif.: Sage.

Grasmick, Harold, and Robert J. Bursik, Jr. 1990. "Conscience, Significant Others, and Rational Choice: Extending the Deterrence Model." *Law and Society Review* 24:837–861.

————. 1993. "Reduction in Drunk Driving as a Response to Increased Threats of Shame, Embarrassment, and Legal Sanction." *Criminology* 31:41–67.

Grasmick, Harold G., and Donald Green. 1980. "Legal Punishment, Social Disapproval, and Internalization as Inhibitors of Illegal Behavior." *Journal of Criminal Law and Criminology* 71:325–335.

Grasmick, Harold G., and Herman Milligan, Jr. 1976. "Deterrence Theory Approach to Socioeconomic/Demographic Correlates of Crime." *Social Science Quarterly* 57:608–617.

Grasmick, Harold G., Charles R. Tittle, Robert J. Bursik, Jr., and Bruce J. Arneklev. 1993. "Testing the Core Empirical Implications of Gottfredson and Hirschi's General Theory of Crime." *Journal of Research in Crime and Delinquency* 30:5–29.

Gray, Louis, and Irving Tallman. 1984. "A Satisfaction Balance Model of Decision Making and Choice Behavior." *Social Psychology Quarterly* 47:146–159.

Greenberg, David F. 1985. "Age, Crime, and Social Explanation." *American Journal of Sociology* 91:1–21.

Grinnell, George Bird. 1972. *The Cheyenne Indians: Their History and Ways of Life.* 2 vols. Lincoln: University of Nebraska Press.

Gross, Llewellyn, ed. 1959. *Symposium on Sociological Theory.* White Plains, N.Y.: Row, Peterson.

Guttentag, Marcia, and Paul F. Secord. 1983. *Too Many Women? The Sex Ratio Question.* Beverly Hills, Calif.: Sage.

Hagan, John. 1989. *Structural Criminology.* New Brunswick, N.J.: Rutgers University Press.

_____. 1991. "Destiny and Drift: Subcultural Preferences, Status Attainment, and the Risks and Rewards of Youth." *American Sociological Review* 56:567–582.

_____. 1992. "The Poverty of a Classless Criminology." *Criminology* 30:1–19.

_____. 1994. *Crime and Disrepute.* Thousand Oaks, Calif.: Pine Forge Press.

Hagan, John, A. R. Gillis, and John Simpson. 1985. "The Class Structure of Gender and Delinquency: Toward a Power-Control Theory of Common Delinquent Behavior." *American Journal of Sociology* 90:1151–1178.

Haines, Michael. 1979. *Fertility and Occupation: Population Patterns in Industrialization.* New York: Academic Press.

Hall, John R. 1987. *Gone from the Promised Land: Jonestown in American Cultural History.* New Brunswick, N.J.: Transaction Publishers.

Hall, Susan, and Bob Adelman. 1972. *Gentleman of Leisure.* New York: New American Library.

Hamm, Mark S. 1993. *American Skinheads: The Criminology and Control of Hate Crime.* Westport, Conn.: Praeger.

Hammer, Joshua. 1990. "Obscene Calls from Academe." *Newsweek,* May 7, p. 26.

Heckathorn, Douglas D. 1990. "Collective Sanctions and Compliance Norms: A Formal Theory." *American Sociological Review* 55:366–384.

Heimer, Karen, and Ross Matsueda. 1994. "Role Taking, Role Commitment, and Delinquency: A Theory of Differential Social Control." *American Sociological Review* 59:365–390.

Hepburn, John R. 1984. "Occasional Property Crime." Pp. 73–94 in *Major Forms of Crime,* edited by Robert F. Meier. Beverly Hills, Calif.: Sage.

Hindelang, Michael J. 1978. "Race and Involvement in Common Law Personal Crimes." *American Sociological Review* 43:93–109.

_____. 1981. "Variations in Sex-Race-Age-Specific Incidence Rates of Offending." *American Sociological Review* 46:461–474.

Hindelang, Michael J., Travis Hirschi, and Joseph G. Weis. 1979. "Correlates of Delinquency: The Illusion of Discrepancy Between Self-Report and Official Measures." *American Sociological Review* 44:995–1014.

Hirschi, Travis. 1969. *Causes of Delinquency.* Berkeley: University of California Press.

_____. 1972. "Social Class and Crime." Pp. 503–520 in *Issues in Social Inequality,* edited by Gerald W. Thielbar and Saul D. Feldman. Boston: Little, Brown.

_____. 1979. "Separate and Unequal Is Better." *Journal of Research in Crime and Delinquency* 16:34–37.

_____. 1989. "Exploring Alternatives to Integrated Theory." Pp. 37–49 in *Theoretical Integration in the Study of Deviance and Crime,* edited by Steven F. Messner, Marvin D. Krohn, and Allen E. Liska. Albany: State University of New York Press.

_____. 1992. "From Social Control to Self Control." Paper presented at the annual meeting of the American Society of Criminology, New Orleans, November.

Hirschi, Travis, and Michael Gottfredson. 1983. "Age and the Explanation of Crime." *American Journal of Sociology* 89:552–584.

_____. 1987. "Causes of White Collar Crime." *Criminology* 25:949–974.

_____. 1993. "Commentary: Testing the General Theory of Crime." *Journal of Research in Crime and Delinquency* 30:47–54.

Hoebel, E. Adamson. 1968. *The Law of Primitive Man.* New York: Atheneum.

Homans, George C. 1961. *Social Behavior: Its Elementary Forms.* New York: Harcourt, Brace, and World.

Horney, Julie, and Ineke Haen Marshall. 1992. "Risk Perceptions Among Serious Offenders: The Role of Crime and Punishment." *Criminology* 30:575–594.

Hostetler, John A. 1980. *Amish Society.* Baltimore: Johns Hopkins University Press.

Jackson, Elton F., Charles R. Tittle, and Mary Jean Burke. 1986. "Offense Specific Models of Differential Association." *Social Problems* 33:335–356.

Jamieson, Katherine M. 1994. *The Organization of Corporate Crime: Dynamics of Antitrust Violation.* Thousand Oaks, Calif.: Sage.

Jeffery, C. Ray. 1990. *Criminology: An Interdisciplinary Approach.* Englewood Cliffs, N.J.: Prentice-Hall.

Jenness, Valerie. 1993. *Making It Work: The Prostitutes' Rights Movement in Perspective.* New York: Aldine De Gruyter.

Johnson, Richard E. 1979. *Juvenile Delinquency and Its Origins: An Integrated Theoretical Approach.* New York: Cambridge University Press.

Jungermann, Helmut. 1983. "Two Camps on Rationality." Pp. 63–86 in *Decision Making Under Uncertainty,* edited by R. Sholz. New York: North Holland.

Kaplan, Howard B. 1975. *Self-Attitudes and Deviant Behavior.* Pacific Palisades, Calif.: Goodyear.

_____. 1980. *Deviant Behavior in Defense of the Self.* New York: Academic Press.

Kasarda, John D., and Morris Janowitz. 1974. "Community Attachment in Mass Society." *American Sociological Review* 39:328–339.

Katz, Jack. 1988. *The Seductions of Crime: Moral and Sensual Attractions in Doing Evil.* New York: Basic Books.

Kaufman, Gershen. 1989. *The Psychology of Shame: Theory and Treatment of Shame-Based Syndromes.* New York: Springer Publishing Co.

Kempf, Kimberly L., ed. 1990. *Measurement Issues in Criminology.* New York: Springer-Verlag.

Kephardt, William M., and William W. Zellner. 1994. *Extraordinary Groups.* 5th ed. New York: St. Martin's Press.

Keyfitz, Nathan. 1982. *Population Change and Social Policy.* Cambridge, Mass.: Abt Books.

Kleck, Gary. 1982. "On the Use of Self-Report Data to Determine the Class Distribution of Criminal and Delinquent Behavior." *American Sociological Review* 47:427–433.

Kohlberg, Lawrence. 1969. *Stages in the Development of Moral Thought and Action.* New York: Holt, Rinehart and Winston.

Kohn, Melvin L. 1977. *Class and Conformity: A Study in Values.* Chicago: University of Chicago Press.

Kornhauser, Ruth Rosner. 1978. *Social Sources of Delinquency: An Appraisal of Analytic Models.* Chicago: University of Chicago Press.

La Barre, Weston. 1969. *They Shall Take Up Serpents: Psychology of the Southern Snake-Handling Cult.* New York: Schocken.

LaFree, Gary, Kriss A. Drass, and Patrick O'Day. 1992. "Race and Crime in Postwar America: Determinants of African-American and White Rates, 1957–1988." *Criminology* 30:157–185.

Laub, John, and Robert J. Sampson. 1993. "Turning Points in the Life Course: Why Change Matters to the Study of Crime." *Criminology* 31:301–325.

Lester, David, and Margot Tallmer. 1994. *Now I Lay Me Down: Suicide in the Elderly.* Philadelphia: Charles Press.

Levine, Martin P., ed. 1979. *Gay Men: The Sociology of Male Homosexuality.* New York: Harper and Row.

Lewis, Oscar. 1961. *The Children of Sanchez.* New York: Random House.

Liska, Allen E. 1969. "Uses and Misuses of Tautologies in Social Psychology." *Sociometry* 32:444–457.

_____. 1987. *Perspectives on Deviance.* 2d ed. Englewood Cliffs, N.J.: Prentice-Hall.
Llewellyn, Karl N., and E. Adamson Hoebel. 1941. *The Cheyenne Way.* Norman: University of Oklahoma Press.
Lofland, John. 1967. *Doomsday Cult: A Study of Conversion, Proselytization, and Maintenance of Faith.* Englewood Cliffs, N.J.: Prentice-Hall.
_____. 1969. *Deviance and Identity.* Englewood Cliffs, N.J.: Prentice-Hall.
Luckenbill, David F. 1977. "Criminal Homicide as a Situated Transaction." *Social Problems* 25:176–186.
_____. 1984. "Character Coercion, Instrumental Coercion, and Gun Control." *Journal of Applied Behavioral Science* 20:181–192.
MacKenzie, Doris L., Phyllis J. Baunach, and Roy R. Roberg, eds. 1990. *Measuring Crime: Large Scale, Long Range Efforts.* Albany: State University of New York Press.
Matsueda, Ross. 1992. "Reflected Appraisals, Parental Labeling, and Delinquency: Specifying a Symbolic Interactionists Theory." *American Journal of Sociology* 97:1577–1611.
McCaghy, Charles H. 1985. *Deviant Behavior: Crime, Conflict, and Interest Groups.* 2d ed. New York: Macmillan.
McCall, Nathan. 1994a. "Makes Me Wanna Holler." *Newsweek,* February 7, pp. 46–52.
_____. 1994b. *Makes Me Wanna Holler: A Young Black Man in America.* New York: Random House.
McClelland, David C. 1975. *Power: The Inner Experience.* New York: Irvington.
Mednick, Sarnoff, and Karl O. Christiansen, eds. 1977. *Biosocial Bases of Criminal Behavior.* New York: Gardner.
Meehl, Paul E. 1971. "Law and the Fireside Inductions: Some Reflections of a Clinical Psychologist." *Journal of Social Issues* 27 (4):65–100.
Megargee, E. I., and J. E. Hokanson, eds. 1970. *The Dynamics of Aggression.* New York: Harper and Row.
Merlo, Alida V. 1995. "Female Criminality in the 1990s." Pp. 119–134 in *Women, Law, and Social Control,* edited by Alida V. Merlo and Joycelyn M. Pollock. Boston: Allyn and Bacon.
Merton, Robert K. 1938. "Social Structure and Anomie." *American Sociological Review* 3:672–682.
_____. 1949a. "Social Structure and Anomie: Revisions and Extensions." Pp. 226–257 in *The Family: Its Function and Destiny,* edited by Ruth Anshen. New York: Harper and Row.
_____. 1949b. "Social Structure and Anomie." In *Social Theory and Social Structure.* Glencoe, Ill.: The Free Press.
_____. 1956. "The Socio-Cultural Environment and Anomie." Pp. 24–50 in *New Perspectives for Research on Juvenile Delinquency,* edited by H. L. Witmer and R. Kotinsky. Washington, D.C.: U.S. Government Printing Office.
_____. 1957a. "Social Structure and Anomie." Pp. 131–160 in *Social Theory and Social Structure.* Glencoe, Ill.: The Free Press.
_____. 1957b. "Continuities in the Theory of Social Structure and Anomie." Pp. 161–194 in *Social Theory and Social Structure.* Glencoe, Ill.: The Free Press.
_____. 1964. "Anomie, Anomia, and Social Interaction: Contexts of Deviant Behavior." Pp. 213–242 in *Anomie and Deviant Behavior,* edited by Marshall B. Clinard. New York: The Free Press.
_____. 1968. "Social Structure and Anomie." Pp. 185–214 in *Social Theory and Social Structure.* Glencoe, Ill.: The Free Press.

Messerschmidt, James W. 1986. *Capitalism, Patriarchy, and Crime.* Totowa, N.J.: Rowman and Littlefield.

Messner, Steven F., Marvin D. Krohn, and Allen E. Liska, eds. 1989. *Theoretical Integration in the Study of Deviance and Crime: Problems and Prospects.* Albany: State University of New York Press.

Messner, Steven F., and Richard Rosenfeld. 1994. *Crime and the American Dream.* Belmont, Calif.: Wadsworth.

Middleton, Russell. 1962. "Brother-Sister and Father-Daughter Marriage in Ancient Egypt." *American Sociological Review* 27:603–611.

Miller, Walter B. 1958. "Lower Class Culture as a Generating Milieu of Gang Delinquency." *Journal of Social Issues* 14 (3):5–19.

Mizrahi, Terry. 1984. "Coping with Patients: Subcultural Adjustments to the Conditions of Work Among Internists in Training." *Social Problems* 32:156–166.

Nagel, Ilene H., and John Hagan. 1983. "Gender and Crime: Offense Patterns and Criminal Court Sanctions." Pp. 91–144 in *Crime and Justice: An Annual Review of Research,* vol. 4, edited by Michael Tonry and Norval Morris. Chicago: University of Chicago Press.

Nagin, Daniel S., and Raymond Paternoster. 1991. "On the Relationship of Past to Future Participation in Delinquency." *Criminology* 29:163–189.

Nardi, Peter M., ed. 1992. *Men's Friendships.* Newbury Park, Calif.: Sage.

Nettler, Gwynn. 1978. "Social Status and Self-Reported Criminality." *Social Forces* 57:304–305.

————. 1985. "Social Class and Crime, One More Time." *Social Forces* 63:1076–1077.

Nisbett, Richard E., and L. Ross. 1980. *Human Inference: Strategies and Shortcomings of Social Judgment.* Englewood Cliffs, N.J.: Prentice-Hall.

Nye, F. Ivan. 1958. *Family Relationships and Delinquent Behavior.* New York: John Wiley.

O'Brien, Robert M. 1985. *Crime and Victimization Data.* Beverly Hills, Calif.: Sage.

Pagelow, Mildred Daley. 1981. *Woman-Battering: Victims and Their Experiences.* Beverly Hills, Calif.: Sage.

Parsons, Talcott. 1951. *The Social System.* New York: The Free Press.

————. 1955. *Family, Socialization and Interaction Process.* With Robert F. Bales, James Olds, Morris Zelditch, and Philip E. Slater. New York: The Free Press.

Paternoster, Raymond. 1987. "The Deterrent Effect of the Perceived Certainty and Severity of Punishment: A Review of the Evidence and Issues." *Justice Quarterly* 4:173–217.

Paternoster, Raymond, and Charles R. Tittle. 1990. "Parental Work Control and Delinquency: A Theoretical and Empirical Critique." Pp. 39–70 in *Advances in Criminological Theory,* vol. 2, edited by William S. Laufer and Freda Adler. Newark, N.J.: Transaction Publishers.

Paternoster, Raymond, Linda E. Saltzman, Gordon P. Waldo, and Theodore Chiricos. 1983. "Perceived Risk and Social Control: Do Sanctions Really Deter?" *Law and Society Review* 17:457–479.

Patterson, Gerald R. 1980. "Children Who Steal." In *Understanding Crime: Current Theory and Research,* edited by Travis Hirschi and Michael Gottfredson. Beverly Hills, Calif.: Sage.

Pearson, Frank S., and Neil Alan Weiner. 1985. "Toward an Integration of Criminological Theories." *Journal of Criminal Law and Criminology* 76:116–150.

Pervin, Lawrence A. 1985. "Personality: Current Controversies, Issues, and Direction." *Annual Review of Psychology* 36:83–114.

———. 1990. "A Brief History of Modern Personality." Pp. 3–18 in *Handbook of Personality: Theory and Research*, edited by Lawrence A. Pervin. New York: Guilford.

Petersen, William. 1969. *Population*. 2d ed. Toronto: Macmillan.

Pfohl, Stephen. 1994. *Images of Deviance and Social Control: A Social History*. 2d ed. New York: McGraw-Hill.

Plamenatz, John. 1958. *The English Utilitarians*. Oxford: Basil Blackwell.

Podolsky, E. 1955. "The Chemical Brew of Criminal Behavior." *Journal of Criminal Law, Criminology and Police Science* 45:675–678.

Polsky, Nelson. 1967. *Hustlers, Beats, and Others*. Chicago: Aldine.

Quinney, Richard. 1970. *The Social Reality of Crime*. Boston: Little, Brown.

Reckless, Walter C. 1967. *The Crime Problem*. 4th ed. New York: Appleton-Century-Crofts.

Reiss, Albert J., Jr. 1951. "Delinquency as the Failure of Personal and Social Controls." *American Sociological Review* 16:196–208.

Retherford, Robert D. 1975. *The Changing Sex Differentials in Mortality*. Westport, Conn.: Greenwood Press.

Richards, Pamela, and Charles R. Tittle. 1981. "Gender and Perceived Chances of Arrest." *Social Forces* 59:1182–1199.

———. 1982. "Socioeconomic Status and Perceptions of Personal Arrest Probabilities." *Criminology* 20:329–346.

Rowe, David C., and D. Wayne Osgood. 1984. "Heredity and Sociological Theories of Delinquency: A Reconsideration." *American Sociological Review* 49:526–540.

Salinger, Lawrence M. 1992. *Anti-Trust Enforcement: An Analysis of Ninety-Nine Years of Federal Criminal Price-Fixing Cases, 1890–1988*. Ph.D. diss., Washington State University, Pullman, Washington.

Saltzman, Linda, Raymond Paternoster, Gordon P. Waldo, and Theodore Chiricos. 1982. "Deterrent and Experiential Effects: The Problem of Causal Order in Perceptual Deterrence Research." *Journal of Research in Crime and Delinquency* 19:172–189.

Sampson, Robert J. 1988. "Local Friendship Ties and Community Attachment in Mass Society." *American Sociological Review* 53:766–779.

Sampson, Robert J., and John H. Laub. 1992. "Crime and Deviance in the Life Course." *Annual Review of Sociology* 24:509–525.

———. 1993. *Crime in the Making: Pathways and Turning Points Through Life*. Cambridge, Mass.: Harvard University Press.

Sanders, William B. 1981. "Delinquent Occasions." Pp. 81–95 in *Juvenile Delinquency; Causes, Patterns and Reactions*, by William B. Sanders. Dallas: Holt, Rinehart and Winston.

Sarnecki, Jerzy. 1986. *Delinquent Networks*. Stockholm: The National Council for Crime Prevention Sweden, report no. 1986:1.

Scheff, Thomas J., and Suzanne M. Retzinger. 1991. *Emotions and Violence: Shame and Rage in Destructive Conflicts*. Lexington, Mass.: Lexington Books.

Scheff, Thomas J., Suzanne M. Retzinger, and Michael T. Ryan. 1989. "Crime, Violence, and Self-Esteem: Review and Proposals." Pp. 165–199 in *The Social Importance of Self-Esteem*, edited by Andrew M. Mecca, Neil J. Smelser, and J. Vasconcellos. Berkeley: University of California Press.

Schur, Edwin. 1968. *Law and Society: A Sociological View*. New York: Random House.

_____. 1971. *Labeling Deviant Behavior: Its Sociological Implications.* New York: Harper and Row.

_____. 1984. *Labeling Women Deviant: Gender, Stigma, and Social Control.* Philadelphia: Temple University Press.

Schwartz, Richard D., and Sonya Orleans. 1969. "On Legal Sanctions." *University of Chicago Law Review* 34:274–300.

Schwendinger, Herman, and Julia Siegel Schwendinger. 1985. *Adolescent Subcultures and Delinquency.* New York: Praeger.

Sebald, Hans. 1992. *Adolescence: A Social Psychological Analysis.* 4th ed. Englewood Cliffs, N.J.: Prentice-Hall.

Sheley, Joseph F. 1983. "Critical Elements of Criminal Behavior Explanations." *Sociological Quarterly* 24:509–525.

Sherman, Lawrence W. 1993. "Defiance, Deterrence, and Irrelevance: A Theory of the Criminal Sanction." *Journal of Research in Crime and Delinquency* 30:445–473.

Sherman, Lawrence W., and Richard A. Berk. 1984. "The Specific Deterrent Effects of Arrest for Domestic Assault." *American Sociological Review* 49:261–272.

Sherman, Lawrence W., Douglas A. Smith, Janell D. Schmidt, and Dennis Rogan. 1992. "Crime, Punishment, and Stake in Conformity: Legal and Informal Control of Domestic Violence." *American Sociological Review* 57:680–690.

Short, James F., Jr., and Fred L. Strodbeck. 1974. *Group Process and Gang Delinquency.* Chicago: University of Chicago Press.

Simon, Rita J. 1975. *Women and Crime.* Lexington, Mass.: D. C. Heath and Company.

Simon, William, and John H. Gagnon. 1976. "The Anomie of Affluence: A Post-Mertonian Conception." *American Journal of Sociology* 82:356–378.

Simpson, Sally S. 1987. "Cycles of Illegality: Antitrust Violations in Corporate America." *Social Forces* 65:943–963.

Smart, Carol. 1979. "The New Female Criminal: Reality or Myth?" *British Journal of Criminology* 19:50–59.

Smith, Douglas A., and Christy A. Visher. 1980. "Sex and Involvement in Deviance/Crime: A Quantitative Review of the Empirical Literature." *American Sociological Review* 45:691–701.

Stack, Steven. 1984. "Income Inequality and Property Crime." *Criminology* 22:229–257.

Stafford, Mark. 1984. "Gang Delinquency." Pp. 167–190 in *Major Forms of Crime,* edited by Robert F. Meier. Beverly Hills, Calif.: Sage.

Stark, Rodney. 1979. "Whose Status Counts?" *American Sociological Review* 44:668–669.

_____. 1989. *Sociology.* 3d ed. Belmont, Calif.: Wadsworth.

Stark, Rodney, and James McEvoy III. 1970. "Middle-Class Violence." *Psychology Today* 4:52–54.

Steffensmeier, Darrell. 1978. "Crime and the Contemporary Woman: An Analysis of Changing Levels of Female Property Crime, 1960–1975." *Social Forces* 57:566–584.

Steffensmeier, Darrell, and Michael J. Cobb. 1981. "Sex Differences in Urban Arrest Patterns, 1934–1979." *Social Problems* 29:37–50.

Steffensmeier, Darrell, and Cathy Streifel. 1991. "Age, Gender, and Crime Across Three Historical Periods: 1935, 1960, 1985." *Social Forces* 69:869–894.

Steffensmeier, Darrell, Emilie Allen, and Cathy Streifel. 1989a. "Development and Female Crime: A Cross-National Test of Alternative Explanations." *Social Forces* 68:262–283.

Steffensmeier, Darrell, Emilie Andersen Allen, Miles D. Harer, and Cathy Streifel. 1989b. "Age and the Distribution of Crime." *American Journal of Sociology* 94:803–831.

Stets, Jan E. 1991. "Cohabiting and Marital Aggression: The Role of Social Isolation." *Journal of Marriage and Family* 53:669–680.

Stouffer, Samuel, et al. 1949. *The American Soldier.* 3 vols. Princeton: Princeton University Press.

Sutherland, Edwin H. 1937. *The Professional Thief.* Chicago: University of Chicago Press.

Sutherland, Edwin H., and Donald R. Cressey. 1978. *Principles of Criminology.* 10th ed. Philadelphia: J. B. Lippincott.

Sutherland, Edwin H., Donald R. Cressey, and David F. Luckenbill. 1992. *Principles of Criminology.* 11th ed. Dix Hills, N.Y.: General Hall.

Sykes, Gresham M. 1958. *The Society of Captives.* Princeton: Princeton University Press.

Sykes, Gresham, and David Matza. 1957. "Techniques of Neutralization: A Theory of Delinquency." *American Journal of Sociology* 22:664–670.

Tallman, Irving, and Louis N. Gray. 1990. "Choices, Decisions, and Problem-Solving." *Annual Review of Sociology* 16:405–433.

Taylor, Ian, Paul Walton, and Jock Young. 1973. *The New Criminology.* London: Routledge and Kegan Paul.

Thio, Alex. 1988. *Deviant Behavior.* 3d ed. New York: Harper and Row.

Thomlinson, Ralph. 1965. *Population Dynamics: Causes and Consequences of World Demographic Change.* New York: Random House.

Thornberry, Terence P. 1987. "Toward an Interactional Theory of Delinquency." *Criminology* 25:863–892.

———. 1989. "Reflections on the Advantages and Disadvantages of Theoretical Integration." Pp. 51–60 in *Theoretical Integration in the Study of Deviance and Crime,* edited by Steven F. Messner, Marvin D. Krohn, and Allen E. Liska. Albany: State University of New York Press.

Thornberry, Terence P., Alan J. Lizotte, Marvin D. Krohn, Margaret Farnworth, and Sung Joon Jang. 1994. "Delinquent Peers, Beliefs, and Delinquent Behavior: A Longitudinal Test of Interactional Theory." *Criminology* 32:47–83.

Tittle, Charles R. 1972. *Society of Subordinates: Inmate Organization in a Narcotic Hospital.* Bloomington: Indiana University Press.

———. 1975a. "Deterrents or Labeling." *Social Forces* 53:399–410.

———. 1975b. "Labelling and Crime: An Empirical Evaluation." Pp. 157–179 in *The Labelling of Deviance: Evaluating a Perspective,* edited by Walter R. Gove. New York: John Wiley.

———. 1980a. *Sanctions and Social Deviance: The Question of Deterrence.* New York: Praeger.

———. 1980b. "Evaluating the Deterrent Effects of Criminal Sanctions." Pp. 381–402 in *Handbook of Criminal Justice Evaluation,* edited by Malcolm Klein and Kathie Teilman. Beverly Hills, Calif.: Sage.

———. 1983. "Social Class and Criminal Behavior: A Critique of the Theoretical Foundation." *Social Forces* 61:334–358.

———. 1985a. "A Plea for Open Minds, One More Time: Response to Nettler." *Social Forces* 63:1078–1080.

———. 1985b. "The Assumption That General Theories Are Not Possible." Pp. 93–121 in *Theoretical Methods in Criminology,* edited by Robert F. Meier. Beverly Hills, Calif.: Sage.

———. 1989a. "Influences on Urbanism: A Test of Predictions from Three Perspectives." *Social Problems* 36:270–288.

———. 1989b. "Prospects for Synthetic Theory: A Consideration of Macro-Level Criminological Activity." Pp. 161–178 in *Theoretical Integration in the Study of Deviance and Crime: Problems and Prospects*, edited by Steven F. Messner, Marvin D. Krohn, and Allen E. Liska. Albany: State University of New York Press.

———. 1989c. "Urbanness and Unconventional Behavior: A Partial Test of Claude Fischer's Subcultural Theory." *Criminology* 27:273–306.

Tittle, Charles R., and Robert F. Meier. 1990. "Specifying the SES/Delinquency Relationship." *Criminology* 28:271–299.

———. 1991. "Specifying the SES/Delinquency Relationship by Social Characteristics of Contexts." *Journal of Research in Crime and Delinquency* 28:430–455.

Tittle, Charles R., and Raymond Paternoster. 1988. "Geographic Mobility and Criminal Behavior." *Journal of Research in Crime and Delinquency* 25:301–343.

Tittle, Charles R., and Mark C. Stafford. 1991. "Urban Theory, Urbanism, and Suburban Residence." *Social Forces* 70:725–744.

Tittle, Charles R., and Wayne J. Villemez. 1978. "Response to Gwynn Nettler." *Social Forces* 57:306–307.

Tittle, Charles R., and David A. Ward. 1993. "The Interaction of Age with the Correlates and Causes of Crime." *Journal of Quantitative Criminology* 9:3–53.

Tittle, Charles R., and Michael R. Welch. 1983. "Religiosity and Deviance: Toward a Contingency Theory of Constraining Effects." *Social Forces* 61:653–682.

Tittle, Charles R., Elton F. Jackson, and Mary Jean Burke. 1986. "Modeling Sutherland's Theory of Differential Association: Toward an Empirical Clarification." *Social Forces* 65:405–432.

Tittle, Charles R., Wayne J. Villemez, and Douglas A. Smith. 1978. "The Myth of Social Class and Criminality: An Empirical Assessment of the Empirical Evidence." *American Sociological Review* 43:643–656.

———. 1979. "Reply to Stark." *American Sociological Review* 44:669–670.

———. 1982. "One Step Forward, Two Steps Back: More on the Class/Criminality Controversy." *American Sociological Review* 47:435–438.

Tunnell, Kenneth D. 1992. *Choosing Crime: The Criminal Calculus of Property Offenders*. Chicago: Nelson-Hall Publishers.

Turk, Austin T. 1969. *Criminality and the Legal Order*. Chicago: Rand McNally.

———. 1992. "Theoretical Integration: Models vs. Explanations." Paper presented at the annual meeting of the American Society of Criminology, New Orleans.

Turner, Francis J. 1992. *Mental Health and the Elderly: A Social Work Perspective*. New York: The Free Press.

Turner, Jonathan H., ed. 1989. *Theory Building in Sociology: Assessing Theoretical Cumulation*. Newbury Park, Calif.: Sage.

Tversky, Amos, and Daniel Kahneman. 1974. "Judgment Under Uncertainty: Heuristics and Biases." *Science* 185:1124–1131.

Tyler, Tom R. 1980. "Impact of Directly and Indirectly Experienced Events: The Origin of Crime Related Judgments and Behaviors." *Journal of Personality and Social Psychology* 39:13–28.

van den Berghe, Pierre. 1973. "Dialectic and Functionalism: Toward a Theoretical Synthesis." Pp. 44–61 in *Sociological Readings in the Conflict Perspective*, edited by William J. Chambliss. Reading, Mass.: Addison-Wesley.

Walker, Henry A., and Bernard P. Cohen. 1985. "Scope Statements: Imperatives for Evaluating Theory." *American Sociological Review* 50:288–301.

Walker, Leonore. 1979. *The Battered Woman Syndrome*. New York: Harper and Row.

Ward, David A., and Charles R. Tittle. 1993. "Deterrence or Secondary Deviation?:

The Effect of Informal Sanctions." *Deviant Behavior* 14:43–64.

Warren, Marguerite. 1981. *Comparing Male and Female Offenders.* Beverly Hills, Calif.: Sage.

Wattenberg, Ben J. 1987. *The Birth Dearth.* New York: Pharos Books.

Weeks, John R. 1981. *Population.* 2d ed. Belmont, Calif.: Wadsworth.

Wells, L. Edward, and Joseph H. Rankin. 1988. "Direct Parental Controls and Delinquency." *Criminology* 26:263–285.

Wilbanks, William, and Paul K. H. Kim, eds. 1984. *Elderly Criminals.* Lanham, Md.: University Press of America.

Willer, David, and Murray Webster. 1970. "Theoretical Concepts and Observables." *American Sociological Review* 35:748–757.

Williams, Kirk, and Richard Hawkins. 1986. "Perceptual Research on General Deterrence: A Critical Review." *Law and Society Review* 20:545–572.

Wilsnack, Richard, Sharon Wilsnack, and Albert Klassen. 1984. "Women's Drinking and Drinking Problems: Patterns from a 1981 National Survey." *American Journal of Public Health* 74:1231–1238.

Wilson, Glenn Daniel, and David N. Cox. 1983. *The Child Lovers: A Study of Paedophiles in Society.* London: P. Owen.

Wilson, James Q., and Richard Herrnstein. 1985. *Crime and Human Nature.* New York: Simon and Schuster.

Wilson, Thomas C. 1985. "Urbanism and Tolerance." *American Sociological Review* 50:117–123.

Wirth, Louis. [1938] 1969. "Urbanism as a Way of Life." Pp. 143–164 in *Classic Essays on the Culture of Cities,* edited by Richard Sennett. Reprint, New York: Appleton-Century-Crofts.

Wolfgang, Marvin, and Franco Ferracuti. 1967. *The Subculture of Violence: Towards an Integrated Theory in Criminology.* Beverly Hills, Calif.: Sage.

Wolfgang, Marvin E., Robert M. Figlio, and Thorsten Sellin. 1972. *Delinquency in a Birth Cohort.* Chicago: University of Chicago Press.

Wright, Erik Olin. 1979. *Class Structure and Income Determination.* New York: Academic Press.

Yates, Aubrey J. 1962. *Frustration and Conflict.* London: Methuen.

Yunker, James A. 1977. "An Old Controversy Renewed: Introduction to the Journal of Behavioral Economics Capital Punishment Symposium." *Journal of Behavioral Economics* 6:1–32.

Zimring, Franklin E., and Gordon Hawkins. 1973. *Deterrence: The Legal Threat in Crime Control.* Chicago: University of Chicago Press.

———. 1981. "Kids, Groups and Crime: Some Implications of a Well-Known Secret." *Journal of Criminal Law and Criminology* 72:867–885.

About the Book and Author

A major contribution to the field of crime/deviance, this volume by noted criminologist Charles R. Tittle puts forth an integrated theory of deviance—control balance. Its central premise is that the total amount of control people are subjected to, relative to the control they can exercise, will affect the probability and type of their deviant behavior.

In developing control balance, Tittle critically reviews other general theories such as anomie, Marxian conflict, social control, differential association/social learning, labelling, and routine activities and offers reasons why those theories are insufficient. Using real-world examples to illustrate his argument, he contends that deviance results from the convergence of four variables, each of which represents an interactive nexus of several inputs, including most prominently a control imbalance. The variables are predisposition, motivation, opportunity, and constraint. Control balance theory also explains six basic types of deviance, ranging from predation, defiance, and submissiveness on one end of a control ratio continuum to exploitation, plunder, and decadence on the other.

Tittle conceives of control balance as a continuation, or temporary culmination, of the collective efforts of crime/deviance scholars who have gone before, presenting it as a vehicle for trying to achieve a fully adequate general theory of deviance.

Charles R. Tittle is professor of sociology at Washington State University–Pullman. He is the editor of *Criminology,* the journal of the American Society of Criminology, and the author of *Society of Subordinates* and *Sanctions and Social Deviance.*

Index